Praise for Ali Rahnema's previous books

Islamic Economic Systems

'The strength of this volume is evident: it is both theoretical and concrete. The authors write in a style that is welcoming to non-Islamic readers.' – *Iranian Studies*, 29, 1996

'The authors approach their subject with remarkable clarity and balance.' – *The Henry Martyn Institute of Islamic Studies*, Vol. 13, India, July–December 1994

The Secular Miracle

'... an enjoyable book with a significant and provocative argument and a vivid description of events that is overwhelmingly grounded on primary and Persian sources.' – *International Journal of Middle East Studies*, Vol. 25, 4

'Rahnema and Nomani present a keen and forceful analysis of the development process of the Iranian revolution.' – *Iranian Studies*, Vol. 25, 3-5, 1992

'Rahnema and Nomani have written what is undoubtedly an intelligent book ... an important book.' – *Iran Bulletin*, 1993

'This is a readable, enjoyable, and instructive book. It is based almost entirely on primary Iranian sources, which makes for many novel insights. It deserves to be read, though with a critical eye, by anyone interested in recent Iranian history.' – *Journal of Islamic Studies*, 1992

'This is a well-researched study in which the authors do an admirable job of weaving together the diverse developments that have swept across Iran since the fall of the Shah. It provides a detailed and fascinating account of the Islamic republic's economic, political and diplomatic policies over the last decade, revealing the underlying rivalries and power struggles within the regime, and their implications for Iran's future.' – *Middle East Journal*, Vol. 45, 3, 1991

'... an interesting but descriptive book about the dynamics of Iran's Islamic revolution ... the discussion of the economic measures, reforms and controversies is perhaps the most valuable contribution. Overall, this is a useful and well-written work.' – *Choice*, June 1991

'... a useful handbook to try and understand the complexities of Iran and where it is going.' – *Ta'ali News & Views*, June 1991

Reviews of the first edition

'This is a judicious and well-conceived collection of studies by experts on prominent figures in the modern Islamic political revival ... Anyone concerned with the politics of the modern Islamic world will find it useful to have this detailed Who's Who within reach.' – Middle East Studies Association (MESA) *Bulletin*

'Well written articles on nine of the best known Islamic ideologues of the past century, the majority authored by a scholar who has published major work on the figures of the movement ... The articles are appropriate for undergraduates and the book could well serve to structure an introductory course in modern Islamic thought.' – *Religious Studies Review*

'The scholarly profiles in *Pioneers of Islamic Revival* give readers an opportunity to judge for themselves where the truth lies.' – *Third World Resources*

'This is an excellent anthology about nine of the most influential thinkers of the past century who have contributed significantly to the shape of popular Islamic thought.' – American Sufi Muslim Association (ASMA)

Pioneers of Islamic Revival

NEW UPDATED EDITION WITH
MAJOR NEW INTRODUCTION

edited by Ali Rahnema

SIRD
KUALA LUMPUR

WBP
BEIRUT

Zed Books
LONDON | NEW YORK

Pioneers of Islamic Revival – New Updated Edition – was first published by Zed Books Ltd, 7 Cynthia Street, London N1 9JF, UK, and Room 400, 175 Fifth Avenue, New York, NY 10010, in 2005.

www.zedbooks.co.uk

First edition, 1994

Second impression of this edition, 2008

Published in Malaysia by Strategic Information Research Development (SIRD), No. 11/4E Petaling Jaya, 46200 Selangor.

Published in Lebanon, Bahrain, Egypt, Jordan, Kuwait, Qatar, Saudi Arabia and United Arab Emirates by World Book Publishing, 282 Emile Eddeh Street, Ben Salem Building, PO Box 3176, Beirut, Lebanon
www.wbpbooks.com

A catalogue record for this book is available from the British Library.

US CIP is available from the Library of Congress.

ISBN 978-1-84277-614-8 hb
ISBN 978-1-84277-615-5 pb

Malaysian ISBN Number: 983 2535 69 7 pb

Contents

List of Contributors

David Commins is Professor of History at Dickinson College. His publications include *Islamic Reform: Politics and Social Change in Late Ottoman Syria; Historical Dictionary of Syria;* and *The Wahhabi Mission and Saudi Arabia.* He has authored numerous articles and regularly offers courses on Islamic Civilization, Modern Middle East History, the Arab-Israeli Conflict and Islam.

Yvonne Yazbeck Haddad is Professor of the History of Islam and Christian-Muslim relations at the Center for Muslim-Christian Understanding at Georgetown University. Among her publications are *Muslims in the West: From Sojourners to Citizens* (editor); *Islam and the West Post 9/11*(co-editor); *Becoming American: Immigration and Religious Life in the United States* (editor); *Contemporary Islam and the Challenge of History; The Muslims of America; Women, Religion and Social Change; Islamic Impact* and *Not Quite American?*

Nikki K. Keddie is a prolific scholar of Iran and the Middle East. She won the international Balzan Foundation prize, which enabled her to bring two post-doctoral fellows to UCLA. She is the author of more than 100 articles. Her numerous single-authored, edited and co-edited books include, *Sayyid Jamal al-Din 'al-Afghani': A Political Biography; An Islamic Response to Imperialism, Roots of Revolution, Iran and the Muslim World; Qajar Iran and the Rise of Reza Shah* and *Modern Iran: Roots and Results of Revolution.*

Chibli Mallat holds the EU Jean Monnet Chair in European Law at Université Saint-Joseph in Beirut. His books include *The Middle East into the 21st Century; The Renewal of Islamic Law: Muhammad Baqer as-Sadr, Najaf, and the Shi'i International* (co-winner of the Middle East Studies Association Albert Hourani Prize in 1994); *Democracy in America* (in Arabic) and *L'Union Européenne et le Moyen-Orient* (editor). He is currently Senior Fellow at the Yale Law School.

Baqer Moin is an author and broadcaster. He has written a number of papers on contemporary themes and has contributed extensively as an analyst and an expert on Islam, Iran, Afghanistan and the region. He has been a member of a UN Media Commission with the Afghan Election Commission in Kabul and produced a report for the European Commission on public service broadcasting in Afghanistan. His publications include *Khomeini: Life of the Ayatollah*.

S. Vali R. Nasr is Professor of Middle East and South Asia Politics and Associate Chair of Research in the Department of National Security Affairs at the Naval Postgraduate School. He is the author of *Democracy in Iran: History and the Quest for Liberty*; *The Shi'a Revival: How Conflicts within Islam will Shape the Future*; *The Islamic Leviathan: Islam and the Making of State Power*; *Mawdudi and the Making of Islamic Revivalism* and *The Vanguard of the Islamic Revolution: The Jama'at-i Islami of Pakistan*. He is also the co-editor of *Expectation of the Millennium: Shi'ism in History*.

Augustus Richard Norton is Professor of International Relations and Anthropology at Boston University. Among his publications are *Amal and the Shi'i: Struggle for the Soul of Lebanon*; *Extremist Ideals vs. Mundane Politics*; *The International Relations of the PLO* (senior editor); *Political Tides in the Arab World* (co-author); *UN Peacekeepers* (co-author); *Security in the Middle East: New Perspectives* (in Arabic) and the two volume collection *Civil Society in the Middle East*. His current research interests focus on strategies of reform in authoritarian regimes of the Middle East.

Ali Rahnema is Professor of Economics at the American University of Paris. His publications include, *The Secular Miracle: Religion, Politics and Economic Policy in Iran*; *Islamic Economic Systems* – both co-authored with Farhad Nomani; *An Islamic Utopian: A Political Biography of Ali Shari'ati* and *Religious Forces on the Riverbed of the Oil Nationalization Movement in Iran* (forthcoming in Persian).

Charles Tripp is a Reader in Politics with reference to the Middle East at the School of Oriental and African Studies, London University. His publications include *Iran and Iraq at War* (co-author); *Iran-Saudi Arabia Relations and Regional Order* (co-author); *A History of Iraq* and *Islamic Responses to Capitalism* (forthcoming).

Introduction to 2nd Edition: Contextualizing the Pioneers of Islamic Revival

Ali Rahnema

From the Wall of Mistrust to the Fortress of Contempt

On 4 November 1979 the American embassy in Tehran was occupied by a group of militant Muslim students, tipsy with anti-imperialist revolutionary zeal and demanding the extradition of the Shah from the USA. Fifty-two American embassy employees were taken hostage for 444 days. The main street on which the embassy was located became the bustling venue of huge anti-imperialist demonstrations and rallies. Inside the embassy, dubbed 'the spying nest', the students were busy recovering and piecing back together the classified and highly confidential embassy documents that had been shredded prior to the takeover. These documents, which were finally published in many volumes, demonstrated the meddling and intervention of the USA in Iranian affairs.

The crisis proved to be a most difficult ordeal for the captives and their families, but its impact went well beyond the closed circle of those directly concerned. Even though it occurred thousands of miles away from the American soil, it marked the collective memory of the American public in an undeniably negative manner. It was a humiliating blow to the pride and vanity of the American public, who considered their country to be the most mighty military power of the world, serving the righteous cause of 'freedom' and 'democracy' worldwide. On that historic date, something broke between the two nations. The American public felt insulted by Iran and its newly asserted Islamic identity. This was the beginning of a vicious spiral of indignation, suspicion and mistrust on the part of the average American towards Iran and Islam. Over 22 years (1979–2001) what had started as an internationally illegal act by a group of students in a country caught in the post-tremors of a revolution developed into an overwhelming feeling of rage and disdain towards everything Islamic.

To the American masses, the reason why their embassy and their diplomats had been attacked was totally incomprehensible. To them the whole history of how, from the Iranian perspective, the USA had denied Iran its most rudimentary right of self-determination and political choice on 19 August 1953 was not clear at all. Ignorance or a politically driven conscious denial of a possible link between past US political actions generating historical grievances and present reactions by those subjected to such actions gave rise to the notion that the confrontational spiral was triggered by an irrational sense of anti-Americanism and anti-Westernism. The USA denied or ignored any possible responsibility for what may have driven the Iranians to act as they did. The morally and internationally unacceptable act of taking the American embassy hostage has to be placed in the context of the CIA coup against Mosaddeq, 26 years earlier. Having condemned the act as an aberration in a volatile and semi-anarchic political environment, one can abstract from the event and assess the message it was trying to convey. The signal intended by the hostage-taking could have been sent more forcefully and in a much less costly manner, as Mosaddeq had done with the closing of the British embassy in Tehran. The move against the embassy and its employees was sending the simple message that a people and their government may decide that their national interests do not correspond with the politico-economic agenda of the USA, imposed on their country. The irrational violence of hostage-taking could be considered as a response to the coup. The incompatibility of national interests should not necessarily be viewed as irrational anti-Americanism and readily traced to the amorphous concept of the culprit's 'Islamic culture'.

Short-circuiting the historical flow of events and identifying the cause of the crisis as the anti-Western Islamic 'peculiarity' of the Iranians placed the entire responsibility of the conflict on the other. The long list of indictments and accusations against US foreign policy in the Middle East seemed irrelevant and immaterial to the US public so long as it did not affect their everyday lives.

The Middle East, its nations, people and religions begin to take shape and become relevant in the minds of the American people at large only when others react to the US government's policies in the region in a manner that makes news or hurts their pride. The fact that nations in different continents and of different races and religions were subjected to the US government's intervention in their affairs seems to have been erased from the US public's collective memory. On numerous historically well-documented occasions the US government has violated the right of self-determination of independent and sometimes democratically elected sovereign states across different continents, inflicting death, pain and agony on those people whose political and economic decisions did not coincide with the American world view.

In view of the public's political amnesia about the US government's past political record, during the hostage crisis the American public was suddenly woken up and exposed to the threat of 'Islamic Iran'. The troubling images of blindfolded embassy employees paraded through the embassy compound and throngs of clenched-fisted Iranians burning the American flag while chanting 'death to America' was an insulting experience to those Americans who witnessed these events from thousands of kilometres away. To them, this was the beginning of a macabre story in which a group of rebellious extremists had 'for no reason' and 'without any provocation' attacked the embassy, taken innocent people hostage, humiliated and maltreated them and broken international law in the process. The historical context in which the hostage crisis occurred does not justify the act, but could shed some light on why it occurred and what could have been done to decrease or prevent the chances of the recurrence of such hostile acts. To the American public, it seemed as if Iran–US relations in the twentieth century had veritably started with Iran's belligerent act of hostage-taking. This preception, incomplete and imperfect as it was, shaped the minds and general attitude of the American public. For those receiving their first exposure to Iran, the plight of their countrymen must have generated a strong sense of pain, indignation and contempt. Such a bitter and ahistorical point of entry into the on-going stream of Iran–US relations foreclosed a fair and cool-headed examination and analysis of the roots of the crisis. Had the American public taken an interest in Iran–US relations some 26 years earlier, their verdict on the hostage crisis may have been far less categorical and their disdain more attenuated.

After November 1979 and 11 September 2001, even though the two were very different, the American public were not interested in a course on history, politics, international affairs, religion or economics to shed light on the events. The weight and magnitude of the events were far more overwhelming than the curiosity to search for the roots. The American public had no time, patience or interest in examining the course of events that had led to those incidents. In the first case the hostages suffered psychological pain, and in the second case blood was spilt. Both cases caused anger as feelings were hurt and emotions ran high. The public expected rapid retaliation and the politicians wished to demonstrate their patriotism and mastery of crisis management. In the case of the hostage crisis, the failure of President Carter's rescue operation added insult to injury and the whole affair ushered Ronald Reagan to the Oval Office. But 22 years later, under different conditions and in the absence of the Soviet superpower, President Bush made a promise to his vice-president when he first spoke to him less than 45 minutes after he was informed that a second plane had hit the second tower. President Bush said, 'Sounds like we have a minor war going on here ... We are at war ... somebody's going to pay.'[1] The president kept his promise.

Nearly two decades after the hostage crisis, a hostage-taker and a hostage, both of whom had sought to examine and understand the underlying reasons for the event, replacing pride and preju- dice with intellectual reflection and examination, overcame their intolerance and exorcized their bigoted demons. Each had humbly put himself in the place of the other in order to understand the circumstances and conditions leading to the occasion. The 31 July 1998 meeting in Paris between Barry Rosen, the US embassy press attaché at the time, and Abbas Abdi, one of the three radical student leaders who led the seizure of the embassy, proved that understanding the views and grievances of the other with the aid of a sense of history allowed for a much more transparent, measured and objective view of reality. Rosen and Abdi hoped that their meeting and a review of Iran–US relations would help inform and sensitize their respective people, thereby reducing hostilities between them. Their bold and noble attempt at dismantling the 'wall of mistrust' between Iran and the USA, a term coined by the reformist President Khatami earlier that year, did not succeed as it was overshadowed by swiftly unfold- ing events in the region with colossal political and international implications. A wider, thicker and taller wall of disdain was being built between the USA and Islam.

The US Military Intervention in Iraq and Its Consequences

The annexation of Kuwait by Iraq in August 1990 prompted the Saudi government to seek US military aid to oust Saddam's army from Kuwait. The presence of US troops in the region and the war against Iraq in 1991 once again aroused emotions over US intervention and imperialism in the Middle East. Even though Saddam Hussein was hardly anyone's hero or role model in the region, the US military intervention turned him into a victim of US aggression and therefore a *cause célebre* to be defended. In the wake of the invasion of Kuwait, Osama Bin Laden proposed the dispatching of his Mujahedin to take part in a *jihad* to retake Kuwait.[2] With the withdrawal of the Soviets from Afghanistan, Bin Laden and the Mujahedin, well armed and trained in their battle against the Soviets, were ready and willing to engage in another holy war and lend a helping hand to the Saudis, who had been their benefactors, friends and mentors. Bin Laden's offer to resolve Iraq's invasion of Kuwait 'internally' was rejected by the Saudi monarchy and instead US armed forces were allowed to be based in Saudi Arabia.[3] The presence of American and coalition troops in Saudi Arabia and the first Persian Gulf war had major long-term political ramifications in the region and beyond.

Five months before the Rosen–Abdi reconciliation meeting, a statement entitled 'Jihad against Jews and Crusaders' was issued in the name of a 'World Islamic Front'.[4] Following up on his passionate plea on 23 August 1996 for the expulsion of Americans from Muslim lands and the overthrow of those Muslim governments who collaborated with them, Bin Laden raised the stakes. In his new statement of 23 February 1998, he accused the Americans of 'occupying the land of Islam in the holiest of the places, the Arabian peninsular, plundering its riches, dictating to its rulers … turning its bases in the Peninsula into a spearhead through which to fight the neighboring Muslim people … continuing aggression against the Iraqi people' and diverting attention from Israel's 'occupation of Jerusalem and murder of Muslims there'.[5] The statement claimed that 'these crimes and sins committed by the Americans' constituted 'a clear declaration of war on Allah, his messenger, and Muslims'. Osama Bin Laden and Ayman al-Zawahiri, heading the list of five signatories, commanded Muslims to kill Americans and their allies – civilians and military – in any country where it was possible. They maintained that their *fatwa* was incumbent upon every Muslim as their 'individual duty'. The object of this outright declaration of war on Americans and their allies in the region was claimed to be the liberation of the Al-Aqsa Mosque and the holy mosque (Mecca) as well as forcing the American army 'to move out of all the lands of Islam'.

The stationing of American troops in the Arabian peninsula and their subsequent engagement in Kuwait and Iraq was construed as an act of crusade against Islam. The response of Bin Laden and his allies was composed of two parts. First, in the tradition of all anti-colonial or anti-imperialist liberation organizations or movements, irrespective of their religion or ideology, his statement called for an all-out war against the 'occupying' or 'invading' troops. There is nothing exceptional or novel about this position. The second and rather unprecedented part of the statement placed civilians and non-combatants, posing no conceivable threat and away from the theatre of war, on the same footing as warring military personnel. The so-called fatwa ordered Muslims, in the name of *jihad*, to indiscriminately kill American non-combatants going about their daily lives maybe thousands of kilometres away from the theatre of war and perhaps even opposed to US intervention overseas.

Camped in Afghanistan, cut off from reality, far from the real theatre of war and without a proper national base to recruit from, a constituency to appeal to and a tangible socio-political programme to offer, Bin Laden, entirely dependent on his international Muslim corps, was uncertain of the military feasibility of attaining his objective of liberating Muslim lands through a regular or irregular war. Effectively foregoing the idea of a military victory in the classical sense of the term, Bin Laden's zeal and voluntarism prompted him to opt for a tactic of gratuitous and wanton use of terror to foster panic. The fact that the adoption of such a tactic separated him from attaining his original polito-military objective even more than before could not have eluded him. By substituting the imposition of a permanent state of horror and alarm on defenceless civilians, instead of attaining specific military targets, Bin Laden introduced an unequal relation of forces between his armed followers and unarmed civilians. This may have been a response to the unequal relation of military forces between US military might and that of Iraq in 1991. An indiscriminate war on unconcerned civilians was furthermore a breach of that unwritten chivalrous code of conduct and honour of selfless freedom fighters, whose strong sense of compassion for justice and protection of the weak and powerless had compelled them to confront the intimidating occupying forces. Mercy towards the weak and defenceless and fury in the face of aggressors had distinguished murderers and mercenaries from freedom fighters, endearing the freedom fighters to the masses whom they were supposed to be defending.

Unable to validate the killing of defenceless people on moral and ethical grounds, Bin Laden justified his this-worldly tactic with an other-worldly argument. This was an instrumental abuse of religion for political ends. The so-called *fatwa* by Bin Laden and his supporters falsely attributed to Islam their own tactic of killing innocent and defenceless people. However, attacking defenceless citizens in another country is an act for which no justification can be found in Islam. From a technical point of view, none of the five signatories of the so-called *fatwa* was known to be a *mujtahid*, eligible to deduce directives from the sources and proofs of the Shari'a. As such, their opinion did not constitute a religious obligation incumbent on believers. Had all five signatories even been established *mujtahid*s, their highly uncommon and irregular opinion on the necessity of killing non-combatants in the name of *jihad* would have been strongly contested by mainstream Islamic jurists and *mujtahids*. In view of the highly complex topic of *jihad* and the constrained prerequisites in pronouncing it, such a call was cavalier and rash.

Desperation and Irrationality Prevail

Having publicly told the US government to withdraw its forces from the region or accept the consequence of a possible attack on its civilian population, Bin Laden probably found himself locked into a discourse and a path from which he could, yet chose not to, escape. On 11, September 2001 (9/11) the deadly threat was carried out killing nearly three thousand people in New York city. Essentially one man's argument that Islam commanded such a killing laid the foundations of a wrathful reaction against Islam.

He had transferred what he believed to be the horrors of an unjust war in the Middle East on to US soil. In the name of Islam, Bin Laden and his followers misrepresented a fundamental description of God in the Qur'an. In a pivotal Qur'anic verse that Muslims are required to repeat in their daily prayers so that it may become their guiding torch in private and social conduct, believers are reminded that their acts should be: 'In the name of God the compassionate and the caring, lord sustainer of the worlds, the compassionate, the caring master of the day of reckoning.'[6]

The Muslim community's denunciation of 9/11 was unequivocal and clear. From the politically conservative Sunni muftis of Saudi Arabia to the old revolutionary Shi'i clerics of Iran and even the fiery spiritual leaders of Muslim guerrilla organizations actively fighting Israel, the message of condemnation was explicit. At the Friday congregational prayers in Tehran on 14 September, Ayatollah Emami-Kashani referred to 'a catastrophic act of terrorism which could only be condemned by all Muslims'. He added that 'the whole world should mobilize against terrorism'. In his sermon against terrorism, however, Emami-Kashani did not lose the opportunity to accuse Israel of being a 'terrorist state which was killing children'.[7] Sheikh Muhammad Sayyed Tantawi, the prominent head of Al-Azhar University in Egypt, where muftis across the world are trained, called the attack 'an odious crime which cost the lives of thousands of innocents'.[8] Sheikh Fazlollah, the spiritual leader of the Lebanese Hizballah, whose organization had been fighting against Israel since 1982, called the attacks 'barbaric acts'.[9] Hizballah's foreign minister, Nawaf al-Musawi, maintained that 9/11 was an act of terrorism.[10] The renowned Egyptian-born Muslim scholar, Sheikh Yusuf al-Qaradawi, who lives in Qatar, categorically condemned the attack on civilians as 'a grave sin' and 'totally forbidden in Islam'. In the name of Islam, he called for punishment of the aggressor 'irrespective of his religion, race or gender'.[11] Sheikh Muawith Mabrook Abbas, the head of Al-Azhar's *fatwa* committee, reacted to people such as Bin Laden who felt qualified to issue a *fatwa* and said: 'These kinds of *fatwa*s have no basis in religion. Anyone just issuing a *fatwa* like that should not be trusted. It should be considered neither the religion of Islam or the teachings of Islam.'[12] Established religious leaders of the Muslim community, irrespective of their political tendencies and their stance in relation to the USA, made it clearly known that in their view 9/11 could not be justified or legitimized by invoking Islam. For them, it was important to de-link it from an Islamic calling.

On Sunday 16 September, President Bush warned Americans and the world that 'this crusade, this war on terrorism is going to take a while'.[13] Two days later, White House Press Secretary Ari Fliesher announced that Bush had regretted using the word 'crusade'. Assuming that the president was not predisposed to the use of such language, reflecting a particularly aggressive and revanchist choice of terminology, it must be concluded that Bin Laden had succeeded in imposing on the president his discourse and language of settling grievances and disputes through a crusade. The president's designation of the war on terrorism as a crusade seemed to have affirmed and adopted, as a policy position, Samuel Huntington's key argument. Rejecting the notion that only a small minority of Muslims are involved in the 'quasi-war' with the West, Huntington makes the ideologically important assertion that: 'The underlying problem for the West is not Islamic fundamentalism. It is Islam, a different civilization whose people are convinced of the superiority of their culture and are obsessed with the inferiority of their power.'[14] Even though later, probably due to domestic and international political considerations, Bush reminded the American people that the terrorists had to be distinguished from mainstream Muslims and publicly spoke on behalf of Muslims and against hatred, the damage was done.

The 9/11 attack provided an ideal excuse for a coalition of Christian Right evangelists and an assortment of angry, intolerant and jingoistic groups to focus on Islam as the new enemy of the West. The attack on America, taken within the context of Huntington's simple and reductionist formula, gave credence to the inevitability of a clash of civilizations between Islam and the West. In order to demonstrate the grave danger of Islam, Huntington had refused to distinguish between shades of Islam and the variety of opinions claiming to be rooted in it. Stereotyping made it possible to ignore the crucial nuances and differences, and to emphasize the false notion of a single monolithic Islam characterized by fundamentalism, extremism and fanaticism. To those in the West who wished to popularize the notion of a monolithic and violent Islam bent on destroying Western civilization, 9/11 provided a theoretically ideal opportunity. Back in 1996, Bin Laden had argued that the war between 'the crusader–Zionist alliance' and Islam was under way and since 1998 he had been calling on Muslims to rally to the cause of what he perceived to be a holy war. Yet his call to arms and holy war did not fall on receptive ears in the Muslim community. Faced with the apathy of the broad Muslim community, Bin Laden could rely only on the blind obedience of his international Islamic corps, hardened in the Afghan war, to launch his desperate vanguard action.

Amalgams, aggregations, generalizations and homogenizations naturally obfuscate the diversity and multitude of shades in Islam and help to present a simple black-and-white picture. The process of vilifying Islam and glorifying Western values facilitates converting into hatred the feeling of mistrust and fear among those who had been afflicted by an immoral act of mass murder. As the sound of war drums in the post-9/11 America reached a crescendo, the *groupuscules* of desperate men hiding in the Hindu Kush mountains, constituting a small drop in the more than a billion-strong Muslim community, rejoiced at having convinced policy-makers and the public in the USA that Huntington was correct in his observation that: 'The problem for Islam is ... the West, a different civilization whose people are convinced of the universality of their culture and believe that their superior, if declining, power imposes on them the obligation to extend that culture throughout the world.'[15] Sabre-rattling and the rhetoric of war could be the diplomatic means of preventing wars, but for those who believe in the necessity of crusades it is a warm-up process, preparing the disbelieving majority for the final showdown. To prepare the hearts and minds of their respective communities for a transnational holy war, the two reductionist and aggressive discourses of Islam-phobia and West-phobia desperately need each other as the living proof of the legitimacy and pressing relevance of their shared principles of fear and hatred of the other.

The men of desperation hoped that reductionist theory, enacted through a bloody attack, would provoke yet another bloody retaliation by the USA. Such an attack could in turn convince the great majority of Muslims who had refused to accept the holy war argument that there really was a crusade under way. If the crusade-lovers could further polarize the situation by arguing that whoever was not with them was against them, and if the rational majority were to fall into this trap, then the clash of civilizations could become a self-fulfilling prophecy. An important hurdle along this war path was the intellectual effort of people of ideas and reflection, irrespective of their religion, nationality, colour and gender. It was their responsibility to show through their reading, examination, analysis and synthesis that naive generalizations and crude assertions about Islam and the West were outright incorrect and politically motivated. On the same day that President Bush categorized his war on terrorism as a crusade, Hubert Védrine, another Western politician with a different culture and outlook, grasped the magnitude of the danger and reacted differently. The French foreign minister expressed the position later adopted by many European governments and the view of an overwhelming majority of all Europeans when he said, 'We have to avoid a clash of civilizations at all costs. One has to avoid falling into this huge trap, this monstrous trap conceived by the instigators of the assault.'[16]

Politics and Rhetoric of Rage and Arrogance

Notwithstanding the cautions and warnings of the world community and apparently in pursuit of the war against terrorism, the Bush administration waged war in two countries. With the support of the UK and Australia and the active participation of the Afghan Northern Alliance, the USA attacked Afghanistan in October 2001. The goal of 'Operation Infinite Justice', which was quickly renamed 'Operation Enduring Freedom', was to remove the Taliban government from power. The Taliban, under the leadership of Mullah Omar, had provided a sanctuary for Bin Laden and his al-Qaeda members since 1996. The war in Afghanistan was followed up with 'Operation Anaconda' in March 2002. This operation was designed 'to squeeze the life out of a Taliban and al-Qaeda stronghold, dug deep into the Shah-i-Kot mountains of eastern Afghanistan'.[17] In March 2003, the USA and the UK, with minor contributions from Australia, Poland, Denmark and Spain, invaded Iraq. The justification for this pre-emptive war was to remove Iraq's weapons of mass destruction and overthrow Saddam Hussain, who was said to be linked to al-Qaeda. About three weeks after the USA launched its campaigns of 'Shock and Awe' within the framework of 'Operation Iraqi Freedom', the Ba'athist government fell. The Taliban in Afghanistan and Saddam Hussain in Iraq, both financially and militarily backed and aided by the USA before turning against their benefactor, were removed from power. Saddam Hussain's totalitarian regime folded and the dictator was captured. No weapons of mass destruction were ever found in Iraq and no operational links between Saddam Hussein's government and al-Qaeda were established. Iraq was plunged into turmoil, devastation and insecurity, with armed resistance to the invading forces proving to be far more staunch, violent and bloody than the USA had expected. The first free legislative elections, held in Iraq on 27 January 2005, gave an absolute majority to the Shi'i, whose political power the USA had wished to contain ever since the Iranian revolution.

By 11 January 2005, the number of US military casualties from daily attacks by Iraqi opposition forces had reached 1,350 deaths and 10,252 wounded, and the number of civilians reported killed by the US intervention in Iraq stood between 15,229 and 17,443.[18] Today, the USA finds itself in a most difficult political and military quagmire. Irrespective of its mighty military presence and its highly sophisticated weaponry, it seems incapable of restoring security to Iraq. Even after the elections, the USA can neither repress the Iraqi guerrilla opposition forces nor is it willing to withdraw its forces before having pacified the 'insurgents'. A hasty retreat would not only highlight the unpopularity of American intervention in Iraq, but would also demonstrate the inability of the US military to overcome a small, unorganized and relatively poorly armed band of guerrillas. The Army of Muhammad (Jaysh Muhammad), one of the prominent Sunni guerrilla groups fighting the coalition forces in Iraq, has pledged to 'drive the polytheists from the Arabian peninsula'.[19] The Armed Vanguard of Muhammad's Second Army has also vowed to 'continue to fight every foreigner until ... victory or martyrdom', and to 'make the Americans regret their occupation of Muhammad's land'.[20]

To crush the increasingly embarrassing Iraqi resistance, the administration and the military opted for the use of heavy-handed methods in search of a quick solution. The decision led only to scandalous revelations concerning the maltreatment of prisoners. Iraqi resistance did not wane, but grave moral and ethical charges were brought against the US military and government concerning 'sadistic, blatant, and wanton criminal abuses' at Abu Ghraib prison in Iraq.[21] At Camp X-ray in Guantanamo Bay, Cuba, prisoners from the Afghanistan campaign were kept in cages, and reported that they were repeatedly beaten, subjected to solitary confinement, forced by the guards to race in short leg-shackles and violently punished if they fell.[22] To torture Iraqis, kill civilians and demolish houses in pursuit of the Iraqi opposition forces all in the name of liberating Iraqis from violence, hardship, dictatorship and torture seems vastly hypocritical. Such deeds presented either a logic gone awry due to desperation or the conviction that might is right and that every act is permitted for the attainment of a higher-order objective, understood only by devout partisans of military intervention. The images of the inhuman and perverse manner in which Iraqis were abused at Abu Ghraib prison demonstrate the escalation of unethical conduct by desperate people who have abandoned human compassion and reason for the sake of political expediency, power and glory.

As fear and hatred among Muslims subjected to or witnessing the death and destruction inflicted by the US military machine escalated, similar feelings towards the 'terrorists' threatening the fabric of Western society were also running rampant among the American public. The anger and emotion generated by 9/11 were fanned by the hate discourse of a coalition of forces. Invectives against Muslims resembled the rage and disrespect exercised against Muslim prisoners at Abu Ghraib and Camp X-ray. Islam became synonymous with violence, brutality, terrorism and fanaticism. It was represented as the undesirable 'other', which despised everything Western and towards which those Americans who accepted this discourse could channel all their rage. The feeling of suspicion and mistrust towards Islam after the hostage crisis in Iran became an overwhelming sense of dread, contempt and repulsion after 9/11. The 'red scare' had given way to the 'Muslim scare'. Islam had filled the vacuum that the demise of the 'empire of evil' had created. The categorical association of September 11 with the blanket-term Islam clearly aided those politicians who wished to pursue their hidden agendas under the smoke screen of the 'Green Menace'. Reflection, inquiry and pressing for the nuances and subtleties of the causal relations disrupt the easy dichotomies that homogenization creates and make life difficult for those who wish to manipulate. The further simplified formula equating Islam with terrorism served numerous political purposes. The creation of a common enemy united people behind a cause, distracted them from other possible socio-economic problems and finally justified war against any Muslim country. The crusade mentality was firmly installed.

It seems evident that terrorism as a violent tool predominantly used in pursuit of political objectives could be employed by any conceivable individual or group with a cause. Even an environmental protection organization could resort to terrorism to obtain its desired goal. The use of terrorism by an environmental protection organization does not render the cause of environmental protectionism terroristic or the believers in that cause terrorists. In the name of white Christian people, the Ku Klux Klan seeks to build a new nation of only whites and Christians. Acts of terrorism by the KKK have never led to the conclusion that white Christian Americans are terrorists. Revolutionary Marxism was the source of inspiration for the Italian Red Brigades, the Japanese Red Army and the German Bader-Meinhof, which aimed to further the cause of the international proletarian movement. Marxism–Leninism and Palestinian nationalism were evoked by the Christian Dr George Habbash's Popular Front for the Liberation of Palestine to further the cause of the Palestinian people against the Jewish state. The promised land of the Jewish people, Zion, provided the impetus for Irgun (Zvai Leumi be-Yisrael) and Lehi (Lohami Herut Israel), dubbed the Stern Gang by the British, to further the cause of the Jewish state against the Palestinians and the British through acts of terrorism. Syllogisms and amalgams blur the eye-opening fine points. Just as all white people, Marxists, nationalists, Christians, Jews, Israelis and Palestinians cannot be conceived of as terrorists or their cause as terroristic, nor can Islam and Muslims. Yet for those who wish to sow fear and muster hatred and anger against an enemy, the danger of the foe must be magnified. A small minority, a faction of a fraction of an ideology or a religion does not sound grave and threatening enough for the people to mobilize against. In the name of fighting terrorism, Islamophobic statements and literature are turning uninformed and complaisant people into bigots.

A quick review of some of the literature that can be readily found on the internet while searching for the topic of 'Muslim Threat' demonstrates the extremist position of certain individuals and organizations in the USA with regard to Islam. The basic argument of these writings is that 'in the current war on terrorism it is the Muslims who are the enemy'.[23] The 'Muslim world and its agents of evil' are held responsible for declaring war on the USA, and 'their target is the American way of life'.[24] People are warned about the nature, culture and goals of the 'enemy' and Islam-watchers are asked 'to waken the city of God and to warn against a threat of immense proportion'.[25] Islam is argued to possess 'a distinct culture ... spawning violence everywhere it goes', and Muslims are depicted as zealots whose aim is to convert people to Islam, or kill them in the attempt.[26] It is asserted that 'violence and repression are part and parcel of the basic religious beliefs of Islam'.[27] True Muslims are believed to be extremists, and it is clearly stated that political moderation and peace-seeking are in contradiction to Islamic beliefs.[28] According to this reading, therefore, Islam is incompatible with anything other than violence and extremism. It is presented as a dogmatic, hidebound and intolerant religion with which it is impossible to 'negotiate' and to which it is impossible to apply 'logic'.[29] Islam is also believed to be a threat to Christians, 'their physical freedom ... livelihood ... stated beliefs ... public worship [and] their very lives'. Muslims are also considered to be a danger to all non-Muslims, as it is argued that Muslims consider non-Muslims as 'infidels to be slaughtered in the name of Allah'.[30] Finally in these startling writings where authors feel that there is still a tiny glimmer of hope left for Muslims, 'the minority of more peacefully minded Muslims' are urged to 'split from mainstream Islam', form a recognizable and separate sect and 'not live in the midst of the mainstream Muslims', so that if they are not killed by fellow fundamentalist Muslims, they will be spared by 'Tomahawk missiles'.[31]

Extreme statements by influential figures of the Christian Right denouncing various aspects of Islam buttressed and added fuel to the crusade mentality that was already gaining ground among segments of the American masses. The growing influence of the Christian Right in sensitive national and international policy formulating circles was a special issue of concern in the aftermath of 9/11. Their predominantly anti-Islamic rhetoric set the tone for resuscitating the ancient holy war between the crescent and the cross dating back some 910 years. By the end of 2003 it was not surprising to find an article in the US press referring – perhaps even in jest – to the vitality of 'the crusader spirit' among Americans and designating the objective of this crusade led by the Americans as 'bringing civilization and salvation [to] a backward people'.[32] On 14 October 2002, the Muslim Public Affairs Council in the USA issued a statement asking President Bush to distance himself from statements by Jerry Falwell, Pat Robertson and Franklin Graham.[33] While the president, Attor-

PIONEERS OF ISLAMIC REVIVAL

ney-General John Ashcroft and numerous senators and House representatives were born-again Christians and affiliated with the Christian Right, outspoken leaders of the Christian Right were indiscriminately attacking Islam and Muslims.[34] The transparent and commonly known bond between the Christian Right and key members of the executive and legislative gave the impression that while official US policy sought to dampen the anti-Islam fervour, the spiritual friends, if not gurus, of some of these policy makers were openly instigating hatred against Muslims.

The evangelist Reverend Franklin Graham, who delivered the benediction at George W. Bush's first inauguration and was a close friend of the family, began attacking Islam after 9/11. Graham's stream of invective against Muslims included his infamous statement on 16 November 2001 that: 'The God of Islam is not the same God of the Christian or the Judeo-Christian faith. It is a different God, and I believe it [Islam] is a very evil and a very wicked religion.'[35] During 2002, while the USA was waging war in Afghanistan and planning to attack Iraq, Jerry Falwell, Pat Robertson, Jimmy Swaggart and a host of other Christian ministers conducted a vicious smear campaign against the person of Muhammad, the Prophet.[36] The bigoted language of Christian Right leaders was undoubtedly offensive to the sensitivities of Muslims, just as any personal attack on Moses or Jesus would have been repulsive to Jews or Christians. The concerted verbal abuse of Islam by so-called men of faith was an intimidation and humiliation campaign against the besieged Muslim community. Fostering and capitalizing on the fear of the 'abject and dangerous other' constituted the salient feature of an exclusivist drive that justified US interventions in the Muslim world not only on political but also on religious grounds. To many people, Huntington's wordy and at times complex formulations on the threat of Islam were not readily comprehensible, while the straightforward sermons of the ministers and pastors of the Christian Right made much more sense. After 9/11, the Christian Right and various neo-conservative organizations who spoke the language and addressed the anxieties of the panic-stricken masses embarked on their mission of identifying Islam as the culprit and hence as the 'enemy'. Through their endeavours a coarse and propagandist discourse of Islamophobia gained popularity, eclipsing the clash of civilizations scenario. A reductionist discourse was replaced by an even more stereotyped and clichéd view of 'the other'. The danger with this new exclusivist-driven discourse was that, exactly like its Islamic homologue, it provided a religious justification for the elimination of the other. Pastor Benny Hinn told thousands of Christians in Dallas, Texas, that: 'We are on God's side. This is not a war between Arabs and Jews. It's a war between God and the devil.' Later at the same convention, it is reported that a few conservative Christian ministers had opined that: 'The line between Christians and Muslims is the difference between good and evil.'[37]

A Rough Road Map to Understanding

It may be foolhardy to believe that those who have made up their minds and firmly believe that Islam is a religion based on terrorism, and that Muslims are terrorists and enemies of all non-Muslims, bent on a wanton war path to destroy Westerners and their way of life, could be easily swayed by counter-arguments and analysis. To them, the simplistic argument by Reverend Franklin Graham makes perfect sense and forecloses all other explanations. Graham repeatedly argues that: 'It wasn't Methodists flying into those buildings, it wasn't Lutherans, it was an attack on this country by people of the Islamic faith.'[38] To cut through the thick layers of misconception, misunderstanding, myth and prejudice that have veiled Islam by both Muslims and non-Muslims, it is necessary to review and trace through the intellectual and political developments that contextualize the present crusade mentality prevailing among a relatively small, but active and vocal minority of chauvinist Muslims and Christians.

To provide a preliminary explanation of how the Muslim people of reflection and desperation have responded to the West, it is necessary to follow a historical trail. In trekking through this historical road map, it will become clear that the interaction, negotiation and reaction to the opportunities, challenges and threats that Western ideas posed sometimes resulted in the adjustment and modification of the position and mind-frame of the Muslims and sometimes resulted in their rejection of the Western discourse. The plurality of Islamic responses and discourses reflects the continuous engagement of Islamic thinkers with varying existential and socio-political problems during different historical epochs. The particularity and novelty of analyses by people of reflection is based on an understanding of the times, conditions and the prevalent ideals and aspirations, both national and international.

European Colonization and Islam's Resistance (1800–1924)

In 1492, the last Islamic enclave in Granada was retaken by Europeans and the exceptionally rich experience of Muslim Spain, where Jews, Christians and Muslims interacted and produced a unique intellectual and material product, came to an end. This historical turning point symbolized the complete return of Spain into Europe's Christian fold. Following the expulsion of the Arabs, the forced conversion of Muslims and Jews by the Spanish Inquisition demonstrated the iron will of the Christian Church to impose its hegemony. It seemed as if Europe wished to cleanse itself from what it believed to have been the misfortune that had befallen it in 711, when the Arabs conquered Spain. In 732, the Arab advance into Europe was halted at the battle of Poitiers in France. Some 750 years later they were rolled back and forced out of Spain. The vibrant Jewish community that had thrived under Arab Muslim rule and refused to convert to Christianity was expelled from Spain after its reconquest by the Christians. The Spanish Jewish community took two separate paths. One group spread out into different parts of Europe, and another moved into Muslim lands.[39] The Muslims who escaped execution by the Spanish Inquisition took refuge in Muslim North Africa. By 1492, while a substantial part of the Balkans remained under Ottoman rule, a new geographical map based on religious confession was being redrawn.

It was not until the 1800s that Europeans made an attempt once again to redraw the geographical map in their own favour and subsequently visited Muslims living in a long geographical stretch from Morocco to Indonesia. This time they came as conquerors. The Europe of the 1800s was going through its own revolutionary turbulence and political rivalries, yet its people shared a common experience of unprecedented achievements in the humanities, social and pure sciences. The rationalist, utilitarian and also humanist Enlightenment experience had a technical and scientific corollary that impacted industry and commerce, unleashed the energies and capacities of capitalism and finally shaped the European commercial and political penetration around the world. In 1880, the per capita income in the 'developed' world was approximately double that in the 'underdeveloped' world, while the population of Germany was more than twice that of the Ottoman Empire and that of France was almost twice that of the Ottoman Empire.[40] As the nineteenth century unfolded it became evident that, owing to their technical superiority in the field of armaments, high explosives and steam transport, the spillovers of the Industrial Revolution, the European powers could readily defeat the peripheral countries they wished to colonize. According to Eric Hobsbawm, by the mid-1880s 'nothing stood in the way of western conquest of any territory that western governments or businessmen might find it to their advantage to occupy'.[41]

North Africa

Napoleon's military victory over the Mamelukes and his short-lived invasion of Egypt on 1 July 1798 marks the new wave of Europe's colonization of the Muslim world. Even though in 1801 the French were expelled, the British Royal Navy, instrumental in the French withdrawal, effectively replaced the French and imposed its economic and political domination over Egypt. The construction and financing of the Suez Canal (1859–69), loan repayments, the integration of Egypt into the world market economy as an exporter of cotton and a major importer of British cloth, capital goods and military equipment led to a huge national debt and eventually bankruptcy. According to the contract between Egypt's ruler, Saeed, and the French Ferdinand de Lesseps and his financial supporters, the Suez Canal and large areas of agricultural land beside it were leased to the company for 99 years free of charge, while Egypt was obliged to use forced labour in the construction of the canal. Until the expiration of the 99-year lease, Egypt, like other foreign shareholders, would receive only dividend on the capital it had invested in the canal company.[42] From 1876 Egypt was placed under the 'dual control' of British and French controllers to oversee and manage Egyptian revenues and expenditures. The deterioration in the economic conditions of the common people led to the short but significant riot of 18 February 1879 led by an Egyptian army colonel, Arabi. The demonstrators claimed that their families were starving. Their wrath was aimed at the Armenian Christian Nubar Pasha, the powerful president of the Council or the effective prime minister of Egypt and the minister of finance, an English taxation expert, Rivers Wilson. These two men, 'politically the most powerful in the country', symbolized a new coalition force ruling over the people. The symbiotic relationship between accommodating domestic elites and the imperialist intruders necessitated a dual struggle on the part of the colonized. The anti-imperialist struggle became fused with the anti-despotic struggle. Having roughed up the two signifiers of unwanted dominance, the protestors forced their way into Wilson's office as they shouted 'Death to the dogs of Christians'.[43] The language of political protestation and denunciation against foreign intervention employed by Egyptian Muslim masses was rooted in their common culture. The most simple and common line of demarcation between them and the intruder was their sense of being Egyptian imbued with their religion. Looking back some 125 years, the chant seemed to send a simple message to the foreign intruders and their allies: 'End your misrule and leave us alone.'

In July 1882, about a month after the bloody riots in Alexandria, with the killing of 50 Europeans or European-protected people and the burning of property, Admiral Seymour of the British Navy shelled Alexandria, and General Wolseley's well-armed and seasoned force of 25,000 men equipped with the latest artillery overran the Egyptian army of only 18,000.[44] Even though Britain's direct colonial rule was abandoned after the First World War (1922), its control of Egypt effectively lasted until 1952. While the British took comfort in their occupation of Egypt, in the Sudan, occupied by Egypt since 1820, a man of humble origins claimed to be the awaited Mahdi or the Messiah. Muhammad Ahmad was a zealous ascetic, who had broken with his Sufi master after he had permitted music and dancing at a family celebration.[45] Muhammad Ahmad believed in the simple, puritanical and un-corrupt life of early Islam, epitomized by the golden age of the Prophet. In the general spirit of anti-colonial movements of the time, his *jihad* was against local collaborators with the colonizers as well as against the colonizers. He promised to rid the Sudan of the Egyptians, Turks and British. It is said that the Mahdi ruled that participation in the *jihad* was incumbent upon all Muslims, replacing pilgrimage to Mecca. In 1882 his warriors, armed with spears and swords, defeated an army of 10,000 Egyptians at Al Ubayyid (El Obeid) and equipped themselves with their rifles and ammunition. The Mahdi's ever-growing army subsequently seized Darfur. Muhammad Ahmad promised to export his revolution to 'other corrupt Islamic states – to Cairo, Mecca and beyond'.[46] In January 1885 his army captured Khartoum, the capital of Sudan. Five months later, before he could spread his *jihad* to Egypt and beyond, the Mahdi died of typhus. By the end of 1885 all of Sudan except Swakin and Wadi Halfa was in the hands of the Mahdi's followers. During his rule, smoking, the consumption of alcohol, dancing and bad language were forbidden and punished.[47] It was not until 1898 that the British recaptured Sudan.

In July 1830, French forces landed in Algeria, occupied the country and placed it under the rule of the military. From 1871, Algeria became a part of mainland France and remained so until 1962, when Algeria obtained its independence. From the outset the French intrusion faced strong resistance from the population, who organized their efforts around their religious leaders. In 1832, under the influence of his father, a religious leader, Abd al-Qadir declared himself the 'Commander of the Faithful' of a Muslim state in western Algeria. Abd al-Qadir proclaimed *jihad* against the French and engaged them in battle until December 1847, when he surrendered to the French General de la Moriciere. In their war against Abd al-Qadir, the French smoked out the resistance fighters hiding in caves and razed villages. The smoking out of some thousand men from the Ouled Riah tribe led a member of the French commission investigating this atrocity to claim that: 'We have surpassed in barbarism the barbarians we came to civilize.'[48] The logic of expansion necessitated securing the colonies from future threats by potential enemies. Just as the security of India led the British to invade Egypt, the safeguarding of Algeria led the French to invade Tunisia in April 1881 and impose a protectorate. By June, southern Tunisia was in rebellion and in July the town of Sfax was bombarded by the navy before it was attacked by the marines.[49]

The Indian Subcontinent

Far away from North Africa, the powerful Moghul empire ruled over the Indian subcontinent. The Moghuls, who had invaded India in the sixteenth century, were Muslims and their official court language was Persian. Their tolerence and respect for the Hindu religion of the local population fostered allegiance from the people and loyalty from the Hindu princes, who served the Moghuls as local rulers. From the mid-1700s dissent and division among the ruling family, the growing military power of an independent Hindu state on the west coast and the Afghan threat had enfeebled the Moghul empire's grip. In June 1757, the British East India Company's army had defeated the provincial governor, the *nawab* of Bengal, at Plassy. According to Jawaharlal Nehru, Robert Clive's victory at Plassy was obtained through 'promoting treason and forgery'.[50] The United Company of Merchants of England trading to the East Indies, known as the East India Company, was established in 1600 through a charter of Queen Elizabeth. The Moghul emperors' enthusiasm for international trade, particularly with the Europeans, had brought the British and French East India Company into India. The commercial greed and rivalry of the British and French over Indian trade led to their in-fighting on Indian soil, and it was eventually the British who prevailed because of their advanced military technology.

Gradually the British East India Company, a commercial entity, became a state within a state. By 1764 the East India Company had taken control of Bengal and received the right to collect taxes from the Moghul emperor in exchange for its support of the shaky empire. After the Regulating Act of 1773, reducing the powers of the company directors in India, in 1784 Prime Minister William Pitt's India Bill placed all the activities of the company, civil, military and commercial, under the dual control of the company and the British Crown. In 1857 the Hindu and Muslim Company soldiers rebelled in Bengal. The Indian Mutiny, also known as the Sepoy Rebellion, had a widespread anti-British dimension and lasted for 14 months.[51] It was not until after the rebellion was crushed in 1858 that the government in London decided to abolish the Moghul empire by deposing Emperor Bahadur Shah Zafar. The British government also ended the powers of the company in India and imposed its direct rule on the subcontinent. In 1877, Queen Victoria officially became empress of India and Britain. The defeat of the 1857 rebellion also ushered in an important modification in the political approach of Muslim leaders to the British presence in India.

With the disintegration of the Moghul empire, Muslim leaders began to react to the ascendant British power that was poised to rule India. The pressing problem confronting them was rather simple. Confronted with the growing hegemony of non-Muslim intruders seeking to impose their own socio-judicial mediation mechanisms, how could Muslims protect their identity, consciousness and selfhood? The first reaction of Indian Muslims, similar to that of their co-believers in Northern Africa, was to assert their identity and regain their rights by force and rebellion against the invaders. In 1803 Shah Abd al-Aziz issued a *fatwa*, arguing that Islamic law no longer prevailed and 'the law of the Christian overlord is current without check and hindrance in the sense of administration and in civil cases'.[52] Declaring the subcontinent to be a *dar al-harb* or a territory under the hegemony of unbelievers and hostile to the Muslims living in its domain, Shah Abd al-Aziz ruled that Indian Muslims should wage *jihad* against British rule. Sayyid Ahmad of Rai Baraili (Barelwi/Bareilly), a disciple of Shah Abd al-Aziz, followed the politico-religious instructions of his teacher, took on the anti-British struggle and preached the doctrine of *jihad*. In 1831, after he had adopted the title of Imam, he was killed along with a group of his followers fighting the Sikh ruler.[53] Sayyid Baraili's *jihad* movement continued in the rural areas of Bengal until 1870. The failure of his movement and later the repression of the widespread anti-British revolt of 1857 must have convinced the Muslim leaders of India that the British could not be easily evicted, armed resistance was incapable of removing them, and confrontation and *jihad* were futile. Other solutions had to be found if Muslims were to continue to practise their religion in a British-dominated land. The pragmatic alternative for the preservation of an Islamic identity was a path of peaceful cooperation and co-existence with the new political and military masters. In the eyes of the Islamic leaders, Islam had to become de-politicized in order to survive.

It has been argued that after the 1857 rebellion, considered a benchmark for Islamic revivalism, the jihadist strategy of Sayyid Baraili was effectively abandoned if not discredited among Indian Islamic leaders. In turn, they opted for a new political strategy based on 'reconciliation and cooperation' with the British.[54] A collaborationist Muslim discourse repudiating *jihad* against the British prevailed. This new accommodating strategy was equipped with the religious justifications and legal opinions that were needed to explain the paradigm shift. The notion that India under British rule was a *dar al-harb* was rejected, and in 1871 the term *dar al-aman*, or abode of protection, where the free exercise of religion is secured, came to characterize the situation of Muslims in British-ruled India.[55] Resistance to or *jihad* against British authorities, who were redefined as the rulers of India, were considered 'rebellion pure and simple' deserving death, according to Islam.[56]

Sir Sayyid Ahmad Khan, one of the most prominent Muslim reformers of India, was a strong opponent of *jihad* against the British and a major proponent of political quietism. He was a key figure in justifying and legitimizing the new cooperation and accommodation strategy. During the 1857 mutiny, Sayyid Ahmad Khan was a civil judge under the East India Company in Bijnaur.[57] There he witnessed the mutiny at first hand and was shocked by the persecution of the Muslims in the wave of repression that followed. The acceptance of British rule by Indian Muslim leaders for the purpose of saving the identity and consciousness of their flock was most pleasing to the colonizers. The price for an unmolested and well-protected Muslim space or community was resignation and complete detachment from political activities that could possibly lead to conflict or confrontation with British rule. Some, such as the Deobandis and Barelvis, wanted this space to be cloistered and sealed off from outside influences, while others, such as Sayyid Ahmad Khan, wished for greater understanding and interaction between Muslims and the British.

Dissatisfied with the relegation of Muslims to second-class citizens, leaders who had pledged their allegiance to the British and renounced political activism found solace in 'cleansing', 'reforming' or 'modernizing' a traditional Islam that had proved to be incapable of resisting the colonizers. Ever since 1813, the Christian missionaries under the protection and patronage of the British government had expanded their following while vilifying Islam. Their arguments centred around the notion that 'Islam had outlived its day, that it could not stand scientific and intellectual scrutiny, that its appeal lay to the grosser impulses of the human race, and that it had kept the Muslim communities all over the world in a state of chronic backwardness'.[58] Those Muslim leaders who had invested in a peaceful *modus vivendi* with the British turned to education as the most effective means of fending off attacks on their faith. The educational defence mechanism took two forms. It either generated an introversion process, shielding the Muslim community from modern 'outside' knowledge, or by embracing and internalizing such knowledge, it demonstrated that Islam was perfectly compatible with modernity.

In 1864 Sayyid Ahmad Khan (1817–98) founded his Scientific Society, first at Ghazipur and then at Aligarh, where English books on history, political economy, agriculture, mathematics and other topics were translated into Urdu. In 1875, he established the Muhammadan Anglo-Oriental College at Aligarh, where he hoped to educate the modern rational Muslim pupil. In 1920, the college became the Muslim University of Aligarh. Sayyid Ahmad Khan was convinced that the key to revitalizing Muslims and restoring their waning self-esteem was to arm them with modern Western education. Aligarh hoped to train good Muslims steeped in the knowledge of Western science and culture, who would become 'civil servants, government functionaries and a new crop of Muslim politicians'.[59] To facilitate the integration of Western education, Sayyid Ahmad Khan needed to 'reform' Islam, which under the historical auspices of the traditionalist 'ulema had become ossified and highly averse to new and foreign ideas. Rejecting the iron grip and monopoly of the traditional four Sunni schools of jurisprudence over the Islamic 'truth' and refusing to accept blind imitation or taqlid as an acceptable method of imparting knowledge, Sayyid Ahmad Khan advocated the opening of the door of ijtihad and engagement in the process of reviewing, rethinking and reinterpreting the interface and relation between life and religion in modern times. Having dispensed with Tradition, Hadith and ijma' (consensus) and armed with only the Qur'an and independent reasoning, Sayyid Ahmad Khan produced numerous innovative exegeses. He rejected stoning to death (rajm) for adultery and the concept of abrogation in the Qur'an.[60]

Among the modernist and liberal revivalists of India, the Shi'i Sayyid Amir Ali (1849–1928), whose ancestors had migrated from Mashhad to India with the army of Nader Shah Afshar, stands out for his efforts to break radically with conservative Islamic traditions.[61] In his book The Spirit of Islam, Sayyid Amir Ali evokes the controversial view that the Qur'an was 'the work of Muhammad', in contrast to the 'orthodox doctrine of the Qur'an as the literal Word of God'.[62] Sayyid Amir Ali presented a rational defence of prayer, fasting, almsgiving and pilgrimage on grounds of social and individual utility. However, he argued that certain customs practised in the Muslim community, such as slavery, polygamy and divorce by repudiation, ran counter to true Qur'anic teachings. He blamed the canonists for the preseverence of such practices. Amir Ali further eulogized the golden ages of Islam and emphasized

the achievements of the faith in Baghdad and Cordova in terms
of 'the advancement of learning and science, religious tolerance
and reception of Greek philosophy'.[63] He argued that Islamic
culture played an important role in stimulating the European
renaissance. In 1877, Sayyid Amir Ali, who was a loyal supporter of
the British Raj, founded the National Mohammedan Association,
which was renamed Central National Muhamedan Association
and campaigned for the Muslim League and a separate electorate
for Muslims. Sir Sayyid Ahmad Khan and Sayyid Amir Ali were
discontent with Islam as it had evolved up until their times and
wished to reform it with an eye to Western achievements, and
were thus modernist and rationalist.

In 1866 Maulana Muhammad Qasim Nanotyi/Nanautawi
(1833–1877) and Maulana Rashid Ahmad Gangohi/Kankoohi
(1828–1905), who are said to have played a role in the 1857
rebellion against the British, founded a different kind of Islamic
educational institution.[64] This *madrasa* or religious school, constructed in a town called Deoband, some 90 miles north-east of
New Delhi was called the abode of knowledge or *dar al-'ulum*
in 1867. Even though the Deoband school of higher learning
combined philosophy and science with the mainstream study
of the sources of Islamic law, the primal influence of 'ulema in
curriculum development led to the prevalence of traditional legal
education. The school trained Arabic-speaking scholars entitled
to issue legal opinion on the proper practice of the faith. The
Deobandi school aimed at teaching the Muslim youth the 'ways
of their masters', providing them with an anchor in the 'reassuring
and comforting values of Islam'.[65] The particular legal training
of Deoband students who later, as *'alim* (singular for *'ulema*),
shaped the proper Islamic perception of believers through their
own network of schools, soon produced a particular brand or
sub-school of Islam, known as Deobandi. Before long, Deobandi
Muslims became the second most influential sub-school of Muslim
thought in India. Today, some 15 per cent of South Asia's Sunni
Muslims and some 20 per cent of Pakistan's Sunni Muslims are
said to be followers of the Deobandi school.[66] By 1967 there
were some 9,000 Deobandi schools in South-East Asia. This
figure had reached some 15,000 by 2000. The Taliban, who ruled
Afghanistan from 1996 to 2001, were students of Deobandi schools
and belonged to the Deobandi Sunnis.

Similar to the Aligarh school, the Deobandis strictly believed in non-participation and non-involvement in politics. Contrary to Sayyid Ahmad Khan, the Deobandis believed in *taqlid* or blind following of the old interpretations and rulings, while they desisted from engaging in *ijtihad*. It followed that the Deobandis avoided using human knowledge and rationality, basing their religious rulings and exegesis on a literal reading of the Qur'an and particularly on the practice of the Prophet. The Deoband school is said to have been established by the *'ulema* to counter the influence of Sayyid Ahmad Khan's modernist and rationalist approach to Islam.[67] The Deobandis have an internationalist rather than a nationalist view of Islam and consider the *ummah* or Muslim community rather than their own country as the fundamental Islamic political unit of analysis. While Sayyid Ahmad Khan sought to incorporate Western education and culture as a means of combating the weakness of existent Islam faced with British colonialism, the Deobandis viewed deviation from the original Islam and the Muslims' attraction to Westernization as the source of Islam's demise. The objective of the Deobandis was to return to the 'pure' idealized Islam of the historical past. In this sense, they were backward-looking reformists. The Deobandis have been considered to be the watered-down Wahhabis of the Indian subcontinent.

Muhammad Ahmad Reza Khan Barelvi/Barelwi (1856–1921) is the founder of Barelvi Sunnism. Today, the Barelvis constitute about 85 per cent of South Asia's Sunni Muslims. In contrast to the Deobandis and Sayyid Ahmad Khan, the Barelvi *'ulema* were intent on preserving Islam as 'it had evolved to the present'.[68] They did not wish to 'transform standards of practice and belief' but 'emerged out of opposition to the Ahl-i Hadis and the Deobandis'.[69] Barelvis were the custodians of actually existing Islam, warding off attacks from the backward- and forward-looking Islamic reformists. The conflict between the Barelvis and Deobandis dates back to the late nineteenth century. In a *fatwa*, Ahmad Reza Barelvi ruled that Deobandis were unbelievers (*kafir*) and that those who doubted that they were unbelievers were also unbelievers.[70] In return, the Deobandis issued *fatwa*s against certain practices of the Barelvis, such as celebrating the anniversary of saints or Sufi teachers (*pirs*) and offerings at graves.[71] The Barelvis held the Prophet in the highest esteem, arguing that he is a superhuman figure, made of flesh and blood and light derived from God's own light, present at all times, infallible and endowed with knowledge of the unknown. They were firm believers in a hierarchical religious structure and considered the 'ulema as capable of intercession. Ahmad Reza Khan Barlevi was also a Sufi Sheikh in the Qadiri order.[72] Sufi practices such as the use of music and excessive respect for the power and position of pirs, shrine and grave worshipping along with esoteric practices became imbued with Barlevi Sunnism. Even though Barlevis are believed to be more superstitious than the Deobandis they are said to be the more tolerant of the Indian Muslims.[73]

Iran

Napoleon's military invasion of Egypt in 1798 and the subsequent interest of France, Britain and Russia in the Indian subcontinent alarmed the Iranians. The European presence in the region convinced Iranian Crown Prince Abbas Mirza Qajar that the scientific and technological superiority of the Europeans was at the root of their supremacy. Abbas Mirza concluded that if Iran was to survive the shock, it had to reform. In 1806, Abbas Mirza told the French envoy, Amédée Jaubert, that: 'The Persians are eager to receive all the useful inventions that you may bring them and do not seek to justify their ignorance or their mistakes by saying, "it is the custom".'[74] Abbas Mirza wanted to learn Western ways and not simply reap the windfall economic and financial gains of surrendering his country to them. He invited the French to train the army, students were sent to Europe to study and a printing house was set up in Tabriz in 1812. With the premature death of Abbas Mirza, an enlightened modernizer, in battle against the Russians, the fate of Iran took a different turn. From 1865 numerous concessions were given by the Shah of Iran to French, German, Austrian and British firms. By 1872, Naser al-din Shah handed a handsome concession to the British subject Baron Julius de Reuter, giving him control over custom revenues, a monopoly over mining certain minerals and metals and the construction of railways, canals and irrigation works, as well as a number of other rights. According to Lord Curzon, it 'literally took away the breath of Europe and handed over the entire resources of Persia to foreign hands for a period of seventy years'.[75] Under growing pressure from a court–'ulema coalition, the Shah was forced to repeal the concession in 1873.

In 1890 another British subject, Major G. F. Talbot, received a monopoly over all activities of the Iranian tobacco industry for a period of 50 years. Under pressure from the *'ulema*, the merchants and the intelligentsia and after three hours of rioting in Tehran, Naser al-din Shah Qajar finally revoked the tobacco concession in January 1892. The power of Mirza Hasan Shirazi's *fatwa* against the use of tobacco, the production, sale and export of which was given to the British, was so effective that even the Shah's wives in the harem joined in the national boycott. It was during the anti-tobacco movement (1891–92) that the influential role of Iranian dissidents of all shades and convictions came to the foreground. These dissident groups – religious, secular and interesting mixtures of both – seem to have coalesced around two key issues, both triggered off by Europeans. First, Iranian dissidents came together to challenge the economic plunder of their country by the British, which had been effectuated by their own Shah. This constituted the anti-tobacco campaign. Second, they had observed the key role of the rule of law in Europe and appreciated its power to harness tyranny in their own country; these disparate political groups, having experienced the power of their unity in the anti-tobacco movement, came together to launch the Iranian Constitutional Revolution.

In 1891 a circle of Islamic modernists, organized essentially around Sayyid Jamal ad-Din Assadabadi (Afghani) and Mirza Malkom Khan, played an important role securing Shirazi's famous *fatwa* and propagating ideas against the tobacco concession. In 1889, Mirza Malkom Khan (1833–1908) began publishing a newspaper called *The Law* in London. Malkom Khan was a firm believer in Westernization, a secular education and abandonment of the Arabic alphabet. Yet he was also well aware of the deep-rooted importance of the public's religious beliefs. In his works he emphasized the coordination and blending of modern ideas with Islamic tenets.[76] Sheikh Hadi Najmabadi (1834–1902), who had connections with Malkom Khan, was an active member of Tehran's Pan-Islamic Centre. This Centre worked closely with Afghani's head organization in Istanbul. As a *mujtahid*, he held the controversial belief that reason was the most noteworthy prophet that guided human beings in the right direction. Najmabadi believed that superstition, blind imitation, fear of criticism and harmful customs and traditions were the worst afflictions of society. In his opinion, the root of his compatriots' decline was to be found in their neglect and deviation from the word of God and the interpretation of the Qur'an according to their own will and incorrect impressions. Those primarily responsible for this failure of actually existing Islam were the clergy. Najmabadi's criticism of the prevalent practices of his contemporary Shi'i clerics was bitter and harsh. He accused them of being power-mongers who manipulated Muslims and the faith for their own personal ends. Najmabadi argued that the clergy would brand whoever dared to discuss their deviations publicly as an unbeliever. Demonstrating the clergy's line of argumentation when confronted with criticism, he argued that they would contend that 'whoever is impolite towards the shoes of an 'alim, would be considered as irreverent towards him and whoever is disrespectful towards an 'alim, will be regarded as discourteous to he who has appointed him as an heir and would therefore be considered as irreverent towards God and the Prophet'.[77] Najmabadi was an opponent of the autocratic rule of the Qajars as well as a rationalist and modernist mujtahid. He believed in the power of reason and was finally branded as an unbeliever and excommunicated by Sayyid Sadeq Tabatabaie, the prominent 'alim in Tehran. Even though Iran was never officially colonized, the presence of Europeans in the region and their economic incursions created the same kind of reactions among the people as in the colonized countries. Islamic modernists rallied in opposition to such incursions, engaged in the critique of actually existing Islam as defined and practised by mainstream clerics while concomitantly contesting the autocratic political system in place. The ideas of these reformists played an important role in the constitutional revolution of Iran.

In Iran, just as in the Ottoman and Egyptian cases, European intervention and presence also gave rise to the emergence of a liberal, secular and anti-religious group of modernist intellectuals longing for a thorough Westernization of their country in all respects. By the early 1900s, the Young Turks and the Committee for Union and Progress had surpassed the modernist Islam of Namik Kemal (1840–88) and the Young Ottomans, who were opting for a secular state in Turkey. Mustafa Kemal represented the secular perception, which found little use in the religious tradition of his country. The secularization of those key institutions such as the judiciary and the educational system, along with an overhaul of the religious rites and practices of the people, became the most pressing concern of the modern Turkish state. In Egypt, Mustafa Kamil (1874–1908) and Lutfi al-Sayyid (1872–1963), nationalist secular reformists, combined their dislike for foreign rule with a strong desire for independence, a constitutional form of government and Westernized education.[78] In Iran, secular and nationalist ideas found their most radical manifestation in the ideas of Mirza Fatali Akhondov (Akhoundzadeh). Akhoundzadeh (1812–78) believed that modernization and political concepts associated with it such as democracy were incompatible with Islam, and that the time had passed when people were obliged to sacrifice their lives for their religion. He argued that to safeguard the motherland from foreigners and to overcome backwardness, the people should become educated and trained in loving and worshipping their country.[79] The secular nationalists generally believed that Islam needed to be erased from the collective memory of the people, so that they could become modernized. They further believed that they could simply erase the Islamic identity of their people and rewrite a Western identity in its place.

The Borderless Pan-Islamists

Even though towards the end of the nineteenth century Muslim leaders in India made their peace with the British intruders and opted for a reconciliatory approach based on keeping their community out of politics, another militant Islamic trend was in the making. It is said that Sayyid Jamal ad-Din Assadabadi (1838–97), generally known as al-Afghani, was probably in India during the Indian Mutiny of 1857.[80] His reaction to this watershed event was different from those of the Indian Muslim leaders. From their reaction he may have learnt that Islam as the ideology of a nationalist movement confronted with an overwhelming power such as that of the British could prove insufficient to expel the intruders and deter them from future intervention. By 1881, Assadabadi's anti-British drive convinced him that Islamic internationalism or pan-Islamism was the only viable tool for confronting imperialism. Pan-Islamism had been embraced by Namik Kemal and the Young Ottomans in the early 1870s. Assadabadi's membership in a Masonic lodge in 1875, while he was in Cairo, may have contributed to this perception. The pan-Islamic movement, an exclusion-based defensive idea, became popular for its appeal to neutralize the effects of the exclusion-based policy of the colonialists. As such it was an antidote to Western colonialism. Assadabadi's political voluntarism and adventurism took him through a vertiginous criss-crossing of Asia, North Africa and Europe. Assadabadi, the popularizer of pan-Islamism and a staunch proponent of Sunni–Shi'i reconciliation and unity, went through cycles of irreligiosity, agnosticism and then Islamic zeal and fervour. He sometimes praised Westernizing reforms and called on Muslims to emulate 'civilized nations' of the West, then he became a staunch and passionate defender of Islam, glorifying the faith. Again, in his response to Renan in 1882, he criticized all religions including Islam for stifling philosophy, science, free thought and progress. Was Assadabadi, usually seen as one of the first pioneers of Islamic revivalism, simply using the popularity and appeal of Islam among the masses to further a secular and anti-imperialist cause? As a roaming anti-British agitator-cum-revolutionary who did not shy away from bargaining with highly placed British politicians such as Randolph Churchill, he travelled from Iran to India, Mecca, the Shi'i shrines in Iraq, back to Iran and then to Afghanistan, Bombay, Cairo and Istanbul. In 1871, the 'ulema in Istanbul expelled him for having 'called prophecy a craft'. From Istanbul he went to Cairo, where he was again expelled for his 'inflammatory antiforeign speeches and his political intrigues'. From Cairo he went to Hyderabad, London, Paris, London, Tehran, Russia, Munich, St Petersburg, Tehran, Baghdad, Basra, London and finally to Istanbul, where he died of cancer of the chin in 1897. During his life, Assadabadi played a role in the Tanzimat reforms in the Ottoman Empire (1869–70), the nationalist uprising of Arabi in Egypt (1879), the campaign against Sir Sayyid Ahmad Khan for his position on cooperation with the British (1881), the anti-British Tobacco Movement in Iran (1891) and the assassination of Nasir ad-Din Shah of Iran (1896).

In 1884 Muhammad Abduh (1849–1905), the broad-minded sheikh who had studied at al-Azhar and had joined Assadabadi's circle in Cairo (1869), joined Assadabadi in Paris. In the city of lights, the two men, one raised as a Shi'i and the other as a Sunni, together published the pan-Islamic, anti-British Arabic newspaper *The Strongest Link*, which was banned in Egypt and India by the British.[81] In 1888, Abduh returned to Egypt. Aware of Egypt's backwardness, a feeling heightened by British dominance and critical of the West, Abduh sought to reform Islam as the engine for renewing the country. In this quest, he emphasized the use of the Qur'an and reason.[82] Abduh formulated a forward-looking modernist Islam based on the reduction of the foundations of

Islam to monotheism and affirmation of Muhammad's message as truth, the predominance of rationality over transmitted reports, the openness of Islam to a multiplicity of interpretations, the cleansing of the faith of supernatural superstitions and blind imitation of temporal and religious authority, the favouring of peace, oneness, forgiveness and friendship towards those with a different doctrine, the combination of welfare in this world and felicity in the hereafter and finally the call on Muslims to abandon the vulgar understanding of predetermination and assume their responsibility in building their civilization. Abduh sought to separate what he believed to be the chaff representing actually existing Islam from the real grain, which represented the true Islam of the time of the Prophet and his immediate followers, the *salaf*.

To confront and respond to foreign occupation and rule, Muslims mobilized around a shared historical sense of identity rooted in the religion of their lands. Islam was a secure, familiar and tested compass that indicated the way to solving existing and emerging problems resulting from exposure to the new ideas of the outside world and foreign rule. Put into the service of politics, a new Islamic interpretation constituted a homespun anti-colonial ideology providing a tool for action. But the reformists and revolutionaries, both foward- and backward-looking, needed to settle scores with actually existing Islam, hence the call on both sides for reviewing the Islam that had come to be. The assertion of the Islamic sense of identity was not, however, hostile towards the achievements of the Europeans. The notion of a dual or a Janus-faced West, one creative and healing and the other destructive and afflicting, was known to the people of reflection in the colonies. The most simple response to the dual complexity of the West was to emphasize one attribute and negate the other. Subsequently, some in the colonies came to perceive the West as the beacon of progress, ignoring or turning a blind eye to its destructive influence on the colonized. Some among this group argued that realism and the immediate safety and welfare of the Muslims necessitated pragmatism, resignation and collaboration. Muhammad Ali, ruler of Egypt from 1805 to 1848 was an ardent admirer of France. He established French schools in Egypt and sent Egyptians to Paris to receive a French education.[83] His grandson, Ismael, who inaugurated the Suez Canal, viewed the canal as a bridge between continents and proudly commented that: 'We are not a country of Africa but a country of Europe.'[84] To the

Muhammad Alis, Ismaels, Abbas Mirzas, Sayyid Ahmad Khans and Sayyid Amir Alis of the Muslim world, the West was the model to be emulated. Others in the colonies perceived the West as the god of destruction and havoc, and held that to fight it effectively they had to close their eyes to its healing powers. The Mahdis, Abd-el-Kaders, Sayyid Ahmad of Rai Barailis and their followers could not objectively weigh and consider the merits of the Westerners whose survival in the heat of the battle implied their own demise. Then there were the people of reflection who could not rid themselves of the temptation to see both the negative and positive attributes of the Westerner as well as the strengths and weaknesses of Islam as it had evolved through time. Malkom Khan, Najmabadi, Assadabadi and Abduh saw the complexity of the historical conjunction they were in. For them the transition from what was to what may be better, while resisting Western political penetration, was not a simple and swift task.

One clear similarity among all men of reflection in this period, irrespective of their political disposition in relation to the colonialists, was their deep belief in the central role that the application of reason could play in the determination of religious truth. Men such as Ahmad Khan, Amir Ali, Abduh, Assadabadi and Najmabadi make a clear attempt at redefining the Islam of their epoch through the revival of independent reasoning. In this sense, one can talk about an Islamic age of reason as an outcome of Muslims confronting the colonialists. The methodology and subsequently the discourse of the people of reflection quickly drifted apart from the traditional 'ulema, whose main concern was to preserve Islam and assure the freedom of its practice among believers. The greater emphasis on and use of rational thought by the revivalists lent itself to their greater involvement with the issues and problems of the social and political sphere. Guided by rational thought, as the revivalists steered religion more towards the socio-political sphere, the traditionalists tried to protect religion from the success and failures of politics. For the traditionalists, in view of the hegemony of non-Muslims in their lands, religion was essentially a private matter, concerned with the correct rites and rituals for the purposes of the here and now and with eschatalogical concepts for the hereafter. For the traditionalists, rationalizing and politicizing Islam would temporalize the faith and subject it to the ebb and flow of worldly fortunes and misfortunes.

The Gestation Period (1925–78)

Mustafa Kemal's decision to abolish the Sultanate in 1923 and the Caliphate in 1924 was a watershed in the modern history of the Islamic world. It signified the official abandonment of an effectively defunct symbol of centralized Islamic power that traced itself to the four Rightly Guided Caliphs. The shockwaves of abolishing the Caliphate travelled throughout the Muslim world, forcing Muslims to conceive of other ways to organize and administer themselves. Reflecting on the reasons why the Caliphate was abolished generated a complete review and reassessment of what it meant to be a Muslim in the early twentieth century. The end of the Caliphate, in an international political environment where a large majority of Muslim countries continued to be colonized, also heralded the impracticality and bankruptcy of Pan-Islamism as an anti-colonial tool. The abolition of the Caliphate symbolized the eclipsing of religious internationalism and the resurgence of secular nationalism to counter the colonial powers. Westernization and modernization to catch up with the West were on the ascent. Each political entity in the Muslim world seemed to be dealing with its Muslim identity in relation to Western ideas, practices and political hegemony in a different way.

By 1925 Turkey, under the iron fist of Mustafa Kemal, was well on its way to a forced path of secularization and modernization. A new family law based on the Swiss legal code had already replaced the Shari'a, abolishing polygamy. The wearing of the fez would be prohibited, a Latin script would replace the Arabic script and women would be given the right to vote in national elections.[85] In Iran, Reza Khan became the first Shah of the Pahlavi dynasty in December 1925. Reza Shah's role model was Kemal Attaturk, whose drive for secularization and modernization he sought to emulate. After approximately a century of penetration and rule by the British, India attained its independence in August 1947. At the same time, a new Islamic state with the name of Pakistan was carved out of it. Indonesia had been under Dutch political, economic and military control since 1816. In 1942 it was occupied by the Japanese, and it finally obtained its independence in August 1945. The Dutch disputed the independence of Indonesia and did not officially recognize it until August 1950. Egypt was given nominal independence by the British in February 1922. But it was not until 1952, when anti-British feelings forced them out of the Canal zone, that the country became truly independent. In July 1952, the Free Officers under the leadership of Gemal Abdel Nasser forced King Farouk to abdicate and in 1956 Nasser was elected President.

The secret Sykes–Picot agreement in 1916 divided the Arab Near East into two zones of colonial rule. After the San Remo conference in 1920, the agreement was put into effect. Lebanon and Syria fell under the control of the French, while Iraq, Palestine and Transjordan went to the British. The new colonial division was legitimized by Article 22 of the League of Nations, under which the League entrusted France and Britain with the responsibility of governing these states. In 1927 the British, who had long supported ('Abdul al-'Aziz) Ibn Saud against the Ottomans, recognized him as the sovereign and independent ruler of Saudi Arabia. In 1925, he had taken control of the Hejaz and the holy places. In the heat of redividing the Middle East, South-West Africa and the Pacific Islands into new colonies, the British and the League of Nations also committed themselves to creating a new nation, based on the Jewish religion. The problem with the creation of the Jewish state in Palestine was that the Jewish community at the time constituted a very small minority among a predominantly Muslim and Arab community. Britain's Balfour Declaration of 1917 promised to support the establishment of a Jewish National Home in Palestine. When in 1922 Britain was accorded a mandate over Palestine, it initially honoured its promise by allowing Jewish migration into the region, the purchase of land and the provision of protection for Jewish political and military activities. On 30 November 1947, the United Nations announced the establishment of separate Arab and Jewish states in Palestine. A guerrilla struggle of attacks and counter-attacks between the Arabs and the Jews ensued immediately, while the British tried to maintain their neutrality.[86] The hunt for land began. On 15 May 1948 Arab armies entered Palestine and were defeated. The map of the modern Middle East was gradually taking shape under the auspices of the British and the French. Iraq received its nominal independence in 1932, but was militarily occupied by the British again in 1941 and effectively remained a British colony until 'Abd al-Karim Qasem's coup against the Hashemite King Faisal of Makkan origin in 1958. Syria and Lebanon obtained their independence in 1941 and Jordan in 1946. In North Africa, independence did not come until the 1950s and 1960s. Libya attained independence in 1951, followed by Tunisia and Morocco in 1956 and Algeria in 1962.

Islamic Ideologues

Between the 1920s and 1940s an important Islamic perception took shape. Islam as it had developed by the 1800s was devoid of an ideological system with clear socio-political objectives and ideals, capable of mobilizing the people around a cause. While existing Islam had not prevented the defeat of the Muslims at the hands of the colonialists, the Russian Revolution had demonstrated the anti-absolutist and anti-colonial force of Marxism–Leninism as a revolutionary ideology. The failure of existing Islam as a socio-political paradigm and the ascent of other galvanizing ideologies initiated a movement in two opposite directions. This was not a simple bifurcation: it was a bi-polarization process. Moving from the position of a critique of Islam as it had evolved at the hands of the jurists (*fuqaha*), one perception looked back to the Islam of the forefathers (*salaf*) as a source of inspiration. The other response looked forward to an Islam incorporating and synthesizing modern ideas, arguing that their essence existed in Islam, but was thwarted by the rigid hold of the conservative custodians of existing Islam. To attain their objective of seeking Islamic solutions, each perception could employ reformist or revolutionary tactics.

The Syrian Muhammad Rashid Rida (1865–1935), who had migrated to Egypt, was a student and disciple of Abduh. In the teachings of Abduh a curious combination of seeming opposites allowed for the emergence of what could be considered as a backward-looking Islamic view in search of modernity. This regressive brand of Islam in search of solutions to modern problems and concerns preached 'a return to primeval Islam conceived as a religion in perfect harmony with the humanism and rationalism of modern Man'.[87] The Salafiyyah movement adopted the notion of a return to the forefathers as the proper and unique source of Islamic inspiration. This notion became a dogmatic principle. The consequent Salafiyyah blend of Islam was in turn highly influenced by Rashid Rida's ideas. At first, Rida's intention to return to the forefathers did not imply the negation of what was modern and the embracing of all that was in the distant past. In contrast to the pre-modern and hence cleansed form of Islam, Rida's ideas represented a mixture of the modern and the traditional.

In response to an anti-Bolshevik *fatwa* by the Mufti of Egypt in 1919, Rida drew up a balanced account of Bolshevism from a modernist Islamic point of view. He argued that it is not for Muslims to follow the Bolsheviks, as they should not follow any positivist laws violating Islamic laws. Yet Rida praised Bolshevism and posited that it aimed at eliminating the 'authority of the greedy lords of wealth and their helpers, the rulers who support them, who have imposed their materialist laws that are based on devouring the rights of the workers in their own countries and on colonization of the countries of other weaker people'.[88] By disaggregating Bolshevism, Rida as a Muslim could identify positive elements within it that he found applicable to modern problems. Like Abduh, Rida was critical of the *'ulema*, especially of their role in distorting the institution of the Caliphate from its ideal form under the Four Rightfully Guided Caliphs.[89] He believed that the *'ulema* justified and legitimized tyrannical forms of government. Rida firmly believed in a constitutional form of government, conceding that this political idea was 'the greatest benefit that the peoples of the Orient have derived from the Europeans'.[90] However, as Enayat argues, on the two central testing grounds of the principle of popular sovereignty and the possibility of man-made laws, Rida remains constrained by the Islamic framework in which he is operating.[91] Yet in his concept of an Islamic state, the scope of the Shari'a and the role that it would play in such a state, Rida introduced elements particular to a dynamic modern state into the seemingly static confines provided for by the traditional Islamic legal apparatus. This merging of ideas displayed the internal duality that characterized the early Salafiyyah.

In the tradition of all reformers, Rida was a chief proponent of the necessity of *ijtihad*. He contended that the eternal nature of the faith could be guaranteed by the regular application of reason to the Text. To ensure the adaptability of the Shari'a to changing times, Rida emphasized the importance of those juristic tools and concepts providing the greatest latitude to interpreters and legislators. To guarantee the public interest of Muslims even at the cost of bending the rigid rules of jurists, Rida promoted flexible Islamic axioms. He upheld the principles that 'the necessary legitimizes or justifies the forbidden', 'need takes precedence over prohibitions', 'rules change with time' and 'if principles of the Shari'a are not in conformity with custom, they do not constitute a reliable legal principle'.[92] Rida believed that if full use was made of the Shari'a's 'inherent mechanism for renovation', the Islamic system would prove capable of adjusting itself to unforseen and emerging problems.[93] Convinced that the Shari'a provided sufficient flexibility to meet and respond to the everyday problems of believers in a practical and up-to-date manner, Rida saw no need to look elsewhere for legal sources of inspiration. In contrast to his faith in *ijtihad*, Rida remained critical of Hadiths. He accepted legal decisions based on 'true' Hadith 'as long as it was not inconsistent with public interest'.[94] The usefulness or utility of a Hadith as well as its rationality thus became the measure of acceptance of a Hadith. Rida, like many of his contemporary reformers was in essence reducing the traditionally established sources of the Shari'a to only the Qur'an and human reasoning.

Rashid Rida was the editor of Abduh's commentaries on the Qur'an as well as the editor of the reformist journal *al-Manar*. After the death of Rida, it was Hasan al-Banna who resumed the publication of *al-Manar* in the late 1930s. The Egyptian Hasan al-Banna, founder of the Muslim Brothers (Ikhwan al-Muslemin) in March 1928, believed in spreading and popularizing the ideas of his predecessors, Assadabadi (Afghani), Abduh and Rida. Banna, however, firmly rejected Europe's political, economic and cultural inroads and hegemony and placed his emphasis on the formal implementation of Islamic law and the founding of an Islamic state. As such, Banna put an end to the duality and balance of looking both to Islam and to the West as sources of inspiration that had existed in the analysis of Abduh and had partially continued with Rida. The Muslim Brothers chose to seal off the vision of an ideal Islamic society from the inroads of modernism and Westernism. Explicit in their negative reaction to modernism was an attempt to limit and roll back the ascendent role of rational thought within Islam. The application and scope of human reasoning was perceived by them as a Trojan horse, destabilizing the traditional certitudes. The Muslim Brothers believed that Islam was an all-embracing concept, regulating all aspects of life, 'adjudicating on every one of its concerns and prescribing for it a solid and rigorous order'.[95] Seeking to revive the Islamic Caliphate and the past Islamic empire, the total ideology of the

Muslim Brothers sought to surpass national borders, appealing to an international and universal brotherhood rooted in the traditional concept of the *ummah*. To further and spread the cause of his perception of Islam, Banna argued that *jihad* and warfare were obligations on every Muslim, and martyrdom a lofty act that would be rewarded in the hereafter. Banna attributed his formulation to Allah.[96] Banna's backward-looking revivalism led to an exclusion-based discourse, deviating from the teachings of Islam. By cleansing the faith, Banna was in effect limiting Islam to those notions and principles important to him. Banna's anti-colonial anger towards the dominant position of foreigners over Muslims took an excessive bent as he called for the obligation of *jihad* not only against infidels, but also against the People of the Book. 'Jihad is not against polytheists alone, but against all who do not embrace Islam.'[97] This was a clear break with Islam's established view of *jihad*.

The rise and success of Banna's radical message of rejecting non-Islamic ideas, while glorifying those notions that he thought exemplified a twentieth-century Muslim, echoed throughout the Muslim world. The rise of an exclusion-based, backward-looking Islamic discourse may be attributed to two developments. First, the ascendency of secularism and Westernization in the Muslim world placed considerable pressure on traditional and orthodox views and beliefs. On the heels of the abolition of the Caliphate and Attaturk's attempt at erasing Turkey's Islamic identity and memory, followed by Reza Shah's similar but weaker attempts, Islam felt under siege. In Egypt, Banna lamented the post-war 'orientations to apostasy and nihilism'.[98] Traditional Islamic beliefs were questioned from all sides, without a new set of Islamic responses taking shape. The crisis of identity and faith created a belief vacuum, exposing Islam to a popularized discourse aimed at bringing a simplified version of traditional Islam to an anchoring position in the private and social life of Muslims. The distinguishing feature of this revived Islam was the politicizing of the faith by reading *jihad* and martyrdom into it and leaving the appropriate time for such engagements in the hands of those who claimed leadership of the faithful. Second, the gradual unfolding of the Palestinian crisis allowed the Muslim Brothers to define and situate themselves in relation to the British colonialists, the Jewish state, their own compatriots and the Muslim *ummah* at large. The long-drawn-out historical events leading to the creation of Israel and the struggle that ensued created a conducive environment for the popularity of the Muslim Brothers and their shift from propaganda and preaching to political action. In November 1935 Sheikh Izz al-Din Al-Qassam, a member of the Muslim Brothers who preached *jihad* against the British and Zionists in Palestine, was killed in a guerrilla operation against the British. His death triggered the Palestinian Revolt of 1936–39 against the British. The revolt is said to have shifted public opinion in Egypt from 'secular Egyptian nationalism and Westernization towards an Arab Islamic orientation'.[99] In honour of Sheikh Al-Qassam, the first 'martyr' of the Palestinian cause, the Islamic Resistance Movement, Hamas, formed in late 1987, called its armed wing the Izz al-Din Al-Qassam Brigades. In the 1930s Al-Qassam relied on concepts such as martyrdom (*shahadah*), martyr (*shahid*) and the person who engages in holy war (*mujahid*) to mobilize the people against the British and Zionists.

The initial British intelligence reports on the Muslim Brothers in 1936 indicate their strong anti-imperialist stance and elucidate their objective of purging 'all Islamic countries of the presence and control of Europeans'. At their meetings, the Muslim Brothers chanted, 'Down with imperialism'.[100] The Muslim people were in need of a shock to jolt them out of their apathy, resignation and submissiveness to foreign and domestic oppressors. *Jihad*, or the duty to wage war against the foreign occupying forces and subsequently the forces of new *jahilliyah* (age of ignorance), therefore became one of the main pillars of their ideology. By 1938, Banna encapsulated the demands of the Muslim Brothers and declared that, having placed their programme in the hands of the leadership of the country, they were expecting their response. 'If they respond to our call and adopt the path to our aim, we will support them. But if they resort to double-crossing and evasion and hide behind false excuses and pretexts, then we are at war with every leader, every president of a party and every organization that does not work for the victory of Islam and does not move in the direction of re-establishing the rule of Islam [*hukm al-Islam*]'.[101] In 1948, Egyptian Prime Minister Mahmud al-Nuqrashi was assassinated by one of the Muslim Brothers, and in February 1949 Banna was assassinated.[102]

Banna's Islamic ideology and his method of attaining those objectives profoundly affected leaders, organizations and movements across the Muslim world, seeking to ascertain their Islamic identity against the ascendence of Westernization. The Syrian Muslim Brotherhood, founded in 1935, followed Banna's ideological orientation. The two Brotherhoods, Egyptian and Syrian, considered themselves to be a single movement.[103] Sayyid Abu'l-A'la Mawdudi, the founder of Pakistan's Jama'at al-Islami party (1941), was deeply influenced by Banna. In turn Mawdudi influenced Sayyid Qutb, whose ideas had a deep impact on a whole generation of Muslim activists. Members of the *jihad* organization, claiming responsibility for the assassination of the Egyptian President Anwar al-Sadat in 1981, made references to the writings of Qutb on the necessity to wage *jihad* on behalf of God. Because of his insurrectionary writings, in August 1966 Qutb was charged with attempting to overthrow the Egyptian government and was hanged along with two of his brethren.

Influenced by the objectives, aspirations and methods of the Muslim Brothers, Sayyid Mojtaba Mirlowhi, better known as Navab-Safavi, founded the Devotees of Islam (Fadaian Islam) in 1945. Like the Muslim Brothers, the Iranian Devotees of Islam had a programme, which they too first circulated among the ruling circles. In it, they called for the application of Islamic law in its entirety, the administration of punishments according to Islamic law, the immediate abolition of all un-Islamic laws and the prohibition of man-made legislation, and finally the immediate prohibition of alcoholic beverages, cigarettes, gambling, prostitution, music, films, cabarets, nightclubs and unveiled women.[104] The Devotees of Islam's disdain for man-made laws reflected the Muslim Brothers' axiom that the Qur'an was their constitution. Navab-Safavi was, like Banna, a staunch supporter of the re-establishment of the Caliphate and the unity of all Muslims. After Banna's assassination, the Devotees of Islam translated one of his articles and published it, accompanied by his picture, in their newspaper.[105] In the introduction, Banna was admired for his steadfast courage and will in conducting the holy *jihad* against foreigners. He was also exalted as the founder of a school of thought that had trained tens of thousands of volunteers willing to sacrifice their lives for the glory of Islam. In 1946, the Devotees of Islam started their assassination campaign by killing the deist historian and outspoken critic of Shi'ism, Sufism and Baha'ism, Ahmad Kasravi. To the Devotees of Islam, Kasravi was shaking the pillars of Shi'i faith and fanning a wave of apostasy and disbelief. While the Devotees justified the assassination of

Kasravi by accusing him of making injurious and insulting comments about the faith and of turning the youth against Shi'ism, the motive for their subsequent assassinations was purely political. They followed up their string of assassinations by killing Minister of Court Hajir (1949) and Prime Minister Razm Ara (1951). Their last two attempts led to the injury of the newly elected member of parliament, Fatemi (1952), and Prime Minister Ala (1956). On 17 January 1956, Navab-Safavi and three of his brethren were executed by firing squad.

The ideology of the Iranian Devotees of Islam, the Pakistani Jama'at al-Islami and the Egyptian Muslim Brothers, which became the sources of inspiration of the radical Islamic groups and tendencies of the late 1980s and 1990s, heralded a fundamental rupture with the mainstream ideas of the first-generation revivalists such as Assadabadi (Afghani), Abduh and partially Rida. While the first troika of revivalists were reason-oriented, inclusion-based, outward- and forward-looking and interested in combining Islam with the intellectual achievements of others including the West, their radical successors were inward- and backward-looking and subsequently exclusion-based. Their 'asabiyyah or solidarity, based on a narrowly defined religious sectarianism, was to be propagated by the use of force and compulsion. Banna, Mawdudi and Qutb, the second troika, were men of reflection who codified a discourse of aggression, desperation and intolerance. Navab-Safavi epitomized the zealous and ascetic militant who put into practice the teachings of the second troika. He could be considered as a link in the 180-year chain connecting Muhammad Ahmad (mahdi) of the Sudan to Bin Laden. Those who fought in Afghanistan (1980s) under the banner of Islam and later became international jihadists were ideological disciples of the second troika. The anti-colonial Islamic discourse of the first troika gradually evolved into a bigoted, xenophobic and anti-foreign discourse. Those who articulated and sought to enforce this violence-prone, monolithic and totalistic discourse confronted Muslims with the false choice of either Islamic monotheism or polytheism. According to this distorted and Islamically fallacious argument the People of the Book also fell into the category of polytheists. This was a non-Islamic trade-off veiled as the ultimate Islamic choice. Deep-seated anti-colonial rage constituted the bait attracting believers to the cause of bigoted and blind violence. In the name of Islam, an ideology was concocted that encouraged the oppressed to internalize the anti-values of the oppressors to assuage their anger and humiliation. The second troika diluted and undermined the emphasis on reasoning and *ijtihad*, replacing it with *taqlid*, or obedience to the views of the religious leaders, and *jihad* against the 'enemies of God'. The mechanical and distorted *jihad* mentality popularized by the second troika was the outcome of the colonial mentality, with some similarities to it. The colonialists and jihadists sought domination through coercion. The subjects of their oppression and violence were considered worthless chattel that needed to be sacrificed at the altar of their designs. For both, the sanctity of their very different ends, one material and the other spiritual-material, justified the means.

Muslim Countries and Islamic Opposition

From the mid-1950s to the end of the 1970s, Muslims, Islamic movements and their ideologues were influenced and affected by those colossal international ideas and events that came to shape and define this tumultuous epoch. This was a period marked by the ascent of liberation and guerrilla organizations, both nationalist and socialist, in the colonies, and civil movements in the old and new colonial countries. In the 1960s, the anti-racist and civil liberties movement in the USA also found an Islamic expression. Ousted from Elijah Muhammad's 'Nation of Islam', Malcolm X sought to resolve the problems of black Americans through inviting them to Islam. He adopted the name Malik El Shabazz after he returned from *hajj*. On 21 February 1965 Malcolm X was assassinated.

In the colonies, 1954 witnessed the fall of Dien Bien Phu and the rise of Ho Chi Minh as the role model of anti-imperialist and socialist leaders. During the same year, Algerian nationalists revolted against the French and anti-French riots in Morocco intensified. The emerging power of the newly independent nations, scared and injured by European colonialism and sceptical of its mighty successor, the USA, was making its debut on the world political scene. The Islamic movements, somewhat submerged by the new ideological contenders, had to come to terms with nationalism and socialism. The Western bloc was busy recruiting friends. The Baghdad Pact initiated by Great Britain in February 1955 was a defensive security pact against Soviet expansionism between Great Britain, Iraq, Turkey, Pakistan and Iran, all of which except Great Britain had a common border with the Soviet Union. The USA promised economic aid to the signatories of the pact. Two months later, the Bandung Conference convened 29 Asian and African countries. The conference gave birth to the 'Third World' and non-aligned bloc of countries united in their anti-colonial, anti-imperialist and, to various degrees, socialist convictions. At Bandung, Nasser of Egypt rubbed shoulders with Chou En-lai of China, Sukarno of Indonesia and Nehru of India, bringing the cause of the Palestinian people to the attention of the newly independent countries.

Nasser's embracing of Arab socialism and pan-Arabism placed him in the radical internationalist camp, feared and suspected by both the conservative pro-Western governments of the region and the Western superpowers. Nasser's purchase of arms from Czechoslovakia in 1955, nationalization of the Suez Canal in 1956, the founding of the Palestine Liberation Organization in Cairo and heightened anti-imperialist rhetoric turned him into a hero of the anti-colonial people of the region and the nemesis of governments such as those of Iran and Saudi Arabia. King Faisal of Saudi Arabia sought to counter and neutralize Nasser's growing appeal by upholding pan-Islamism and securing a *fatwa* from the *'ulema*, effectively rejecting nationalism and other isms.[106] In Egypt, however, the prominent and highly respected rector of al-Azhar, Sheikh Mahmud Shaltut, a driving force in reconciling differences among various Islamic schools of thought, argued that Islam was compatible with socialism. In effect, Nasser combined all the required elements of Arab Socialism, pan-Arabism and Islam to ensure his political popularity in Egypt as well as his stature as the leading radical figure in the region. While from 1955 to 1967 pan-Arabism and Arab Socialism had played an important role in galvanizing a sense of pride and identity among the people of the region, the defeat of Egypt in the Six Day War against Israel brought shame not only to Nasser, but to the ideology that had fuelled his radical discourse and paradigm. At home, the Muslim Brothers turned against Nasser after realizing that he was not going to impose an Islamic government with Islamic laws on the nation. In turn, Nasser repressed the Muslim Brothers brutally. In 1969, the burning of the al-Aqsa Mosque in Jerusalem radicalized King Faisal of Saudi Arabia. Against the background of a weakened Nasser, King Faisal called for *jihad* against Israel and began supporting the PLO, which he had previously shunned because of its presumed dependence on Egypt.

After Nasser's death in 1970, his successor, Anwar al-Sadat, sought to accommodate and appease the Muslim Brothers, repressed by Nasser. The 1971 Egyptian Constitution affirmed Islam as the official religion of the state and stipulated that the Shari'a was a source of legislation.[107] After a short honeymoon, during 1977, the Muslim Brothers attacked Sadat's rapprochement with Israel and the Peace Treaty. Sadat sought to neutralize his critics by emphasizing the Islamic nature of his rule. Having toyed with the idea of implementing Islamic penalties, in 1980, through a plebiscite, Sadat made the Shari'a the main source of legislation. Sadat, who was addressed as the al-Ra'is al-Mu'min (the Believer President) in the Egyptian media, turned against the Muslim Brothers and their radical Islamic cohorts in September 1981. Less than a month later Sadat was assassinated by Lieutenant Khalid al-Islambuli, a member of Tanzim al-Jihad (Organization of Jihad). Under the presidency of Hosni Mubarak, Islambuli and four other Muslim militants were put on trial and later executed.[108] Later, in 1985–86, Egyptian sympathizers of the 'Organization of Jihad' and those who had been arrested in relation to Sadat's assassination joined the Mujahedin in Afghanistan. Most notable among them was the physician Ayman al-Zawahiri.[109]

In Pakistan, Ayub Khan came to power in 1958. He believed in cleansing Islam of superstition and stagnation and moving the country forward by incorporating modern science and knowledge.[110] Ayub Khan's modernization drive and especially his reform of Muslim family law provoked a strong backlash from the religious establishment. The debates that followed the reforms demonstrated the religious establishment's strong intent on maintaining its ultimate power over interpretation and final decision-making in all religion-related domains. They argued that only the qualified members of the religious establishment possessed the necessary knowledge of Islamic law. The non-clerical modernists, intent on rejecting the monopoly of the 'ulema over 'Islamic learning and interpretation', argued that 'all informed Muslims have the right to exercise interpretation', since Islam does not possess or recognize a separate class of priests.[111] During this period, an obvious tug of war between the official custodians of the religious establishment and Islamic modernists and even secular forces over the right and legitimacy to interpret and opine on

Islamic topics and issues is observable across the Muslim world. General Zia al-Haq's ascent to power in 1978 and his attempt to transform Pakistan into a truly Islamic state provided ideal conditions for the growth of Islamic parties in Pakistan and neighbouring Afghanistan. At home, Zia's government included members of Mawdudi's Jama'at al-Islami party. Zia al-Haq's goal of creating an Islamic bloc in the region against India played an important role in the flourishing of Mujahedin groups in Afghanistan, after the Soviet invasion.

In Iran Ayatollah Khomeini opposed Mohammad Reza Shah's White Revolution, which included land reform, the nationalization of forests, the privatization of nationalized industries, profit-sharing schemes for factory workers, women's suffrage and the creation of a literacy corps. Parallel to his criticism of the Shah's internal politics in 1963, Khomeini campaigned against the provision of diplomatic immunity to US personnel in Iran and argued that the Capitulation Agreement 'reduced the status of the Iranian people to a level lower than that of an American dog'.[112] Khomeini's claim that Islam was being endangered by the Shah's policies resulted in a two-day anti-government demonstration that was brutally repressed by the army. Ayatollah Khomeini was imprisoned and exiled to Turkey and subsequently to Iraq, where he resided until his triumphant return to Iran via France in February 1979.

During Khomeini's absence from Iran, aside from the official religious establishment, the Islamic cause branched into three different tendencies. First, the modernist Islam of men of reflection such as Mehdi Bazargan, Mahmud Taleqani and Ali Shari'ati represented an extroverted, forward-looking, relatively flexible and open Islam largely based on human reasoning. While the Islamic modernism of Bazargan was a liberal, forward-looking Islam, that of Shari'ati and Taleqani, while equally forward-looking, was much more inspired by and anchored in the socialist ideals of a just and classless society, free of national and international exploitation. Shari'ati and Taleqani also fought against the religious status quo, seeking to liberate Muslims from the stupefying powers of the religious establishment. The Islam of this group was an inclusive and subsequently tolerant Islam. Second, the Organization of the Iranian Peoples' Holy Warriors (Sazeman-e Mujahedin Khalq Iran) was a radical, revolutionary and clandestine vanguard group, deeply marked by the success of Marxist guerrilla movements worldwide and committed to armed insurrection. The founding fathers of the Mujahedin were disciples of both Bazargan and Taleqani. The Islam that appealed to their generation was revolutionary, egalitarian and anti-imperialist. Their ideology was essentially based on a revolutionary Marxism in the political, social and economic realm, effectively couched and formulated in Islamic terms and symbols. While Bazargan, Taleqani and Shari'ati were reformist modernists, the early Mujahedin were revolutionary modernists. The third tendency, the Islamic Coalition of Mourning Associations (Hey'athay-e Mo'talefeh Eslami), was a continuation of Navab-Safavi's Devotees of Islam. The Islamic Coalition of Mourning Associations followed the Devotees of Islam both theoretically and tactically. Their Islam was exclusion-based and intolerant. Some of the founding members of the Coalition of Islamic Mourning Associations were active members of Navab-Safavi's group. This tendency came to occupy an important place in the power structure of the Islamic Republic of Iran.

Tension between the governments of Muslim states and their Islamic political movements constituted an intrinsic feature of the political life of this period. In Syria, since the mid-1960s, the Muslim Brothers had challenged the power of the Ba'ath party, through both peaceful and armed resistance. Two years after his ascent to the presidency in February 1971, Hafiz al-Asad's introduced a secular constitution, triggering rioting and demonstrations led by the Muslim Brothers. In 1976, the Brotherhood began its *jihad* against the government. The anti-governmental military operations multiplied and came to include attacks against Soviet military advisers and an attempt on Assad's life. The government responded brutally. In July 1980 a law was passed 'making membership or association with the Brethren punishable by death'. [113] In October 1980, the Syrian Islamic Front was established and called for the overthrow of Assad's regime through *jihad*. It sought an Islamic state committed to 'Islamic socialism', promoting 'social justice under Islamic law', and was uncompromisingly opposed to Israel and Zionism. [114] By 1985, Assad tried to accomodate his Islamic opposition by freeing hundreds of prisoners.

In 1958, President 'Abd al-Karim Qasem of Iraq allowed the establishment of the Hizb al-Da'wa al-Islamiyyah (Party of Islamic Call). [115] This mass Shi'i organization, benefited from the theoretical writings and teachings of the distinguished cleric Muhammad Baqir Sadr. In his major works, *Our Philosophy* and *Our Economics*,

Sadr argued that Islam was compatible with a modern society based on popular sovereignty, social justice and the abolition of exploitation. Legislature, however, had to be compatible with Islamic law. With the seizure of power by the secular Ba'athists in 1968, the Shi'i Party of Islamic Call or Da'wa adopted a more aggressive posture against the state. The Ba'athist government, intent on keeping religion out of politics, reacted aggressively to Shi'i radicalism by imprisoning clerical leaders and expelling Shi'i Iranians who were active in the Da'wa and who had lived in Iraq for a long time. Between 1973 and 1974, members of Da'wa were killed in prison, arrested and sentenced to death. In 1977 and after the Iranian revolution in 1979, the Shi'i religious mourning ceremonies of 'Ashura turned into anti-regime demonstrations calling for the overthrow of the regime. When in 1979 the Shi'i demonstrators demanded the establishment of an Islamic state, Baqir Sadr and his family were arrested. In response to the harsh repression against Da'wa, a military branch was founded in late 1979. In April 1980, five months before Iraq's attack on Iran and the beginning of the eight-year Iran–Iraq war, Muhammad Baqir Sadr and his sister Bint Huda were executed. The military wing of Da'wa was named Shahid al-Sadr or the Martyr Sadr. In 1982, Da'wa and other Shi'i groups gathered in Tehran and founded the Supreme Council of the Islamic Revolution in Iraq. Another notable Shi'i cleric, Musa al-Sadr, Muhammad Baqir al-Sadr's cousin and brother-in-law, who was born in Qum, returned to Lebanon, his ancestral home, in 1960. Musa al-Sadr founded the Movement of the Deprived (Harakat al-Mahrumin) in 1974. Believing in the necessity of an armed wing, in 1975 Musa al-Sadr organized the Amal (Afwaj al-Muqawma al-Lubnaniya). It was in August 1978 that Musa al-Sadr mysteriously disappeared in Libya.

Islam on the Offensive (1979–Present)

Shortly after a heterogenous and spontaneously formed coalition of Nationalist, Islamic and Marxist forces brought the Iranian revolution to victory and an Islamic Republic was established, the West realized that it was confronted with a new and powerful insurrectionary world outlook. This was an ideology that appealed to the dispossessed, the humiliated, the discredited and the disavowed. The culturally, economically and politically dispossessed were taking revenge on those who had ignored them. Among this rainbow of forces there existed those who were neither culturally nor economically dispossessed, but sought political empowerment. The natural victims of the modernization and secularization process, relatively pauperized by a polarizing market economy and culturally marginalized in their own country, stood side by side with those who favoured the secularization and modernization process, against the Shah's autocratic regime. The stark differences between the slogans, ideals, discourses, demeanour and prevailing mass psychology of the anti-absolutist revolutionary stage with the period after the consolidation of power by the clergy loyal to Khomeini sowed confusion not only among foreign observers of Iran but even among those Iranians who were the actors and not the managers of the revolution. The magic of the Iranian revolution during its anti-autocratic period was that it appealed to and attracted all social strata and classes. It was an all-inclusive, all-embracing broad-based mass movement with the single objective of dethroning a king who had come to epitomize all that was undesirable to a majority of his subjects. By all accounts, this was a relatively bloodless revolution. Right before the eventual transfer of power to the 'revolutionaries', even the Shah's mighty army, whose generals and soldiers had sworn allegiance to 'God, Shah and the motherland', officially declared its 'impartiality and nonpartisanship' in the confrontation between the people and the Shah.

The broad-based anti-autocratic Popular Front that formed the engine of the revolution came to take shape because a significantly large social group firmly believed in the anti-imperialist, democratic and social justice-oriented discourse that was often repeated by the spiritual leader of the revolution, Ayatollah Khomeini. In the early days of the revolution, Khomeini attacked the Shah as a 'slavish servant of the foreigners and imperialists', who was squandering the fortunes of the nation. In his fiery declarations, Khomeini wrote that the Shah, who was supposed to be the 'guardian of freedoms', did not 'allow anyone, anywhere in the country to utter a word of criticism' and added that, 'the shadow of his abominable police force' hovered over the country. Finally, Khomeini accused the Shah of massacring his people.[116] Three months before the victory of the revolution, Ayatollah Khomeini, residing in Paris, told anxious reporters who were concerned with democratic rights and freedoms of Marxists in an Islamic Republic that: 'An Islamic republic is a democratic state in the true sense of the word and ... everyone can voice his opinion ... and the Islamic state will respond with logic to all the arguments put forward'.[117] The consolidation of power by Ayatollah Khomeini proved that socio-political concepts had different meanings in different discourses pronounced at different times and places. Democratic rights and freedom of expression came to be redefined after the institutionalization of the rule of the jurisconsult (velayat-e faqih).

The Challenge of the Iranian Revolution

The complexity of the Iranian revolution was not evident. It is not surprising that initially Western intellectuals responded rather favourably to the revolution. Michel Foucault considered the Iranian revolution as 'the renewal of an entire nation's total existence through the resumption of a spiritual experience found at the heart of Shi'i Islam'.[118] Foucault reminded his public of the seldom-cited lines that preceded Marx's famous statement on religion as the opium of the masses. According to Foucault, Marx had written that religion was the spirit of a world without spirit. He then concluded that: 'We should therefore say that Islam in 1978 was not the opium of the people, exactly because it was the spirit of a world without spirit.'[119] Western fascination with what seemed like a spiritually induced anti-imperialist and anti-despotic mass revolutionary experience was not unexpected. Western intellectuals, critical of their own society, identified with a revolution that claimed to place spiritualism on the agenda of an individualist, materialist and consumerist world.

Certain Western governments began to distance themselves from the Islamic Republic of Iran because its tumultuous spiritual experience had resulted in a radical and religiously anchored challenge to an identity, culture and way of life associated with the West. The rejection of that which was conceived as being imposed from the outside, politically, economically and culturally, necessitated a return to indigenous sources of inspiration and interpretation. The Iranian revolution, not without bitter internal disputes, turned to its Islamic heritage, a privately familiar, yet politically and socio-economically unfathomed alternative, as an ideology. This was a classic case of the oppressed discovering a new force and power within, which it had come to recognize as having always possessed without awareness of its potency, and using it to challenge the oppressors. The mentally colonized was taking revenge on the colonizer, without caring to identify the merit-worthy elements in his intellectual and material achievements. The question posed by the new challenger was simple. What has the West done for the non-Westerner and why do we, the non-Western, today stand so disadvantaged compared to them? In practice, the rebirth of a model Islamic human being, free of the shortcomings of the so-called Western individual, remained an unfulfilled utopian dream, quickly marred and blemished by inhuman acts committed by the new Republic.

The revolution deprived the USA of a highly Westernized, minerally rich and politically close partner in the region. Before the revolution, Iran was considered to be the US 'gendarme' of the region, intervening in Oman to repress the Marxist guerrillas in Dhofar. The Iranians' belief in their absolute right to reject US political and economic intervention was construed as an attack on the USA. According to Huntington, 'it is hardly surprising that following the 1979 Iranian Revolution, an intercivilizational quasi war developed between Islam and the West'.[120] The key slogans of the Iranian revolution were 'independence, freedom, an Islamic Republic'. Does Huntington imply that the anti-despotic, anti-imperialist and Islamic demands of the Iranian revolution should be construed as a declaration of war against the West? The appearance of a new anti-imperialist force, appealing to the culturally, economically and politically disinherited at a time when the fervour of old Marxist–Leninist forces were fading away, presented a major political challenge to the international political position of the USA, especially in the oil-rich Middle East region. Promoting a scenario based on an inevitable war between Islam and the West, instigated by Islam, provided the USA with a perfect excuse for planning and executing policies aimed at enfeebling this new brand of anti-imperialist and populist force.

While the debate raged over the Islamic discourse or Shi'i sub-system that was to represent the new Islamic Republic and provide the substance of its constitution, the fragility of a monolithic Islamic discourse became readily apparent in Iran. Islam in power was confronted with the same issues and problematics of any post-revolutionary society. What kind of society is to be built? What is the relation of the people to the state? What are their rights and responsibilities? How is power distributed, redistributed and transferred? What was different in the Islamic Republic of Iran was that the questions, responses and critiques were mainly phrased in an Islamic jargon. Islam, this potent political identity and tool for action, cascaded into a panoply of paths and courses of action and modes of conducting the socio-political, cultural and economic livelihood of a nation. When the debate became bloody and gruesome in Iran, it became clear that political Islam, like all things political, could not be saved by the spirituality, mysticism and moral ethics of the faith. In order to obtain its earthly objective of political and economic power, Islam became a tool in the hands of those who had obtained power. It was used to justify and legitimize the policies of the new ruling elite. The failure of political Islam to deliver those democratic rights and liberties denied by the previous regime, while prohibiting certain rights and liberties provided by the previous regime, triggered a natural de-politicization process of Islam in Iran, where it had all started. The intellectual process of secularization in Iran started when the Islamic government produced a new autocratic ruling class seeking its earthly self-interest while proclaiming to rule in the name of Islam.

For Muslims around the world, Sunnis as well as Shi'is, witnessing the Iranian experience and the rise to power of a revolutionary Islamic state in the second half of the twentieth century was a powerful source of inspiration, awakening long-felt yearnings. It seemed as if the dreams and aspirations of the pioneers of Islamic revivalism as well as the historical longing of Muslims to impose their cultural identity in their our homes had come true. During its early euphoric days, the Iranian revolution held a desirable and clear mirror before all Muslims who opposed their rulers and system of government. The Iranian revolution proved that movements could rely on Islam as a potent mobilizing force to overthrow regimes. The Iranian revolution revived the historically worn-out self-respect and confidence of Muslims in their faith as a tool for political change as well as a means of social, economic and cultural transformation and improvement. Irrespective of the content and direction of the Islamic Republic, which immediately became a bitter bone of contention within Iran, to discontented Muslims the Iranian revolution became the symbol of what the Soviet, Chinese and Cuban revolutions had presented to revolutionary Marxists across the world.

Neutralizing the Iranian Revolution

It was not long after the Iranian revolution that the fear of a wave of Islamic revolutions throughout the region surfaced. The exporting of revolutionary Islam and the domino effect that it could produce presented a major ideological challenge to the USA, which was the major loser in this situation. If political Islam could evoke such mass enthusiasm and mobilize such passion and fervour in non-Arab Iran, could it not generate equal if not greater fervour and passion in the rest of the Muslim non-Arab as well as Arab world, where Islam as a revolutionary force had long been poised to take power? A radical Islamic challenge to Western political and economic interests in the region proved realistic when, at the end of the 1979 *hajj*, the Grand Mosque in Mecca was taken over by several hundred radical Muslims, challenging the authority of the Saudi royal family. With one royal ally gone and the other under siege, the USA was understandably alarmed by the tidal waves that Islam could produce. The threat of radical Islam as a force capable of destabilizing Western-friendly oil-producing monarchies as well as geo-politically important allies such as Egypt clearly posed a new kind of international problem. Saudi authorities, probably with the blessing and technical support of their US allies, responded categorically. First they obtained a religious *fatwa* to retake the mosque, then they laid siege to it for two weeks and finally attacked the insurgents. The Saudi commando raid left behind 127 dead soldiers and took 170 prisoners. In a huge bloodbath, 63 of the 170 surviving insurgents were beheaded. The Saudis witnessed how Islam could wage war on Islam, and a sense of bewilderment and shock passed through the well-protected and cloistered Saudi society.

The conservative but Western-friendly Islam of the Saudi royal family had to be protected from the radical Islam of the insurgents. It seemed as if the guardians of puritan and cleansed Wahabbism needed re-cleansing. Ever since the dawn of humanity, individuals, groups and classes, societies and nations had fought over issues of justice, equity, fairness and ethical principles of right and wrong. This was no different. The Islamic dimension of the conflict presented the plurality of Islam embedded in the faith. The threat was not against the West directly, but against the Islam and the power of the West's allies in the region. This dangerous trend had to be contained, in order to safeguard Western interests in a highly sensitive region. The self-assertiveness of a dominated people, re-armed with a deep-rooted and newly redefined religion-cum-ideology, seeking to control and map out their present – even at the risk of their future – was taken as a sign of belligerence and intolerance towards the West. An economic and political struggle somewhat similar to the one engaged in by the USA during its war of independence and civil war was given a new spin as a 'quasi-intercivilizational war'. Either impervious to the rich plurality of Islam or intentionally turning a blind eye to it, a rudimentary and clichéd classification of good and bad Islam came to prevail. This simplistic stereotyping was rooted in a more elementary logic, devoid of any ethical or moral considerations. Muslim leaders, governments and forces friendly towards the USA were considered 'good Muslims' and those neutral, unfriendly or anti-USA were considered 'bad Muslims'. Long before President Bush informed the world community in late September 2001 that: 'Either you are with us or you are with the terrorists', US foreign policy functioned on the basis of these same unuttered lines. The 'good Muslim', irrespective of his record on human and civil rights, was one who accepted and followed the US lead.

The War in Afghanistan: A Different Model of Islamic Struggle

It can be argued that the string of events in Afghanistan triggered off by the Soviet invasion was directly related to the Soviet perception of an Islamic threat to its southern republics after the victory of the Iranian revolution. In turn, the Soviet invasion of Afghanistan provided the ideal solution for harnessing the rising tide of Islamic radicalism in the region. Why not galvanize and channel the anger and rage of a newly politicized Islam, primarily sensitive to US foreign policy in the region, against the other oppressor and colonizer, which was furthermore atheist and 'Godless'? Identifying the anti-Soviet war in Afghanistan as a religious war against the atheists not only deflected the wrath of militant Muslims from their own pro-Western governments, but forged bonds of cooperation and alliance between radical Muslims and the USA. As long as such militant Muslim forces were battling the USA's main military and ideological rival, they were considered friendly 'freedom fighters'. To attract the young and angry Muslims of the world to this theatre of religious war, a war of liberation against foreign invasion had to be passed off as a religious crusade or *jihad* against communism. This new crusade gave rise to a new type of sectarian, fundamentalist, hidebound, military-minded, puritan and violent Islamic force, fuelled and manned by a new crop of Fedaian (devotees) or Mujahedin (holy warriors) of Islam. This international and zealous Islamic corps, which was to become militarily professional and technologically savvy on Afghan soil, was the USA's trump card in its new foreign policy position: turning the Islamic upsurge to its own advantage by implementing a green Islamic belt around the southern flank of the Soviet Empire.

From 1979 the USA provided covert aid, but by 1982, through the intermediary of Pakistan, one of its closest allies in the region, it was providing $600 million per year to the Mujahedin in Afghanistan, with a matching sum provided by the Gulf states.[121] Soon, 'huge consignments of light weapons were delivered by the CIA and unloaded at the port of Karachi', and heroin was exported via Karachi.[122] By 1985, the USA was supplying the Mujahedin with Stinger missiles, which are said to have turned the tide against the Soviet army.[123] The massive US and Saudi contribution of some $6.5 billion to the war effort of the Islamic forces in Afghanistan had numerous rewards. By emphasizing the religious nature of the new anti-communist crusade and the sacrifices that success in such a campaign would necessitate, the West, in the very short run, successfully utilized the Mujahedin for its own political ends. Yet its call appealed to the most conservative and dogmatic trends and factions of the Islamic radicals. Mullah Omar, who later became the leader of the Taliban, joined Mohammad Yunis Khalis' Hizb Islami between 1989 and 1992 to fight the Soviets. This group had splintered from Golbuddin Hekmatyar's Hizb-e Islami (Islamic Party), and was one of the organizations receiving aid through Pakistan. Subsequently around 15,000 warriors, predominantly from Saudi Arabia (5,000), Yemen (3,000), Algeria (2,800) and Egypt (2,000), joined the *jihad* in Afghanistan.[124] The 'Islamic international corps' pouring into Pakistan to fight in Afghanistan and stationed in Pishawar received a salary of some $1,500 per month while fighting alongside the Mujahedin.[125]

The predominantly Sunni Islamic international brigade served several crucial and useful purposes in the large geo-political theatre of US interest in the Middle East. The first was to use fanatical Islam to roll back communism. The second was to show the oppressed and politically frustrated people of the Arab and non-Arab world that the real theatre of war, where Muslims could demonstrate their prowess, selflessness and superiority, was not Palestine but Afghanistan. It was in Afghanistan that Muslims could enforce their identity and create their ideal state. Third, focusing the wrath of Muslims on the communists served to deflect and deform the original anti-colonial and anti-US message of the Iranian revolution, which at times smacked of anti-capitalism. Fourth, by appealing to Sunni Muslims and pursing the policy of isolating Shi'i Iran, it successfully fuelled the Shi'i–Sunni, Iran–Arab schism, thus preventing the formation of an Islamic United Front. Finally, the USA came to salvage its status as the most trustworthy friend of the leaders of the conservative Arab world. The theatre of war in Afghanistan, far away from the frontiers of Arab states, allowed for the wrath of disinherited Muslims to be vented and deflected from targeting their own governments and that of the USA. On another front, the USA actively participated in, if not prompted, yet another theatre of war to enfeeble and destroy the Islamic Republic of Iran. In September 1980, Muslim Iraq, backed militarily, technologically and financially by the West, attacked Muslim Iran.

The US objective was more than successfully obtained in Afghanistan. Not only did the Soviet troops withdraw in 1989, but the retreat of Soviet forces and the internal ramifications of defeat in Afghanistan set off a chain reaction that played an important role in the collapse of the Soviet Empire. In the eight-year Iran–Iraq war, however, the main US objective, which was the military and political defeat of the Islamic Republic and an eventual regime change, did not materialize. The war, however, weakened both Saddam Hussein, the US protagonist and ally at the time, and the Islamic Republic of Iran. In the Iran–Iraq theatre of war, the West not only provided money and arms to Iraq, but in July 1988 USS *Vincennes* shot down an Iranian civilian Airbus on its way to Dubai, killing all 290 passengers on board. This event played an important role in Khomeini's decision to accept a ceasefire with Iraq in August 1988. The aftermath of these two wars, in which the USA had handpicked its 'good Muslim' partners, proved to be catastrophic. For the first time in US history, the ramifications of erroneous and unrealistic policy-making based on simplistic and short-sighted considerations rather than well-reflected long-term analysis brought the horror of blood and terror on to US soil.

Six months after Iran's acceptance of the ceasefire with Iraq, the Red Army withdrew from Afghanistan and less than four months after this event, Ayatollah Khomeini died on 4 June 1989. After the departure of the Soviets, the weakening of the Islamic Republic and the death of Khomeini, the fate of Afghanistan was no longer of major importance to the USA, Saudi Arabia and the Gulf States that had been financing the war. Subsequently, the USA began to alter its policies with regard to certain Mujahedin groups in Afghanistan. All aid to Golbuddin Hekmatyar, the leader of Hisb-e Islami (Islamic Party) and Abdul Rasoul Sayyaf, the founder of Ittihad-e Islami (Islamic Unity), both pro-Wahhabi, was cut off by Washington on grounds of their extremist positions.[126] The drying up of the flow of financial resources that had regularly nurtured the Mujahedin groups during the 1980s provoked the wrath of the holy warriors, who viewed the change in policy as 'Washington's abandonment of the *jihad*' and Riyadh's betrayal of it.[127] Following Iraq's invasion of Kuwait, King Fahd of Saudi Arabia requested the assistance of the West. The military build-up in Saudi Arabia during the end of 1990, followed by the start of the first Persian Gulf War on 17 January 1991, added insult to the injury of the Mujahedin. Their benefactors seemed to have turned against them. To the dismay of US policy-makers, the 'good Muslims', who had been cultivated, befriended and financially supported, reacted and suddenly turned against the hand that had fed them.

The war in Afghanistan had created a new international breed of zealous Muslim warriors, who eventually wreaked havoc on US soil. The true products of globalization, these guerrilla fighters of the cyber age have no home base, no national allegiance or responsibility, no palpable geographical military objectives and no confined geographical headquarters. The world is their arena and their target is spread out wherever the USA and its allies have a political, financial, cultural or religious interest or presence. Their religion makes a claim to a universal Islam, but it is primarily based on an exclusion-driven, sectarian and essentially militaristic outlook, which could have any or no religion or ideology as its base. They believe in an all-out war, excluding no weapons or methods for inflicting loss on their enemies. The objectives and intentions of the Mujahedin, beyond their claim of establishing a world Islamic order and securing the departure of non-Muslim troops from the region, remain vague. According to Gilles Kepel: 'This milieu was cut off from social reality; its inhabitants perceived the world in the light of religious doctrine and armed violence. It bred a new, hybrid Islamist ideology whose first doctrinal principle was to rationalize the existence and behaviour of militants. This was jihadist-salafism.'[128]

The withdrawal of the Soviets and the fall of the Soviet empire fuelled the myth of the invincibility of the holy warriors and the righteousness of their cause as well as their methods. The experience of Afghanistan was believed to be applicable to all Muslim countries where governments did not implement the Shari'a according to the perception of the young holy warriors. The passion and fervour of waging war for a holy cause and an overwhelming sense of power and glory as a result of victory filled the veterans of the Afghan war. Between 1989 and 1992, this voluntarist and extremist group sought to clone its 'successful experience' elsewhere. Some, such as the Algerians, returned to their own countries to impose an Islamic order; some took an internationalist view and set off either to export the Islamic revolution to Bosnia, Tajikestan, Chechnya, Kashmir and the Philippines or simply spread the faith through sowing fear and terror in Western cities. Finally, others remained in Afghanistan to finish the internal war and impose an Islamic state.

The experience of the Afghan war presented an alternative model to the Iranian revolution for those who sought to usher in an Islamic state in their countries. The Iranian revolution was an inclusive, popular, national and broad-based socio-political movement, which had relied essentially on civil disobedience, national strikes and mass demonstrations for obtaining its ends. This movement was not based on blind violence, military campaigns, fratricides and proclamations of holy war. The Iranian clergy were very careful not to evoke the concept of *jihad* against the Pahlavi regime. This was a popular revolution, cutting across class, gender and ideology, for the success of which no military commander of a regular or irregular army could take credit. The Afghan victory was a different story. It was the result of long-drawn-out military campaigns in which the willpower and firepower of the holy warriors, a good number of whom came from abroad, were backed by handsome monthly paycheques and sophisticated military hardware, also from abroad. The principal engine of success in the Afghan experience seemed to be its reliance on violence and the gun, readily shrouded in a simplified notion of waging holy war or *jihad*. Voluntarism and the will to power through holy war was an important lesson learnt by the Islamic International Corps. They took home with them the notion that political power in the name of Islam was attainable through waging holy war and shedding blood, as it had proved successful back in Afghanistan. Three key concepts could be identified as the backbone of this new type of Islamic holy warrior. All means are permitted in the cause of establishing an Islamic state and obliterating the enemies. Power was within the range of the guns of those holy warriors ready for martyrdom. In the war waged against illegitimate powers, the heretics, the collaborators and the infidels, all except those who actively supported the holy warriors, were considered enemies. In this exclusion-based war of desperation there was no room for neutrality or passive by-standers.[129]

In the 1980s and 1990s two broad types of Islamic movements and organizations emerged. Both spoke on behalf of Islam and aimed at establishing an Islamic state, while relying on the concept of *jihad* to advance their military and political cause. The first group discovered that creating and nurturing a broad-based social network system alongside its military activities provided it with a solid political basis on which it could construct its long-term objectives. The socially inclined, welfare-oriented Islamic movements or organizations emphasize the provision of community services and recognize the importance of meeting the basic needs of the population as well as recruiting holy warriors among them. The Lebanese Hizballah represents this type of socially inclined, welfare-oriented Islamic organization, balancing its military activities with the construction of hospitals, schools, medical centres, public assistance facilities, food distribution centres for the needy and even firms and productive units.[130] The second type of Islamic organization was that of the voluntarist holy warriors who felt that through blood, bullets and martyrdom they could realize their special brand of Islam. This was a purely vanguard militarist organization, uninterested in and too impatient with creating a social base by engaging the community or society in a dialogue. These military types of Islamic organizations were greatly influenced by the Afghan war and are best represented by the GIA in Algeria and al-Qaida. In time, community-based and socially inclined Islamic movements became increasingly involved in national politics as the proper arena for representing their community and religious interests. The Islamic Salvation Front (FIS) in Algeria and even Hamas in Palestine can be considered community-based welfare-oriented organizations. While the sectarian martial features of socially in-clined Islamic movements diluted as they became integrated in national politics, closed militaristic Islamic organizations, cut off from social reality and respresentation, become more extremist, desperate and marginalized as their message of violence and blood was reciprocated by more blood-letting and destruction.

The Algerian Bloodbath

On 15 February 1989 the Soviet army withdrew from Afghanistan, and on 21 February 1989 the Islamic Salvation Front was born at the Sunna Mosque in Bab el-Oued in Algiers. The political objective of the FIS was the establishment of an Islamic republic and the return of the 'religious aspects of the Algerian state'.[131] Within the FIS, while Abbasi Madani, its leader, favoured the ballot box, the democratic road to power and political participation and dialogue, Ali Belhaj, a radical *salafist*, denounced democracy as alien to Islam. According to Belhaj, the second-in-command of the FIS, 'Muslims could not support a pluralistic system that was "in conflict with the ideology [of the FIS] and that contradicts the beliefs of our people"'.[132] Ten months after the creation of the FIS, a huge crowd of veiled women converged on the National Assembly in Algiers demanding the application of the Shari'a. The social programmes of the FIS among the poor assured it of popular support. The provincial and municipal elections of June 1990 gave a landslide victory to FIS. The FIS-controlled councils subsequently sought to ban shorts and swimwear in the streets, concerts of rai music, the sale of alcohol and mixed-sex education.[133]

It was not until after the first Persian Gulf War, the arrest and imprisonment of Abbasi Madani and Ali Belhaj, the landslide victory of the FIS in the first democratically held legislative elections, the annulment of these elections by the military, the banning of the FIS and finally the sentencing of Madani and Benhaj to 12 years in prison that the bloodbath in Algeria began. The Algerian military's decision to block the political participation and victory of the FIS strenghtened the hand of the extremists, who had opposed the parliamentary road to power. However, violence started before the intervention of the military in January 1992 to terminate the legislative elections. By November 1991, the 'Afghans' had entered into action in Algeria.[134] Tayeb Messaoudi, whose *nom de guerre* was Tayeb al-Afghani, and Abderrahman Dahane, whose *nom de guerre* was Dahane al-Afghani, two Algerian veterans of the Afghan war, attacked the military post at Guemmar in south-eastern Algeria, killing 15 young conscripts and escaped with arms and ammunition.[135] On 29 June 1992, the Algerian President Mohammad Boudiaf was assassinated and a wave of violence, executions and destruction was unleashed on nearly every segment of society. In the mayhem, which lasted until 1999, somewhere between 100,000 to 120,000 people lost their lives to 'terrorist violence' in Algeria.[136] A considerable number of murders ascribed to terrorists were, however, the result of 'the settling of scores' during times of widespread insecurity and instability.[137]

The Armed Islamic Group (GIA) is said to have been created by the Algerian members of the Islamic international corps in Peshawar in 1989.[138] The GIA was dominated by the veterans of the Afghan war. Its members were usually unemployed and poorly educated young men. The GIA was intent on overthrowing the Algerian government, which it deemed 'impious and illegitimate', and imposing an Islamic state through *jihad*, 'blood and martyrdom'.[139] According to Abdelhaq Layada, the first military commander of the GIA: 'The ungodly had everywhere succeeded in clinging to power, because the movements opposing them had hesitated to embrace *jihad* and to resort to armed struggle.'[140] The activities of the GIA at times became intertwined with those of the Armed Islamic Movement (MIA) and the Islamic Salvation Army (AIS). Mustafa Bouyali, a veteran of the Algerian war of independence, a follower of Sayyid Qutb and the founder of the MIA, was killed in 1987.[141] His hardline followers joined the GIA once the military activities of the Algerian Afghans had started in November 1991. The AIS, the official military wing of the FIS, was created in 1994 in response to concerns over the GIA's claim to the leadership of the Islamic movement and as a means to pressure the government to lift its ban on the FIS and allow its legal activities.[142] While the AIS primarily targeted the security forces, the GIA focused its violence on the regime's officials, intellectuals, secular activists and foreign citizens, and even engaged in 'liquidating' 70 MIA fighters, suspected of 'cooperation with the regime'.[143] The 1994 merger between the AIS and the GIA lasted a year. Upon the collapse of the merger, the GIA pronounced a death sentence on Madani and Belhaj.[144]

The model of a successful Islamic movement for the military commanders of the GIA was Afghanistan. In 1994, another veteran of the Afghan war, the 26-year-old Sherif Gousmi, known as Abu Abdallah Ahmad, became the military commander of the GIA. He established a special assassination unit known as the 'Death Brigades', recruited entirely from the Afghans.[145] From 1994, the GIA under Djamel Zitouni carried its violence on to French soil. The extremist goals and strategies of the GIA were different from those of the FIS. The GIA not only challenged the Algerian regime, but threatened all other segments of the population, including moderate Muslims who sought to participate in the political process. The GIA was the heir to Banna's 'Special Apparatus' of the Muslim Brothers and Navab Safavi's 'Devotees of Islam'. According to Kepel, the GIA's political and organizational departure from the Algerian scene in 1997 was 'even more confused and mysterious than the one whereby it came into existence in 1992'.[146]

Lebanese Hizballah

In July 1982 Syria allowed some 1,500 Iranian Revolutionary Guards, originally dispatched to Syria with the intention of repelling the Israeli invasion of southern Lebanon, to establish a base in Ba'albak. The founding of a new and radical Shi'i force in Lebanon was also in the interest of Syria, as Hafez al-Assad feared a possible rapprochement between Nabih Berri's Shi'i Amal movement and the USA. With the disappearance of Musa al-Sadr, radical Shi'i resistance was to be carried out by the Hizballah. The Party of God, which had effectively splintered from the moderate Amal movement, was intended to become Iran's Islamic spearhead in the Arab world, exporting and disseminating a revolutionary Islam. The Shi'i Hizballah, which officially proclaimed its allegiance to Ayatollah Khomeini, was implanted in a land that had provided the Iranian Safavid dynasty with its Shi'i clerics and where Shi'is constituted 40 per cent of the population. The two-fold thrust of Hizballah was to challenge the oppressive Arab regimes of the region as well as to combat the hegemonic role and interests of all the superpowers in the area. The main targets of Hizballah, however, were the USA and Israel. In the 1990s, Iran's primary concern with domestic reconstruction and regaining international legitimacy and recognition after the war with Iraq translated into a step-by-step process of disengagement in Lebanon. Concomitantly, the Revolutionary Guards were gradually withdrawn from the region and by 1998 the last of them had left Lebanon.

The rapid pace at which Iran increased its funding of Hizballah in the 1980s slowed down considerably in the 1990s. Iran's contribution of $30 million in 1985 more than doubled in two years, reaching $64 million in 1987. After a decade – by 1997 – Iran's financial assistance stood at $80 million. By 2004, Iran's financial support of Hizballah varied between $60 and $100 million according to different sources. These figures indicate that since 1997 Iran's assistance to Hizballah has either flattened or, more probably, decreased. Today, even though the organization considers Ayatollah Ali Khamenei its ultimate leader and maintains close ties with Tehran, it is far from being an Iranian-controlled militia. Sheikh Muhammad Husain Fadlallah, one of Hizballah's major spiritual figures, does not toe the official organizational line and recognizes Ayatollah Sistani of Najaf as his *marji taqlid* (source of imitation).

Hizballah's spree of kidnapping, hijacking and suicide-bombing against Western military and civilian targets in the 1980s subsided in the 1990s. In October 1983, Hizballah was suspected of involvement in the car-bomb attacks on the US Marine barracks and French military installations in Beirut. These attacks killed 243 US Marines and 50 French soldiers. This bloody attack resulted in the withdrawal of US troops from Lebanon. While the 1990s witnessed a suspension of Hizballah attacks against Western interests in the region, the organization focused its military activities essentially on operations against Israel. From 1985 Hizballah waged a forceful and effective guerrilla war against the state of Israel. By 1990 Hizballah had developed into a serious anti-Israeli military machine, not only constantly fighting in the field, but also training members of Hamas and Islamic Jihad. The important military role of Hizballah in the second intifada is undeniable. In 1992 Sheikh Abbas Musavi, the militant leader of Hizballah, was killed along with his wife and son by an Israeli gunship attack. In retaliation, Hizballah is said to have bombed the Israeli embassy in Buenos Aires in March of the same year, killing 29 people. In July 1994 Hizballah was once again implicated in the bombing of a Jewish community centre, killing 95 civilians. In May 2000, Israel withdrew its forces from southern Lebanon and Hizballah attained its most important military and political objective, the liberation of Lebanese soil.

The ascent of Sheikh Hassan Nasrallah, one of the four founding clerical members of Hizballah, to power as Musavi's successor took Hizballah along a different path. Parallel to Hizballah's social welfare orientation, reflected in the wide range of essential services it provided in the region, the new Hizballah leadership chose to participate actively in the Lebanese political process. Ten years of social mobilization was to be put to the service of obtaining a strong foothold in the Lebanese political system. Having effectively employed the concepts of *jihad*, self-sacrifice and 'martyrdom operations', Hizballah turned its attention to becoming an efficient, popular and modern political party. Its image was also to change from that of a one-dimensional terrorist organization to one that also believed in a political and peaceful path of building an ideal state in Lebanon. Nasrallah, who was re-elected as secretary-general for a third term in July 1998, claimed that the USA was not a target of Hizballah, and there were rumours about a dialogue between Hizballah and the USA. Without disbanding his military wing or weakening his military forces, Nasrallah embarked on the parliamentary road to power. In 1992, Hizballah participated in Lebanon's first parliamentary election in 20 years and with its allies won 12 seats. Today, Hizballah and the Amal occupy 35 seats in the Lebanese parliament. By 2005, the pioneers of 'martyrdom operations', essentially acting on behalf of Iran and Syria in the region, had shed their extremist principles and evolved into a different organization with deep national interests. After the withdrawal of Syrian troops from Lebanon on 17 March 2005, Nasrallah rejected US pressure on Hizballah to disarm. He reminded the international community that Hizballah's military power constituted a guarantee against Israel's possible violation of Lebanese territory, and that his organization did not take orders from Syria or Iran.[147] In response to a journalist's question on his view on an Islamic state, Nasrallah responded, 'We believe the requirements for an Islamic state is to have an overwhelming popular desire, and we're not talking about fifty per cent plus one, but a large majority. And this is not available in Lebanon and probably never will be.'[148] Irrespective of the fact that only the USA, Canada and Israel continue to consider Hizballah a terrorist organization, the Hizballah of 2005 is a well-entrenched, broad-based, popular force, which has heavily invested in the democratic political process in Lebanon.

In 23 years, Hizballah has undergone major transformations and its success is primarily due to its ability to adapt its tactics and goals in view of the welfare of its constituency. In contrast to the men of desperation and violence in the GIA, totally consumed by activism and voluntarism in the name of Islam and uninterested in and unconcerned with the life and security, let alone well-being, of Algerians, Hizballah came to realize that the call to Islam in the absence of receptive ears remains mute. Hizballah reached out to the community and created the social base that inevitably responded to its call, whereas the GIA took revenge and punished those who did not understand or did not share its ideals. Unable to communicate with the people, the GIA became ever more isolated, sectarian and intolerant, even alienating Algerian Muslims. Hizballah's inclusiveness, in contrast, attracted Sunnis and Christians. In the previous Lebanese parliament, three of the 12 seats held by Hizballah and its allied parties belonged to a Christian and two Sunnis.[149]

Conclusion

The purpose of this book is to provide an understanding of what Islamic thinkers and ideologues thought about the position, role and possible contributions of Islam in the modern world. It is the story of how intellectuals, teachers and practitioners of the Muslim faith sought to provide socio-political and cultural responses anchored in their faith to the anxieties, contradictions, dichotomies and needs of their co-believers and compatriots. These were all men of reflection at first, aware of their times, yet, like all visionaries, not always content with what they saw. These men, in their own minds and those of their followers, were, at one level, social healers, peacemakers and reformers (*muslehun*). As men of ideas, they had a socio-political and cultural vision of what ought to be. Seldom did they know how to get there or what would be the social consequences of the inapplicability of their ideals.

Those among the pioneers of Islamic revival who pursued their dreams by entering the practical world of politics and power committed acts not expected of social healers. They, as all politicians do, convinced themselves that human sacrifice, when necessary, was only for the good of a higher cause. For them all acts could be justified by claiming that it safeguarded the rule of God. Consumed by power, they lost patience and sacrificed the objects of the exercise, namely human beings who were to be properly guided. The loss of innocence of those pioneers who became politicians is now a part of their political biographies, but does not take away from the fact that they remained respected as men of ideas who intended to heal socio-political and economic ills and to promote social, national and international felicity. Their notion of felicity was grounded in what they understood to be the essence of their faith.

While on the surface the world was exposed to the newsbreaking and often bloody events involving Muslims, scarcely any attention was being paid to the evolution, soul-searching, brainstorming and rethinking that was in progress among Muslim intellectuals. An important current of Muslim intellectuals, whose true impact will be felt only in the years to come, reflected on how Islam had been presented, interpreted, applied and used in the last two decades of the twentieth century. A silent and deep-rooted in-house transformation was taking place among Muslim intellectuals. The official Islams of political groups, movements, parties and states were placed under scrutinizing magnifying glasses and carefully analysed by a new breed of Muslim intellectuals. This new breed was equipped with a different intellectual baggage, steeped in Islamic as well as Western knowledge and directly affected and impacted by the manner in which official Islams had reacted towards emerging situations and problems. This new generation of Muslim intellectuals was conscious of the theoretical developments and transformation in the West and mindful of the repercussions of these developments on their co-believers and compatriots. They presented new Islamic paradigms reflecting the evolving international conjuncture. Just as the pioneers of the late nineteenth and early twentieth centuries had reconfigured and reformed their faith, the new pioneers were naturally pushing beyond the constructions and interpretations of their predecessors.

In view of politicized Islam's recent record and performance, a group of Muslim intellectuals are reassessing its theoretical validity and practical appropriateness as a viable project for governing and administering societies in the modern world. While in the West politicians and the media focus on the simplistic association of Islam with terrorism, fundamentalism and violence, the new pioneers of Islamic revivalism are questioning and challenging the political Islam their predecessors developed. Islam was used by first-generation pioneers as the source material of a potent discourse, the objective of which was to shatter those socio-political and economic systems that seemed neither just and fair nor moral and ethical. The appeal of political Islam, not to be confused with Islam as a belief system, was fundamentally due to its promise of providing a better and brighter alternative to the one that prevailed in both the material and spiritual realm. After some 25 years of experience with inefficient, stifling and corrupt political causes and systems that came to power in the name of Islam and failed to deliver their material and spiritual promises, it became evident to Muslim reformists that religion needed to be separated from government and state. The ruling classes of Islamic states, seeking to legitimize and justify their particular politico-economic interest by evoking religion, had to be unmasked. The impious acts of power politicians, motivated by fortune, fame and glory, had to be de-linked from their false claim to religiosity and exposed as what they truly were. The de-politicizing of Islam, or freeing Islam from the monopoly of its new official clerical-political custodians, has begun in earnest. The objective of this soul-searching process was not only to return to the people their legitimate rights and liberties, but to save the spirituality and import of the faith from being sullied by political mismanagement.

At another level, in contrast to the dogmatic and exclusion-based Islam of the present-day zealous holy warriors who encap-sulate the faith only in holy war, blood and martyrdom and those clerical custodians of a static historical Islamic jurisprudence, who resist all change as innovation and apostasy, when it suits them, another group of Muslim intellectuals have sought to break the monopolistic hold of single eternally valid interpretations of the faith. This re-reading of Islam has legitimized Islamic pluralism and placed the custodians of all single interpretations and readings on the defensive. Some of these men and women of reflection have taken their contemplative analysis to the roots of the faith, re-reading the primary sources, namely the Qur'an and the Sunna.

Some have questioned the process by which the faith became an 'official', 'orthodox' and a 'dogmatic enclosure'.[150] The essential and inherent structure of Islam and Islamic thought is argued by the new pioneers to be an open one in which the interface between 'God's message' and 'human beings' takes place without any official interpreter. In this new discourse 'the people to whom God's message is addressed are themselves the interpreters of the message'.[151] The meaning of the Text will be revealed only through its interpretation and exegesis.[152] The subjectivity of the interpreter, based on his or her assumptions, hypotheses and previously acquired body of knowledge and ideology, opens the door to a variety of Islamic interpretations and Islamic pluralism. The key to ending official mono-interpretations of Islamic knowledge is obtained through the application of the modernist formula that in the process of evolution of human understanding of the content of the revealed Text, Islamic knowledge evolves.[153] For some of these reformers, 'the Qur'an is a living phenomenon' and therefore 'a humanistic hermeneutics of the Qur'an has to take seriously the living phenomenon and stop reducing the Qur'an to be only a text'.[154]

The profile of present-day Muslim reformists, framing a twenty-first century Islam, is as rich as the plurality of their discourse. Their names, nationalities, sex and occupation reveals the fact that a broad-based global re-examination and dialogue is under way among Muslims of reflection as Muslims of desperation seemingly play out their last acts.[155] In this process of dialogue and intellectual interaction, non-Muslims and laymen are not excluded. It is important to note that women have entered the debate, while enlightened clerics continue to apply their expertise to the task of reform and modernization. Certain clerics are even de-frocked, placed under house arrest and imprisoned as a result of their efforts. In addition to prominent intellectuals from the traditional Muslim world, one comes across the name of Amina Wadud, an African-American woman who converted to Islam in 1972 and whose works on women and the Qur'an have been translated into Turkish, Persian and Indonesian. Wadud is an Islamic scholar and academic, whose study of the Qur'an revealed to her an overwhelming 'confirmation of women's equality'.[156] In March 2005, Amina Wadud led a mixed Friday congregational prayer for Muslims in New York City's Cathedral Church of St John the Divine, since no major mosque would host such an event.

In defiance of an exclusion-driven, intolerant and violent mono-interpretation of Islam, the door of Islamic pluralism reclaiming oneness, inclusiveness, tolerance, peace and universalism as the essence of the faith, has been opened by the new pioneers.

Notes

1. *The 9/11 Commission Report*, New York: W.W. Norton, 1st edn, n.d., p. 39.
2. Ibid., p. 57.
3. Ibid.
4. http://www.fas.org/irp/world/para/docs/980223-fatwa.htm
5. Ibid.
6. M. Sells, *Approaching the Qur'an*, Ashland: White Cloud Press, 1999, p. 42.
7. http://news.bbc.co.uk/&/hi/world/americas/1544955.stm
8. http://www.dawn.com/2001/10/30/top 17.htm
9. http://news.bbc.co.uk/&/hi/world/americas/1544955.stm
10. Adam Shatz, 'In Search of Hizbollah', *New York Review of Books*, 29 April 2004.
11. http://www.islam-online.net/English/News/2001-09/13article25.shtml
12. http://www.pbs.org/wgbh/pages/frontline/shows/muslims/portraits/egypt.html
13. http://www.crescentlife.com/heal%20the%20world/crusade_a_freudian_slip.htm
14. S. Huntington, *The Clash of Civilizations*, London: Touchstone, 1998, p. 217.
15. Ibid., pp. 217–18.
16. http://www.crescentlife.com/heal%20the%20world/crusade_a_freudian_slip.htm
17. http://www.time.com/time/covers/1101020318/popup/
18. http://www.antiwar.com/casualities/
19. http://www.iwpr.net/index.pl?archive/irq/irq_63_1_eng.txt
20. Armed Vanguard of Mohammad's Second Army, http://www.globalsecurity.org
21. S. Hirsh, 'Torture at Abu Ghraib, *The New Yorker*, http://www.newyorker.com/fact/content/?04051fa_fact
22. J. Franklin, 'Guantanamo Prison', http://www.historiansagainstwar.org/resources/torture/janefranklin.html
23. D. Champion, 'The Muslim Threat', http://www.jpfo.org/unpopularsp-champion-muslim.htm
24. D. Gibson, 'Today's Muslim Threat', http://www.american-partisan.com/cols/2002/gibson/qtr4/1025.htm
25. Champion, 'The Muslim Threat'; K. B. Napier, 'The Muslim Threat',

http://www.Christiandoctrine.net/doctrine/outlines/outline_00046_the_muslim_threat_web.htm

26. Champion, 'The Muslim Threat'.

27. Napier, 'The Muslim Threat'.

28. Ibid.

29. Champion, 'The Muslim Threat'.

30. Napier, 'The Muslim Threat'.

31. Champion, 'The Muslim Threat'.

32. James Pinkerton, 'Century In, Century out – it's Crusade Time', http://www.newsamerica.net

33. http://www.religioustolerance.org/reac_ter18b.htm

34. http://www.grist.org/news/maindish/2004/10/27/scherer-christian/. Forty-five senators and 186 representatives in 2003 earned 80 to 100 per cent approval ratings from the nation's three most influential Christian Right advocacy groups – the Christian Coalition, the Eagle Forum and the Family Resource Council.

35. http://www.pbs.org/wnet/religionandethics/week616/p-cover.html

36. For a chronological acccount of their anti-Islam invective see http://www.religioustolerance.org/reac_ter18b.htm

37. Ibid.

38. http://www.jesusjournal.com/articles/publish/printer_121.html

39. I. M. Lapidus, History of Islamic Societies, Cambridge: Cambridge University Press, 1995, p. 389.

40. E. Hobsbawm, The Age of Empire, London: Weidenfeld & Nicolson, 1995, pp. 15, 342.

41. E. Hobsbawm, The Age of Revolution, London: Weidenfeld & Nicolson, 1995, p. 3.

42. T. Pakenham, The Scramble for Africa, London: Abacus, 1994, p. 78.

43. Ibid., pp. 72–3.

44. Ibid., p. 135.

45. Ibid., p. 227.

46. Ibid., p. 228.

47. Ibid., p. 274.

48. B. Stora, Algeria, Ithaca, NY: Cornell University Press, 2001, p. 5.

49. Pakenham, The Scramble for Africa, p. 121.

50. http://www.sscnet.ucla.edu/southasia/History/British/Plassey.html

51. Sepoys were the Indian soldiers of the British East India Company.

52. Ghulam Mohammad Jaffar, 'The Repudiation of Jihad by the Indian Scholars in the Nineteenth Century', Hamdard Islamicus, Autumn 1992, No. 3.

53. Sayyid Ahmad Baraili (1833–77) should not be confused with Mohammad Ahmad Reza Khan Barelvi (1856–1921), founder of the Barelvi school of Islam.

54. Jaffar, 'The Repudiation of Jihad'.

55. Ibid.

56. Ibid.

57. The information on Sir Sayyid Ahmad Khan is largely drawn from the learned articles of Abdul Hamid and B. A. Dar at http://www.muslimphilosophy.com/hmp/default.htm

58. Abdul Hamid, 'Sir Sayyid Ahmad Khan as a Politician, Historian and Reformist', http://www.muslimphilosophy.com/hmp/default.htm

59. http://pakistanlink.com/sah/040202001.html

60. B. A. Dar, Sir Sayyid Ahmad Khan as a Religio-Philosophical Thinker, http://www.muslimphilosophy.com/hmp/default.htm

61. The information on Sayyid Amir Ali is based on http://banglapedia.search.com.bd/HT/A_0186.HTM and http://www.islam4all.com/new_page_60.htm

62. http://www.islam4all.com/new_page_60.htm

63. Ibid.

64. R. Upadhyay, Fatwa – An Instrument of Ulema Politics in India? http://www.saag.org/papers10/paper990.html

65. http://pakistanlink.com/sah/040202001.html

66. http://www.globalsecurity.org/military/intro/islam-barelvi.htm

67. http://pakistanlink.com/sah/040202001.html

68. B. D. Metcalf, Islamic Revival in British India: Deoband, 1860–1900, Princeton, NJ: Princeton University Press, 1982, p. 296.

69. Ibid., p. 265.

70. Upadhyay, Fatwa.

71. Ibid.

72. Metcalf, pp. 267, 307.

73. http://www.globalsecurity.org/military/intro/islam-barelvi.htm

74. I. Amini, Napoleon and Persia, Washington: Mage Publishers, 1999, p. 78.

75. J. Afary, The Iranian Constitutional Revolution, New York: Columbia University Press, 1996, p. 29.

76. A.-H. Haeri, Shi'ism and Constitutionalism in Iran, Tehran: Amir Kabir, AH 1364, pp. 42–3.

77. The section on Najmabadi is based on ibid., pp. 91–6.

78. I. M. Lapidus, History of Islamic Societies, Cambridge: Cambridge University Press, 1995, pp. 602–8, 622.

79. The section on Akhoundzadeh is based on A. H. Haeri, Shi'ism and Constitutionalism in Iran, pp.28–9.

80. The information in this section is based on N. Keddie, An Islamic Response to Imperialism, Berkeley, CA: University of California Press, 1968, pp.3–35.

81. Keddie, An Islamic Response to Imperialism, p. 24.

82 Yvonne Haddad, 'Muhammad Abduh: Pioneer of Islamic Revival', in this volume, p.36.

83. Pakenham, The Scramble for Africa, p. 74.

84. Ibid., p. 75.

85. Lapidus, *History of Islamic Societies*, pp. 608–10.

86. M. Rodinson, *Israel*, New York: Pathfinder Press, 1973, pp. 72–3.

87. H. Enayat, *Modern Islamic Political Thought*, London: Macmillan, 1986, p. 69.

88. M. R. Rida, 'Socialism, Bolshevism and Religion', http://www.freearabvoice.org

89. Enayat, *Modern Islamic Political Thought*, pp. 72–3.

90. Y. M. Choueiri, *Islamic Fundamentalism*, London: Pinter, 1990, p. 54.

91. Enayat, *Modern Islamic Political Thought*, pp. 77–80.

92. A. Al-Azmeh, *Islams and Modernities*, London: Verso, 1996, p. 112.

93. Enayat, *Modern Islamic Political Thought*, p. 80.

94. Al-Azmeh, *Islams and Modernities*, p. 114.

95. B. Lia, *The Society of the Muslim Brothers in Egypt*, Reading: Garnet Publishing, 1998, p. 76.

96. Hasan al-Banna, 'Jihad', http://www.youngmuslims.ca/online_library/books/jihad/

97. http://www.nmhschool.org/tthornton/hasan_al.htm

98. Enayat, *Modern Islamic Political Thought*, p. 84.

99. Lia, *Muslim Brothers*, p. 235.

100. Ibid., p. 81.

101. Ibid., p. 206.

102. Choueiri, *Islamic Fundamentalism*, London: Pinter, 1990, p. 49.

103. R. H. Dekmejian, *Islam in Revolution*, Syracuse, NY: Syracuse University Press, 1995, p. 106.

104. A. Rahnema and F. Nomani, *The Secular Miracle: Religion, Politics and Economic Policy in Iran*, London: Zed Books, 1990, p. 81.

105. *Nabard-e Mellat*, No. 35, 7 Dey.

106. J. L. Esposito, *Islam and Politics*, Syracuse, NY: Syracuse University Press, 1991, p. 109.

107. Dekmejian, *Islam in Revolution*, p. 80.

108. The section on Sadat is based on Dekmejian, *Islam in Revolution*, pp. 80–3.

109. G. Kepel, *Jihad*, London: I.B. Tauris, 2003, p. 221.

110. Esposito, *Islam and Politics*, p. 116.

111. Ibid., p. 119.

112. A. Rahnema and F. Nomani, *The Secular Miracle*, p. 303.

113. The section on Syria is based on Dekmejian, *Islam in Revolution*, pp. 108–18.

114. Dekmejian, *Islam in Revolution*, pp. 110–11.

115. October 1957 has also been suggested as the founding date of Da'wa.

116. H. Algar, *Islam and Revolution*, London: KPI, 1985, p. 228.

117. Rahnema and Nomani, *The Secular Miracle*, p. 5.

118. Y. Richard, *L'Islam Chi'ite*, Paris: Fayard, 1991, p. 267.

119. Ibid.

120. Huntington, *The Clash of Civilizations*, p. 216.

121. Kepel, *Jihad*, p. 143; P. Marsden, *The Taliban*, London: Zed Books, 1998, p. 29.

122. Kepel, *Jihad*, pp. 143–4.

123. Marsden, *The Taliban*, p. 35.

124. J. Bruce, 'Arab Veterans of the Afghan War', *Jane's Intelligence Review*, April 1995, Vol. 7, No. 4.

125. M. Stone, *The Agony of Algeria*, London: Hurst, p. 183.

126. Kepel, *Jihad*, p. 217.

127. Ibid., p. 219.

128. Ibid.

129. See R. Takyeh, 'Islamism in Algeria: A Struggle Between Hope and Agony', *Middle East Policy*, Summer 2003.

130. R. A. Norton, *Hizballah of Lebanon: Extremist Ideals vs. Mundane Politics*, Council on Foreign Relations, pp. 2–3.

131. Stone, *The Agony of Algeria*, pp. 163–4.

132. Ibid., p. 165.

133. Ibid., pp. 167–8.

134. Ibid., p. 171.

135. G. Swart and H. Solomon, *Algeria: The Politics of Fundamentalism and Extremism*, Center for International Political Studies, p. 6.

136. Stone, *The Agony of Algeria*, p. 178.

137. Ibid.

138. M. Boudjemaa, 'Terrorism in Algeria: Ten Years of Day-to-day Genocide', http://www.iss.co.za/pubs/monographs/No74/Chap6.html

139. Swart and Solomon, *Algeria*, pp. 5-7.

140. Kepel, *Jihad*, p. 260.

141. Ibid., pp. 163, 254–5.

142. Stone, *The Agony of Algeria*, p.184; Swart and Solomon, *Algeria*, p. 4.

143. Swart and Solomon, *Algeria*, pp. 4, 6; Takyeh, 'Islamism in Algeria'; Stone, *The Agony of Algeria*, p. 188.

144. Stone, *The Agony of Algeria*, p. 189.

145. Ibid., p. 188; and Bruce, 'Arab Veterans of the Afghan War'.

146. Kepel, *Jihad*, p. 273.

147. *Le Monde*, 18 March 2005.

148. Adam Shatz, 'In Search of Hizbollah', *New York Review of Books*, 29 April 2004.

149. The information on Hizballah is based on Norton, *Hizballah of Lebanon*; Shatz, 'In Search of Hizbollah'; Information Division, Israel Foreign Ministry, *Iran and Hizbullah*, 1997; Information, Analysis and Advice for the Parliament, Commonwealth of Australia, *Hizballah in Profile*, 2 June 2003; Rahnema and Nomani, *The Secular Miracle*.

150. Terms used by Mohammed Arkoun. See *Rethinking Islam*, Oxford: Westview, 1994, p. 22; Ursula Gunther in S. Taji-Farouki (ed.), *Modern Muslim Intellectuals and the Qur'an*, Oxford: Oxford University Press, 2004, p. 132.

151. M. Mojtahed Shabestari, *Naqdi bar Qeraat Rasmi az Din*, Tehran: Tarh-e No, AH 1379, p. 95.

152. M. Mojtahed Shabestari, *Hermeneutic, Ketab va Sunat*, Tehran: Tarh-e No, AH 1377, p. 15.

153. A. Soroush, *Qabz va Bast Teorik Shari'at*, Tehran: Sarat, AH 1370, pp. 118–19.

154. N. Abu Zayd, *Rethinking the Qur'an: Towards a Humanistic Hermeneutics*, Utrecht: Humanistics University Press, 2004, pp. 62–3.

155. The names of a selected few, whose works have been translated into, analysed or reviewed in the Anglo-Saxon world (readily acknowledging that many more who should also be mentioned in a comprehensive list have been omitted) include Mohammad Mojthed Shabestari, Abdolkarim Soroush, Mohammed Arkoun, Nasr Hamid Abu Zayd, Mohammed Arkoun, Mohamed Talbi and Fatima Mernissi.

156. Asma Barlas in Taji-Farouki (ed.), *Modern Muslim Intellectuals and the Qur'an*, pp. 99, 101. Wadud's leading of a mixed Friday congregational prayer is reported in *Time*, 28 March 2005.

1

Introduction

Ali Rahnema

The 1979 Iranian revolution, which brought an Islamic government to power, catapulted revolutionary Islam as a potent ideology on to the international political scene. The events since that date bear witness to the fact that Islam, as a political force, is not a passing fad. It appeals to the socially, politically and economically disinherited. It provides a moral shield against the 'onslaught' of western 'anti-values'. Finally, it acts as an anchor for individuals and social groups caught in the tempest of incertitude, relativism and an identity crisis. The political and socio-economic conditions in the third world provide an ideal breeding ground for its rapid spread. In Afghanistan and the Sudan, Islamic governments have been in power since 1992. In Algeria, the electoral victory of the Islamic Salvation Front in December 1991 confronted the world with the 'paradox of democracy'. The prospect of an Islamic government forced the traditional bastions and proponents of parliamentary democracy to invoke individual human rights as a universal principle of 'a higher order' than the will of the majority, thus justifying their open support for a military coup. In crisis-ridden Tadjikestan, Islamic forces, seem poised to win political power. In Egypt, Morocco, Tunisia, Syria, Iraq, Jordan, Lebanon, Kuwait, the Occupied Territories, India, Sri Lanka, Indonesia, Burma and Malaysia, politicized Islam remains an important force to be reckoned with. It pursues the road to power through all the political means available to it, parliamentary and extra-parliamentary. Even in Turkey, the show-case of 'successful transition' from Islam to modern-day secularism and westernization, outward appearances are belied by the latent power of Islam, repressed ever since Mustafa Kemal. In the local elections of October 1992, the Islamic Welfare Party came in a strong second place. Finally, the events in Albania and disintegrating Yugoslavia have brought the issue of Islam even to Europe.

Islam is now a major force on the international scene, and observers, teachers and students of political economy in the classical sense of the term have had to learn, understand and follow the logic and implications of its message. Two general cognitive phases can be identified in the process of the western public's reflection on Islam. At first, the absence of information and relative ignorance of the subject matter led to a mono-Islamic perception. Later, faced with different interpretations and therefore different policy implications by Muslims of the same or different movements, issues such as 'whose Islam' and 'which Islam' indicated a growing understanding of the complexity and multiplicity of Islam. Even though consensus exists on the spiritual nature of the Islamic state, and the religious obligations of its members according to the Shari'a, there is scant agreement on the political and economic form of such a state. Different and sometimes opposing social, economic, political and even legal Islamic discourses can and are presented by equally pious Muslims.

The newly re-born ideological contender claims a long and rich historical past. It is replete with epics of struggle, sacrifice and martyrdom by heroes defending values, ideals and aspirations conceived by God, against disbelievers. It possesses its own language, jargon, methodology, set of definitions, assumptions and arguments. It presents a belief-system with what seems at first a clearly delineated contour of the ideal individual, life and society. It also identifies the barriers to, as well as the means of, their attainment.

This book attempts to introduce and analyse the lives and contributions of a number of men whose religio-political and economic writings as well as political practice have played a crucial role in reviving Islam as a potent political force. The object of the book is to provide a balanced account of these men, their political environment, life, ideas, and contributions to the contemporary Islamic movement. This collection does not focus on the original theoreticians and practitioners of the faith, but on those nineteenth- and twentieth-century figures who believed that the Islamic doctrine (maktab) was capable of providing practical solutions to the emerging problems of the modern world.

This collection makes no claim to comprehensiveness. Certain recent influential Islamic revivalists such as Muhammad Iqbal, Abd ar-Rahman al-Kwakibi and Muhammad Rashid Rida (Reza) could have been included. The reader can be consoled, however, with the thought that a significant part of the ideas of these men is either rooted or echoed in the works of those discussed here.

Abd ar-Rahman al-Kwakibi was born in Halab, Syria, in 1854. He was a true disciple of Sayyid Jamal al-din al-Afghani and Abduh. Kwakibi's criticism of and outspokenness against the tyranny of the Ottoman sultan, Abdul-Hamid, resulted in the closure of his journal and his imprisonment. In his book, *Tabay' al-Estebdad*, Kwakibi, explained that any government can become despotic, unless it is made responsible to the people and placed under their direct control and scrutiny. Kwakibi believed that despots had always depended on religion as a crutch to exercise their arbitrary rule. His thoughts on economic relations in an Islamic society lent themselves to a radical analysis. Finally, he firmly believed that Islam was in need of a movement similar to Protestantism in Christianity to return it to its original purity.

In 1865, Muhammad Rashid Rida was born in Syria. He became a staunch follower of Abduh, after he migrated to Egypt. Rida wrote a comprehensive biography of Abduh and co-authored with him an exegesis of the Qur'an. In 1898, Rida published a journal called *al-Minar* in Cairo. *Al-Minar* which was conscientiously published for 35 years, became the organ of Islamic modernists. Its pages on Islamic thought and practice reflected the idea of Sayyid Jamal al-din al-Afghani and Abduh. According to Hamid Enayat, 'there is essentially nothing in the writings of Rida that has not been previously said by Sayyid Jamal or Abduh.'[1]

Muhammad Iqbal Lahouri, better known as Allameh Iqbal, was born in 1877. Iqbal was greatly influenced by Mowlavi, the famous Persian mystical poet. His poetry and prose in Urdu, Persian and English were his effective medium of disseminating his world outlook. The philosopher-poet reflected on the human condition which he witnessed in his own country, India. He lamented the national and international systems which had perpetuated the suffering of his people. The West, in his opinion, had given birth to two inhuman and spiritually bankrupt systems, capitalism and imperialism. Islam on the other hand, he argued, had fostered obedience and submission instead of challenging the status quo. In response to Islam's inertia, Iqbal felt the necessity of reinvigorating Islam and thus wrote his book *The Reconstruction of Religious Thought in Islam.* Iqbal appealed to Muslims to search for their 'real' Islamic self whereby, he believed, they would unearth the means for their temporal liberation. Iqbal's objective, according to Ali Shariati, was to transform Islam from an individualized creed simply constructed around a moral relation between man and God into an all-encompassing ideology which would regulate all aspects of human conduct.[2]

Certain Attributes of Islamic Revivalists

Islamic revivalism in Islamic lands, during its first phase of manifestation, is characterized by a renewed interest in Islam as an endogenous ideology with redeeming powers. For the born-again Muslim the Qur'an and the Tradition of the Prophet provide fundamental sources from which solutions for pressing contemporary socio-political and economic problems could be deduced. The Islam of private practices and rituals is socialized and publicized. The lives, struggles and sacrifices of the worthy companions and successors of the Prophet are glorified and presented as exemplary role-models for present-day Muslims. During this stage public compliance with, and belief in, a common Islamic heritage becomes the bond that distinguishes between 'them' and 'us'. This ground-preparing phase is succeeded by the inevitable drive to reinstate Islam as the principal coordinating mechanism of society. The establishment of an Islamic state is probably the most important objective of all Islamic revivalists. This, however, does not mean that all revivalists share a common view of what constitutes an Islamic state and how it should function.

Since Islamic revival has taken roots in lands where Islam has been and is the majority or the official state religion, the question remains as to why Islam needs to be reinstated where it is already respected and largely practised? Reviving Islam in an Islamic country is preparing the way for the Phoenix to rise from its own ashes. Although this may be considered as a rejection of the way Islam is actually practised and interpreted by its official custodians and the ruling classes it can also be construed as the negation of the social, political, economic and cultural practices in place. In this sense it becomes a powerful and angry voice of discontent against the perceived upholders of an un-Islamic if not polytheistic status quo. Islamic revivalism ultimately aims at the overthrow or radical transformation of a social system which it believes engenders decadence, corruption, deprivation, social injustice, repression and impiety. Islamic revivalists identify four primary causes for the plight of the Muslim people. First, the erosion of Islamic values and the complicity of governments in ignoring the implementation of Islam's socio-economic and ethical ordinances. Second, the quietism and frequent collaboration of the institutionalized clergy with essentially non-Islamic governments. Third, the corruption and evil-doing (*zulm*) of the ruling classes or families. Finally the latters' collaboration with and dependence on non-Islamic and imperialistic powers.

Concern with an Islamic renaissance and the need for change is by no means a novel or recent idea. The means of attaining such a transformation, reform or revolution, has long been the subject of controversial debate. Imam Muhammad Ghazali (1058–1111) was one of the earliest pioneers of Islamic revival. In his book *The Revival of Religious Science*, Ghazali provides a clear explanation for the necessity of Islamic revival even in an Islamic state. Sultan Malikshah-e Saljouqi reigned over a vast empire as the defender of the Islamic faith. Ghazali, who lived in Baghdad during his rule, argued that the corruption of the Islamic jurists, or the ulama, corrupted the ruling princes and their corruption, in turn, corrupted their subjects, the masses.[3] Ghazali argued that formal or apparent legal purity veiled intrinsic impurities. What seemed pure on the outside was not on the inside. What was prohibited had become permissible and what was permissible had become forbidden.[4] Ghazali maintained that the greatest part of the wealth, from which the princes gave away gifts to the jurisconsults and functionaries, was ill-gotten or attained in an Islamically-forbidden manner.[5] Ghazali identified the clergy and the ruling class as the two forces that perpetuated the plight of the people. His solution was to reform the type of Islam that was upheld and propagated by the official clergy, thereby unearthing the pure and authentic Islam and changing the people and finally the ruling elite. It should also be pointed out that having criticized both the actually existing clergy and the political leadership, Ghazali argued that the Law demands obedience to God, His Prophet and to those who are in power.[6] Fearful of the consequences of civil war and anarchy, Ghazali abandoned any thought of armed resistance or revolution against a tyrranical ruler.

Ghazali separated the first stage, of reawakening Islamic fervour, from the second stage, of radical political action and change. While he rejected revolutionary change as a means of redressing socio-political problems, he considered intellectual dissent and reform as permissible and necessary. Modern Islamic revivalists, however, view the Islamic re-education of the people as a prelude to revolution and the attainment of political power, when possible. They invoke the concept of rebellion against unjust unislamic rulers. They thus choose to challenge the call for submission and obedience to whomever is in authority, a concept which had long been evoked to justify servitude to unjust rulers.

All Islamic revivalists are nostalgic about Islam's spirit of compassion, solidarity, fraternity and social justice. This spirit has been associated with the 'Golden Age' of the Prophet's rule in Medina. Longing for the order established by the early pious upholders of the faith, however, becomes meaningful in the context of the radically transformed actually existing socio-economic environment. The task of these men became one of reconstructing, reforming, reviving or synthesizing Islam in order to make it relevant to the needs, demands and predicaments of those whom they considered the victims of modern civilization. The revivalists proclaim to be committed to the material and spiritual salvation of the wretched Muslims of the earth. Their Islam combines a critical discourse of the status quo with a call for reconciliation and unity among all Muslims. To confront the 'outside' world and its growing influence, the power and glory of Islam has to be secured by putting an end to the incessant infighting between various Islamic sects. Theoretically, Islamic revivalists seek to heal previous wounds inflicted by Muslims themselves. Their object is to synchronize what they believe to be a historical dislocation between the spiritual and material spheres. Their success hinges not only on understanding, analysing and criticizing the problems of the modern era but also on the provision of more useful and applicable solutions than those of their rival schools.

Islamic revivalists use the substance of Islam in order to develop their new ideological structure. Their construction is modern in the sense that it addresses the universal themes and problems of the post-industrial revolution era. Naturally, in this process, certain novelties, if not innovations, are incorporated and certain dispensable residues are abandoned. Islam at the hands of these men is adapting itself to changing times. More importantly, however, it seeks to re-define and re-shape certain aspects of the modern era according to its own vision. The posture of Islamic revivalists towards modern political, social and economic systems, their material achievements, their social relations and their institutions is thus both accommodating and confrontationist.

For Islamic revivalists, the products of modern civilization may be divided into two distinct types: the attractive which has to be incorporated and co-opted and the repulsive which has to be cleansed and obliterated. On the one hand, the adoption of human rationality as the ultimate source of Truth and the total abandonment of Divine injunctions is held responsible for social, moral and ethical degeneration and corruption. On the other hand, technological development is considered acceptable since it is not believed to impair the ideal Islamic spirit or undermine the Shari‘a. Figuratively speaking, modern Islamic revivalists have no theoretical problem with decapitating the head yet retaining the dexterous hands and fingers that ushered in the age of science and technology.

The Islamic revivalists were confronted with the task of articulating an Islamic ideology, with which they intended to attract disciples and thus foster change. Islam, therefore, had to be actualized. Whereas, the rewards for being a good Muslim were traditionally deferred to the hereafter, the revivalists had to establish a relation between piety and temporal rewards and impiety and temporal punishments. For the traditional ulama, religious disobedience was ultimately punished by eternal damnation in the hereafter. The majority of revivalists argued that rebellion against the absolute sovereignty of God or deviation from His correct path was punished in this world by subjecting the guilty or the impious to social injustice, economic exploitation and political tyranny. Quietism and acquiescence were thus branded as impiety. The religious realm was subsequently politicized.

The term 'revivalist' ascribed to the Islamic theoreticians and practitioners presented in this volume veils the usual distinction between modernists and traditionalists. The fact of the matter is that these men are both modernists and traditionalists. They believe in a basket of legal sources which are both dynamic and static. They are firm believers in the primary sources of the Qur'an and the Sunna, the secondary sources of consensus (ijma') and analogy (qiyas), or reason (aql), and finally ijtihad, or the legal practice whereby a jurist applies his independent effort to deduce unavailable laws from the sources. *Ijtihad* implies the application of human reason and rationality. It constitutes a bridge between eternally valid divine injunctions and time-specific requirements of every age. It is the key to providing an Islamic interpretation of modern developments and circumstances. It is also a means through which religion can become intricately interwoven with politics.

Since the thirteenth century (tenth according to some), the Sunnis have prohibited the application of *ijtihad*. One of the main disputes between modern Sunni revivalists and the traditional Sunni ulama is over the issue of *ijtihad*. The position of Sunni revivalists is best illustrated in the stance of Iqbal Lahouri, who maintained that the closure of the gate of *ijtihad* was 'a pure fiction' and that 'modern Islam was not bound by this voluntary surrender of intellectual independence.'[7]

The recent history of Islamic governments has also demonstrated that aspiration to and the maintenance of political power, ultimately necessitates pragmatism. Islamists can be rigidly loyal to the canon, only if they remain as social critics and not as contenders for power. Without the tool of *ijtihad* the gap between Islamic theory or aspirations and contemporary reality or constraints becomes impossible to bridge. The Islamic traditionalist who seeks to create and run an 'authentic' Islamic state in the modern world and initially holds a low opinion of the pragmatic means and tools that are used to circumvent the letter of the Law to facilitate everyday life is soon forced to become an Islamic modernist to assure the survival of the Islamic state.

Other than being Islamic revivalists and preachers of Islamic righteousness, the figures discussed in this book differ in their Islamic interpretations of social, political and economic issues and concerns. The concept of the right to *ikhtilaf*, to differ in opinion on legal issues pertaining to non-primary sources, legitimizes such diversity of opinion. Traditionally, however, differences of opinion are only allowed among trained Islamic jurists, the ulama.

Among the revivalists discussed in this book, some attained the summits of classical Islamic legal training and some were essentially autodidacts. Some were Islamic jurists and clerics, others were laymen and Islamologists. Some wore the traditional clerical garb, others the western suit and tie. Some were familiar only with their own language and that of the Qur'an, others also with western languages and literature. The difference in training could shed some light on how each interpreted Islam, viewed its role and assessed its potential in securing the objective of an Islamic government in the modern world. The 'outsiders', those without an official Islamic training, were less bound by certain axiomatic, jurisprudential principles, less confined to a specific procedural framework, more inclined towards innovation and more critical of the official clergy. For them a synthesis between Islamic concepts and modern values was possible and necessary. The 'insiders', those with a formal Islamic training, were concerned with reviving Islam but not at the cost of sacrificing what they considered to be its essence. As much as they might have believed in actualizing and politicizing Islam, they could not tolerate a socio-political Islam devoid of its rites, rituals and religious obligations. For them all pronouncements and actions had to be subjected to the close scrutiny of all the evidence on which any Islamic legal opinion has to be based. For the 'insiders', the clerical institution was the historical defender of the faith.

Sayyid Jamal al-din Afghani received his classical religious studies at Najaf and Karbala, the hub of Shi'i thought and education. It is said that at the age of sixteen he became a jurist and obtained his right to exercise *ijtihad* from Shaykh Morteza Ansari, the prominent Shi'i jurist.[8] Ayatollahs Khomeini and Muhammad-Baqir Sadr and Hojat al-Islam Musa Sadr attended Shi'i seminary schools, became Islamic jurists and subsequently sources of imitation (*marja'-e taqlid*) in Iran, Iraq and Lebanon respectively. Shaykh Abduh received his formal Islamic education at Ahmadi and Al-Azhar, the two foremost centres of Islamic studies in Egypt. Later in his life, Abduh attained the highest religious position in the land and became the Mufti of Egypt. Mulana Mawdudi never attended a religious school in his youth and started to work as a journalist at the age of sixteen and then went back to religious studies at the age of twenty-one. Hassan al-Banna's formal education was at the Dar al-Ulum, Egypt's teacher training college. Sayyid Qutb is said to have memorized the Qur'an by the age of ten. Yet he too, like Hassan al-Banna, did not receive a formal Islamic education. Both men graduated from Dar al-Ulum. Shariati graduated from Mashhad's teacher training college and went on to receive his doctorate from the Faculté des Lettres of the University of Paris.

Each man has left his own imprint on the contemporary Islamic movement and its national or regional intellectual leaders. Their writings have been translated into the many languages spread across the Muslim world. To varying degrees and among different social groups in different Islamic countries, their names have attained an aura of eminence and grandeur. Their pictures adorn homes, offices and governmental buildings. To generalize, one can say that in the Islamic world they are often praised as heroes and idols, while in the West they are usually vilified as Islamic fundamentalists, threatening the fabrics of western life-style. Seldom, however, are they studied or analysed.

Notes

1. Enayat, H., *Modern Islamic Political Thought*, London, Macmillan, 1370/1982, p. 157.
2. Shariati, *Collected Works*, vol. 5, p. 154.
3. Al-Ghazali, *Kitab Ihya' 'Ulum al-din*, 4 vols., Cairo, Ottoman Printing Press, 1352/1933, vol. 2, p. 211, 1933.
4. Ibid., vol. 1, pp. 111–29.
5. Ibid., vol. 2, p. 120.
6. Laoust, H., *La politique de Gazali*, Paul Geuthner, Paris, vol. 1, p. 376.
7. Iqbal, M., *The Reconstruction of Religious Thought in Islam*, Lahore, Sh. Muhammad Ashraf, reprint 1982, p. 178; and Kamali, M.H., *Principles of Islamic Jurisprudence*, Cambridge, Islamic Texts Society, 1991, p. 390.
8. *Tarikh-e Farhang-e Moaser*, vol. 1, pp. 20–2.

2

Sayyid Jamal al-Din 'al-Afghani'

Nikki R Keddie

Sayyid Jamal al-Din al-Afghani (the name by which he is best known, although he was born and brought up in Iran) was a pioneer of Islamic modernism and especially of anti-imperialist activism, known both for his wide-ranging life and thought and for his advocacy, from 1883 on, of pan-Islamic unity as a means to strengthen the Muslim world against the West. It is only since the 1960s that accurate biographies of Afghani have been written. Earlier biographies were based largely on stories told by him and his followers. These biographies were distorted largely for political reasons. Recent scholarly biographies, based largely on irrefutable primary sources like Afghani's own letters and papers first catalogued and made available to the public in 1963, demonstrate that Afghani was born in Iran and had a Shi'i education, rather than being an Afghan Sunni as he usually claimed. The newer biographies also show that many other elements in the pre-1960s biographies, still current in the Sunni world, are inaccurate.

It is therefore important to come to a study of Afghani with an open mind, and, if one is interested in pursuing his story further, to read works that are based on sources independent of his word and contemporaneous with his life, rather than accepting the numerous largely mythological and hero-worshipping works that often have more in common with hagiography than accurate history. Even when the mythology that often surrounds him is stripped away, Sayyid Jamal al-Din will be found to be a man of important ideas and activities, and of major and continuing influence.

Sayyid Jamal al-Din al-Afghani (1838/9-1897) was one of the first figures to restate Muslim traditions in ways that met the important problems brought about by the increasing encroachments of the West on the nineteenth-century Middle East. Rejecting both pure traditionalism with its uncritical defence of inherited Islam on the one hand, and blind imitation of the West on the other, Afghani became a pioneer in the reinterpretation of Islam, with an emphasis on qualities needed in the modern world, such as the use of human reason, political activism, and military and political strength. By finding such values within Islam, Afghani was able, and for many Muslims who admire him is still able, to attain an influence on Muslim believers not achieved by those who simply and more openly borrowed western ideas. Afghani's widespread travels, and especially the years he spent in Egypt and India, both pioneering areas for Islamic reform, gave him an influence not matched by many who spent their lives and put forward their ideas in one country. This was true especially because several of his Egyptian disciples first published Afghani's articles in Arabic, the most important language in the Muslim world, and later became influential in their own right, thus carrying forward Afghani's influence. On a lesser scale the same kind of role for Afghani was experienced in Iran, Afghanistan, and South Asia, where most of his important followers came on the scene only later.

The importance of such international discipleship is shown by the relative lack of international influence of those slightly earlier thinkers and activists known as the Young Ottomans, especially their leading intellectual, Namik Kemal. These thinkers wrote in Ottoman Turkish, a language that Arabs and even Turks stopped reading in the early twentieth century, and the fact that they pioneered in many important aspects of Islamic reformism, including a number of ideas put forth later by Afghani, is widely ignored, even by most specialists on the Middle East, down to today. It was Namik Kemal who first wrote a modern intellectual defence of Islamic unity, a phrase translated in the West as pan-Islam, and it is very likely that Jamal al-Din heard of this Young Ottoman idea, which he later promoted. Muslims and western scholars are much more likely to see Jamal al-Din than Namik Kemal as the main pioneer of intellectual pan-Islamism, even though Afghani did not originate it.

As the first Islamic modernist whose influence was felt in several countries, Afghani influenced a variety of trends that reject both pure traditionalism and pure westernism. Although Afghani in his later life and since his death has been associated especially with pan-Islam, his pan-Islamic writings occupied only part of the key decade of the 1880s. In the course of his lifetime he promoted a variety of often contradictory viewpoints and causes, and his thought has some affinity with various trends in the Muslim world. These include the Islamic liberalism advocated especially by his Egyptian disciple Muhammad Abduh; the conservative Islamic revivalism proposed in different forms by Abduh's follower Rashid Rida, by the Muslim Brethren, and by various contemporary Islamist movements; and also pan-Arabism and other forms of nationalism. Although Afghani's influence on these movements is often exaggerated, his interpretation of Islam in modern and often political terms displayed a mode of thought that was to become increasingly popular in the Muslim world.

Much of Afghani's reputation in the Muslim world is posthumous, and he was far less known in his own lifetime than after his death, but the same is true of many influential historical figures.

The early biographies of Afghani, written in Arabic by his disciples, were skewed both for expedient reasons and because Afghani often distorted his own life, hiding, for example, his Iranian Shi'i background, and, especially in his last fifteen years, not wishing to publicize those of his ideas that were at odds with normative Islam. As Afghani after his death became increasingly an icon in the Muslim world, more and more mythological features were added to most of the biographies and other works written about him.

Jamal al-Din's Biography

Regarding Afghani's birthplace there is no primary source that supports the Afghan birthplace or upbringing usually claimed by him, and there are now a variety of sources showing that he could not have been Afghani, but was born and given a Shi'i education in Iran. These include letters to the Iranian nephew who wrote the only early biography based on his actual birth and childhood. The dated books and treatises found among Afghani's papers show that as a result of his education in Iran and, almost certainly, in the Shi'i shrine cities in Iraq, he was well-versed in Islamic philosophy and in the Shaikhi school of Shi'ism, which was an unusually philosophical variety of Shi'ism that developed in the eighteenth and nineteenth centuries.

Unlike the Arab and Turkish world, where most Greek-inspired philosophy had for centuries been untaught as heretical, Iran had an uninterrupted philosophical tradition, with books by Avicenna and later Iranian philosophers taught even in religious schools. The medieval Islamic philosophers were disciples of ancient Greek and Hellenistic trends, generally following Plato, Aristotle, or neo-Platonism, and giving an essentially rationalist explanation of the world that included a rather deistic and distant deity who did not interfere arbitrarily in the workings of the universe. They tended to reconcile this Greek-based rationalism with Islam by saying, and occasionally writing, that God had given hints, which they noted, in the Qur'an, that this form of rationalism was the truth. They, like the deity, thought that the rational truth was only for an elite, while the masses could be made to behave, believe, and not cause trouble only by a religion that said that conduct in this world would be physically rewarded and punished in the next world, and that God acted directly on the world. This theory, which western thinkers associated with the western Arab philosopher Averroes and called the 'double truth' (a misnomer, as there is only one true truth – the philosophical one) was equally characteristic of Avicenna and several other Iranian philosophers.

When Afghani went to Istanbul, in 1869-70, he put forward ideas coming from the Islamic philosophers. And when he went to Egypt in the 1870s he taught his young disciples these mainly Iranian philosophers. There is considerable evidence that his teaching included not only rationalism, but also the philosophers' distinction between what should be taught the intellectual elite (namely, the rational truth) and what should be said to the masses (what was suited to their understanding and emotions).

In addition to knowing the philosophers, Afghani, it is clear from his papers, was well-acquainted not only with the innovative Shaikhi school of Shi'ism, but also with the mid-nineteenth century Iranian Babi movement, an offshoot of the Shaikhis whose founder claimed to bring a new dispensation that superseded the Qur'an. (The Babis in turn engendered the rather different Bahai religion in the 1860s.)

After almost certainly continuing his education in the Shi'i shrine cities of Najaf and Karbala, Afghani went to India in his late teens, at around the time of the Indian mutiny of 1857. From the time of his first recorded utterances in the 1860s until his death, the most consistent theme in Afghani's life is hostility to British rule in Muslim lands. It seems unlikely that this developed significantly in Iran or Iraq, where British control was less than overwhelming, and very probable that it was a reaction to British rule and policy in India. His belief that the British were out to undermine Islam and substitute Christianity was one that was current among many Indian Muslims, and later among other Muslims who experienced or witnessed British direct rule of Muslims.

Afghani apparently also had his first important contact with western thought in India, and according to one Arab disciple it was in India that Afghani became sceptical about all positive religions, which he saw mainly as a means of consoling people over death and other problems of this world.

After his stay in India, Afghani apparently went on pilgrimage to Mecca, then to the Shi'i shrine cities, probably to Istanbul, and then to Afghanistan via Iran. Both Afghani's papers and British documents from Afghanistan show that Afghani was not returning home when he entered Afghanistan in 1866, but was known to be a foreigner, unknown to the Afghans and speaking Persian like an Iranian. Afghani, partly on the basis of papers he brought with him, entered into close relations with the Afghan emir A'zam Khan. His advice to the emir did not concern reform, as is often said, but was to ally himself with Russia and fight Britain. He appears in the considerable documentation from this period as a fiercely anti-British political figure, and there is no mention of his discussing either religion or reform. The fall of A'zam Khan and the rise of the more pro-British Shir Ali led to Afghani's expulsion from Afghanistan by the latter in December 1868. He went to Bombay, Cairo, and then Istanbul in 1869.

In Istanbul Afghani was able once again to enter into high circles. His contacts were with leading westernizers and secularists, like Munif, president of the Council of Education, and Tahsin, the scientifically-minded director of the new university. It is probable, as Niyazi Berkes suggests, that Afghani, with his religious training and claims, was useful to such men in giving a religious colouring to westernized educational projects, which were opposed by the Ottoman ulama. Afghani was chosen to give one of the opening speeches at the new university in 1870. Here he praised westernizing reforms, urging Muslims to emulate the 'civilized nations' of the West. In this talk he showed his lifelong concern with Muslim self-strengthening, which he was not always to express in such westernizing terms.

Also in 1870 Afghani was appointed to the reformist official Ottoman Council of Education, and, owing to his ties with prominent educationalists, was invited to give a public lecture which, however, brought about his expulsion on grounds of heresy. This embarrassing incident has been distorted by Abduh and other biographers. The talk was one of a series open to volunteer speakers, not the great individual event that it is often claimed to be. While the talk would have been acceptable had it been limited to dealing, however positively, with modern science and technology, its intended subject, Afghani brought in themes long condemned as heretical, including referring to prophecy as a craft. (The standard pre-1960 biographies treat this as a false charge, but contemporary evidence shows that Afghani did say this.) This gave the ulama a chance to attack their real target – the modern university – which was closed somewhat later. Afghani was expelled from Istanbul and the head of the university was ousted from his post as a result of ulama reaction to Afghani's talk.

Afghani then went to Cairo, where he had his longest stay, from 1871 to his expulsion in 1879. The prominent Egyptian politician Riyad Pasha apparently invited him and arranged for him to have a stipend. For most of his stay he was mainly involved in informal teaching of young men, several of whom became his disciples. The young Muhammad Abduh and several others later prominent in Egyptian life were among these devoted disciples. Apart from Afghani's personal magnetism and intelligence, the stress on teaching Islamic philosophy, documented in Afghani's books and papers, was no doubt important in making him a popular teacher.

The 1870s were a period in which a spendthrift Egyptian ruler, Khedive Ismail, together with European lenders and consuls, were creating a debt problem of major crisis proportions resulting in overtaxation and other exactions on the population. In such a situation the time was ripe for an indigenous ideology that could bring about the reform and self-strengthening that intellectuals in particular desired. In some ways medieval Muslim philosophy could provide a basis for such an ideology. It exalted reason above literal revelation and could be used to attack the pretensions of the religious classes to true knowledge. It also showed how to develop a rationalist and non-literal interpretation of the Qur'an. The style of interpretation used by Muslim philosophers to advocate Aristotelian rationalism could equally be used to show that the Qur'an and Muslim traditions enjoined modern science, parliaments, and national armies. Islamic philosophers also advocated, and showed how to use, radically different arguments for the masses and for the intellectual elite. Afghani and his followers could mobilize the masses' traditional and religious sentiments by stressing the western threat to Islam, while emphasizing to the elite the need of modernizing reform of society and religion. Based on such different approaches, elite and masses could unite in a struggle against western Christian domination. Islamic philosophy, as presented by Afghani, provided an indigenous ideological basis, not borrowed from western oppressors, for building a reformed and independent community.

Afghani encouraged his followers in the late 1870s to publish newspapers in which they stressed current political issues. In these years there was a dramatic increase among Egyptians in political interest and involvement. The problems of finance and taxation combined with other internal and foreign events to create a growing political crisis. In this period Afghani came forward as a political figure in two ways: by using a Freemasonic lodge as a vehicle for political intrigue and change, and by influencing people through oratory. His political plotting involved plans to overthrow the Egyptian ruler, Khedive Ismail, and replace him with his heir, Taufiq. However, when Ismail was ousted and Taufiq put in power, in 1879, it was with British and French backing. Afghani had no influence on Taufiq, and was soon expelled by him.

Afghani also got a public reputation via his fiery anti-British speeches. It was largely these popular public speeches that moved the pro-British and pro-order Khedive Taufiq to expel Afghani in August 1879. Many of Afghani's followers were involved in Egyptian nationalist politics after his 1879 expulsion, but, contrary to stories tying Afghani and his followers to 'Urabi's rise, they were not tied to the 'Urabi nationalist movement until after it temporarily took power, long after Afghani's expulsion. Taufiq's sudden expulsion of Afghani in August 1879 though tied to anti-British speeches was not, as Afghani said, instigated by the British.

From Egypt Afghani went to the Muslim-ruled princely state of Hyderabad in south India, where he stayed for two years. Here he wrote in Persian several articles and his only treatise, known from the title of its Arabic translation as 'The Refutation of the Materialists'. In this work we find a considerable transformation in Afghani's public persona. Here he presents himself for the first time as a strong defender of religion in general and Islam in particular against attacks by the unorthodox. Although a close analysis of this work shows that the virtues claimed for religion are purely pragmatic ones, such as group solidarity, it is worth asking why at this time Afghani, who, evidence suggests, had not changed his private views, chose to present himself in public as a passionate defender of religion and of Islam.

The 'religious' Afghani of the 1880s is so enshrined in the public perception of him that it is worth stressing that until then references to Afghani by those who knew him emphasize rather his religious scepticism. Why might Afghani in the early 1880s have wished to present himself for the first time as a great defender of Islam, and later of pan-Islam? It is unlikely that there was any great religious conversion, especially since the anti-religious 'Answer to Renan' was written two years *after* the 'Refutation'. Yet he was probably affected by some of the same trends as had turned others, like the Young Ottoman Namik Kemal, into defenders of Islam. These trends may be compared to those a century later, in the 1970s and 1980s, which again turned many Muslim secularists into real or apparent defenders of Islam. Just as today's contemporary Islamism followed upon non-Muslim encroachments, and notably Israeli victories against the Arabs, so Islamic and pan-Islamic trends in the 1880s followed closely upon western conquests in the Muslim world: of Russia against the Ottomans in 1878, of the French in Tunisia in 1881, and of the British in Egypt in 1882. And, again as in the 1970s and 1980s, there was disillusionment with the West as a model and a revulsion within the largest area of the Middle East, the Ottoman Empire, toward westernizing reformers. All the westernizing innovations of these reformers had not saved the empire from defeat by the Russians, from further carving up by the European powers at the 1878 Congress of Berlin, from rising discontent among the Christian subjects who had most benefited by westernizing reforms, or from growing economic subjugation to the West. In Egypt there was a similar reaction against western creditors and conquerors. Afghani, who had always opposed British encroachments in Muslim lands, was quick to utilize the resulting pro-Islamic and anti-western sentiment to strengthen the unity of the Muslim world against foreign, especially British, incursions.

In addition, in India there were dramatic divisions between pro-British Muslim reformers, led by Sayyid Ahmad Khan, and anti-British Muslims, most of whom stressed a more traditional Islam. As a lifetime opponent of British incursions in Muslim lands, Afghani was ready to align himself with more traditionally Muslim groups against Sayyid Ahmad Khan and his followers. His 'Refutation of the Materialists', ostensibly an attack on internal opponents of Islam, including radical reformers, is in fact mainly aimed at pro-British reformers like Sayyid Ahmad Khan, not because they are reformers but because they are pro-British. In the 1880s, in this work and others, Afghani picked up the trend for Islamic revival and solidarity as a weapon against British rule in Muslim lands. Again there are contemporary parallels in people like the recent Iranian ideologist Ali Shariati, who utilized Islam against the West while remaining a reformer. It should be added, however, that there is strong evidence that Afghani was far less of a believer than he claimed in the 1880s, while Shariati was apparently a real believer; also Shariati never formed tactical alliances with people as conservative as some of Afghani's allies. However, Afghani's writings are intellectually superior to Shariati's (although not as brilliantly original as some of his followers claim), and it seems likely that Afghani's works will have a longer life and influence.

From India Afghani went briefly to London, and then in 1883 to Paris. Here he was joined by Muhammad Abduh and the two published an Arabic newspaper, al-'Urwa al-Wuthga ('The Strongest Link', a reference to the Qur'an or Islam) which was subsidized by admirers and sent free to leading figures throughout the Muslim world. In this paper Afghani continued his anti-British polemics, writing especially against British incursions in Egypt and Sudan. He also began to put forth arguments favouring unity among Islamic countries as a means to stem further foreign encroachments, and wrote in praise of the Ottoman sultan, Abdul Hamid, as well as authoring or inspiring a number of more theoretical articles.

Also in Paris Afghani wrote a response to a talk, published as a journal article, by Ernest Renan, who claimed that Islam was particularly hostile to science. Although Afghani's talk was later presented in the Muslim world as a defence of Islam, he in fact agreed with Renan that religions in general, including Islam, were hostile to science, and even added that only a few of the elite could appreciate the real, scientific rather than religious truth. His only defence of Islam was to point out that it was several hundred years younger than Christianity, and hence might progress equally in time. This article may be taken as evidence of Afghani's true ideas, as there was no reason why he should invent a line of argument that could only harm him if it became known in the Muslim world. (His followers took steps to ensure that no translation be published and that his true line of argument not become known.)

Discontinuing his newspaper after less than a year, probably due to a drying up of its subsidy rather than to the British prohibition of its entry into India and Egypt as is usually stressed, Afghani entered into high-level schemes, led by the philo-Muslim Briton Wilfrid Blunt, to get the British out of Egypt and the Sudan. Since these plans involved contact with leading British politicians, the anti-British Afghani came, ironically, to be considered a British agent by some Muslims. In this period, seeing Blunt and other Britons preoccupied with the rebellious Mahdi of the Sudan, Afghani claimed to be an agent of the Mahdi, a claim for which there is not one shred of documentary evidence.

The only significant result of these negotiations was to put Afghani in contact with the Ottoman sultan Abdul Hamid II, with whom he tried to ingratiate himself. Afghani had already written well of the sultan in his Paris newspaper. Other progressive or formerly progressive Muslim activists also turned to this sultan, often considered a reactionary, as the strongest force against further European encroachment in Muslim lands.

When nothing came, for a time, of Afghani's ties to the British or to the sultan, he accepted an invitation from the Russian chauvinist editor Katkov to come to Russia. He went by way of Iran, where he unexpectedly spent several months, first in the southern port of Bushire and then in Tehran, where he received an invitation from the shah via the Iranian minister of publications. The shah soon turned against Afghani, possibly because of his violent anti-British views, and pressured him out of Iran, into Russia. There Afghani tried to influence prominent Russians into promoting an anti-British war in India and elsewhere, but without success.

In 1889 the shah went to Europe via St. Petersburg and Afghani managed to see some of the men in his entourage.
Afghani then located the shah in Munich where, probably in the hope of appeasing Russian anger over his recent concessions to the British, he apparently invited Afghani to Iran. Afghani first returned to St. Petersburg, saying he had been given a mission by Iran's prime minister to improve relations, though the prime minister denied this when Afghani returned to Iran. Once Afghani saw he could have no influence on Iran's government, he gathered a group of reformers to whom he taught methods of oppositional action. As had been true in Egypt the time was ripe for oppositional activity, as growing economic concessions to foreigners were arousing opposition among merchants, intellectuals, and the clergy. Hearing of a plan to exile him, Afghani took refuge at an inviolable shrine just south of Tehran, where he continued his teaching.

In January 1891, alarmed by a leaflet attacking the government over its concessions, Iran's rulers violated Afghani's sanctuary and had him forcibly taken from Iran into Iraq. This degrading treatment, especially for a *sayyid* in sanctuary, contributed to Afghani's desire for vengeance on the shah. While in Iraq Afghani wrote letters to disciples and ulama against Iran's concessions to foreigners; after that he continued his propaganda against the Iranian government from London.

Iran was then ideal terrain for Afghani's tactic of using religious appeals to stop foreign incursions. The Iranian ulama were more independent and hierarchically organized than were the Sunni ulama of other countries. The issue of concessions to Christian foreigners united religious figures, nationalists, and reformers. Afghani was thus able to be one of several forces in the Iranian mass movement against a tobacco concession to a British company in 1891, which forced the shah to cancel the concession, although his role here and elsewhere was considerably smaller than is stated in many biographies.

Going from Iraq to London, Afghani joined Malkam Khan, an Iranian reformer, in propaganda against the Iranian regime. Sultan Abdulhamid then conveyed to him an invitation to come to Istanbul, and Afghani soon agreed. In Istanbul Afghani was at first well treated, but was never given important tasks. He worked with a group of Iranians to send letters and gifts to non-Ottoman Shi'i ulama, asking them to support the pan-Islamic claims of the sultan. This further aroused Iran's rulers against Afghani, and many among the sultan's retinue

were also hostile to him. Then one of Afghani's Iranian
followers who had been imprisoned for oppositional activities
in Iran, Mirza Reza Kermani, visited Afghani in Istanbul.
Afghani appears to have suggested to Mirza Reza that he return
to Iran and kill the shah, which he did in the spring of 1896.
Three of Afghani's followers already imprisoned on the late
shah's request were extradited to Iran and killed for a crime with
which they had no connection. The Iranian rulers also made
lengthy efforts to extradite Jamal al-Din, but the Ottomans
claimed he was an Afghan and not extraditable to Iran –
probably in order to keep him from revealing Ottoman court
secrets in Iran.

In 1897 Afghani died of cancer of the chin. Among the many
myths about him is that he was poisoned by the sultan, but his
illness and the operation he had for it are well documented. By
this time, Afghani had not been allowed to publish anything, to
travel, or to speak publicly for five years, and he was fading
from general consciousness, until his death brought a brief
flurry of notices. His real fame came later, however, when a
number of causes he championed, such as Islamic modernism,
militant activism, and especially anti-imperialism, became more
widespread in the Muslim world, and many looked back to him
as a pioneer of such causes.

In describing Afghani's character, those who knew him often
noted his boldness, devotion to causes, and indifference to
material considerations. In addition we may note less generally
admired characteristics like delusions of grandeur, distorted
views of reality, and hostility to any ties to women. His
personal magnetism, now often called charisma, was extraordinary, and he had an uncanny ability to enter into high
governmental circles. But he nearly always quickly lost the
favour of the powerful. This seems to have been for two
reasons: his propensity for oppositional plotting at the same
time as he was dealing with men in government, and his
penchant for grandiose anti-foreign schemes. His bluntness,
temper, and lack of deference also played a role. He favoured
quick and violent acts like assassinations, wars, intrigues, and
revolts.

The growing power of the West over Muslims continued
after Afghani's death and brought forth increasing defensive or
assertive reactions, some of which were based on unrealistic
notions of Christian or other persecution of Muslims, rather
than on a deeper understanding of imperialism.

Despite his faults and partial unrealism, Afghani contributed to the Muslim world several things: after a long denigration of that world and of Islam by westerners he helped emphasize parts of the Muslim tradition that were worthy of pride, and suggested that reform could occur via a reinterpretation of Islam. By his boldness he helped give courage to many who had felt there was no alternative to submitting to existing power structures. He helped introduce and disseminate tools of political education and action including the journal or newspaper of opinion, the leaflet, and the secret political society. Although he was not a leader in pushing for specific internal reforms, and spent much more time and effort fighting foreign control of Muslim lands, he did at times speak and write of such reforms as constitutions and parliaments. One may speak of two sides of his words and actions – political intrigue on the one hand, and organization and political education on the other. He probably would have been a more effective figure had he concentrated more on the latter rather than spending so much time on ultimately fruitless grandiose political acts. Had he done so his legacy might have been less ambiguous.

Afghani was the most important initiator of a growing trend toward changing Islam from, primarily, a religious faith (with elements of social control by the ulama and the powerful) into a primarily politico-religious ideology that emphasizes aims not traditionally considered religious. Islam was seen by him and many who came after him largely as a source of solidarity, in particular solidarity against the encroachments of western governments. This emphasis on anti-imperialist ideology and solidarity has continued to be in the forefront of a number of Islamic and nationalist movements in the Muslim world ever since Afghani's time.

In Pakistan and a number of other Islamic countries the ideologization of Islam is partly recognized, and the term 'Islamic ideology' has a positive connotation, whereas terms including 'ideology' in the West usually imply that something false and instrumental is involved. For western thinkers it is overwhelmingly other people who have ideologies, not oneself, and one cannot imagine a western government having, or sponsoring, an organization for the promotion of 'Democratic Ideology', 'Liberal Ideology', or 'Christian Ideology', as is found in Pakistan regarding Islamic ideology. But ideology, however understood, is certainly an apt term for many of the intellectual movements of the past century.

It is important to realize that few of the trained ulama, Shi'i or Sunni, past or present, have accepted the teachings of Afghani, whose deviations from classical Islam they recognize. He is a precursor not of religious trends, but rather of a series of ideological movements, especially those designed to utilize Islam for primarily political goals. He was the first of a line of ideological modernizers – many of them laymen with little religious training – who have tried to interpret Islam in new ways to inculcate in Muslims the values of reform and self-strengthening in order to reform the Muslim world and regain its independence from the West.

Sayyid Jamal al-Din's Influence

The question of what influence a thinker or activist has had is nearly always trickier than it might appear at first sight. As already noted, Afghani voiced ideas, including reformist pan-Islam, that were first put forward by the Young Ottomans, yet the latter had very little influence among non-Turkish speakers, while Afghani's publications in Arabic and Persian meant that most people found these ideas in Afghani rather than in the Young Ottomans. Beyond such misattributions, however, there is the fact that many aspects of Afghani's persona and ideas were more attractive to later thinkers than they were in, say, the 1890s, and this, plus Afghani's already existing stature, encouraged many later reformers to read back into Afghani their own values. Hence, for example, much is made by later writers of Afghani as an internal reformer and constitutionalist, but many of the examples given are simply false. The only writings by Afghani favouring constitutionalism came during a short period in Egypt when this was a live issue with anti-imperialist implications, and was associated with some of Afghani's political allies, as against his political enemies. Other than that there are numerous examples of Afghani working with, not against, autocratic rulers, and the actual reforms he wrote about have more to do with modern rationality and strength than with popular sovereignty. More than either he wrote of freeing the Muslim world from western control, which clearly concerned him far more than did constitutionalism.

Liberation from western control became an increasingly popular cause over time, and Afghani's words could and can be cited in support of such liberation, whether advocated by

Islamic modernists, nationalists, or contemporary Islamists. Afghani was also attractive to later activists because of his unusually active political life. Also contributing to the Afghani legend was the large number of prominent people, Muslim and western, with whom he had contact. Writers like E.G. Browne and Wilfred Blunt wrote admiringly of Afghani, and such western recognition strengthened his standing in the Muslim world. The notion that Afghani had impressed, and even debated with, prominent westerners added to his stature and importance in the eyes of Muslim intellectuals.

Finally, Afghani's continuing popularity owes something to the fact that he is not seen as compromised by pro–western positions, as, for example, is his ex–disciple Muhammad Abduh. Nor is he today generally tied to the now–declining cause of nationalism, even though in the 1870s and early 1880s he in fact wrote many articles in support of nationalism, including praising the unity of Muslims and Christians in Egypt and of Muslims and Hindus in India. These writings, although significant in number, are far less known than his pan-Islamic and pro-Islamic writings of the 1880s. (Far more is known, for instance, of his totally mythical 'support' for a Muslim state like Pakistan in South Asia than of his actual articles in Persian calling for Hindu-Muslim unity against the British.)

As is the case with many important ideologists, it is difficult to argue that later trends would have been significantly different had he never lived. Within the limits of the way 'influence' is usually understood, Afghani may be said to have been, and still to be, very influential. Much, if not most, of this influence, however, has been based on a largely mythical biography and interpretation of his ideas.

Afghani's main influence may be traced in a line going back chiefly to two men, his Egyptian disciple Muhammad Abduh, and the latter's follower Rashid Rida. As noted, Abduh was the most important of several direct Egyptian disciples and pupils of Afghani who were influenced, among other things, by Afghani's Egyptian teaching of rationalist Islamic philosophy and by his use of one argument for the elite and another for the masses. It is very possible also that Abduh's adoption of a rationalist type of theology associated with the early Islamic theologians 'the Mu'tazilites' was influenced by Afghani. Just as Islamic philosophy remained alive in the Iranian and Shi'i world, so Mu'tazilite theology remained the theology of the Twelver Shi'i long after it had essentially died out among

Sunnis. This theology stressed the independent existence of such categories as justice, and believed that God was obliged to act justly, while the later school of theology that became dominant among Sunnis believed that God, being omnipotent, could do whatever he wished, and that whatever he did became justice. In addition, the Mu'tazilites, unlike the dominant school, believed in free will, and this became the position of modernists like Abduh.

Rashid Rida (1865–1935) was early attracted to Afghani's words but came to know him only at second hand, chiefly via Abduh. Rida developed a more conservative and islamically-oriented interpretation of Afghani, in accord with his own views. Afghani, Abduh, and Rida are generally, for all their differences, considered Islamic modernists. This school of thought, prominent in the late nineteenth and early twentieth centuries and still very much alive, especially in South and Southeast Asia, sought to reinterpret Islam on the basis of returning to the Qur'an and to early Muslim leaders and reinterpreting them in liberal modernist ways. This had been done before Afghani, but he encouraged it, and it was carried out even more systematically by some of his followers. A return to reinterpreted scripture is characteristic of religious reforms in many traditions, particularly since the Protestants (and Afghani compared himself to Luther). Such a procedure has the advantage for reformers of cutting away many centuries of religious practice and leadership and reducing the essence of religion to a manageable body of ideas which can then be reinterpreted.

It is also true that the Qur'an, like many prophetic scriptures, has strong reforming and humanistic elements that can easily fit into modern thought, however intractable some of its legal aspects may be. In essence most Islamic modernists, including Afghani and Abduh, wanted to make Islam compatible with modern western thought and science.

The name and example of Afghani spread in the early twentieth century, and all sorts of biographical details and ideas were attributed to him. The Afghans, who wrote nothing about Afghani until the First World War (and that was a translation of an existing biography) soon began to make him a national hero, and succeeded in getting his (reputed) body sent back to Afghanistan. He was given an Afghan childhood biography that lacked nothing except documentation. Similarly Afghani was made a precursor of the idea of an independent Pakistan despite the fact that his talks in India show him to be an unequivocal supporter of pan-Indian nationalism, who praised especially the achievements of the Hindus.

Although Afghani's Islamic modernism sounded similar to that of the people who invoked his name in the 1930s, the different role of similar-sounding ideas in different periods should be noted. Writing before western ideas had spread widely among Muslims, Afghani was mainly addressing people whose primary commitment was to traditional Islamic values, and in saying that modern western virtues were to be found in Islam he was trying to obtain Muslim acceptance of those modern ideas. By the 1930s, however, Islamic liberals were addressing an audience most of whom were educated in western ideas, and when these people conflated Islamic and western values they were largely trying to reinstate Islam with that audience and to build an Islam acceptable to it. Or else their audience was torn between Islam and secular, western-based loyalties, and the modernists were trying to indicate that their newer ideas could be reconciled with Islam. These people have been characterized as apologists, who try to build pride in Islam while very largely adhering to western values. Afghani, however, was mainly calling people to action, not to increased admiration of Islam.

Very different from liberal apologetics, but often including writers and leaders who looked to Afghani, was the type of Islamic revivalism that began in the late 1920s and has had a strong recrudescence from the 1970s on. The Muslim Brethren in Egypt and the organizations led by Maududi in Muslim India developed between and since the two world wars. Theirs was not liberalism in Islamic clothing, but it was also not a restatement of traditional Islamic trends. Rather it favoured a politicized Islam along with a return to selected aspects of Islamic law and practice, in the name of a complete return to Islamic law. Secular nationalism was eschewed and borrowings from the West by the Islamists were not admitted, although they were and are in fact huge. These movements are in part a reaction against imitation of the West and against western control in Muslim lands. Such movements could appeal to another side of Afghani – his resistance in the name of Islam to western control of Muslim lands. With the growth of Zionist immigration to the Palestine mandate (held by Britain) between the wars and the creation and victories of Israel after the Second World War, the feeling of Islam besieged increased, despite the formal independence of most Muslim states. After the 1967

Israeli victory many Muslims began to say that Israel's Jewish identity helped its conquests, and that Muslims must similarly identify with Islam.

Just as liberalism and apologetics represent one side of Afghani's life and actions and leave out another side, the same is true for Islamic revival. Like the revivalists, Afghani wished to mobilize Muslims to fight against western conquest and control and to strengthen Islamic countries. Unlike the revivalists, however, he did not stress Islamic laws or practices; he was open to new ideas and not concerned with strengthening the type of Islam that had been dominant in the past, which he strongly criticized. Afghani was similar to the revivalists in that both believed or believe in anti-western activism, but Afghani did not share their ultimate Islamist goals.

Today both liberals and Islamic revivalists, as well as a number of others, find something to appeal to in Afghani, and biographies of him and reprints of his books and articles continue to pour off the presses in the Muslim world. The great majority of these works do not incorporate the newer scholarship of the past twenty-five years. It is worth noting that an Egyptian Christian author who introduced into Egypt some ideas and research findings about Afghani found in recent works, including those by the present author, was strongly attacked by several Egyptian Muslim writers. Not only the idea that Afghani might have been other than a completely pious Muslim but even the evidence that he was born in Iran and had a Shi'i upbringing often brings forth heated denial in Sunni countries. It is as if the undermining of any significant part of the Afghani myth would make all the rest crumble and threaten a number of current ideological positions. Although the major documentation, including many documents in Arabic, on Afghani's life have been available for thirty years, no Arab author seems to have ordered and used microfilms of these documents, or even the catalogue that reproduces many of them. It appears that what is important is to protect the ramparts against recent scholarship rather than even to try to see whether the newer documents can be interpreted so as to support positions acceptable to Afghani's Muslim disciples.

Even without the mythology that surrounds him, however, Afghani may be seen as a truly major figure in a number of trends in the Muslim world. His emphasis on Islam as a crucial force in warding off the West and increasing the solidarity of Muslim peoples, his calls for reform and change within despotic political systems under the banner of Islam, and his attacks on those who sided with western imperialists or otherwise split the Muslim community are all themes that have found a long-lived and considerable success and succession since his time.

In his own time Afghani was, first of all, a defender of the Islamic world against growing western encroachments; secondly, he believed that reform was necessary to make the Muslim world strong enough to resist the West and restore its independence, and only thirdly, if at all, was he concerned with a revival of Islam as a religion. His preoccupation with self-strengthening against the West is a theme that has continued in a whole series of movements, including the modernist liberals (some of whom were, however, less concerned with this than with internal reform), nationalists, leftists, and Islamic revivalists. Even when the mythology is stripped away, Afghani will be found to have expressed himself forcefully on issues that remain of primary concern to the Muslim world. In this sense, his influence may be said to be of both central and seminal importance.

3

Muhammad Abduh: Pioneer of Islamic Reform

Yvonne Haddad

While there may be a certain fickleness in the way historians choose to recognize certain individuals as formative in the various stages of a nation's history, there is little doubt that anyone writing about Egypt as it emerged from the nineteenth century and plunged its way into the twentieth could imagine not acknowledging the enormous contribution of Muhammad Abduh to modern Islamic thought. Scholar, pedagogue, mufti, *'alim*, theologian and reformer, he was controversial in the context in which he operated, and continues to be influential both on his disciples and on those who thought that his compromises with the West went too far. In many ways he reflects the life and commitments of the great Abu Hamid al-Ghazali, whose teachings are so reminiscent of his own.

Muhammad Abduh's roots were deep in the soil of rural Egypt. He was born in a village on the Nile delta in 1849, of a family renowned for its commitment to learning and to religion. His father had two wives, and young Muhammad learned early the difficulties of living in a polygamous family, a subject he addressed with great conviction in later years when he spoke out strongly for family reform and the rights of women. As a boy Abduh studied reading and writing at home, and by the time he was twelve had read the Qur'an so many times that he had memorized it. One of his biographers notes that, because he was spared the environment of a Qur'an school, Abduh never suffered the fate of others who knew the Qur'an by heart, that of swaying back and forth while lecturing or reciting from the holy book.[1]

When he was thirteen Abduh was sent to Tanta to study at the Ahmadi mosque, considered second only to the great al-Azhar University as the place to learn the Qur'an and recitation. His first experience with learning by rote, memorizing texts and commentaries and laws for which he was given no tools of understanding, was formative in his later commitment to a thoroughgoing reform of the Egyptian educational system. Perplexed and unhappy, he fled the Tanta mosque convinced that he would never again take up academic life. At the age of sixteen he married.

It was shortly after this that Abduh's uncle, one Shaykh Darwish Khadr, came into the young man's life. A Sufi of the Shadhili Brotherhood, he rekindled the flame of enthusiasm for learning and for religion in Abduh by teaching him the ethical and moral disciplines and ascetic practices of his order.[2] Although Abduh spent only a brief time with Shaykh Darwish, an interest in the inner life of Sufism remained with him throughout his life. Later, however, he was to become critical of many of its external forms as well as its teachings. For a while he even adopted an ascetic lifestyle, but abandoned it both through the urgings of the Shaykh and in the later excitement of coming into the orbit of the charismatic Jamal al-Din al-Afghani.

In 1866 Abduh left his family and his wife and set out for Cairo to study at al-Azhar. High hopes for real learning were again sorely disappointed when he encountered the same kind of pedantry and rote memorization without understanding that he had found at Tanta. Shaykh Muhammad Mustafa al-Maraghi describes the general atmosphere at al-Azhar at the time that Abduh was a student: '[Muhammad Abduh] grew up in a lustreless age ... he, and others like him, went on studying dull, lifeless rules cut off from their wellsprings in the Qur'an and the canonical writings, shorn of their roots in the language of the Arabs ...'[3] Little wonder that reform of this system of learning was to become a lifelong passion for Abduh.

Three years after Abduh began his work at al-Azhar, the enigmatic and exciting reformer Jamal al-Din al-Afghani came to Egypt. Quickly Abduh was drawn into his sphere, and under al-Afghani he began to broaden his study to embrace philosophy as well as the social and political sciences. Afghani gathered around him in Cairo a group of young Azhar students including future Egyptian leader Sa'd Zaghlul and led them in discussions of theology, law, philosophy and mysticism. But his was not the dry academics of the university; Afghani was an activist who instilled in his students the urgency of resisting European intervention in the life of their country and the importance of seeing the Islamic peoples as one unified community.[4] Abduh cast off the last vestiges of world-denying asceticism and entered the world of socio-political activism from which he never retired, although ultimately he was to eschew Afghani's revolutionism in favour of a more conciliatory and evolutionary approach.

In 1878 Abduh accepted a teaching assignment at the newly established Dar al-'Ulum college. He used this as an opportunity to speak and write on political and social matters, and especially national education, during this period of heightened national consciousness in Egypt. By the following year his mentor al-Afghani was considered too politically incendiary, and was expelled from the country. At the same time Abduh was removed from his teaching post at Dar al-'Ulum and ordered into retirement. He was soon reactivated by the prime minister, however, and appointed one of the editors, and then chief editor, of *al-Waqa'i' al-Misriyya*, the official Egyptian Gazette. In that position he became a major influence in shaping public opinion.

As Abduh became increasingly critical of the methods and actions of the political and military leaders of the country his position was seriously jeopardized. Finally he was forced to choose between the nationalist cause and the pro-British occupation policies of the Khedive. His choice of the former led to his three-year exile from Egypt, beginning in 1882. Deeply discouraged at the apparent failure of nationalism, Abduh entered a dark period of his life. First finding refuge in Beirut, he received an invitation from his old friend al-Afghani to join him in Paris. There they founded the short-lived but greatly influential society 'al-'Urwa al-Wuthqa', the 'strongest link', whose purpose was to unite Muslims and rid them of the causes of their apparent disunity. The society, as well as its newspaper of the same name (of which eighteen issues were published), was dedicated to the general task of warning non-western people of the dangers of European intervention, and the specific cause of freeing Egypt from the bonds of British occupation. 'The focus on Muslims is due to the fact that the majority of nations who are betrayed and humiliated, and whose resources have been usurped by the foreigners, are Muslim.'[5]

Abduh himself indicated the purposes of their publication to be: (1) identifying ways in which to rectify the problems of the past which had led to decline; (2) infusing Muslims with a hope of victory and eradication of despair; (3) calling to steadfastness in adherence to the principles of the fathers and forebears; (4) defending against the accusation levied against Muslims that they cannot progress as long as they adhere to the principles of Islam; (5) providing information on important political events; and (6) enhancing relations between nations and improving public welfare.[6]

The society eventually was dissolved, and Abduh returned to Beirut where he became a teacher in a Muslim school. His home was a centre for young men of all faiths – Muslims, Christians, Druze – captivated by his magnetic teaching style. His most important theological work, *Risalat al-Tawhid*, was based on the lectures he gave during this time in Beirut. In 1888 the Khedive gave him permission to return to Cairo. Forbidden from teaching, where he was considered to be too influential over the young, he was made a judge in the 'native courts' established to apply the new lawcodes of the Khedive.[7] He proceeded to become a member of the administrative council of al-Azhar in 1895, and just before the turn of the century was appointed Grand Mufti of Egypt. From that position he worked to introduce changes in the system of religious courts, and continued his lifelong struggle for reforms of Egyptian education, particularly in al-Azhar. As Mufti he brought back the practice of issuing personal opinions or *fatwas* to private individuals on matters of law and conscience. It is in these *fatwas* that some of the most interesting glimpses into the thought of this complex man are to be found.

Muhammad Abduh died on 11 July 1905. The number of people who paid their respects in Cairo and Alexandria attests to the deep regard in which he was held. His earlier attachment to al-Afghani seems to have moderated; in later life he rarely mentioned the man who had been so influential on him. Although Abduh was attacked sharply for his outspoken views and his actions, particularly in the last years of his life, there was deep recognition of the loss that both Egypt and Islam suffered with the death of a leader noted for his gentle demeanour and deep spirituality. Persons of the three monotheistic faiths Judaism, Christianity and Islam came together to honour him as scholar, patriot and man of faith.

Abduh's Milieu

During the early part of the nineteenth century, Europe, practically speaking, had been quite distant from the Islamic world, known really only to those few who were able to travel to European capitals and discover first-hand the ideas that were current in western thought. Eager to adopt European military technology whose superiority had been proven on the battlefield, Muslim rulers encouraged visitors and students sent to Europe to attempt to replicate European civilization in their own countries. They became the kernel of a new social order, which actually diminished the power of the Ulama, merchants and craftsmen.[8] Until that time many Muslims concerned about the condition of Islamic nations had been tempted to borrow indiscriminately from the West, hoping that the importation of ideas from an obviously flourishing civilization would help bring Muslim countries back to their former state of glory. Such visitors to Europe as Khayr al-Din of Tunisia, Rifa'a al-Tahtawi of Egypt, Sayyid Ahmad Khan of India and Malkum Khan of Iran were urging their compatriots to find what was best in European ideology and try to incorporate it into their own societies. Philosophers such as Voltaire and Montesquieu were studied with great interest, along with positive law and forms of secular thought.

Thus after the middle of the century, western thought became accessible to far greater numbers of Muslims. Significant amounts of material were translated into Arabic, making European ideas available to intellectuals across the Muslim world. Muslims were able to ponder the ideals of European liberalism and see more clearly whether or not they were applicable to their own circumstances. At the same time the actual European presence in Muslim countries was becoming more evident with the immediacy of colonialism, changing the very nature of the encounter between East and West. By 1870 it became obvious that Europeans were actually taking over major parts of the Muslim world, ruling their economies and interfering in the political processes. The teachings of Jamal al-Din al-Afghani warning about western penetration and control were beginning to find response among a growing number of the elite of Muslim nations. As a result the effort to infuse the heritage of Islam with new, liberal western ideas became subsidiary to, perhaps even co-opted by, the need to face issues of nationalism and independence from European hegemony. There was a clearer sense of the dangers of the indiscriminate importation of ideas and of the need to shore up Muslim defences against undue encroachment. Muhammad Abduh was influenced by this change in mood; he was also instrumental in shaping it.

Abduh's Analysis of the Problem

Abduh was aware of the state of decay in Muslim societies when contrasted with that of Europe. According to his analyses the condition of weakness and backwardness was due both to external factors, a consequence of European hegemony that threatened the very existence of Muslim societies, and to internal realities, the situation which the Muslims brought about themselves.

Abduh recognized the seriousness of the European challenge. European nations, he said, have entered a new phase characterized by a thriving civilization based on scientific knowledge, arts, industry, wealth and order, and a new political organization based on conquest buttressed by new means of conducting war and by weaponry capable of wiping out more numerous armies.[9] That, however, does not mean that Muslims have to succumb to their power or emulate their ways. European strength makes the challenge more forbidding since Muslims can never be subservient to British rule regardless of the force the colonial powers may employ to cow the inhabitants or the tricks they utilize to placate the citizens. They are to be treated as aggressors since they seek the possession of other people's land. Furthermore, they are not fit to govern Muslim society since 'they are different in religion and it is inappropriate to submit to them even if they establish justice'.[10]

Abduh insisted that Europeans must be resisted because their lofty principles do not tally with their treatment of their subject people. Egyptians suffer from blind confidence in foreigners without distinguishing whether they are deceptive or sincere, truthful or liars, faithful or traitors. In one celebrated meeting with a representative of the government in England, Abduh argued boldly for his cause. Asked his opinion on the present state of Egypt and British policies there he responded: 'We Egyptians of the Liberal Party believed once in English liberalism and English sympathy; but we believe no longer, for facts are stronger than words. Your liberalness we see plainly is only for yourselves, and your sympathy with us is that of the wolf for the lamb which he designs to eat.'[11]

Abduh was the first Egyptian to point to the backwardness of Egyptian society and the fact that it had lost its capacity to renew itself. The social and political problems of Egypt, he said, are due to its own heritage which has made it incapable of responding to the challenge of the age.[12] He saw Muslim weakness as due to the internal division within their community, the bifurcation of the caliphate and the carving up of the Muslim *ummah* into small nations with a variety of sects and beliefs, fighting against one another in allegiance to various leaders. Islamic teachings, he said, show that the fate that has befallen the Muslims is a test from God, a punishment for their lack of diligence. The decline of Muslim societies is a punishment promised in the Qur'an.[13] It is also due to ignorance and misunderstanding of the faith, to sectarian divisions on the whole, to a closing of *ijtihad* or individual interpretation, and to misguided policies of Islamic leaders.[14]

For Abduh, as for others, the truly ideal time of Islam was the time of the Prophet Muhammad and his immediate followers before divisions, schools of thought, and intellectual trends borrowed from other nations penetrated the early Muslim community. Thus he insisted that in order to initiate reform, it is necessary to return to the minimum essentials of the faith that all schools of law, all sections and factions, can identify as true Islam. He advocated making use of the best of the traditions but condemned blind imitation, *taqlid*, as an impediment to progress. He asserted that there is a need to be selective in re-appropriating the teachings of the past. Urging that special criteria be established to ascertain what texts are truly authoritative, he determined that three principles should be used: (a) the *salaf*, forebears whose authority is to be sought, must be identified; (b) there must be careful analysis of the texts to be consulted. Unlike other *salafis*, Abduh felt that every ancient text except the Qur'an is open to questioning and discussion. All opinions of scholars have to be judged by the Qur'an. If what they say is compatible with Qur'anic teachings, then their teachings can be utilized; (c) given the prevailing condition of sectarian division, political authorities should not be aligned to any particular school. In all of this Abduh urged the use of reason and what he saw as the essential freedom of man to understand the laws that govern human life.[15]

Thus he advocated a return to the one true source of Islam,

the Qur'an, on which Muslims cannot disagree.[16] He affirmed that the Qur'an has unequivocally identified the *sunan* of Allah, the immutable laws of God which determine the cycles of decay and decline and the rise and ascendency of nations. Following these laws is the only means of the revival of the nation. The establishment of a righteous and just society must be in accordance with the teachings of the Qur'an.

Abduh spent considerable time in seeking to refute the French Minister of Foreign Affairs, M. Gabriel Hanoteaux. Hanoteaux's accusation that Muslims advocated a confrontation between Islam and the West merited extensive comment. Abduh argued that it is obvious that in this case the West set itself up as a confrontational civilization, saying, 'we are superior because we are Christian and you are inferior because you are Muslim.' Thus for Abduh, the Islamic affirmation of the relevance of Islamic civilization is a response to the gauntlet that was thrown down by the West in its claims to superiority. Hanoteaux had argued that the source of the creativity and brilliance of European civilization was its Aryan origins. He further claimed that the problem with Islamic civilization is that its roots are Semitic. This Abduh strongly refuted by accusing Europeans of being imitators rather than innovators. The truth, he said, is that Europe appears superior because it has borrowed extensively from Islamic civilization.[17] The Aryan heritage, so prized by Hanoteaux, Abduh saw as polytheistic and undemocratic. Its adherents discriminate according to class, he said, and are noted for bloodletting rather than peace. 'The eyes of the observer of history,' wrote Abduh, 'become red from looking at the blood that has coalesced on the ice of time, because of what those associated with the religion of the Aryan civilization did as they opposed that civilization and tried to douse its fire.'[18]

He questioned the claim that nineteenth-century European civilization was brought by the first wave of Aryan immigrants and affirmed that it was Semitic in origin, brought in by Muslims who distilled and purified the knowledge they received from Persia, Egypt, Rome and Greece. The setting was Andalusia, despite the fact that the Christian clergy did their best to eradicate it because it set up a threat to their authority.[19] Abduh defended the contributions of the Semitic race and eastern civilizations in general, especially those of the Phoenicians and the Pharaonic Egyptians. The Semitic race and their religion are grounded on the belief in the one God, he said.

The Aryan civilization which Europeans brought from Asia, on the other hand, carried with it polytheism and barbarism. He denied that there was much influence of Greek and Roman civilizations on Europe and insisted that Christianity was born weak and continued so until the coming of Islam.[20]

Abduh was sharply critical of European Christianity as a religion and a civilization. Arguing against the accusation that Islam must be judged to be stupid because Muslims are currently backward, Abduh charged that if a religion is assessed on the basis of the condition of its adherents one would have to say that there is no connection between Christianity and modern civilization. Muslims have access to the Christian Gospel which they can read and comprehend, and none of its subtle meaning escapes them. It is clear to them that rather than affirming the creation of a world civilization, the Gospel orders Christians to separate themselves from the world and be ascetic. The Gospel enjoins the Christian to give up his robe if someone steals his shirt, and if he is struck on the right cheek to turn the left one too. Christians are asked to renounce this world and seek that which is eternal. They are ordered to give to God what is God's and to Caesar what is Caesar's. Does this in any way characterize the Christian society of Europe? demanded Abduh. Modern Christian civilization is in fact one of power and conquest, a civilization of gold and silver, of ostentation and pleasure. Its chief ruler is the sterling pound or the lira, and it is clear that the Gospel has nothing to do with it.[21]

In the process of rebuttal of European attacks on Islam, he said, a new form of refutation has emerged. Unlike the medieval encounter with Byzantine Christianity which focused on the nature of Christ, the trinity, incarnation and resurrection, and which hurled epithets on the person of Muhammad and pointed to the carnal nature of Islam, the focus in the twentieth century shifted to the relationship of religion to the world and the role and efficacy of both Christianity and Islam in creating, fostering and nurturing modern civilization. From a dispute over which religious beliefs represent true revelation and provide for felicity in the hereafter, the debate changed to which religion can empower its adherents to be successful in refashioning the material world.

Abduh argued that the teachings of the Gospel are world-renouncing, while those of the Qur'an are world affirming. He identified the main principles of each religion; the framework that he provided has become the standard for twentieth-century Muslim depiction of Christianity:

(1) Christianity is founded on the belief in miracles. The Gospel teaches that the proof of the validity of Christianity is the way in which such miracles confound nature and its laws. This shows that Christianity is unscientific and has nothing to do with European civilization, since every study shows that the universe has eternal laws and that behind all movements there are causes and reasons. Anyone who believed that he could change things through prayer alone would have no need of scientific research.[22]

(2) The second principle of Christianity is the authority of its clergy as noted in Matthew 16:19: 'I give you the keys of the kingdom of heaven. Whatever you bind on earth will be bound, and whatever you loosen will be loosened.' This argues against the claim that Christianity is a rational religion that encourages freedom of thought. The fact is that Christian clergy actually have the power to determine whether a person is a Christian and to excommunicate. The believer is not really free in what he believes, nor is he able to act according to the rational decisions of his intellect. He is in fact bound by the judgement of the religious leaders.[23]

Even Protestants who claim a freedom to interpret the scripture have not changed the claim that the Bible is the source of knowledge for humanity. The human intellect is constrained; it is not allowed to supercede what is taught in the books.[24]

(3) Christianity advocated the abandonment of the world. Christians are ordered to be devoted to the kingdom of God and to run away from the world, as in Matthew 6:10,19. The Gospel [sic] even advocates celibacy, an obvious contradiction of God's commandment to procreate and fill the earth.[25]

(4) The fourth principle shared by all Christians, whether Orthodox, Protestant or Catholic, is belief in the primacy of the irrational. Christianity affirms that faith is a gift in which rationality has no input. Consequently, religion is above reason and refutes rational thought.

(5) The fifth principle that Christians affirm is that the scriptures contain all that is necessary for humanity concerning this life and the next. Everything concerned with religious beliefs, ethical existence and physical activity and all that is necessary for human happiness is contained in the Old Testament and the New Testament. Some, for example, have gone so far as to prove that metallurgy is found in the Bible.

(6) The sixth principle distinguishes between Christians and

others, as depicted in Matthew 10. 'I came not to bring peace to the earth but a sword, to separate a man from his father, a daughter from her mother, and a wife from her mother-in-law.' Christian teachings encourage the disruption of the family and the social order. The enemies of a person can be his immediate family. When Jesus was told that his mother and brothers were waiting for him outside he said that the disciples were his mother and brothers.[26]

To offset the attacks against Islam Abduh set out to redefine and re-invent Islamic teachings in contra-distinction to Christianity. The contentious nature of the debate appears to determine the scope, tone and content of his efforts which are manifestly defensive in nature. They are clearly structured to prove Islam's superiority over Christianity. In actual fact, the Islam he defined had little to do with what obtained at his time:

(1) Abduh asserted that Islam is based on two foundations: belief in God's unicity and the affirmation of Muhammad's message as truth. The first seeks to alert the human mind and point individuals toward the universe and its order and laws of causation. It helps one understand that he has a maker who has created the heavens and the earth, day and night, the movement of the wind which man can utilize to navigate his ships. Therefore when Islam calls men to state belief in God it asks them to look at rational proof and not supernatural miracles as does Christianity. There is consensus in Islam that belief in God precedes the message of the prophets and the books. One cannot believe that there are books revealed by God until one accepts the existence of God in the first place. The only supernatural thing Muslims are asked to believe in is the Qur'an which has been proved to be the revelation of God, not something concocted by humans as is the Bible. Thus the first principle of Islam is that rational proof is the foundation and the means of true belief.[27]

(2) There is consensus among most Muslims that the second principle that undergirds Islam is that if there is a discrepancy between reason and what is reported, that which is rational predominates.

(3) The third principle proves the openness of Islam to various interpretations. If someone says something and his statement appears in a hundred ways to make him a *kafir* or unbeliever, if there is even one way of accepting what he said as belief then it is unacceptable to call him an unbeliever.[28]

(4) The fourth principle affirms that since the time when the prophets delivered their message one cannot call others to the truth without a proof. This proof cannot be in miracles or strange occurrences.

(5) Islam is enjoined to overthrow religious authority because the only true relationship is that between man and God. Elimination of the power of religious authority sets the believer free from any supervision.[29]

(6) The sixth principle is that of protecting the *da'wa*, the message of Islam, and stopping *fitna*, discord. While Europeans have accused Islam of being bound by *jihad* and legislating warfare, the truth is that Islam favours forgiveness. Fighting is sanctioned under restricted conditions in order to stop aggression against the truth and its people, as well as to maintain peace. It has never been to force people to convert to the religion nor to take revenge on those who disagree with them. This is the reason why conquests in the history of Islam do not record the same kinds of things you hear about Christian wars in terms of the killing of old men, women and children.[30] There has not been a single Islamic war, he argued, where the annihilation of others is sought as in Christian wars. When Muslims conquered a territory they allowed its people to worship and practise their faith. Christians have been free in their places of worship and in following their own customs. It is true that they paid *jizya*, but that was to ensure their security and protection. Elsewhere Abduh said that *jizya* is justified since its aim is to help those who pay it and to preserve their security and because it actually amounts to less than Christians paid prior to Islam.[31] Caliphs have asked their military leaders to respect those who were in convents and monasteries, and they proclaimed the sanctity of the blood of women and children and non-combatants. The Sunna forbids hurting *dhimmis*; there are mutual duties and rights between them and the Muslim community. Thus the Prophet Muhammad said: 'He who harms a *dhimmi* is not one of us.'[32]

It is of course true, Abduh admitted, that some Muslims may have deviated from these principles, especially at the time when Islamic power began to wane. But he insisted that that was of no concern to him because it is not of the essence of Islam. The so-called Christianity of peace assumed for itself authority over other religions under its power. It persecuted the adherents of other faiths, expelling them when it could not convert them to Christianity and baptize them. As history bears witness, nothing protects non-Christians from Christians except the power of numbers or the strength of the community. That is because Christianity did not come to bring peace, but rather the sword.[33]

(7)The seventh principle of Islam is its amity, *mawadda*, toward those who are different in doctrine. This characteristic is evident in the fact that Islam allowed Muslim men to marry Christian and Jewish women who would raise their children. They did not force these women to convert, but allowed them to practise the tenets of their faith, attend religious services, and fulfil their religious duties. Furthermore, Islamic law, Abduh contended, does not distinguish between the rights of wives, whether Muslim or People of the Book.[34]

(8) The eighth principle is that Islam joins the welfare of the world with that of the hereafter. The teachings of Islam do not deny the enjoyment of this world or command the renunciation of pleasure in order to assure felicity in the world to come. Islam, unlike Christianity, affirms the importance of life in this world.[35]

It is important to note, however, that despite his harsh criticism of Europeans and western Christianity, Abduh was in many ways drawn to European learning and culture. He even mastered French in later life and read much French literature and philosophy, coming to believe that material change for the good can actually result from interaction with the West. He recognized, however, that while the achievements of modern Europe were impressive they could not be imported wholesale into non-European countries with any hope of success. He was deeply concerned about the secularization of Egypt and saw it splitting his people apart. Abduh felt that his task was to awaken Muslims to their condition, challenging them to assume responsibility to bring about change and infusing them with the belief that theirs was not a permanent condition caused by the backwardness of their religion. Islam itself calls for social progress. The strength of Islam, he said, is contingent on the answers it is able to offer to social and intellectual problems.[36] At the same time, however, he believed that change must come only in accord with the deepest principles of Islam. Reform has to come from within Islam itself and not by erecting a new and alien system.[37]

Abduh understood clearly the need for the reform of Islamic societies. He saw the problem of his time to be the consequence of the ossification of Islamic thought. Aware of the urgent need for a total transformation of society, he attempted to initiate a process for an intellectual revolution. He tried to distinguish between what can be changed without destroying the core of Islam, and what is the essential part that cannot be subject to change.[38] The method of bringing about change is to make sure that Muslims do not give way to despair and wallow in their decay; rather, they are to be empowered by hope and challenged to seek glory. (Surah 12:87; 15:56).[39] The greatest innovation, bid'a, is the claim that Islam is the cause of the condition in which Muslims find themselves, a reality that has led to despair and the belief that the corruption of the common people has no cure. 'It is the secret disease of their soul, a malady that has taken hold of their hearts, because they abandoned the book of their Lord and the way of their Prophet and accepted wrong reports or misunderstood the truth. That is a disease more deadly to the spirit than the body.'[40]

Abduh's Reform Project

Abduh perceived one of his main tasks to be a response to those Egyptians who, influenced both by the success of secular Europe and by its attacks against Islam, were persuaded that religion was a prime element in the retardation of Muslim societies. Of paramount concern to him was the problem of the decline of the Muslim ummah, and the enormous temptation to reverse that decline by trying to emulate the West. On the one hand he refuted the charges that Christians, both colonialists and missionaries, were making against Islam. On the other hand, he affirmed the superiority of the Muslim faith, the true interpretation of God's message. He never claimed that the West was not in ascendency at that time in history. What he did say is that the reason for its superiority was because it took the best of Islam and appropriated it to itself. Muslims, he said, were in an inferior position because they had abandoned true Islam. Once they had reappropriated the initial impetus that set them on the world stage and built their great civilization they would be able to resume their rightful position of superiority.

The decay of Muslim societies, as depicted by Europeans, was due primarily to the Islamic contention that God predetermines human actions, which leads to a lack of initiative on the part of Muslims to build a civilization and compete in a changing world. Europeans also charged that Islamic teachings about obedience to those in power led to despotism, that Muslim clergy were corrupting the faith, and that a primary reason for the backwardness of Islamic countries was to be found in teachings related to women, specifically those concerning polygamy and easy divorce. These attacks charged Muslim people with backwardness, which Abduh accepted. What he could not accept, and spent a lifetime arguing against, was the critique that this backwardness was due to the religion of Islam itself and its inability to adapt to the modern world.

Muslims, he said, had lost their independence and the ability to determine or chart their own destiny. Some areas were under direct occupation, others under the hegemony of foreign influence. His mammoth task was to awaken Muslims to their condition, challenge them to assume responsibility to bring about change, infuse them with the belief that the current state of decline was not a permanent condition due to their inability to bring about change or to the inadequacy of Islam to meet the challenges of the modern world.

The issue for Abduh was not whether it is possible to be Muslim and still accept the modern world, but whether Islam is in fact really relevant to modernity. His intent, therefore, was to prove that Islam is indeed a rational religion which can serve as the basis of life in the modern world.[41] He saw no conflict between Islam and the principles of modern civilization. 'It is for Islam', he said, 'to rectify modern civilization and purify it from its filth.' When modern civilization comes to know true Islam it will become one of its greatest defenders and a source of empowerment. Ossification will disappear, and the greatest proof of that is that the Qur'an stands as a witness over Islam.[42]

That which binds people together is religion since it prescribes what is ordained by God. A return to the principles of the religion will empower the people since it will purify the heart, uphold the moral fibre, and inspire devotion and unity in the defence of the *ummah*. Religion is rooted in the soul of the individual through heredity over the centuries. Hearts are contented with it. He who seeks to revive the *ummah* need only blow on the flickering fire and it will permeate all souls. 'Should they assume the management of their affairs, set their feet on the road to victory and assume the true foundations of the faith as their goals, nothing will impede their march toward human perfection.'[43]

When Muslims call for the return to religion and its reform, Abduh said, it is not something that Europeans should fear as an insurrection against Europe. However, when Christians hear the mention of religion, they often create for themselves the vision of a monster which they fear. Responding to the accusation that the pilgrimage itself is an occasion for Muslim conspiracy, Abduh insisted that rather it is a means of honest communication and should not be misunderstood. Its aim is for Muslims to learn about each other's experience and what is useful for the reform of their beliefs, as well as to defend against calamities, injustices and tribulations. He argued that Muslims have erred in their understanding of *tawakkul* and *gadar*, which has led them to give in to laziness. They have ceased working and depended on fate to take care of matters, believing that this was somehow pleasing to God and could fulfil the demands of the religion.[44] Muslims have erred, he said, in understanding that the religion of Islam is the best that exists among the nations, and that power and greatness are conjoined to this religion forever. They have incorrectly imagined that wellbeing would be their fate and that they would achieve an elevated status by mere words, without any comprehension of the meaning. They have also thought that God guarantees victory to his servant without any effort on the part of the latter. If a Muslim is afflicted by a tragedy or calamity he too easily takes solice in predestination and waits for the unknown without taking any action to protect himself.[45]

Abduh's interest was always more in the realities of the human situation and how to amend it than in abstract philosophical or even theological argumentation. He did go beyond the acceptable Ash'arite theology to the extent that he credited the possibility that humans by the use of reason are capable of knowing and choosing between right and wrong. In his two major works, *Risalat at-Tawhid* and *Al-Islam wa'l-Nasraniyya ma'al 'Ilm wa'l-Madaniyya*, he tried to bring reason, revelation and the individual moral temperament into harmony,[46] but in the end reason was clearly emphasized. 'In case of disparity between reason and what has been transmitted by tradition,' he asserted, 'reason predominates. The tradition is then either re-interpreted in order to attune to what is rational or to affirm its genuineness while affirming one's inability to discern God's intent.'[47]

Because of his continuing insistence on the use of reason Abduh was accused by the conservative jurists, with some justification, of being a kind of neo–Mu'tazilite. Insofar as he tried to acknowledge the power of human reason and human choice this charge seems to have some validity, although in the end he accepted the tensions between human free will and divine foreknowledge/predestination, acknowledging that some things are known to God alone. He also used the issue of predestination to levy an attack against Christians, especially the Thomists, saying that they are far more predestinarian than Muslims. To the extent to which Islam contains some predestinarian ideas, it is because they came through Aryan influences, brought in by Persians and Byzantines who hoodwinked Muslims with their fancy words and sowed discord in Islam, and are not part of the innate nature of Islam itself.[48]

In an effort to revitalize the faith, Abduh opted for a novel interpretation of the role of man in the world, depicting him as *khalifat Allah*, agent of God on earth charged with the task of building and constructing a civilization. While most classical exegetical works had emphasized the Qur'anic verse that refers to man as *khalifah* as reference to a subsequent creation or as the designation of the Prophet Muhammad for such a role, Abduh opted for an interpretation in which each individual is responsible and accountable for the building of this civilization.[49]

Qur'anic Exegesis

Having assumed the daunting task of transforming the dominant world view of Islam at his time, Abduh's plan for political and social reform made a reinterpretation of the Qur'an for the modern world of great importance. He felt that the Qur'an must play a central role in elevating society, reforming the condition of the *ummah*, and bringing forth a modern Islamic civilization. Thus he could interpret Islam as the champion of progress and development.[50] It is necessary, he said, to return to the original Qur'anic text. By stripping the text of layers of repetitious and at times conflicting commentary Abduh led the way toward making the text accessible to the growing number of educated people able to read and reflect on its meaning and message. In a sense, he initiated the twentieth-century trend of individual interaction with and interpretation of the Qur'an.

For Abduh, the underlying principle for the resurrection of

the nation was the basic belief that the Qur'anic message is universal and all-encompassing. The Qur'an is distinguished from other books of revelation because it is neither limited in time nor targeted for a specific community; rather it addresses all humanity. He stressed the following points in relation to the Qur'an:

(1) The primary purpose of the Qur'an is to affirm the *tawhid*, the unicity of God, and all other subsequent doctrines that affirm God's action of revelation, the sending of prophets, and the reality of resurrection and human recompense.

(2) The Qur'an is a complete and comprehensive revelation; believers cannot be selective in what portions they choose to adhere to.

(3) The Qur'an is the primary source for legislation for a righteous society. While Abduh endorsed the use of reason and science in understanding the text he insisted that social life is to be organized according to the teachings of the Qur'an.

(4) Muslims should not imitate their forebears in interpreting the Qur'an, but must be authentic and true to their own understanding.[51]

(5) Reason and reflection should be utilized in interpreting the Qur'an. Abduh saw the Qur'an as urging people to search and think about the revelation as well as to know the laws and principles that govern the universe in order to understand. 'The Qur'an is worthy of being called the book of freedom of thought, of respect for reason and for the shaping of the individual through research, knowledge and the use of reason and reflection.'[52]

Abduh believed that the Qur'an has been revealed by God as guidance for the happiness of all humanity in this world and the next. While there have been various attempts to interpret the scriptures by exegetes discussing its inimitability, its foreign words, its esoteric meaning and its grammar, those commentaries he saw as being of little benefit since they do not address the interest of the *ummah*. Every human being is to understand the revelation of the Qur'an according to his ability, whether he is learned or ignorant.[53] People need a *tafsir* that restores their confidence in their religion, one in which they are able to learn about the efficacy of prayer, the prescribed moral life, and how to keep away from evil.

He rejected the type of exegesis prevalent in his time that focused on a convoluted interpretation of text. For him, the urgent need was the creation of a functional interpretation of the Qur'an to aid in understanding legislation, doctrine, ethics and principles so as to attract people and give them the impetus for action. Such exegesis should involve a straightforward understanding of the meaning of the text to encourage Muslims to follow divine teachings. He did not believe that having a commentary accessible to the common people, however, obviates the need for specialists who are dedicated to understanding the truth of the meaning of the words. The experts must have a deeper knowledge of the Qur'an. Abduh set out five particular requirements for these exegetes:

(1) They must learn the meaning of the vocabulary of the Qur'an and interpret it according to the understanding of the community at the time of revelation. The classical exegetes interpreted the vocabulary according to the usage of the time in which they lived during the first three centuries of Islam and consequently their interpretation is conditioned by their circumstances and is not necessarily relevant for modern life.

(2) Exegetes must have an excellent command of Arabic so as to guarantee authenticity of interpretation. The Arabic language, said Abduh, has fallen into decline, no longer the vehicle for great works in the arts and sciences as it once was. In order for the religion of Islam to flourish Arabic must flourish. This can happen not by turning to the books used in al-Azhar, but by going back to the works of the great scholars at the time when Islam was at its zenith.[54]

(3) Exegetes must have a good knowledge of the human condition. The Qur'an talks extensively about human nature, about immutable divine laws, and about the laws that govern the rise and fall of nations. An exegete must learn to be conversant with the teachings of the Qur'an about the development of nations, their strengths and weaknesses, their greatness and degradation, their knowledge and ignorance, their belief and disbelief.

(4) Exegetes must have expertise in the context of the prophetic period in order to understand the Qur'anic condemnations of the life of the communities flourishing at the time, and which of their practices are unacceptable.

(5) They must acquire knowledge about the life of the Prophet.[55]

Thus the basic foundation of the reform project for Abduh was the Qur'an. The scripture must be utilized to re-invigorate Muslim society. Every individual is to encounter God through the revelation and not through the *walis*. He called for a Qur'an-centred life to replace tradition, a Qur'anic theology to replace scholastic deliberations. Conviction, in accord with human nature and informed by the study of the Qur'an, must be able to address and engage the masses and not be restricted to elite concerns. At the same time, the Qur'anic verse that insists that there is no compulsion in religion should underpin the Islamic *da'wah*.[56] To foster such an understanding of Islam, said Abduh, a new kind of religious leadership must be trained, one tied neither to slavish imitation of the past nor to the godless interpretations of the West, one able to understand the benefit of modern sciences and the reality of living in the modern world. This leadership must sit in judgement on the politicians and emphasize substance over traditional rituals.[57]

The ulama are also to act as a dam against the incursions of the foreigners.

> Do they acquiesce to being enslaved by the foreigner after their great dominance? What do they seek in life, disgrace and scorn, poverty, perpetual suffering at the hand of the oppressive enemy? Do they find security under foreign rule? ... If the common people are in ignorance of God's prescriptions, what excuse do the ulama have when their role is to preserve the law and acquire expertise in its teachings? Why do they not seek the unity of the Muslims? Why do they not attempt to unite them? Why do they not attempt to reform corruption? Why do they not propagate what can empower the hopes of the people and remind them of the promises of God?[58]

Education

One of the most significant issues with which Abduh dealt throughout his life and his career was the reform of education. For him education was crucial, scientific knowledge an imperative. Part of his concern was to find an alternative to the kind of stagnation that he himself encountered in the Egyptian religious schools, best typified by his training at al-Azhar.[59] His proposed programme had as one of its major foundations the proper understanding and utilization of Islam in bringing about the empowerment and revival of society. He was critical of the modern schools established by foreign missionaries as well as those set up by the government. In the former, he said, the student was forced to learn about Christianity and in the latter he learned no religion at all.

Abduh's concern for reform in education and for acquiring from Europe that which is of benefit was also tempered by his desire to block indiscriminate borrowing. He believed that the efforts of those who advocated translation and dissemination of European thought, thinking that publication of newspapers can cure the ills that have befallen the nation by raising consciousness and shaping the character of the people, were ineffective. 'What is the use of publishing, if no one reads, and even if people read, do they understand? And those who understand, would they seek the desired goals?'[60] Some Muslims advocated opening schools based on the European system, simultaneously in all Muslim countries, believing that would be the way to disseminate knowledge and assure that morality would be inculcated in the people. This proposal he found impractical unless decreed and supervised by a powerful sultan who would be able to provide the necessary resources. Even then force would be needed to make the people undergo a change that Abduh was convinced they would detest.[61]

He also found other proposals for reform of education to be impractical. Among them was the idea that an elite should be educated in western sciences who in turn would provide the training for the rest of society. While admitting that the proposal might have some potential merit, he nonetheless objected to its adoption on the grounds that the content of the education might not in the end be efficacious. How could this method work, he asked, if the knowledge is alien in its seeds, the manner in which it is germinated, and the soil in which it is nourished?[62] He also questioned this method of disseminating knowledge because of the problem of the transmitters only being able to act according to the knowledge they had received without having the means to integrate it with their own traditions and sources of knowledge. Such persons too easily believe that what they have received is perfect for every occasion. 'They are not masters [of the knowledge]; they are carriers and transmitters.'[63]

Another reason Abduh doubted the efficacy of indiscriminate borrowing was that he recognized that in the several decades in which it had already been tried it had failed to make a difference in Egyptian and Ottoman society. Observing the schools that had been established according to the European model, as well as students who were sent to Europe to bring back knowledge, science, arts, literature, and civilization, he asked: 'Have the Egyptians and the Ottomans benefited from this imported [civilization] now that some time has passed? Has their condition improved over what obtained prior to their attachment to this new way? Have they saved themselves from devouring poverty and penury? Have they been capable of changing the behaviour of which the foreigner has accused them? Have they bolstered their defences? Have they achieved strength to withstand the enemy assault?'[64] His answer, of course, was 'no'.

Furthermore, he said, the dangers of creating a westernized elite have far more serious ramifications. The westernized few have taken to using the slogans of the foreigner such as 'freedom, nationalism, ethnicity'. They have changed the mode of their housing, the styles of their clothing, the kind of food they eat and the furniture and utensils they use so as to appear more western. They compete in buying foreign products which they display proudly. They have undermined indigenous industry and crafts since local craftsmen are unable to compete in making the new luxury products and do not have the financial resources to import the tools necessary for their manufacture. In other words, they have squandered the wealth of the nation.[65]

Abduh's final objection to blind emulation of western education was that experience has shown that those who imitate other nations and appropriate their customs become the opening through which enemies penetrate. They become the indigenous perpetrators, preparing the road and opening up the gates for the foreigners. They appropriate skewed values exalting those they emulate and ridiculing and degrading those who are different. They welcome the colonizers of their country and seek employment with them, considering the foreign victory as a blessing to themselves. 'The imitators become the shock troops of the conquerors, helping them to establish their power. That is because they do not know any other virtue or consider any other power outside their sphere.'[66]

Abduh championed an indigenous functional system of education which was to include universal education for all children, both male and female. All should acquire the rudimentary skills of reading, writing and arithmetic. All were to receive religious instruction that glossed over sectarian differences in Islam and highlighted the differences between Christianity and Islam.

The content and duration of education should vary according to the goals and professions that the students sought. Abduh believed that children of peasants and craftsmen should receive the minimum education to allow them to follow in the footsteps of their fathers. They should not be expected to go beyond elementary school education. The curriculum of these schools should include: a book which is a summary of Islamic doctrines according to the teachings of the Sunnis with no reference to sectarian differences; a brief text outlining the foundations of ethical and moral life and spelling out what is right and what is wrong; and a brief text on the history of the life of the Prophet Muhammad, the life of the sahaba, the companions of the Prophet, and the reasons for Islamic ascendancy.[67]

In Abduh's system, the middle schools are to be attended by those who are seeking to specialize in the Shari'a, the military, medical training or government employment. Their curriculum should include the following: a book that provides an introduction to knowledge, the art of logic, the principles of reasoning and the protocol of disputation; a text on doctrines, addressing such issues as rational proof, the determination of the middle position in an effort to avoid conflict, a more detailed treatment of the differences between Christianity and Islam, and the efficacy of Islamic doctrine in reforming life in the world and in the hereafter; a text that explains right and wrong, the use of reason and the principles of doctrine; and a history text that includes the conquests and spread of Islam.[68]

Higher education should be made available for teachers and principals, with a more comprehensive curriculum including exegesis of the Qur'an, Arabic language and linguistics, the science of Hadith, the study of morality, principles of jurisprudence, historiography, the art of preaching and convincing, theology and rational understanding of doctrine.[69]

Politics

Another of Abduh's antagonists was Farah Antun, the influential Cairene publisher of the journal al-Jami'a. Antun published articles that ascribed the backwardness of Muslims and decay in Islamic civilization to the Islamic teachings that linked religious and civil authority. The progress of the West, he claimed, is due to their ability to separate the two. Abduh's response was on two levels. First, he refuted the claim that Christianity separates religious and secular authority by pointing to Christian teachings which make ordinary beings subservient to the power of the clergy. Second, he focused on a redefinition of the true teachings of Islam which he insisted are not an impediment to progress and development. Islam, unlike Christianity, does not recognize religious authority. The *ummah*, rather than some theocratic entity, is the source of the authority of the ruler. The ruler exists for the welfare of humanity, overseeing its changing and progressing conditions. The *ummah* is a collectivity that decides what is in its own best interests and the means of achieving those interests.

Abduh tended to blame the prevailing conditions of authoritarian governments in the Muslim nations on the ignorance of the jurists and the rulers. He faulted the jurists for not understanding politics and for depending on the rulers, failing to make them accountable for their policies in government. The rulers, on the other hand, not only were ignorant of how to administer government and justice, they had corrupted the jurists and used them for their own purposes by making them produce *fatwas* to vindicate the policies of the government.[70] Of crucial importance for the *ummah* is political unity and justice, neither of which Abduh saw existing because of the neglect of the leadership. All the evils that have befallen the Muslim community are a consequence of this disunity. Muslim leaders assume exalted titles such as princes and sultans, live ostentatiously and oppulently, and seek the protection of foreign non-Muslim governments to support them against their own people. They usurp public funds for personal pleasure and fail to administer justice. In addition they fail to consult the appropriate books or follow the Sunnah. They are thus a cause of the corruption of the ethics of the community.[71]

Abduh was insistent that in Islam there is no final authority besides that of God and the Prophet.[72] 'In Islam', he said, 'there is no authority except ... the call to righteousness and condemnation of evil. This is an authority delegated by God to the humblest of Muslims by which they confront the most haughty, as it is delegated to the most noted among them to judge the lowliest.'[73] Abduh insisted that Muslims have never had the equivalent of a Pope who combines religious and civil roles in his office. The Shari'a has established the rights as well as the constraints of the power of the highest authority in Islam, the ruler, whether Caliph or Sultan. It is a distinct role, different from that of the Qadi. The Sultan is the executor of what the Qadis judge to be just.

Islam set a path, he said, establishing limits and identifying rights. There is no wisdom in legislation if there is no power to administer justice and execute the judgements of the Qadis. This authority lies with the Caliphs and the Sultans. The Caliph is not sinless, does not receive revelation and does not have the right to interpret the Qur'an. He has to know Arabic in order to understand the book and the way of the Prophet so that he is able to distinguish independently between truth and falsehood and thus facilitate the establishment of justice. He is obeyed as long as he adheres to the truth of the book and the way of the Prophet. But Muslims constantly stand in judgement on him. If he veers from the path they hold him accountable. If he deviates they correct him. There should be no obedience to one who transgresses against the creator; he must be replaced. The *ummah* sets him up and the *ummah* has authority over him. It removes him when it sees that it is in its own best interest. By all counts, therefore, the Caliph or Sultan is a civil ruler whose domain is not a theocracy because he does not receive laws from God.[74]

Abduh believed that it is the duty of the Muslims to give advice to the ruler, based on Islamic teachings about *shura*, consultation. Thus he said that when Muslims call for an end to despotism and for consultation on their welfare and destiny, they are following the teachings of the Shari'a and not emulating the foreigner.[75] The readiness of the people to follow the method of *shura* is not contingent on their training in research, reflection or the principles of disputation. It is sufficient that they seek truth and the establishment of a system where public interest is maintained. There should be no illusion that just laws will be based on foreign models. There are laws that are suitable for some people and not for others. In order to be beneficial, laws have to take into consideration the condition of the nation, the nature of its trade, agriculture, its customs and beliefs. Those who legislate the law should not seek to accommodate foreign laws, but must take into account the conditions of their own people and their distinctive nature.[76]

Muslims, he said, do not need to apologize for their insistence that Islam conjoins this world and the next. It is European Christians who are duplicitous on this matter. Voicing a theme that has continued to reverberate throughout this century, Abduh accused the Europeans of having a double standard. The

French, for example, expelled the Jesuits from France to keep them from competing for authority over matters of state. At the same time they provided both military and financial assistance for their work in Lebanon so that they could preach Christianity. It is because Europeans covet Muslim lands that they have tried to say that in order for society to be revitalized religion must be abandoned.[77] Arguing against western criticism of the unity of religion and politics in Islam, Abduh said: 'France calls itself the protector of the Catholics in the East. The Queen of England calls herself the Queen of the Protestants. The Czar of Russia is King and head of the church at the same time. Why, then, is it not permissible for Sultan 'Abd al-Hamid to be called the Caliph of the Muslims or the Commander of the Believers?'[78]

Abduh took many opportunities to criticize Christianity, usually in response to western criticism of Islam, yet he himself had many Christian students and friends, especially during his stay in Lebanon. While he favoured the institution of an Islamic state he nonetheless viewed non-Muslims as full citizens with all rights and privileges. He affirmed that the national party is a secular party whose membership is open to all regardless of religion, one in which Jews and Christians can participate. All are brothers, he said, and the Islamic Shari'a forbids hatred and considers all humans equal in treatment.[79] Despite the fact that Islam is a religion of *jihad* and war, its sanctions are to avoid discord, *fitnah*. The accusation that Ottoman Christians are not trusted by Muslims, he said, is not true, arguing that Coptic nationals participate in all facets of governmental life except the Islamic religious courts. The two religious groups have a congenial relationship except those who have become religious fanatics among the Christians. Rhetorically he asked if any Christian had been expelled from government service, or denied the right to be a lawyer, publish a newspaper, run a printing press, or set up a factory or commercial enterprise because of his Christian faith.[80] It is obvious that Christians have been used in administration, he said; in fact they receive an undue proportion of promotions and awards compared with Muslims. They have received concessions that Muslims are not eligible for. Even the embassies of the Ottoman nations have Christian officials. The Sultan has good relations with the heads of Christian sects and honours them by allowing them into his presence.[81]

The Role of Women

Social reform was important for Abduh and he called for a revision of the Shari'a to make it more attuned to the demands of the modern world. He believed that a strong societal fabric is a crucial element in developing a strong nation and worked for the psychological rearmament of the community in order to withstand the attacks of the foreigners against Islamic society. The most important building block of the new society, he said, is the individual. The *ummah* is composed of family units, and unless these units provide a functioning healthy environment, the society will crumble. 'Its wholeness is contingent on the wellbeing of the homes.'[82] In order to bring forth a new vibrant nation, Abduh felt it was necessary to reform the prevailing customs regarding the role and status of women. He believed that the relationship between husband and wife must be one of mutual respect and consideration in order to raise a healthy generation of citizens who are confident, self-assertive and not cowed by foreigners. 'And know that men who attempt to oppress women in order to be masters in their own homes raise slaves to others.'[83]

Responding to western criticism of Islam as oppressive to women, Abduh insisted that in Islam there is gender equality. 'Man and woman are equal in rights and duties; they are also equal in reason, feelings and sense of self.'[84] He acknowledged that there is a mutuality of rights and duties between men and women, that male and female are equal in responsibility and accountability to God, that they have the same Islamic duties and beliefs, and that they are both enjoined to seek knowledge. He also affirmed that male and female have a covenantal relationship.[85]

This established, he reminded his readers that the Qur'an says that men have a degree above women (S. 2:228),[86] noting that this distinction is necessary in order to avoid discord. For the family is a social institution and every social unit needs a leader. In the case of family management, men are more worthy of leadership because of their strength and the fact that they are responsible to provide for their families from their wealth. By law, the husband is responsible to protect and provide for his wife; in return, she is obedient. This, however, does not mean that women can be coerced or pushed around. Rather, they have complementary functions. 'Woman is to man and man is to woman as organs of the same body. Man is the head and woman is the body.'[87] He did, however, believe that if women actually have the qualities of leadership and decision making, then men's superiority is not operable.[88] In another place, he wrote that according to the Qur'an, there are two kinds of women, the righteous and the rebellious. Men's leadership and distinction is operative only in the case of the disruptive wife.[89]

Abduh saw discord in society as a consequence of men's appetites for pleasure. Unlike other contemporary authors, he did not place the blame on women or their capacity to arouse men sexually. 'Some people claim that women have a stronger desire than men. There is no substance or proof to this claim ... Men were and still are the ones who seek women and pant after them, then they oppress them by manipulating their character and judging their feelings.'[90]

He believed that laws are necessary in order to regulate human society and control men's desires and limit their appetites. Thus he argued for monogamy: 1. If a woman is made available to all males and each female is allowed to be a partner to each man, at any time the fire of jealousy will rage in human hearts and each will attempt to defend what he desires. This will lead to bloodshed. 2. The woman by nature is incapable of providing for her livelihood and of protecting herself from harm, especially during pregnancy and lactation. If the male is not aware of his responsibility in defending her and her rights, she and her progeny will be lost. 3. The new Muslim man will be motivated to work hard and save in order to be a good provider for those who are dependent on him. The most important factor is that man is generally unwilling to risk himself and carry burdens in order to make a living, unless he sees women and sons dependent on him for their livelihood. Their dependency not only functions as a motivation for his hard work, it acts as an incentive for deferred benefits such as the reciprocal care that his family will give him once he wearies of his duties. Unless there are dependent children and a wife, he will not save for the future. If progeny are mixed, this is no longer true. Doubt concerning the paternity of the child would lead to laziness; the man would not struggle to provide for such a child.[91]

As usual, Abduh responded in his discussions concerning women to the anti-Islamic charges of western critics. One was levelled against the practice of polygamy. He did feel that while the practice of polygamous marriages existed in early Islam, it should not be maintained in the modern world. During the formative period of Islam, this practice had great benefit since it helped in forging new kinship groups and in creating and cementing a community.[92] But while the prophet and the *sahaba* were meticulously fair, this is impossible for other humans. Although the Shari'a allows for four wives if the man has capacity and can be just, in the final analysis, it is impossible for ordinary humans to be just. Equality in treatment means in the amount of expenditure, housing, clothing, food, companionship (not intercourse). If a person fully understands the burden of equality of treatment, he will realize that it is impossible to have more than one wife. If the proper understanding of justice and fairness in treatment is taken seriously, there is no way any one can be just.[93] Furthermore, since the Hanafi school of law admits that religion came for the welfare of society, the ulama must realize that because justice is impossible, polygamy should be forbidden.

Another issue raised by critics of Islam was the veiling of women. Abduh believed that the prevalent custom of veiling was not of the essence of Islam since there is no *nass*, or Qur'anic text, for veiling. It is a custom acquired by Muslims from other nations and has nothing to do with religion.[95] On the matter of the education of women, he called it a religious duty decreed by God since knowledge is the essence of what it means to be human. Women's education should not be restricted to religious education but must include exposure to management of the home, the proper means of raising children, and the conditions of the world, as well as a proper understanding of human relations.[96] 'Permitting women to be devoured by ignorance and be tempted by stupidity is a grave crime.'[97]

Another target of the critics of Islam was the prevalent practice of easy divorce. In order to reform the custom, Abduh placed it in a larger context. He interpreted a Qur'anic text (S. 2:230) as saying that God does not approve of divorce. He saw divorce as something that involves the whole *ummah* and requires societal restrictions, rather than just an individual or family concern. He therefore advocated that it be taken from the arbitrary authority of the husband and placed under the jurisdiction and expertise of the Qadi. Society as a whole must restrict the oppression of women. He even formulated a law that gives women the right to seek divorce under certain circumstances, such as desertion by the husband, physical or verbal abuse, or in cases of perpetual fighting with no possibility of resolution.[98]

Conclusion

Abduh was a man of complexity and even contradiction. He was both peasant by birth and elite by training, position, and affinity. While he judged foreign occupation harshly, he nevertheless managed to work co-operatively enough with government officials that he could occupy posts of great prestige and influence. Because his thought was a combination of the new and the old, at times it appeared convoluted and vague. Deeply critical of much Islamic orthodoxy prevalent at the time, he in fact departed little from tradition in his writings and did manage to work with the religious establishment. Dedicated to change, he was in the end not a radical reformer but an educator who felt keenly the need for consensus. His public life was girded by his writing and his teaching, and both were ultimately determined by his primary tasks of reforming Islam and freeing it from the bonds of imitation, of rehabilitating Muslim peoples, and bringing the masses back to the proper practice of true religion.[99]

In many ways his work amounted to a re-interpretation of Islam for the modern world. His was a crucial time when the encounter with Europe was most intense and most urgent. Thus his creative responses both bear the imprint of the heat of the encounter and are tempered by the reality of the weakness and defeat of Muslim nations. Impressed with the importance of the concept of utility in shaping the pragmatic approach of Europeans, he highlighted the Islamic ideal of al-maslaha al-'amma, public welfare, into a position of prominence. It is also clear that he was impressed with the role that democracy plays in providing public constraints on the ruler, hence his emphasis on shura. It is not unfair to say that in his emphasis on Islam as a culture and a civilization he tended to ignore many of the aspects of Islam as personal faith.

Abduh's efforts to infuse the Islamic heritage with modern ideas eventually led to a division among his disciples. Some saw in his vision of a revitalized Islam the only answer for the salvation of Egyptian society. Others advocated a separation between religion and state, and began to press for the secularization of society. Finally, however, the efforts of secularists to offer a viable alternative to an Islamic society were not sufficient to scale what they experienced as a wall of dogmatic and obscurantist opposition. The followers of the early secularists attributed their failure to the fact that they were

few in number and faced a daunting task. They were importing
ideas and concepts that were truly foreign and not the products
of Muslim reflection on the internal history of Islam. Rather
than trying to substitute a new structure wholesale, they
attempted to graft elements of the European model onto what
was already in place, hoping that the new 'patches' would take
hold and grow.

Abduh's legacy in defining Islam for the twentieth century is
evident in the hundreds of texts that reiterate various aspects of
his thought. Although some of the leadership of the Muslim
Brotherhood have accused him of having veered from the
essential affirmations of Islam, his imprint is clear both as they
contest some of his propositions and as his ideas are echoed in
their own formulations of the nature of Islam. Although his
popularity has receded recently, because of the rise of the
Islamists, Muhammad Abduh's ideas continue to shape many of
the new generations of Muslims throughout the world.

Notes

1.   Osman Amin, *Muhammad 'Abduh*, Washington, D.C.: American
Council of Learned Societies, 1953, p. 3.

2.   For a full treatment of the influence of Shaykh Darwish on the life of
Muhammad Abduh see Charles C. Adams, *Islam and Modernism in Egypt*,
London: Oxford University Press, 1933, pp. 23ff.

3.   Cited in Amin, '*Abduh*, p. 14.

4.   See Albert Hourani, *Arabic Thought in the Liberal Age, 1798–1939*,
London: Oxford University Press, 1970, p. 109.

5.   Muhammad 'Abdu, *al-Muslimun wa'l-Islam*, Tahir al-Tanahi (ed.),
Cairo: al-Hilal, 1963, p. 24.

6.   Hasan Al-Shaykhah, *Ma'l-Imam Muhammad 'Abdu fi Madrasatihi
al-Adabiyya*, Cairo: Matba'at al-Azhar, n.d., pp. 28–9.

7.   Malcolm H. Kerr, *Islamic Reform. The Political and Legal Theories of
Muhammad 'Abduh and Rashid Rida*, Berkeley: University of California Press,
1966, p. 104.

8.   Al al-Din Hilal, *al-Tajdid fi al-Fikr al-Siyasi al-Misri al-Hadith*, Cairo:
Ma'had al-Buhuth wa 'l-Dirasat al-'Arabiyya, 1975, p. 20.

9.   Rashid Rida, *Tarikh al-Ustadh al-Imam Muhammad 'Abdu*, Cairo:
Matba'at al-Manar, 1344H, vol. I, p. 153.

10.   Muhammad 'Abduh, *al-A'mal al-Kamila*, (edited by Muhammad
'Amara), Beirut: al-Mu'assasa al-'Arabiyya li 'l-Dirasat wa 'l-Nashr, 1972,
vol. I, p. 637.

11.   Quoted in Amin, '*Abduh*, p. 59.

12.   'Abd al-'Ati Muhammad Ahmad, *al-Fikr al-Siyasi li 'l-Imam Muhammad
'Abdu*, Cairo: al-Hay'a al-Misriyya li 'l-Kitab, 1978, p. 256.

13.   'Do not fight one another, lest you fail and lose your vigour.' S. 8:46.

14. Ahmad, *al-Fikr*, p. 102.

15. 'Abdu, *al-A'mal*, vol. III, p. 386.

16. *Ibid.*, pp. 116–17.

17. *Ibid.*, vol. III, p. 202.

18. *Ibid..*, vol. III, p. 204.

19. *Ibid.*, vol. III, p. 203.

20. Ahmad, *al-Fikr*, p. 149.

21. 'Abdu, *al-A'mal*, vol. III, p. 204.

22. Citing Matthew 10 and Mark 3 he said that if one reads the Gospel it is clear that the proof of Jesus's truth is in his miracles, as miracles are always proof for those who follow a given faith. And in Matthew 17 it says that whoever has the faith of a mustard seed can move a mountain. *Ibid*, vol. III, p. 261.

23. *Ibid.*, vol. III, p. 261.

24. *Ibid.*, vol. III, p. 274.

25. *Ibid.*, vol. III, p. 261.

26. *Ibid.*, vol. III, pp. 261–4.

27. *Ibid.*, vol. III, pp. 278–9, 282.

28. *Ibid.*, vol. III, p. 283.

29. *Ibid.*, vol. III, p. 284.

30. *Ibid.*, vol. III, p. 289.

31. Muhammad 'Abdu, 'al-Idtihad fi al-Nasraniyya wa 'l-Islam,' in *al-A'mal*, vol. III, 291–2.

32. 'Abdu, *al-A'mal*, vol. III, p. 290.

33. *Ibid.*, vol. III, p. 291.

34. *Ibid.*, vol. III, p. 292; 'al-Idtihad,' p. 292.

35. 'Abduh, *al-A'mal*, vol. III, p. 294.

36. 'Abdu, *al-A'mal*, vol. III, p. 321.

37. Rida, *Tarikh*, vol. II, p. 477; Muhammad 'Abdu, *Al-Islam wa'l-Radd 'ala Muntakidih*, Cairo, al-Matba'a al-Rahmaniyya bi-Misr, 1928, p. 76.

38. Ahmad, *al-Fikr*, p. 16.

39. Muhammad 'Abdu, 'al-Amal wa talab al-Magd,' in Tahir Tanahi (ed.), *al-Muslimin wa'l-Islam*, Cairo: Dar al-Islam, 1963, p. 49.

40. 'Abdu, *al-A'mal*, vol. III, p. 230.

41. Hourani, *Arabic Thought*, pp. 139–40.

42. Ahmad, *al-Fikr*, p. 101.

43. Muhammad 'Abdu, 'al-Din Wasilat al-Islah,' in *al-Muslimun wa'l-Islam*, p. 89.

44. 'Abdu, *al-A'mal*, vol. III, p. 229.

45. *Ibid.*, vol. III, p. 230.

46. Kerr, *Islamic Reform*, p. 109.

47. Muhammad 'Abdu, *Al-Islam wa'l-Nasraniyya*, Cairo: al-Manar, 1938, pp. 54–5.

48. 'Abdu, *al-A'mal*, vol. III, pp. 203–11.

49. *Ibid.*, vol. IV, p. 135.

50. *Ibid.*, vol. III, pp. 257–8.

51. Muhammad 'Abdu, *Tafsir al-Fatiha*, Rashid Rida (ed.), Cairo: al-Manar, 1330H, pp. 35–53.

52. He cites S 10:101, 29:19; 22:46; and 18:17 as proof of the Qur'an's insistence on rationality. 'Abdu, *Ibid.*, p. 73.

53. 'Abdu, *Ibid.*, pp. 6–9.

54. Abduh initiated a variety of projects to encourage the reform of the Arabic language. This includes the forming of the Society for the Revival of Arabic Sciences which facilitated the editing of classical texts on rhetoric, Arabic philosophy and linguistics.

55. 'Abdu, *Ibid.*, pp. 10–13.

56. *Ibid.*, p. 74.

57. One author reports that upon his return from the Sudan in 1905, Abduh was met by a throng of people. One of the Shaykhs came up to him and told him that one of the prominent Christians had converted to Islam and he was teaching him the details of ablution. The Imam asked what details he was referring to and he said: 'For instance, I explain the parameters of his face between the two ears widthwise and from the forehead to the chin lengthwise.' The Imam frowned and angrily said, 'O shaykh, every human being knows his face without the need of a surveyor.' al-Shaykha, *Ma' al-Imam*, p. 5.

58. Abduh, 'al-Amal,' in *al-Muslimun*, p. 58.

59. The primary reason why Abduh failed in his attempts to reform al-Azhar was the opposition both of the Azhar shaykhs and of the Khedive Abbas Hilmi. The Khedive ultimately appointed Abduh Mufti in order to keep him from becoming the Shaykh al-Azhar, which position was given to Salim al-Bishri who aborted the entire reform effort. Ahmad, *al-Fikr*, p. 252.

60. Abduh, 'al-Fada'il,' p. 82.

61. *Ibid.*, p. 82.

62. *Ibid.*, p. 83.

63. *Ibid.*, p. 84.

64. *Ibid.*, p. 85.

65. *Ibid.*, p. 86.

66. *Ibid.*, pP. 86–7.

67. 'Abdu, *al-A'mal*, vol. III, pp. 77–8.

68. *Ibid.*, vol. V, p. 79.

69. *Ibid.*, vol. V, pp. 80–2.

70. Muhammad 'Abdu, 'al-Tasawwuf wa-sufiyya,' in *al-A'mal*, vol. III, pp. 530–31.

71. Muhammad 'Abdu, 'Din al-Wahda wa 'l-Siyasa wa 'l-Quwwa,' in *al-Muslimun wa-'l-Islam*, pp. 36–46; cf. 'Abdu, *al-A'mal*, vol. III, p. 230.

72. 'al-Idtihad,' 185–6.

73. *Ibid.*, p. 288.

74. 'Abdu, *al-A'mal*, vol. III, pp. 287–8.

75. *Ibid.*, vol. I, p. 354.

76. *Ibid.*, vol. I, p. 365.

77. 'al-Muslimun wa-'l-Islam,' pp. 144–5.

78. 'Abdu, *al-A'mal*, vol. III, p. 233.

79. *Ibid.*, vol. I, pp. 107–8.

80. *Ibid.*, vol. III, 234–6.

81. *Ibid.*, vol. III, p. 237.

82. Muhammad 'Abdu, *al-Islam wa 'l-Mar'a*, compiled and edited by Muhammad 'Amara, Cairo: al-Qahira li'l-Thaqafa l-'Arabiyya, 1975, p. 11.

83. *Ibid.*, p. 7.

84. *Ibid.*, p. 7.

85. *'Abdu, al-A'mal*, vol. V, p. 193. See S. 4:21.
86. Muhammad 'Abdu, 'al-Shura,' in *al-Muslimin*, pp. 190ff.
87. 'Abdu, *al-Islam wa 'l-Mar'a*, pp. 16–18; cf. 'Abdu *al-A'mal*, vol. IV, pp. 630–5.
88. Muhammad 'Abdu, 'al-Shura,' in *al-Muslimun*, p. 208.
89. 'Abdu, *al-A'mal*, vol. V, pp. 208–211.
90. 'Abdu, *al-Islam wa 'l-Mar'a*, p. 13.
91. Muhammad 'Abdu, 'Hajat al-Insan ila al-Zawaj,' in *al-Muslimun wa al-Islam*, p. 94.
92. 'Abdu, *Tafsir*, p. 187.
93. 'Abduh, 'Hajat al-Insan' pp. 97–100.
94. 'Abdu, *Tafsir*, p. 188.
95. 'Badu, 'Hijab al-Nisa' ', *al-A'mal*, vol. II, pp. 107–115.
96. 'Al-Shura,' p. 211; 'Abdu, *al-A'mal*, vol. IV, pp. 631–2.
97. Quoted by 'Abbas Mahmud al-'Aqqad, *'Abqari al-Islah wa-'l-Ta'lim: al-Ustadh Muhammad 'Abdu*, Cairo: al-Hay'a al-Misriyya al-'Amma li '-Ta'lif wa 'l-Nashr, 1970, p. 214.
98. 'Abdu, *al-A'mal*, vol. IV, p. 641.
99. Adams, *Islam and Modernism*, pp. 96–103.

4

Khomeini's Search for Perfection: Theory and Reality

Baqer Moin

Introduction

Ayatollah Khomeini is the first Islamic theologian to develop and put into practice his idea of an Islamic government in the modern world. As a political practitioner he continues to attract conflicting emotions. For many he is the dark side of Islam, the arch–Caliph of religious orthodoxy. For others he is the defender of the faith, the man who restored power and puritanism to Islam in the face of decadence, corruption and western hegemony. And for the militants who seek to challenge the established order in the name of Islam, Khomeini remains a model. Yet in Iran itself, where Khomeini led the first Islamic Revolution, what is emerging after more than a decade of Islamic rule, are clear signs that Khomeini's Islamic puritanism has lost its appeal. Furthermore, by promising that Islam is able to solve all worldly problems, Khomeini pushed Islam beyond its endurance and exposed its shortcomings. Inadvertently, he may have engineered what amounts to the beginning of the first Islamic reformation. Khomeini's upbringing, his education as theologian, the clergy's humiliation by the Pahlavis and the demise of Islam as a world power have all influenced his thinking. Khomeini's world view is far more coloured by his mystical vision of the 'Perfect Man' and his missionary zeal seems to have been influenced by seeing himself as the 'Perfector of Man'.

Background

On 24 September 1902, Ruhollah Khomeini was born in Khomein – then a small village in central Iran. Khomeini's family are Mussavi Sayyeds, who trace their descent from the Prophet through the line of the seventh Imam of the Shi'i, Musa al-kazem. They were originally from Neyshabur in northeastern Iran. In the early eighteenth century the family migrated to India and settled in the small town of Kintur near Lucknow in the kingdom of Oudh whose rulers were Twelver Shi'i. Ruhollah's grandfather, Sayyed Ahmad Moussavi Hindi, was born in Kintur and was a contemporary and relative of the famous scholar Mir Hamed Hosein Hindi Neyshaburi whose voluminous work *Abaqat al-Anwar* is the pride of Indian Shi'ism.

Ahmad left India in about 1830 for a pilgrimage to the shrine city of Najaf where he met a notable landowner and merchant of Khomein. Accepting his invitation, Ahmad went to Khomein to become the spiritual guide of the village. There he married Sakineh, the daughter of his host. The couple had four children including Mustafa who was born in 1856. Mustafa studied in Najaf, under Mirza Hasan Shirazi, then returned in 1894 to Khomein where he became a prosperous clergyman with a family of six children, of whom Ruhollah was the youngest and the only one to be called Khomeini (of Khomein).

Mustafa was murdered seven months after Ruhollah's birth. Soon after, the country was engulfed by a series of anti-establishment protests, staged by the ulama, the bazaar merchants and the modern educated reformists, which led to the 1905–06 Constitutional Movement. The Shah was forced to grant a western-style parliamentary constitution. However, he died the following year, to be succeeded by his anti-constitutionalist son.

This turbulent period inevitably left its mark on the young Ruhollah, though he enjoyed the love of Sahebeh, his aunt, who had moved in with them to look after her brother's children. Sahebeh was a strong-minded woman. Ruhollah's life was dominated by her as well as by his mother. They both died when he was sixteen.

As a child, Khomeini started to learn Arabic, Persian poetry and calligraphy at government school and the 'maktab'. Maktab, 'place of writing' in Arabic, in effect was a 'place of reading' in Iran. An old mullah or a local woman taught the alphabet and the pronunciation of the Arabic letters. Children squatted on the floor and repeated whatever the teacher said. Discipline in the maktabs was very harsh. Punishment for mispronouncing a Qur'anic word was severe by today's standards. The suffering of children in the maktab was notorious in Iran.

Like other children, Ruhollah was taught to memorize by heart the last few chapters of the Qur'an and a few phrases and words in Arabic about the Prophet and the Imams. Beside books on the lives of the Imams and a book of the Hadith (Traditions) of the Prophet Muhammad, it is the Shi'i version of history that was taught and reinforced. For example, it was believed that neither the Prophet himself nor his family (including the twelve Shi'i imams) died of natural deaths. This is suggested by the Shi'i saying 'We are either poisoned or killed'. This struggle between truth and falsehood, *haq* and *batel*, or seeing things in black and white, was imprinted in Ruhollah's mind. The vocabulary and feeling of being wronged remained with him for the rest of his life. There are no grey areas when it comes to this inbuilt sense of deep tragedy. Only revenge can put things right. Ruhollah heard this over and over in his life from home to maktab, mosque and madraseh. In this interpretation of history, Muhammad was wronged by his enemies. His daughter Fatima, who is revered by the Shi'i, was wronged by Omar. Her husband, Ali, had been wronged by Abu Bakr, Omar and Othman who had deprived him of his right to succeed the Prophet as Caliph. The Sunnis regard Ali as merely the fourth Caliph after Muhammad, while the Shi'i regard him as the first Imam. Having been wronged, Ali was then murdered. It is the duty of all Shi'is to avenge such wrongs.

Education

As Ruhollah grew older he began to take his religious studies more seriously. When fifteen, he started learning Arabic grammar with his brother Mortaza, who had studied some Arabic and theology in Isfahan.[1] Ruhollah was studious, with a particular talent for writing and composition in Persian poetry. He learned a good deal of classical poetry with the emphasis, at least to begin with, on moral and ethical poetry such as the great classic, 'Sa'di's Golistan' (Rose Garden). Hafez's fusion of lyricism and mysticism was also taught. There is hardly a major poet whom Ruhollah has not quoted in his later writings. Nader-e Naderpour, a contemporary Iranian poet who had met Khomeini in the early 1960s in Qom recalls: 'We recited poetry for four hours. Every first line I recited from any poet, he recited the second'.[2] Khomeini also showed interest in Persian calligraphy, learning it from a certain Sheikh Hamzah Mahallati. It was a skill which he practised even in his old age.

Ruhollah was the product of central Iran, which has for centuries supplied Shi'i Islam with a steady stream of religious scholars and clerics and Ruhollah's studies udner Mahallati were very much a part of this tradition. To become a *mojtahed* was what the young Ruhollah then longed for. Khomein was no longer a fertile ground for his aspirations. Najaf would have been an ideal choice, but the collapse of the Ottoman empire and its replacement in Iraq by a British mandate had led to political turmoil. Moreover, he was not yet sufficiently educated to go to Najaf. Isfahan, on the other hand, a centre of Shi'i learning for several centuries, was the nearest important city to Khomein; Ruhollah decided to go there. Once in Isfahan, he heard of Shaykh Abdolkarim Ha'eri-Yazdi, a leading cleric who had left Karbala to avoid the political turmoil which had prompted most of the leading clergy to declare their opposition to British rule in Iraq. Ha'eri was living in the nearby town of Sultanabad or Arak. For a student whose dream was Najaf this was an exciting opportunity. Ruhollah was seventeen when he left for Arak.

In Arak, Ha'eri trained a generation of leading clerics in a madraseh endowed by Haj-Aqa Mohsen Araki (1325/1907), one of the leading anti-constitutionalist clerics.[3] As a beginner in the circle of learning, Ruhollah studied 'Suyuti', an Arabic grammatical text by the Egyptian scholar Jalaluddin Suyuti (or al-Usyuti). Determined as he was to learn, Ruhollah would make few compromises, a quality he retained throughout his life. 'One day when he was studying Suyuti with other students in the courtyard of the school, Ha'eri was teaching advanced studies to other talabehs and the noise disturbed Ruhollah. Having never bothered to mince his words, Ruhollah turned to 'Ha'eri and told him, politely but firmly, to speak more softly'.[4] Ha'eri was astonished to be chided thus by a student. Ruhollah was now a fully-fledged talabeh and wore a black turban.

With the decline of the Ottoman empire, the leading ulama were reluctant to remain in the cities while under British mandate. However, Qom was seen to be a suitable Shi'i city. As an early Shi'i centre, Qom houses the shrine of Ma'sumeh, the sister of Imam Reza the eighth shi'i Imam. The revival of Qom as a major theological centre is essentially associated with Ha'eri who was welcomed to the city when he made a pilgrimage there in 1921. He was subsequently invited to transfer his teaching circles to Qom. After Ha'eri's arrival at Qom, Ahmad Shah, the last Qajar monarch, made a special trip to congratulate him on his decision. Shortly, most of the clergy from Arak as well as a number of leading clerics from other cities gathered in Qom and turned the city into a fully-fledged centre of theology with teachers in all branches of Islamic learning. Some five months later, Ruhollah who was then studying the *Motavval*, a book on rhetoric and semantics, followed Ha'eri to Qom and took up residence in a converted theological school close to the shrine.

One of Khomeini's first teachers in his new residence was Muhammad Reza Masjed-Shahi with whom he studied rhetoric and poetry but who was also to interest him in a new topic – Darwin's theory of evolution – which the anti-clerical secularists were to use to taunt the clergy. Masjed-Shahi was one of the many mullahs who attempted to refute Drawin and Khomeini was soon to learn and discuss his teacher's book *The Critique of Darwin's Philosophy*.

Ruhollah completed his study in *fiqh* and its principles with a teacher from Kashan eleven years his senior, Ayatollah Ali Yasrebi-Kashani (d. 1959). He then attended Ha'eri's classes. Attending such lectures signified one's entrance into the 'third level'. Ha'eri taught the Dars-e Kharej, or 'studies beyond the text', a level at which there are no set books and students work towards forming their own opinions on given legal issues. This was the final stage of Ruhollah's education. By the early 1930s he became a mujtahid and received the *ijazeh* (certificate) to relate the hadith (traditions) from four leading teachers.[5] The first of these was Mohsen Amin 'Ameli (d. 1952), who was a leading cleric from Lebanon. Imam Musa Sadr succeeded Amin in becoming the leader of Lebanese Shi'ites. The second was Shaykh Abbas Qomi (d. 1959), a leading narrator of hadith and Shi'ite historian. Qomi is a bestselling author in modern Iran, especially his book of common prayer known as *Mafatih ul-Jenan* or 'Keys to Paradise'. A copy of 'Keys to Paradise' was given to each war volunteer after the revolution, a practice misinterpreted by opponents of Khomeini and fed to the western press as 'Plastic Keys to Heaven'. The third teacher was Abolqasem Dehkordi Isfahani (d. 1934), who was a leading mullah in Isfahan. The fourth was Muhammad Reza Masjed-Shahi (d. 1943), who came to Qom in 1925 in protest against the anti-Islamic policies of Reza Shah.

At the age of twenty-seven, Ruhollah married Batul, the daughter of an ayatollah from Tehran. Batul remained his life-long wife. They had five children, two sons and three daughters.

In Search of the Perfect Man

While studying law and jurisprudence in Qom, Khomeini also studied two unconventional traditions of Islam – *erfan* and *hekmat*. This was going to have the greatest impact on Khomeini's view of himself and the world. *Erfan*, an Arabic word meaning gnosis, the mystical knowledge of the inner world of Man seeking intimacy with God, is a spiritual tradition found mainly in the Shi'i world which, with some reservations, parallels and shares many doctrines with Sufism. *Hekmat*, characterized both by a thoroughly logical and scholastic system of thought and by an experiential exploration of the nature of ultimate reality, provides the main intellectual stream of *erfan*. Its leading thirteenth-century exponent was the great Shi'i scholar Nasir al-Din Tusi, who systematically defended the metaphysical writings of Avicenna against the attacks of unorthodoxy levelled by theologians, in particular the criticisms of Ghazali, who accused Avicenna and his followers of heresy. For Ibn Arabi, another representative of the more gnostic and mystical aspects of *hekmat*, the central idea of mysticism is a transcendent state which he called 'opening', through which direct knowledge of God and the unseen is achieved. To reach this elevated state it is necessary to discipline oneself through religious law and the practices of the spiritual path, but 'opening' is ultimately a gift of God. He claimed that he had met the beatified Muhammad, that he knew God's greatest name (*esm-e a'zam*) and that he had acquired his knowledge not through his own labour but through direct inspiration.

During the Safavids, Sadr al-Din Shirazi, better known as Mulla Sadra (d. 1641), played an instrumental role in the study and exposition of *hekmat* in Persia. His works, of which *Al-asfar al-arba'a* ('The Four Journeys') is the most masterful representation, are based on what he called the Transcendent Wisdom (*al-hekmat al-muta'aliya*), the source or moment of direct awareness of the true reality of being, which comes with the realization of the oneness of the intellectual subject and object, as well as an awareness of the intellect itself.

Another manifestation of *erfan*, which is also important with respect to Khomeini, is the contribution of Persian mystical poetry, although it was not confined to the Shi'i poets; two of the most renowned Persian poets were Sunnis. The first, Jalal al-Din Rumi (d. 1273), is perhaps the most highly regarded of all Sufi poets. He attracted a large following in Konya and left behind two masterpieces of Persian mystical poetry: the *Masnavi*, a long didactic work, and a collection of lyrical poetry usually referred to as the *Divan of Shams-i Tabriz*, after the wild and ascetic dervish who became the most elevated object of Rumi's mystical love. The second poet, Hafez of Shiraz (d. 1389 or 1390) was a link between *hekmat* and *erfan*, combining the rational issues of his time raised by such philosophers as Omar Khayyam, with the mystical approaches of Sufi poets like Rumi.

Having studied philosophy, Khomeini began to study mysticism. He was particularly interested in the *Sharh-i Fusus*, a commentary by Sharaf al-Din Dawud Ghaisari (d. 1350) on the *Fusus al-Hikam*, one of Ibn Arabi's works, which gives a mystical exposition of the divine attributes reflected in the prophets from Adam to Muhammad. In 1937, Khomeni wrote a commentary on the Fusus.

Khomeini was particularly influenced by one of his teachers, Shahabadi, to whom he once said: 'What you are saying is not in the book. Where is it from?' Shahabadi replied. 'It is said,' by which he implied, 'It is my own opinion.'[6]

Shahabadi, who did not believe in quietism and was one of a small group of mullahs who actively opposed Reza Shah's policies, also influenced Khomeini's political views. Shahabadi emphasized the importance of planning in order to educate and organize Muslims. He would advise his students to simplify difficult subjects for a wider popular appreciation, something which the Prophet had encouraged when he said: 'Talk to people according to the level of their intelligence.' It was a lesson that was to be practised, most effectively, by Khomeini in future years. Constantly urging his students to work towards the salvation of the Muslim community, Shahabadi even set out the following guidelines: (1) to publish a religious magazine in order to propagate religious thought and activities among the people; (2) frugality in everyday life and overcoming harmful habits; (3) to form an Islamic company to produce Islamic and

Iranian goods for domestic consumption and export; (4) to establish a fund for granting interest-free loans. In a reference to Shahabadi, Khomeini acknowledges his influence, stating that he was not only a perfect theologian and mystic but also a combatant (*mobarez*), these being the three key facets of Khomeini's own personality.[7]

In a commentary on a supplication known as 'The Dawn Supplication' (*Do'a al-Sahar*), Khomeini demonstrated the conformity of the Shari'a with the logic of mysticism.[8] He argued that there was no intrinsic contradiction between *erfan* and Sufism on the one hand and a strict adherence to the Shari'a on the other. It is, of course, difficult for a modern Westerner to reconcile what he might regard as two conflicting attitudes: the gentle, contemplative attitude of Sufism and the rule-bound legalistic attitude of the Shari'a.

Khomeini's developing personality conformed with Islamic tradition. As an intelligent, introverted and frustrated young man embittered by the decline and decay of the clerical establishment, discovering the inner illumination of mysticism was a turning point for Khomeini. He was neither satisfied nor fulfilled by the orthodox version of religion so common among the majority of the clergy. However, it is dangerous for any theosophist to reveal the secrets of mystical knowledge. Unpopularity, threats, excommunication, exile, isolation and even death have rewarded many of those who have proclaimed their belief in this secret knowledge. Hallaj was crucified for boastfully telling the world at large: 'I am the truth.' Ibn Arabi was condemned as a heretic for having claimed to have seen the Prophet; Suhrawardi was executed. A'in-al- Qozat of Hamadan, was hanged and his body burnt. Mullah Sadra, the last great philosopher of Islam and the founder of Transcendental Theosophy, a tradition which was followed by Khomeini, was driven out of his home town, Shiraz.

What all of these mystics said can be viewed as echoing, in different ways, what Hallaj had propounded. As Ibn Arabi wrote: 'Everything in the world is nothing but fantasy or imagination, or images in the mirror, or shadows.' Fear of persecution forced many mystics and philosophers in the Islamic world to hide behind a language which the common man would not understand. One such was Mir-Damad (d. 1631) whose work Khomeini came to know in later life. He brought together mysticism and the esoteric aspects of Shi'ism. He remained safe from the zealots' wrath, only because his language was too complicated to be understood.

Khomeini usually wrote in a simple language, while he kept his mystical writings under wraps. His public posture since his early days as a *mojtahed* always conformed to the general trend of the clergy. He appeared to shun suspicious subjects like philosophy and mysticism in favour of the mainstream disciplines of law, jurisprudence, the sciences of the Qur'an and the Traditions of the Prophet and the Imams.

Islamic history is punctuated with incidents in which jurisprudents, mystics and philosophers have fought one another. Jurisprudents value and use revelation, the simplest of the three messages after mysticism and philosophy. However, mysticism in its devotional form is seen to be the most direct path to God, which is why it has been so attractive to converts. The militants, however, have found less to value in it. Khomeini was, in a sense, one of the few to reach the stature of a leading jurisprudent, the highest level of theoretical mysticism and also to become a highly regarded teacher of Islamic philosophy. He is unique in also being regarded as a leading practitioner of militant Islam.

The concept of the Perfect Man captured Khomeini's imagination since it provided him with a new and more effective mode of expressing the decay in Islam. He also accepted the mystics' view of the pre-existence of the Prophet. It is believed by the Shi'is that after the death of the Prophet, the Light passed to Ali and through him to the Imams of his house. Logos is central to the mystical understanding of the universe and man's place in it.

It is important not to confuse the non-Shi'i Sufi treatment of Light and the Perfect Man, the shaykh and the saint, with the Shi'i view, the Imam. For the sufi a *vali*, or 'saint', is designated either by virtue of his inheritance of a position in a chain of esoteric initiation, or, as was supremely the case with Ibn Arabi, by virtue of his inward visions. But for the Shi'i the *vali* is always the Imam. The Shi'i mystic can ultimately only rise to identification with the 'Imam of the Age' whereas the non-Shi'i Sufi takes the Prophet as the model of the Perfect Man. There is arguably a grey area where the 'extremist' view that the Imam is spiritually superior to the Prophet overlaps with the possibility of his rising to a point of imitation of the Prophet. What is most interesting is the theory that after the physical death of the Prophet there are vicegerents, imams, saints and *valis* who carry on the Prophetic torch. Both *valis* and saints feel that they inherit this mystical inward aspect of Muhammad's nature described as Cosmic Guardianship (*Velayat Takvini*) or Creational Guardianship, which as far as they are concerned is far more important than the legalistic and outward appearance of Muhammad as an apostle and a Prophet (*Velayat Tashri'i*, or Legislating Guardianship). Mystical saints are Muhammad's personal representatives to whom he has delegated his functions as vicegerent of God. Without their invisible government (*velayat*) the world will fall into disorder and ruin.

In Khomeini's commentary on 'The Dawn Supplication' he quotes major Islamic mystics such as Ibn Arabi, Mullah Sadra, Hafez and Rumi to support his view that: '... the Perfect Man is the holder of the chain of existence, with which the cycle is completed ... He is God's great sign, created in God's image.'9 Having accepted Ibn Arabi's view on the Perfect Man, Khomeini then turned to his hero, Mullah Sadra, whose transcendental theosophy (*Hekmat-e Mota'aliyeh*) drew on the *erfan* of Ibn Arabi, the illuminationist philosophy (*falsafeh-ye 'ishraq*) of Suhrawardi, the rational philosophy (*falsafeh-ye mashsha'i*) of Avicenna's followers and on Shi'i theology (Kalam). Ibn Arabi believed in a journey of purification, formulated into four journeys, while Mulla Sadra examined the issues involved as an intellectual as well as a spiritual journey, rationalizing his argument with mystical and philosophical explanations. Khomeini took this a step further. For him the first journey was 'from Mankind to God' (*min al-Khalq ila-al-Haqq*), in which the traveller (*sa'lek*) in search of 'Truth' strives to leave the domain of human limitations. The second journey is with God in God. He will acquaint himself with the beauty of God's names and attributes, witnessing their real manifestations, influence and governance. The third journey is one in which the traveller returns to the people, but is no longer separate from God as he can now see His omnipotent essence. The final journey is one in which the traveller has acquired godly attributes with which he can begin to guide and help others to reach God. This is the crucial stage. It is here that *velayat* (vicegerency) and prophethood are realized, giving the traveller the mission to preach God's word. He must guide people from multiplicity to unity, from blasphemy to faith, from polytheism to the oneness of God, from imperfection to perfection. More importantly, by establishing rightful policies, the government of absolute justice and a reign of divinity, the Perfect Man will guide society towards absolute perfection.

'The Ascension of the Traveller and the Prayer of the Mystics' (*Me'raj al-Salekin wa Salat al-'Arefin*), one of the books written by Khomeini, is apparently about the daily prayers of Muslims, but in reality it is a book about the travels of a seeker who embarks upon the four journeys.[10] Deploying a cautious language so as not to alienate the uninitiated, Khomeini uses the mystical terminology of Ibn Arabi, Mullah Sadra and others, though demonstrating that he knows his subject intimately. In his books on jurisprudence Khomeini discusses prayer for ordinary believers. He mentions the type of prayers, the intent, the time, the physical cleanliness of the supplicant and the correct pronunciation of the Arabic words. It is here that one either takes refuge in one's inner self or establishes separate systems for commoners and the elite (*awamm wa khawass*). Several verses of the Qur'an clearly state: 'The majority do not think ... the majority do not understand ... the majority do not appreciate.' This was undoubtedly a problem for a thinker such as Khomeini. His language in this book is very much the language of a mystic imbued with the love of God, and the theosophical belief in the relationship between God and Man is kept always in mind when he discusses this relationship.

Professor Mehdi Ha'eri Yazdi, the son of Ayatollah Ha'eri, a former student of Khomeini and a leading Iranian scholar who is well-versed in both western and Islamic philosophy, is of the opinion that Khomeini, not unlike Hallaj, considered himself as having completed the fourth journey which implies a belief in the words 'I am the truth and people' (*Ana al-haqq wa al-khalq*). The only difference is, says Ha'eri, that Hallaj, 'having secrets in his charge', failed not to tell 'the world at large' and was crucified, but Khomeini succeeded. 'Khomeini is not a philosopher,' says Ha'eri Yazdi. 'He has no mathematical mind. Nor has he a "disinterestedness" to qualify him as having one.' However, in Ha'eri Yazdi's view, Khomeini was 'the greatest living theoretical mystic'.[11]

Khomeini did not publish much from his mystical books before the revolution. Had it not been for the social and political upheaval, and had the traditional clergy been as powerful as in other periods, he himself might have become the victim of the orthodox faction. Khomeini was aware of this antagonism towards the mystics and was careful to justify all his utterances, first through Qur'anic verses and then through the sayings of the Prophet and the Imams. In fact, during his televised commentaries on the Qur'an, broadcast after the revolution, he referred to antagonism towards one of his own teachers, Mirza Ali-Akbar Hakim, implying that the clergy would have considered someone who taught mysticism as being beyond the pale.

Khomeini's relationship with God was something of a puzzle for many people. His son Ahmad says that he understood from his mother and friends that his father had a special relationship with God with whom he was at one, often speaking with frightening enthusiasm about his beloved Lord. [12] Occasionally, after the Revolution, when officials came to see him with great problems or a major crisis, he would talk about God as if nothing else existed.

In his audiences, he would occasionally elaborate on his mystical views of the Universe and Man. On one such occasion he preached to warring members of parliament and officials that selfishness was the cause of their divisions.

'Man', Khomeini told an audience in his little mosque in northern Tehran, 'has certain qualities which do not exist in any other creature. For example, in Man there is an aspiration towards absolute and not finite power, absolute and not finite perfection; and since absolute power and perfection cannot be realized in anything but God the Almighty, Man by nature seeks God without himself knowing that he does. One strong proof for [the existence] of absolute perfection is this very love of Man for it. Man has an actual love for absolute perfection, and there cannot be an actual lover without there also being an actual beloved. Here, there can be no supposition nor invention, for Man's innate nature seeks the reality of absolute perfection and nature cannot be deceived. Human nature demands absolute perfection.

'What is more, it demands this perfection for its own self. All human beings are restrictive in pursuit of perfection. And where they all attain this absolute perfection, they become one. Monopoly then ceases as there is no multiplicity. If a man is the ruler of a city, he is not satisfied in his heart of hearts: he wants to be the ruler of a province. When he has attained this, he still feels unfulfilled for he wants to have the whole of the country in the palm of his hand. And if he comes to be the ruler of a country, he then wants other countries to be under his rule too. The fact is that if you give anyone the whole globe, he will not be content with what he has for he is after absolute perfection. He will not even be content if he has the whole world, the whole galaxy, the entire firmament in his possession, for all this does not constitute absolute perfection. Man will not be assured until and unless he conjoins the ocean of Absolute Perfection and becomes part of it.

'It is through the invocation of God that he finds contentment, not through becoming a President or a Prime Minister, or having the power of the great powers or possessing all there is on earth and in the heavens. What brings confidence and rescues one from this instability and need is the recitation of the name of God. Not the recitation of His name in a mere verbal repetition of *'La illah illa Allah'* (There is no god but God) but an invocation in and from the heart.'[13] Whether Khomeini was reflecting on his own personal progress can only be speculated on.

A student of Khomeini who published his reflections on 'The Dawn Supplication' said of him: 'If the western philosophers consider the world as a mixture of conflicts and strife, it is possible to call this man the centre of contradictions and the pivot of divergent tastes and feelings. The man who talks about issues of theosophy and mysticism (i.e. the mystical path and liberation from all material inclinations) can simultaneously think about the establishment of Islamic government, justice for the oppressed and the implementation of Islamic law'.[14] And Khomeini, at this stage, *was* thinking about it.

Interest in Politics

To move towards the implementation of the Islamic law, and drive society towards perfection, Khomeini had to acquire the means necessary. In theological centres, later to be described by Khomeini himself as the den of snakes, factionalism, lobbying and populism are the norm. Moral authority, financial rewards and character assassination are not ruled out. Teachers and advanced students are the main actors and extras who can turn a teacher into a grand ayatollah or else destroy him. By the age of twenty-seven, Khomeini in effect entered clerical politics and began to have his own circle of admiring students. He was less interested in discussion for its own sake. 'He put forward a topic in a decisive manner, first explaining other opinions on the topic and then his own opinion before looking for arguments.'[15]

Khomeini's devotion to mysticism and his noncomformity did not, however, curb his interest in what was going on in Qom and the country at large. Driven by what he perceived to be the moral degeneration of Iran, in the 1930s he began to teach ethics. He later recalled how during this period the people '... were selfish, feeble and sluggish', so that 'they were unable to resist the dictatorship of Reza Shah.'[16] To Khomeini his fellow countrymen lacked the necessary moral fibre to combat this 'decay, and Iran as a nation thus lay dormant'.[17] Khomeini lectured at Qom's Faiziyeh School. His choice of a prominent public venue next to the Shrine of Fatima in the bazaar, and his choice of Thursdays and Fridays as Muslim public holiday when thousands of pilgrims visited the city, ensured that his reputation spread far beyond religious circles. Indeed, many people travelled from neighbouring towns and villages and even from Tehran just to hear him speak. The authorities soon perceived the threat he posed to public order and attempted to dissuade him from giving lectures, even in theological schools. Khomeini is reported by his students as having replied: 'I am duty-bound to continue with these lectures. If the police want to stop them, they will have to come themselves and physically prevent them from taking place.'[18] Although the police did not take up Khomeini's invitation to intervene they began to exert such pressure on him that he was forced to move his lectures from the prominent Faiziyeh to the more remote Hajj Mullah Sadeq School of Theology. In 1941, when the Allies occupied Iran removing Reza Shah, the anti-clerical policies ceased to be implemented. Khomeini returned to the Faiziyeh and continued his lectures. Unlike most mullahs, who attempt to frighten their congregation with the punishment of Hell and motivate them with the lure of heaven, Khomeini preached about Good and Evil, religious awareness, self-discipline and the roots of decadence in Islam. It was now his fellow clerics who aired their objections to the mystical and philosophical content of his lectures. Having resisted the government's pressure in the 1930s, he was finally to give way to the pressure of fellow clerics in the late 1940s and abandon his public lectures. It was from then on that he began to turn to the teaching of jurisprudence although he did continue to teach ethics, mysticism and philosophy privately. 'They considered my son religiously impure simply because I was teaching philosophy and mysticism,' he complained bitterly many years later.[19] Ali Akbar Hashemi Rafsanjani, a student of Khomeini and later president of Iran says that Khomeini was forced into seclusion by those who were against his teaching of philosophy, including Ayatollah Borujerdi. For almost three years, therefore, Khomeini taught at home, often concealing the fact that he was teaching philosophy and mysticism. However, three of his close students, Ayatollah Mortaza Motahhari, Ayatollah Hosein Ali Montazeri and Ayatollah Javadi Amoli continued their private lectures in transcendental theosophy with him.

Khomeini entered the national political and religious debate, albeit anonymously, after the Second World War when Reza Shah was no longer in power. To survive the anti-clerical rule of Reza Shah, the clergy, after an initial period of struggle, felt they had little choice other than to keep their heads down. 'It was so difficult a time that, had Ha'eri uttered a word, they [Reza Shah's regime] would have destroyed the theological centre of Qom,' explained a close friend of Khomeini, Ayatollah Saduqi.[20] This passive approach was justified by appeals to the Shi'i notion of *taqiyya*, or dissimulation, which is permitted in order to protect the 'pale of Islam' when Muslims face a danger they cannot resist or fight against. There can be no doubt that during the reign of Reza Shah this was the attitude adopted by a majority of the ulama, and there is some evidence that Khomeini himself belonged to this group. One of his students recounts that when Bafqi, an Ayatollah who had incurred the Shah's displeasure, returned to Qom after a period of internal exile, Khomeini went to visit him. Bafqi was upset because mullahs had allowed the authorities to demolish part of the Imam Mosque in Qom in order to build a road and castigated Khomeini, saying: 'You were here and allowed them to demolish the Imam's Mosque?' Upon which Khomeini replied: 'Dissimulation is my path and the path of my forefathers' (*at-taqiyyatu Dini wa Dinu Abaee*).[21]

In the post-Reza Shah period Khomeini was able to throw off his dissimulation. His first written political statement was recorded in 1944 in the visitors' book at a mosque in Yazd. At the top of the page he wrote: 'To be read and put into practice.'[22] He began with the Qur'anic verse: 'Say: I do admonish you on one point: that you do stand up for God, in pairs or singly'. The significant point in the lines which followed was his emphasis on the idea of standing up for or staging an uprising in the name of God. He continued with a comment on what had happened to the nation for not standing up for God: 'It is our selfishness and the abandoning of an uprising for God that has led to our present dark days and subjected us to world domination. It is selfishness that has undermined the Muslim world.'[23] Disappointed with the performance of his fellow Muslims, Khomeini urged them to learn some dedication to and determination in their religion from the Baha'is whom he otherwise regarded as hated heretics. Shortly afterwards Khomeini elaborated his views on Reza Shah's rule in his first political work, *Kashf al-Asrar* ('The Discovery of Secrets'), which he appears to have completed in 1942.

Deploying the polemical style he had learnt at theological school, Khomeini spoke rhetorically of Reza Shah as 'that illiterate soldier who knew that if he did not suffocate them [the ulama] and silence them with the force of bayonets, they would oppose what he was doing to the country and religion.'[24] *Kashf al-Asrar* was not, however, aimed primarily at Reza Shah. Its real target was those who, in Khomeini's eyes, had 'actively collaborated with him', especially renegade clergymen. Indeed, it was a direct response to an attack on the clerical establishment in a pamphlet called *Asrar-e Hezar Saleh* ('Secrets of a Thousand Years') written by Hakamizadeh, the editor of *Homayoun*; Khomeini later recalled that when he saw the work of this 'warped person' he was inflamed with rage. Despite problems he was having with his eyes at the time, Khomeini saw no alternative but to take forty-eight days off from his teaching obligations to reply to the accusations. On the subject of Hakamizadeh and men like him, Khomeini maintained that while the world had been enveloped in the hellfire of war, and nations were trying to salvage themselves, there were some 'mindless' people who were trying their utmost to spread disunity and mischief instead of helping their brethren who had been pushed into war. These people had taken the 'criminal step' of spreading their 'poisonous' ideas against the clergy. He considered it his duty to bring these facts to people's attention so that the sources of Iran's corruption and misery could be traced. One reformist trend that had been gaining ground, and which Khomeini particularly reviled, argued that Shi'i rituals and the rituals of some Sufi sects had little to do with the original religion founded by Muhammad. This view, which was advocated by Kasravi and a number of former mullahs, was not unlike that espoused by the puritanical Wahhabi sect in Saudi Arabia. So Khomeini accused its propagators of being 'the followers of the camel grazers of Riyadh and the barbarians of Najd, the most infamous and the wildest members of the human family.'[25]

Khomeini wrote parts of his pamphlet in a much more sober

fashion. He proceeded systematically, selecting and refuting doubts about 'God's unity, the Imamate and religious leadership, the clergy, government, law and the Hadith'. Demonstrating his knowledge of philosophy, logic and polemics he would challenge his opponents, explain the background to his subject matter and put forward his case. Another technique he employed was to appeal to his readers' sense of patriotism and religious sentiments. Unusual for a mullah of his generation he even made constant use of a philosophical term fashionable at the time among the anti-clerical element, namely *kherad*, or the power of reason: 'This irrational person (Hakamizadeh) has taken it for granted that religious people have trampled upon the rule of "reason" and have no regard for it. This reveals his ignorance and want of information. Is it not religious people who have written all the books on philosophy and the principles of jurisprudence? Have they not looked upon thousands of philosophical and theological issues in the light of reason and intellect? Is it not these leaders of theology who consider reason as one of the binding issues?'[26]

Yet such displays of political sensitivity were interspersed with pure invective. In his counter-attack on the clergy's opponents Khomeini would often lose control, accusing them of stupidity, treachery, ignorance and heresy. But as he embarked upon the final statement of his polemic, in what was undoubtedly an offensive tone, he wrote that those who see themselves as protectors of religion must 'smash in the teeth of this brainless lot with their iron fist' and 'trample upon their heads with courageous strides'.[27] There is yet another layer to *Kashf al-Asrar*. Here we see the first statement of the ideas on the constitution of an Islamic state; Khomeini advised his readers and particularly the clergy to look at the chapters on government.

'Government,' Khomeini argued, 'can only be legitimate when it accepts the rule of God and the rule of God means the implementation of the Shari'a. All laws that are contrary to the Shari'a must be dropped because only the law of God will stay valid and immutable in the face of changing times.' Western civilization and foreigners have, in this respect, 'stolen from the misled Muslims their reason and intelligence.'[28]

The form of government, he said, did not in itself matter as long as the law of Islam was enforced. But if the government were to be a monarchy, the king should be appointed by the mojtaheds who would choose 'a just monarch who does not violate God's laws, will turn from oppression and wrongdoing and will not violate men's property, lives and honour'.[29] Rather chillingly, he expected the government of Islam to 'follow religious rules and regulations and ban publications which were against the law and religion and, in the presence of religious supporters, hang those who wrote such nonsense.'[30] The 'mischief-makers who were corrupters of the earth (*mofsed fi'l-arz*) should', he said, 'be uprooted so that others would avoid betraying religious sanctity.'[31]

Khomeini's past heroes were of different Islamic persuasions. At one extreme was Modarres, an impeccable parliamentarian, and at the other Sheikh Fazlollah Nuri, the anti-constitutionalist and conservative defender of the Shari'a. Khomeini often referred to the execution of the Sheikh along with the overthrow of the Ottoman empire and the intervention of Britain in the affairs of Iraq as the three calamities that had befallen Islam. Khomeini's admiration and praise for the Islamic thinkers and pioneers of change were commensurate with the militancy of their defence of the Shari'a. Although he praised the leading constitutional thinker Ayatollah Na'ini (1860–1936) for resisting the British in Iraq, he had little praise for Na'ini's attempt to reconcile democracy and Islam, Na'ini had written a book on Shi'i political theory which countered the views of the anti-constitutionalist clergy.

By the late 1940s Khomeini began to emerge from his self-imposed seclusion, believing that politics was just as much a part of Islam as philosophy, mysticism and jurisprudence. To further his views he closely observed the two giants of the time, Ayatollah Kashani, who played a prominent role in politics, and Ayatollah Borujerdi, who was the most important *marja'-e taqlid* since 1947.

Khomeini shared Kashani's views on many issues such as anti-colonialism, Islamic universalism, political activism and populism. But they differed in many ways, too. Kashani was the urbane politician willing to be flexible, while Khomeini was more austere and less accommodating. While Kashani severed his links as a teacher at theological centres, Khomeini was an advocate of a united clerical leadership. True, Kashani was perhaps more popular with junior and middle-ranking clerics like Khomeini, but it was the leading ulama in Qom and Najaf who were in charge of the theological centres and not Kashani. Khomeini's admiration for Kashani was second only to that for

Ayatollah Borujerdi, another personality on whom he pinned his hopes for stemming clerical disunity and feebleness.

In fact, Khomeini as a teacher of theology in Qom played an active role in seeking an acceptable, strong man to unite and protect the clergy. He found such a man in Borujerdi, a leading mullah known for his immense knowledge of theology and jurisprudence; he was also considered very pious, a firm believer in the Sunni-Shi'i dialogue and an able administrator. The sheer personality and charisma of Borujerdi as well as his reformist vision soon overshadowed all other Shi'i clerics, making him their almost universal leader. His restraint did create some problems between himself and the political mullahs, jealously guarding as he did his non-political status of *marja'-e taqlid*. Borujerdi's non-interference in politics at a time when Iran was going through a major nationalist upsurge during the premiership of Dr Mosaddeq alienated the nationalists and their Muslim allies who were expecting support from the clergy. However, Kashani ignored Borujerdi's advice and accepted the office of speaker of the Majlis.

The rich mosaic of politics in post-Second World War Iran was dominated more by Dr Mosaddeq than by any other politican. It was in the mid-1940s that Mosaddeq assumed the leadership of the National Front, a loose coalition of liberal nationalist deputies in the Majlis. In Khomeini's view, 'Mosaddeq meant well and wanted to serve the nation but his main mistake was not having got rid of the Shah when he was strong and the Shah was weak.'[32] For his part, Borujerdi never supported Mosaddeq.

In 1953 during the bloody controversy over Seyyed Ali Akbar Borqa'i, a pro-Tudeh cleric, who had allegedly insulted Borujerdi, Islam and the Qur'an at the Peace Partisans' Congress in Vienna, it was Khomeini who emerged as a close aide to Borujerdi. When a reporter on the weekly journal *Taraqqi* went to interview Borujerdi, he referred to Khomeini as his official representative.[33] In the interview Khomeini quoted Borujerdi as saying that Borqa'i must leave Qom and must not take part in the elections. When the reporter asked Khomeini whether he could be photographed, Khomeini refused. This was Khomeini's first interview.

During these years a religious historian wrote: '[Khomeini] is one of the great teachers and a prominent figure of Qom's theological centres.'[34] In the ornate literary style common at the time he described him as 'the learned philosopher, the discerning jurisconsult by whom the eyes of the theological centre are enlightened.'[35] He added that Khomeini '... is the centre of attention for many students and people from Qom, Tehran and other cities, whose lectures on ethics had been attended by hundreds of virtuous people from the centre itself and from other places'. Of Khomeini's lectures on theology, the historian wrote: 'His lectures are better than any others,' and predicting Khomeini's future, he added that 'much hope was now pinned on him'.[36]

By the late 1950s Khomeini was one of the rising stars in the theological teaching centres. Years of teaching ethics, theology, transcendental theosophy and philosophy were bearing fruit as his two hundred or more students were spread all over Iran and among the Shi'i community abroad. Far and wide they had become leading local clerics representing one of the grand ayatollahs, leading prayers, teaching theology and preaching. As a gradualist, Khomeini established his credentials as a prominent religious leader before moving on to the political arena in order both to strengthen his standing within the religious establishment and to widen his power base in general. Khomeini regarded his two main patrons, Kashani and Borujerdi, as two facets of Muhammad: Kashani the political and Borujerdi the religious leader. Neither of them were ideal for Khomeini although both are said to have pointed to Khomeini as Iran's future religious leader. Khomeini's political instinct taught him to express his often unconventional and radical views, persuading others to adopt similar positions while at the same time adhering to the consensus of the Qom establishment under the patronage of Borujerdi.

Theologically speaking, Khomeini was not in a position to become another Borujerdi, as he was young and there were many ageing senior ayatollahs still alive. Many clerics have faced a similar predicament, including Ha'eri and Na'ini, both of whom had reached the highest level of learning but neither of whom had the chance to achieve ultimate leadership, to become senior *marja-e taqlid*, because of the longevity of their seniors. On the other hand, Khomeini did not want to become another Kashani, whom he saw as misunderstood by the Qom and the Tehran clergy, and from whom religious nationalists such as Mehdi Bazargan, Ayatollahs Reza and Abolfazl Zanjani and Taleqani distanced themselves, blaming him for Mosaddeq's downfall. Having the Feda'ian-e Islam and Kashani as examples of forces which did not have the support of the majority of the clerical establishment and which were eventually isolated and defeated, Khomeini did not want to break with the theological circles. In fact, his criticism of Kashani was that instead of trying to Islamize politics, he politicized Islam. Khomeini's aim was to ensure that this did not happen to him.

After the coup against Mosaddeq, the Shah gradually regained his self-confidence, and this subsequently affected his relationship with Borujerdi. The Shah was no longer willing to visit Borujerdi at his home and their last meeting had been a non-event. The sick man was helped out of his bed and taken in a horse-drawn carriage to the Shrine where he was made to sit on a chair for almost an hour to await the Shah. Two officers helped him stand on his feet as the Shah approached. The Shah did not shake the old man's hand, a hand which he had kissed many times in the past, let alone pay him homage. He merely said the customary greeting 'Ahval-e Aqa Chetor Ast' (How is the health of your good self?),[37] but did not wait for a reply, or exchange any other words, before leaving the old man. The meeting was seen as a deliberate humiliation to Borujerdi and the clergy. Khomeini and his students saw the Shah's growing 'arrogance' as an indication of Borujerdi's weakness. Furthermore, in their view, he was now surrounded by the Shah's agents.

Borujerdi died in March 1961 and the battle of succession started. On the seventh day after Borujerdi's death, the pro-Shah Ayatollah Behbahani came to Qom to invite the leading mullahs in Qom to form a group to look after the theological colleges and possibly find a replacement for Borujerdi. At the time, Khomeini was only fifty-nine. Unhappy with Behbahani's role at court and incensed by his non-intervention in the execution of Navvab-Safavi, Khomeini took part in the meeting but not in the discussions. There were more senior clerics in Qom, Mashad and Najaf. He gave the impression that he wanted to be known only as a teacher and not as a 'source of emulation'. Khomeini's students asked him to come forward. Khomeini is said to have declined indicating that there were others more senior than he. Another reason for his reluctance to put his name forward was that some of his teachers were still alive and considered to be more suitable, an important factor in theological centres. Distinguishing himself by absence and apparent lack of ambition, Khomeini became more popular with those who knew him. Khomeini had already placed a good number of his students in key positions throughout Iran and a number of other countries. When the time came to stand up to the Shah's regime, support was forthcoming from everywhere and the influence of his students was such that they could even lobby for further support among reluctant and apolitical clerics.

The death of Borujerdi was in many ways a watershed in clergy-state relations. For the government, Borujerdi's death was a blessing in disguise. In the absence of such a powerful personality the government felt that it would be easier to embark upon social change and thus alleviate both internal and external pressure. Borujerdi, who had earlier supported the Shah, had on several occasions aborted government attempts to introduce reforms, including land reforms.

After Borujerdi's death the Shah seemed to be indirectly intervening in clerical affairs by sending a telegram of condolence to Grand Ayatollah Hakim in Najaf. Hakim, an Arab and an Iraqi citizen, was by no means an obvious choice as Borujerdi's replacement, nor did he ever attain Borujerdi's stature. He was possibly the most popular clergyman among the Shi'i Arabs in Lebanon, Iraq and the Gulf, but he knew little about Iranian politics. Other, possibly more obvious, candidates included Ayatollahs Seyyed Abdolhadi Shirazi, Kho'i and Shahrudi in Iraq, and at least six Ayatollahs in Iran. The departure of Borujerdi also meant that the Shah no longer felt himself bound to consult the clergy over plans that had possible religious implications. It also gave clerics like Khomeini a free hand to act according to their own judgement, as they no longer had a need for Borujerdi's approval.

Moreover, the absence of both Borujerdi and Kashani gave Khomeini an extra incentive to accomplish what they had failed to obtain: a successful fusion of religion and politics. Khomeini campaigned a great deal in private, and, after Borujerdi's death, in public, to eradicate the stigma attached to *Akhund-e siasi*, or 'The political mullah'. Politics and religion is one, he often declared. Khomeini was not unfamiliar with politicians in Tehran. He had met with several ministers and prime ministers in his role as advisor to Borujerdi. Among these were Dr Eqbal and Dr Ali Amini, respectively a former and the current prime minister.

On the morning of 2 January 1962, which coincided with the birthday of Imam Ali, Amini, who was trying to initiate certain reforms and also establish his authority as prime minister in the face of the Shah's increasing autocracy, went to Qom to meet Khomeini, Golpaygani, Shariatmadari and Mar'ashi–Najafi. At about midday along with his aides and deputies, Amini had a meeting with Khomeini as one of the four leading Qom theologians. After the customary greetings, the guests were offered tea and Persian biscuits. Khomeini and Amini indulged in a lively debate on the role of the clergy and government in society as well as on clerical expectations of the government and vice versa. What has been published of Khomeini's conversation with Dr Amini indicates Khomeini's desire for winning concessions from the government when it was trying to enlist the clergy's support for its reforms. In January 1962, some ten months after Borujerdi's death, the government was in a position to go ahead with the land reform plan. The conservative clergy and landowners were disenchanted but neither Khomeini nor the newly established ayatollahs raised any objections. At their meeting Khomeini did not utter a word about land reform. In Amini's words, 'He was unhappy about the divorce procedures, and I assured him of our cooperation to rectify the issue.'[38] Amini, however, was replaced by Asadollah Alam, a well-known landlord and a close personal friend of the Shah.

After some twenty years of relative harmony between the ulama and the Shah, the first clash of wills was to be won by the clergy, with Khomeini as the main benefactor. The challenge was kindled by a report in Tehran's newspapers on 7 October 1962 that women were to be given the right to vote. The new bill also abolished Islamic legal requirements, replacing the Qur'an with the 'Holy Book'. The news caused immediate uproar in Qom. Khomeini, for his part, used the occasion to draw the attention of Muslims to the 'threat' that the government posed for Islam. To avoid any unwarranted breach of protocol, Khomeini decided to invite his clerical rivals to the home of their teacher. Later that evening Khomeini and two other leading clerics in Qom, Ayatollahs Shariatmadari and Golpaygani, met at Haeri's residence and at this extraordinary meeting the three men discussed the issue, its consequences, and possible courses of action.[39] It was at this crucial meeting that some of Khomeini's leadership qualities began to emerge.

After the exchange of a number of terse telegrams between the leading ulama and the state, protest against the bill spread in Qom and Tehran, and two months after it had been passed, the cabinet had to swallow its pride and nullify the bill. Thus, not only did the Shah's determination to carry out his reforms meet a major, although temporary, setback, but a new political-religious militancy with a maximalist leader emerged. The government's retreat over the local election law encouraged the traditional bazaaris to help their clerical allies retrieve an historical power base which had been gradually lost under the Pahlavis. After the repeal of the local election bill a group of bazaaris went to meet with Khomeini in Qom. Their discussions led to an agreement on a more organized system of informing their constituency and criticizing the unislamic practices of the regime. From then on the duplication and distribution of Khomeini's directives were put on a more organized footing. Acting as a link and a guide for different groups of bazaaris, he helped them establish an alliance under the title of *Hey'athay-e Mo'talefeh-e Eslami*, the Islamic Coalition of Mourning Groups.

In January 1963 the Shah took what was possibly the most daring decision of his monarchy by accepting direct responsibility for social reform. Emulating his father, the Shah was intent on implementing change and proving where real power lay, arguing that he alone could tackle the social, political and economic problems of the country without having to ally himself politically with the left or the right. His six-point reform bill, which he had put to a referendum, included land reform and reform of the electoral laws to include women. The programme was a bold attempt to change the face of Iranian society as well as a challenge to the clergy. Certain that a substantial proportion of the leading clergy would not support the militants led by Khomeini, the Shah did not expect a major challenge to his authority. He could not possibly have foreseen the dramatic turn of events that followed.

On 23 January 1963 Qom witnessed the outbreak of the discontent and calculated wrath of the clergy. The clashes and bloody riots that ensued challenged the Shah and finally led to the arrest and transfer of Khomeini to Tehran. When he was brought back to Qom on 7 March 1964, Khomeini was no longer viewed as merely one of the leading ayatollahs but as an ayatollah who had achieved the political leadership of the clergy. Another opportunity for Khomeini to consolidate his political position arose in autumn 1964 when parliament passed a bill granting US military personnel extra-territorial rights. Khomeini's attack on the government and his reference, in a speech on 27 October 1964, to the fact that Iran's sovereignty had been trampled on, were not to be without consequence. Once again he was arrested and taken to Tehran. This time, however, the Shah decided to banish him.

The departure of Khomeini, first to Turkey and from there to

Iraq, rid the Shah of a major obstacle to his reforms as well as an important and powerful source of opposition to his rule. However, Khomeini's influence was not to wane completely. It had merely been driven underground. Khomeini's first general political statement in Najaf proved that SAVAK was justified in fearing his determination. SAVAK tried, though without success, to stem his sources of income in Iran. His direct contact with Iran, however, was considerably curtailed.

Having lost direct contact with his constituency in Iran and hope of mobilizing the mullahs of Najaf, Khomeini began to develop a relationship with Iranian student bodies abroad. Among the members of these groups were students like Abolhassan Bani-Sadr, Ebrahim Yazdi and Sadeq Qotbzadeh, who were to become prominent personalities during the 1979 Islamic Revolution.

Meanwhile Khomeini wrote his *Tahrir al-Wasilah*, a commentary on a traditional theological text which also covered socio-political issues abandoned by his contemporaries – such as holy war, ordering the good and forbidding evil. The book gave Khomeini the status of a jurist. Here, Khomeini returned to the question of Islamic government with vigour, taking up where he had left off in *Kashf al-Asrar*. Khomeini now stated that the Imam, or leader of the Muslim community, has the right to fix prices or impose trade restrictions, if he feels it is in the interest of Islamic society. He also tackles many political issues in terms of foreign policy, aiming to prevent the Muslim community from falling under the influence of foreigners.

Khomeini, the jurisprudent, was now in Najaf and among the rival mullahs whom he did not trust; nor he was trusted by them. It took him five years in the city of Najaf before he felt confident enough to tell the clergy that they were not doing enough. In fact Khomeini did not challenge the Najaf clergy while Ayatollah Sayyed Mohsen Hakim was active and well. In 1970 Hakim's health was in decline and he was under pressure from the Iraqi government. Khomeini, who did not see any of the other leading ayatollahs as real rivals, went back to the topic of Islamic government. He delivered a number of lectures from 21 January to 8 February 1970, presenting a survey of 'the hopelessness and impotence of the Islamic world'.[40] He referred to the manner in which Muslims had been wronged by Jews, Christians, imperialism and colonialism, with the help of servile and corrupt rulers.[41] Criticizing the clergy for indulging in scholastic and pedantic points, on topics such as menstruation and outward cleanliness, he addressed his audience who, he said, were to assume future responsibility for the introduction of Islamic laws and systems.[42]

Khomeini encouraged his students to realize that it was their duty 'to establish an Islamic government', and to have confidence in their own ability to fulfil this task. He urged the clergy to work towards the establishment of an Islamic state by assuming responsibility for executive, legislative and judicial positions. He also set out a programme of action to achieve this, commencing with major reform within the theological centres.

Khomeini's main theoretical position in giving legitimacy to such an Islamic state was his doctrine of *Velayat-e Faqih*, which has been variously translated as the Vicegerency of the Theologian, The Governance of the Jurist or the Guardianship of the Jurisconsult.

Despite occasional activities by the opposition, the Shah was in a powerful position from the mid-1960s to the mid-1970s, when he introduced Iran as 'an island of stability' and prosperity. The fact that Khomeini issued only a dozen statements or so addressing the Iranian people inside the country during this period, reflects the fact that he was not treading on fertile ground.

The first crack in the solid wall of 'stability' and continuity appeared in 1977 as the Shah replaced his loyal prime minister, Amir Abbas Hoveyda who had served him for twelve years, with an apparently more energetic man, Jamshid Amouzegar. At this time, nobody knew that the Shah was suffering from cancer and had undergone a treatment a month before. In October the clerical establishment was shocked to hear that Khomeini's eldest son, Mostafa, had died under mysterious circumstances. This event was to give Khomeini considerable media coverage.[43] People flocked to Khomeini's family home in Qom to offer their condolences to his brother Mortaza Pasandideh and the rest of the family. Responding to telegrams and letters of condolence, Khomeini took the opportunity to depersonalise the issue.[44] Yet he did not hesitate to exploit the situation.

The appearance of an article on 6 January 1978 in the daily *Ettela'at* insulting Khomeini triggered street demonstrations and clashes with the army in Qom, leaving six dead. On the fortieth day (*arba'ain*) of the deaths in Qom, Tabriz revolted and soon each confrontation and death led to uprisings in other cities. As the wildfire spread, the Shah became a target of abuse and vilification. Seizing the hour and reflecting the national mood, in an interview with Le Monde, Khomeini took the internal opposition by surprise, declaring that the Pahlavi dynasty must be overthrown, adding that the ideal would be the establishment of an Islamic state.[45] Sensing his undisputed leadership of the anti-Shah movement, Khomeini distanced himself from the left and called directly on the army to join the people's movement.[46] In Paris, he spoke of a 'progressive Islam' in which even a woman could become president and in which 'Islamic rules of retribution would not be applied unless sufficient preparations had been made to implement Islamic justice in its totality.'[47]

In this period Khomeini did not discuss his theory of the 'Guardianship of the Jurisconsult' let alone his views of mystical guardianship. He referred only to the supervisory role of the clergy. In Khomeini's camp there were just two more goals to be acheived: the departure of the Shah and the return of Khomeini.[48] The first objective came nearer when on 10 and 11 December 1978, the two important religious days of Tasu'a and Ashura, 9 and 10 Muharram, millions of people marched peacefully through Tehran demanding the removal of the Shah and the return of Khomeini. Khomeini took the initiative by publicizing his three-point plan of action which he had already circulated among the candidates for a revolutionary council and provisional government. Unveiling the plan to the Iranian people, he claimed that '... according to religious rights and based on the vote of confidence in me by an absolute majority of the people, a council called the Islamic Revolutionary Council has been formed. Its members will be introduced at the earliest possible opportunity.'[49] The appointment of a Revolutionary Council was the first step towards the establishment of necessary institutions for governing Iran.

On 16 January 1978 an ailing and sad Shah packed his bags and left the country, never to return. Two weeks later, on 1 February, a victorious Khomeini was back in Iran, greeted by millions of Iranians as the leader of the revolution.

The Ruler

The man who had talked about the creation of a perfect government, perfect society and perfect men was now at the helm of authority. The politician, the jurisprudent, the mystic was in power. Once in Tehran, Khomeini's tone began to change. He was well aware that he soon had to be ready to take over the apparatus of the state. Organization was necessary. He had also to establish his own position without alienating those who had helped the revolution. Drawing his legitimacy from the concept of *Velayat-e Faqih*, which had earlier been rejected by Shi'i clerics, Khomeini appointed Mehdi Bazargan as prime minister even before the army declared its neutrality. Khomeini's reference to the concept of *Velayat-e Faqih* went unnoticed at the time.

Khomeini was now planning to establish the Islamic rule he had theorized before. His immediate concern was the consolidation of power. He believed that without power evil could not be eradicated, truth could not be established and Islam could not be implemented. The first step was to purge the revolution from the 'forces of evil' and those who had served the old regime. Within a short period, Amir Abbas Hoveyda, former prime minister, and over two hundred of the Shah's top generals and officials were shot. Execution of lower ranking military personnel, officials and people accused of a variety of 'crimes' followed later.

The new value system introduced by Khomeini was not easily identifiable as traditionally Islamic. Khomeini and his followers used a vocabulary which was essentially that of a 'revolutionary Islam'. The God most revolutionaries were referring to was no longer 'compassionate and merciful', as every chapter of the Qur'an starts with, it was rather a vengeful 'smasher of the tyrants'. The language of class struggle appeared in a religious guise.

The differences between revolutionary Khomeini and gradualist Bazargan were not confined to human rights issues, as had been the case in the early days of the new regime. It was the difference in their attitude, in their world view and their vision of future Iran. The occupation of the American Embassy in Tehran on 4 November 1979 by pro-Khomeini radical students was the last straw for Bazargan. Khomeini readily accepted Bazargan's resignation and charged the Revolutionary Council to take over the responsibilities of the executive and the legislative branch, while preparing for a constitutional referendum and presidential elections.

At this time Khomeini's discourse became both more egalitarian and more radical. He besieged the Revolutionary Council to look after the poor and the homeless, whom he increasingly referred to as the pillar of the revolution. His repeated references to the poor and the homeless was partly idealistic and partly political. Weary of the political criticism of the intellectuals, leftists, nationalists and liberals, Khomeini was intent on silencing them. The hostage taking at the American Embassy allowed him to associate any discontent with and criticism of the Islamic government with American interests. He said that America did not intervene by force but infiltrated through the pen.[50]

Step by step all positions of power were placed under the watchful eyes of the clergy and all opposition effectively was neutralized, suppressed, physically annihilated or co-opted. In October 1981 the position of the president, which had been occupied by non-clerical figures, was also given to a clergyman, Hojjat al-Islam Ali Khamane'i. So internally, Khomeini had attained his primary objectives of Islamizing the state according to his own perception of Islam.

To assure the survival and continuity of the Islamic state, Khomeini turned to the question of succession. In November 1985, following Khomeini's advice, the Assembly of Experts appointed Ayatollah Hossain Ali Montazeri to succeed Khomeini. Montazeri was a distinguished theologian and a former student of Khomeini. Yet his sincere protestations against the abuse of human rights in general, and in Iranian prisons in particular, corruption, the abuse of power by government officials and, finally, red tape in the Islamic republic were seen by Khomeini and the clergy in power as naive, disloyal and ultimately dangerous. In March 1989 Khomeini sought Montazeri's resignation and set up a body to review the constitution.

The removal of Montazeri, who was probably the only leading theologian after Khomeini with the necessary revolutionary credentials, was a turning point. Later the Assembly of Experts had to appoint a lesser man, who lacked the stature of Khomeini, as his successor, as no major *faqih* was available to lead the country according to Khomeini's principle of Guardianship (*velayat*).

Even before the removal of Montazeri, Khomeini was experiencing major difficulties in ruling the country. In the face of growing pressure to find answers to the daily problems of the government in Islamic texts and settle differences between his aides, Khomeini was forced to take drastic measures. In January 1988, Khomeini issued his historical statement on *Velayate Motlaqeh-ye Faqih* or the absolute rule of the theologian. He asserted: 'Islamic government, which stems from the absolute guardianship of the Prophet Muhammad, is one of the primary injunctions in Islam, taking precedence over all subsidiary precepts, even praying, fasting, and performing the Hajj.'[51] In Khomeini's view such an absolute authority could even abrogate the constitution. As an unprecedented move, it seemed that the *faqih* was now able to change, or at least revoke, legal rulings which had been firmly enshrined as part of Islamic law, for the sake of some higher principle. It was an unprecedented statement by any Shi'ite clergyman. Was it Khomeini the jurisprudent who was extending his absolute rule to all paths of life in order to preserve the Islamic government, or was it Khomeini the mystic who was fusing *Velayat-e Motlaqa-y Erfani*, or absolute gnostic rule, with politics? What is obvious is Khomeini's reaction to events was gradually showing itself in his impatience and dissatisfaction with the guiding role of the clergy. This prompted him to justify the *faqih*'s assumption of absolute political power. But he failed to carry the religious centre with him in constructing enduring arguments for extending the *faqih*'s power.

Khomeini's final show of power was his *fatwa* (edict) against the British author Salman Rushdie, on 14 February 1989. The edict called on all zealous Muslims to execute Rushdie for having insulted Islamic sanctities. Khomeini added that whoever was killed in performing this duty would be considered a martyr.[52] For Khomeini who had been deprived of apparently certain victory against Iraq on the war front, the *Satanic Verses* must have seemed as yet another international, imperialist conspiracy against the Islamic Revolution. Whether he used the issue simply to strengthen his flagging popularity remains to be shown. Within Iran there were forces who wanted to bring the issue under control but they failed.

Conclusion

As a statesman Khomeini was bound by the Shari'a and expediency of politics. His vision of Islam was reactive. The emphasis was on what is not Islamic rather than providing a blueprint for an Islamic society. In opposition his vagueness was an asset; in power, a handicap. His interpretation of Islam was that he should not be compromising. Yet the reality of politics made him compromise. His inflexible approach to Iran's relations with other countries cost Iran billions of dollars and many thousands of lives during the war with Iraq. He failed to see the realities of international politics and provoked the animosity of both the USSR and the USA.

Furthermore, he did not travel inside Iran after his return from exile and all his information came from the small group of associates that met with him on a regular basis. Up to the end of his life he was under the impression that the great majority of the Iranian people were supporting him and the other clergy who had formed the new ruling class of Iran.

His most serious shortcoming was in the area of human rights. He considered all those who opposed him and his government as infidels who could and should be liquidated in the interest of Iran and Islam. Iran used to have the dubious distinction of the country with the highest execution rate in the world. In Khomeini's utopian world there was no room for dissent. Dissidents were treated with the same severity that the Spanish Inquisition reserved for heretics in its heyday.

Khomeini's lack of clarity on many non-religious issues, such as inflation, foreign trade, the role of the private sector in the economy, the limits to private property and so on, were a great source of confusion for government officials. These points of contention were also used by different factions in Iran to promote their own cause by giving different and contradictory quotations of Khomeini to justify their own actions.

Khomeini, under international and internal pressure to ensure the survival of the Islamic state, gave supremacy to the state over religious tenets – unheard of in Shi'i Islam. This brought Iran in line with Sunni Islam, where 'those in authority' must be obeyed.

Yet on another level, Khomeini was a believer in the institutionalization of Islam. It was these institutions which enabled the young republic to survive him. What he has left behind is not a democracy. Yet the system is representative of various trends among the Islamicists, reflecting their divisions and pains as they attempt to find an Islamic response to Iran's acute socio-economic problems.

Khomeini, who fervently wanted the survival of the Islamic government was in favour of gradual change from within. Pragmatically, he allowed things considered forbidden in the past like contraception, playing chess, buying and selling musical instruments, and changes in land ownership.

Khomeini felt bound by what he regarded as the rules of religion, but above the law of the land. It was he and he alone who was the final arbiter over the law-makers. Having attempted to impose his own version of Islam on a complicated government machinery and having failed to come up with answers to many social, economic and foreign policy problems, he in effect exposed the inability of religion to cope with many of the problems that Iran is facing today. This has divided his followers into those who believe that religious leaders should leave politics to the politicians, and those who advocate direct clerical intervention. This approach will not absolve the clergy who have been tainted with politics. Another section of Khomeini's followers, such as the present ruling leadership, are of the view that a broad-minded interpretation of Islamic rules and regulations will enable the Islamic state to cater for the spiritual needs of the faithful as well as their worldly needs. In the first case Islam would effectively be subjected to the power of the state now that it had been placed above religion. In the latter, it would be diluted to a degree that would make it difficult to recognize from what it was before the revolution. While the young militant are carrying Khomeini's picture in the streets of Bradford, Baku and Kashmir, Khomeini's subjects are busy reinterpreting his rulings and dismantling his legacy.

Khomeini the politician was a powerful fusion; intoxicated by the cosmic vision of a mystic, yet bound by the firm belief of a jurisprudent who carried out God's command. As a mystic, Khomeini was an elitist but as a theologian he was expedient, while as a politician he was a populist who believed in the use of force and, if need be, violence. He was calculating to the point of opportunism. The three facets of his personality – jurist, mystic and politician – should not be regarded as three separate personalities in one. For him there was no separation between being a jurist, a mystic or a politician. At the same time, driven by his personal experience as a mystic and theologian, even in politics he strove to push the community, as he puts it, towards a state of perfection. In reality the society he ruled over was far from perfect. No one can deny his charisma or role in modern Islamic and Iranian history, but he will eventually be judged on the results of his policies, pronouncements and actions rather than his heart-felt and sincere intentions.

Notes

1. Nour-baksh, Sayyad Hassan; Yadvare-ye Nahzate Eslami (Chehre-ye Enghelab dar Esfahan), Tehran, 1982, p. 6.

2. Personal interview with Nader Naderpour. London, 29 November 1982.

3. Chesmandaz, edited by N. Pakdaman, no. 5, 1988, Paris p. 26.

4. Khomeini, Ahmad; interviewed by Hamid Algar. Tehran, 12 September 1982.

5. Sobhani, Ayatollah Ja'far in *Howzeh*, no. 32, June 1989, Qom. Also Reza Ostadi, in *Keyhan Farhangi*, no. 3, June 1989, Tehran.

6. Khomeini, Ahmad, in *Sargozashthaye Vizheh*, vol. 1, Tehran, Payam-e Azadi Publications, 1985, p. 128.

7. Shahabadi's Biography, *Nour-e Elm* Monthly, no. 9, April 1985, Qom.

8. Fehri, Sayyad Ahmad, introduction to *Sharh-e Do'aye Sahar*, Tehran, 1982, p. 8.

9. Khomeini, Ayatollah Ruhollah, *Sharh Du'a al-Sahar* ('Dawn Supplication'), edited by S.A. Fehri, Beirut, 1982.

10. Khomeini, Ayatollah Ruhollah, in *Yadname-ye Ostad-e Shahid Mortaza Motahhari*, vol. 1, Tehran: Sazemane Entesharat va amouzesh-e Enghelab-e Eslami, pp. 30–100.

11. Personal interview with Mehdi Hae'ri, London, November 1985.

12. Khomeini, Ahmad, in *Sargozashthaye Vizheh*, vol. 1, Tehran, Payam-e Azadi Publications, 1985, p. 128.

13. Khomeini, Ayatollah Ruhollah, *Sahife-ye Nour*, vol. 14, Tehran, Vezarat-e Ershad-e Eslami, 1982, p. 134.

14. A. Ferhi in introduction to 'Dawn Supplication', Beirut, 1982.

15. J. Sobhani in *Keyhan-e Farhangi*, no. 3, Tehran, 1989. Also Sadegh-e Khalkhali in *Yad Quarterly*, no. 4, Tehran, 1986.

16. Khomeini, R, *Kashf-al-Asrar*, n.p, n.d, pp. 8–10.

17. *Ibid.*

18. Rouhani, S.H, *Nahzat-e Imam Khomeini*, vol. 1, Tehran, 1982, p. 39.

19. *Resalat*, 25 February 1989.

20. Saduqi, in *Sargozashthaye Vizheh*, vol. 3, Tehran, Payam-e Azadi Publications, 1983, p. 134.

21. Tehrani, M.S, in *Yad Quarterly*, no. 4, Tehran, 1986.

22. Khomeini, Ayatollah Ruhollah, *Sahife-ye Nour*, vol. 1, Tehran, Vezarat-e Ershad-e Eslami, 1982, pp. 1–4.

23. *Ibid.*

24. Khomeini, R, *Kashf-al-Asrar*, n.p, n.d, p. 9.

25. Khomeini, R, *Kashf-al-Asrar*, n.p, n.d, p. 5.

26. *Ibid.*

27. Khomeini, R, *Kashf-al-Asrar*, n.p, n.d, p. 105.

28. *Ibid.*

29. *Ibid.*

30. *Ibid.*

31. *Ibid.*

32. Khomeini, Ayatollah Ruhollah, *Sahife-ye Nour*, vol. 3, Tehran, Vezarat-e Ershad-e Eslami, 1982, p. 36.

33. Mahallati, F, in *Yad Quarterly*, no. 2–3, Tehran, 1986.

34. Razi, M, *Athar-Al-Hojjah*, vol. 2, Qom, 1374 H, pp. 44–5.

35. *Ibid.*

36. *Ibid.*
37. *Yad Quarterly*, vol. 6, Tehran, 1987, p. 29.
38. Personal interview with Ali Amini, Paris, November 1982.
39. Rouhani, S.H., *Nahzat-e Imam Khomeini*, vol. 1, Tehran, 1982, p. 149.
40. Khomeini, R, *Hokumat-e Eslami*, n.p, 1971, pp. 1–25.
41. *Ibid.*
42. Khomeini, R, *Hokumat-e Eslami*, n.p, 1971, p. 9.
43. Akhavan Towhidi, H, *Dar Pass-e Pardeh-ye Tazvir*, Paris, 1986, p. 52.
44. Khomeini, Ayatollah Ruhollah, *Sahife-ye Nour*, vol. 1, Tehran, Vezarat-e Ershad-e Eslami, 1982, p. 249.
45. Khomeini, Ayatollah Ruhollah, *Sahife-ye Nour*, vol. 2, Tehran, Vezarat-e Ershad-e Eslami, 1982, p. 46.
46. *Ibid.*, p. 98.
47. *Ibid.*, p. 259.
48. Yazdi, E, *Akharin Talashha dar Akharin Rouzha*, Tehran: Entesharat-e Qalam, 1984, p. 119.
49. Khomeini, Ayatollah Ruhollah, *Sahife-ye Nour*, vol. 4, Tehran, Vezarat-e Ershad-e Eslami, 1982, p. 207.
50. *Ibid.*, pp. 148–57.
51. Reported in SWB, BBC Monitoring, Reading, UK, 7 January 1989.
52. Reported in SWB, BBC Monitoring, Reading, UK, 15 February 1989.

5

Mawdudi and the Jama'at-i Islami: The Origins, Theory and Practice of Islamic Revivalism

Seyyed Vali Reza Nasr

Sayyid Abu'l-A'la Mawdudi is a central figure in the revival of Islam in recent decades. His interpretation of Islam has formed the foundation of contemporary Islamic revivalist thought. Prolific and articulate, he has greatly influenced contemporary Muslim thinkers from Mindanao to Morocco. From Sayyid Qutb of Egypt to Algerian, Iranian, Malaysian or Sudanese revivalist activists, Islamic revivalism has evolved around Mawdudi's prolegomenon.[1] In South Asia, where Mawdudi's exegesis found shape, his influence has been most pronounced. The organization that has embodied his ideological vision, the Jama'at-i Islami (the Islamic Party), has over the course of the last fifty years had an important role in the history and politics of Pakistan, India, Bangladesh, Sri Lanka, and the South Asian communities of the Persian Gulf, as well as those resident in the West.[2] The extent of Mawdudi's intellectual influence and political impact makes a study of his biography, the origins of his ideological perspective, his vision of Islamic revolution and the Islamic state, and their manifestation in the politics of the Jama'at important for understanding the politicization of Islamic thought in recent times. This article will examine each of these issues in turn.

The Making of the Revivalist: Mawdudi's Life and Education

Mawdudi was born in the city of Aurangabad in South India on 25 September 1903 (3 Rajab 1321). He was born into a *sharif* (North Indian Muslim notables) family from Delhi who had settled in the Deccan. The family traced its lineage to the great Sufi saints of the Chishti order, who helped plant the seed of Islam in Indian soil.[3] Mawdudi's family had served the Moghuls, and had been especially close to the court during the reign of Bahadur Shah Zafar, the last ruler of that dynasty.[4] The Mawdudis had suffered a loss in status following the Great Mutiny and fall of the Moghul dynasty in 1858. The legacy of their service to Muslim rulers led them to continue to identify with the glories of Muslim history in India; they were therefore not reconciled to British rule.

The Mawdudis eventually moved from Delhi and settled in the Deccan. There they served generations of the Nizams of Hyderabad.[5] Mawdudi's maternal family was also of north Indian origin and had served the Nizams. The family's close identification with the heritage of Muslim rule over India, its aristocratic pretensions, and its dislike of the British played a central role in shaping Mawdudi's world view in later years.

Sayyid Ahmad Hasan, Mawdudi's father, was among the first to attend Sayyid Ahmad Khan's Muslim Anglo-Oriental College at Aligarh, and to participate in that experiment with Islamic modernism.[6] However, he did not remain there for long. He left Aligarh to complete his education in law in Allahabad, and then he settled in the Deccan, first in Hyderabad and later in Aurangabad. In Hyderabad he became a Sufi and for a time moved to Delhi and devoted himself to the shrine of Nizam'uddin Awliya'.[7] Ahmad Hasan's love for Sufism and his puritanical streak created a strongly religious and ascetic environment for the education of his children. Ahmad Hasan took great pains to raise his children in the *sharif* culture. He educated them in the classical educational system, excluding English and modern subjects from their curricula.[8] They were educated at home in Arabic, Persian and Urdu, reading religious and literary texts for a number of years. Mawdudi became well versed in Arabic at a young age. His mastery of Arabic was such that at the age of fourteen he translated Qasim Amin's *Al-Mirat al-Jadidah* ('Modern Women') from Arabic to Urdu.[9]

At the age of eleven Mawdudi was enrolled at a school in

Aurangabad where he was taught modern subjects, especially the sciences, for the first time. Mawdudi was compelled to abandon his formal education altogether five years later at the age of sixteen, after his father fell seriously ill and died.[10] Thenceforth Mawdudi pursued his intellectual interests on his own. He was not interested in religious issues, but purely political ones. His passion then was Indian nationalism. For instance, between 1918 and 1919 he wrote essays in praise of Congress party leaders, particularly Mahatma Gandhi and Madan Muhan Malaviya.[11] In 1918 he moved to Bijnur to join his brother, Abu'l-Khayr, where he embarked on a career in journalism.

Before long the brothers moved to Delhi, and there Mawdudi came into contact with an array of intellectual currents within the Muslim community. He learned about modernist views and became involved in the independence movement. In 1919 he moved to Jubalpur to work for the pro-Congress party weekly, Taj. There he became fully active in the Khilafat movement,[12] and in mobilizing Muslims in support of the Congress Party.[13] He wrote passionately in defence of his cause, which resulted in the closing of the weekly.

Mawdudi then returned to Delhi, where he became acquainted with such important Khilafat leaders as Muhammad 'Ali, with whom Mawdudi briefly cooperated in publishing the nationalist newspaper Hamdard. It was during this period that his political outlook became increasingly religious. He briefly joined the Tahrik-i Hijrat (Migration Movement) protest which encouraged Indian Muslims to emigrate from British India – dar al-harb (abode of war) to Muslim-ruled Afghanistan, itself seen as dar al-Islam (abode of Islam).[14]

It was at this juncture, in 1921, that Mawdudi became acquainted with the leadership of the Jami'at-i 'Ulama-i Hind (Society of Indian Ulama), Mawlanas Mufti Kifayatu'llah and Ahmad Sa'id in particular.[15] The eminent Jami'at ulama were impressed with Mawdudi's talents and invited him to edit their official newspaper, Muslim. Mawdudi remained in the service of the ulama in the Jami'at until 1924 as editor of the Muslim and its successor, al-Jami'at. It was in the service of the Jami'at that he became more acutely aware of Muslim political consciousness, and became openly active in the affairs of his faith. He began to write on issues of concern to Indian Muslims, the plight of Turkey in the face of European imperialism, and the glories of Muslim rule in India. Although his tone became increasingly communalist and overtly political, revival of Islam was not as yet a central focus of his writings.

The stay in Delhi also provided Mawdudi with the opportunity to continue to learn and grow intellectually. For instance, he learned English and read western works. His association with the Jami'at also encouraged him to receive a formal religious education. He commenced the *dars-i nizami* (the syllabus of religious education which has been popular in seminaries in South Asia since the eighteenth century), studying first with 'Abdu'ssalam Niyazi, and later with Deobandi ulama of the Fatihpuri mosque's seminary in Delhi.[16] In 1926 he received his certificate in religious training (*ijazah*) and became one of the ulama. Interestingly, Mawdudi never acknowledged his status as an *'alim*, and his tie to the Deobandi tradition did not come to light until after his death. Most biographies of Mawdudi simply identify him as a journalist who was self-taught in religious subjects.

With the collapse of the Khilafat Movement in 1924, Mawdudi's life took a major turn. He became cynical about nationalism, which he now believed had misguided Turks and Egyptians, leading them to undermine Muslim unity by rejecting the Ottoman empire and Muslim caliphate. He also lost faith in Indian nationalism, believing that the Congress Party was merely parading Hindu interests under the guise of nationalist sentiments. His approach became openly communalist, revealing a dislike for the nationalist movement and its Muslim allies. It was at this time that he found his views at odds with the ulama of the Jami'at, who supported the Congress in its fight to end British rule. Mawdudi left the Jami'at, parting ways with his Deobandi mentors.

It should be noted that his disagreement with the Jami'at and opposition to the Congress did not mean that he was reconciled to British rule. He rather advocated an Islamic as opposed to a nationalist anti-imperialist platform, one which would combat colonialism as it safeguarded Muslim interests. He put forward a communalist platform which was articulated in religious language. Taken to its logical conclusion it soon gave place to a revivalist discourse. The course of events, moreover, soon imbued Mawdudi's persona with a sense of mission, permitting him to clarify his views and produce a new religious and political platform.

In 1925 a Muslim killed Swami Shradhanand, a Hindu revivalist leader who had advocated reconverting low caste converts to Islam back to Hinduism. The Swami had raised the ire of Muslims after he publicly slighted Muslim beliefs. His death led to criticisms of Islam as a religion of violence in the Indian press. Mawdudi was prompted to action by this response, especially after he heard the Khilafat leader, Muhammad 'Ali, invite Muslims to action.[17] It was then that Mawdudi wrote his famous book on war and peace, violence and *jihad* in Islam, *al-Jihad fi'l-Islam*. The book was then the only systematic explanation of the Muslim position on *jihad* to respond to the criticism of Islam, and continues to be one of the most lucid treatments extant of this theme by a revivalist thinker. It was well received by the Muslims,[18] whose accolade confirmed Mawdudi as an intellectual leader of his community.

From this point on Mawdudi dedicated his life to leading his community to political and religious salvation. In 1928 he moved to Hyderabad, where he wrote extensively on an array of subjects.[19] He completed a number of translations of philosophical and exegetic works from Arabic, wrote accounts of the history of Hyderabad, and prepared texts of Islamic studies at the behest of the Nizam's government, the most important of which was his seminal introduction to Islam, *Risalah-i Diniyat* (later translated as *Towards Understanding Islam*). It was in Hyderabad that his greater religiosity first manifested itself. He grew a beard and adopted Indo-Muslim attire. He had 'reconverted' to Islam, assuming a new outlook which was religious in content but was motivated by his reading of political imperatives.

The future of Hyderabad, this last remnant of Muslim rule of India, did not appear certain at the time. Its majority Hindu population was showing signs of unrest, and the Nizam's power was on the wane. Mawdudi was greatly dismayed at what he witnessed in his homeland. He sought to find a reason for the gradual decline of Muslim power in Hyderabad, and concluded that the cause was to be found in the corruption of Islam by the centuries of incorporation of local customs and mores that had obscured that faith's veritable teachings. Salvation of Muslim culture and the preservation of its power lay in the restitution of Islamic institutions and practices after they had been cleansed of the cultural influences that had sapped Muslims of their power. He encouraged the Nizam to reform Hyderabad's Islamic institutions and to implement the true teachings of Islam. The Nizam's government did not adopt Mawdudi's recommendations. Its inaction disheartened Mawdudi and led him to lose trust in the existing Muslim political structures and instead to look for a new all-inclusive socio-political solution to safeguard Muslim interests.

Mawdudi's revivalist position was radical communalism as it articulated Muslim interests and sought to protect their rights, and demanded the severance of all cultural and hence social and political ties with Hindus in the interests of purifying Islam. Mawdudi even went so far as to advocate a separate cultural homeland for Indian Muslims.[20]

In 1932 Mawdudi began to publish *Tarjumanu'l-Qur'an*, a journal which for the following forty-seven years became the most important forum for his views.[21] Mawdudi knew that his writings alone could not have an effect on the political events that were unfolding at a rapid pace at that juncture in Indian history. His intellectual endeavours had to go hand-in-hand with the efforts of an organization based on his ideas. It was this conclusion that in 1938 led him to move to Punjab to head Daru'l-Islam (Abode of Islam), an education project first initiated by Muhammad Iqbal (d.1938), the famous Punjabi poet and thinker, at Pathankut, a small hamlet in Punjab.[22] At Daru'l-Islam, Mawdudi established a model Islamic community which he hoped would lead to large scale reform of Islam in India. Mawdudi, however, remained intensely interested in politics. While pursuing the educational objectives of Daru'l-Islam he also became embroiled in the debates surrounding the Pakistan Movement between the Muslim League and the Muslim supporters of the Congress Party. Mawdudi was eager to make his views known but was careful to maintain his independence of thought. He was initially most critical of the Muslim supporters of the Congress, many of whom were his mentors in the Jami'at-i 'Ulama-i Hind. He accused them of betraying the Muslims of India by allowing their opposition to British imperialism to override their responsibilities to their community. But soon Mawdudi turned his attention to the Muslim League which he criticized for its secular outlook.

As Mawdudi became preoccupied with politics he lost interest in the Daru'l-Islam project, leaving it in 1939 for more directly political activity in Lahore. There he taught Islamic studies at the Islamiyah College and lost no time in joining in debates over the future of the Muslim community.[23] It was in Lahore that the idea of a formal party to embody his ideas took its final shape in Mawdudi's thought and works. In August 1941 Mawdudi, along with a number of young ulama and Muslim

activists founded the Jamaʻat-i Islami (the Islamic Party).[24] Soon
after its establishment the Jamaʻat moved its headquarters to
Pathankot, where Mawdudi and his colleagues and followers
developed the party's structure, political position, ideology, and
plan of action. From Pathankot the Jamaʻat organized across
India. It did not develop quickly and extensively enough,
however, to have a direct effect on the course of events in India.

When India was partitioned, the Jamaʻat too divided, giving
place to independent Indian and Pakistani Jamaʻat-i Islamis.
Mawdudi, along with 385 of Jamaʻat's members, opted for
Pakistan. The Jamaʻat-i Islami of Pakistan set up its headquarters
in Lahore, and Mawdudi assumed its leadership. From this
point on Mawdudi's intellectual and political career were closely
tied to the vicissitudes of Jamaʻat's development, which will be
considered in greater detail later in this essay.

Mawdudi's Thought and Ideology

While Mawdudi's biography tells much about the origins and
impetus for Islamic revivalism, his ideological expositions
capture the essence of this approach to Islam and account for his
significance. Throughout his years of political activity
Mawdudi continued to write, producing a long list of articles,
commentaries, short tracts and books. The intellectual force of
his writings, persistently emphatic in his works, goes a long
way to explain his central role in contemporary Islamic thought.
His works have furthermore been influential in traditional
religious scholarship in South Asia. For instance, his translation
of and commentary on the Qur'an, *Tafhimu'l-Qur'an* ('Understanding the Qur'an'), which was begun in 1942 and was
completed three decades later, in 1972, has become one of the
most widely read sources of its kind in Urdu. Although written
in a popular style, and with a view to furthering the cause of
Islamic revivalism it has found a place among the classical
Islamic scholarship of the subcontinent.

In his numerous works Mawdudi elaborated his views on
Islam – its theology, law, philosophy and mysticism – and on
society, economy and politics. Mawdudi advocated an
interpretative reading of Islam, one which aims to mobilize piety
and faith for the purpose of political action.[25] He placed
emphasis on religious works (the exoteric dimensions of Islam),
discouraged traditional religious practices, and rationalized the
Islamic faith, making salvation the culmination of social action.

Mawdudi viewed Islam as a holistic ideology similar to western ideologies. His notion of Islamic ideology, one of the most prolific and systematic articulations of its kind, has been most influential in giving shape to Islamic revivalism as a distinct reading of Islam, its history, and its purpose across the Muslim world.

Part of the power and appeal of Mawdudi's ideology owes to the fact that its contours were drawn in discourse with socialism and capitalism. Mawdudi developed his notion of Islamic ideology consciously to supplant both of these western ideologies among the Muslim intellectual leaders.[26] Not only were the two ideologies alien to the Muslim world view, but also they were inadequate in addressing Muslim concerns and, moreover, threats to Muslim interests. Capitalism for Mawdudi was symbolized in the British Raj, which he held accountable for the decline of Muslim power in India. Mawdudi began to view socialism as a threat after the communist-inspired Telangana uprising posed a serious challenge to the Nizam's rule in Hyderabad in the 1930s and 1940s. Yet ideological discourse in the Foucaudian sense also involved borrowing and assimilation – the appropriation of western concepts and ideas to construct an Islamic resistance to the West.[27] It was to present Islam as a viable socio-political force, in place of socialism and in opposition to capitalism, to Muslim intellectuals that led Mawdudi to punctuate his discourse with such distinctly western terms as 'Islamic revolution', 'Islamic state', and 'Islamic ideology'.

Mawdudi's reading of Islam began with a radical exegesis. His vision was chiliastic and dialectic in that it saw the battle between Islam and un-Islam (*Kufr*) – the West as well as the traditional Muslim culture of India – as the central force in the historical progression of Muslim societies.[28] Mawdudi, particularly in his early writings, was critical of Sufism and especially of institutions and the popular celebrations and practices associated with it in India.[29] Mawdudi, much like Hasan al-Banna', did not favour eradicating Sufism but wished to reform it, that is, appropriate it. In Mawdudi's writings veritable Sufism, cleansed of its 'un-Islamic' dimension, became none other than a synonym for the form of Islam which he had set forth.

The struggle between Islam and un-Islam, argued Mawdudi, would culminate in an Islamic revolution and the creation of an Islamic state, which would in turn initiate large scale reforms in society, thereby leading to a utopian Islamic order.[30] Unlike Ayatollah Khomeini, Mawdudi was not primarily concerned with charting the path to power, but rather with the shape of the Islamic state. This state at its foundations was based on the Shari'a (holy law). This, however, is a given in any discussion of Islam and politics; Mawdudi's contribution to this discussion lies in the fact that he went beyond the question of the incumbency of the state to address the problematic of its operation. In fact, what distinguishes Mawdudi from the host of other Islamic thinkers is his preoccupation with the administrative functioning and the constitution of the Islamic state. It was his aim to prove that the Islamic state above and beyond an ideal would be a viable entity, superior indeed to western and socialist models. He believed the Islamic state was necessitated by its viability and superiority, and not only by religious sanction. He believed this would facilitate its realization, rendering a prolonged struggle to that end unnecessary. According to Mawdudi, Muslims would eagerly opt for an Islamic state once they learned of Islam's true teachings and the viability and inherent superiority of the Islamic state. Attainment of the Islamic state was nothing more than the culmination of a successful *da'wah* (missionary call); running the Islamic state, preserving and developing it, however, would require more and ought to be the central concern of Muslims. In practice, the Jama'at followed a different course. As Mawdudi's exhortations to Pakistanis failed to realize his aim, the Jama'at became involved in the political process to serve as a catalyst, nudging society and state toward an Islamic end.

In defining the shape of the Islamic state Mawdudi borrowed widely and indiscriminately from the West. The Islamic state would be run by a modern machinery of government: an elected president, a parliament, and an omnipotent judiciary. The relations between these branches would be governed by checks and balances meted out in a constitution.

The success of the Islamic state would hinge on its legitimacy in the eyes of society. It was for this reason that Mawdudi, unlike most Islamic revivalist thinkers who followed him, favoured islamization of society before the creation of the state. It was for this reason that Mawdudi placed a great deal of emphasis on education, and viewed Islamic revolution as a piecemeal effort. If the state were islamized before society, then the state would be compelled to resort to autocracy to impose its will on an unwilling and unprepared population, thus dooming the process of socio-political transformation. The ethical and functional utility of the Islamic state and its utopian image was, however, predicated on the cadence between its ideals and the aspirations of the society, which was essential to Mawdudi's view of the Islamic state as a viable system as well as a democracy – about which Mawdudi was emphatic, mainly because democracy is the most desired form of government in the West. It is important to note that Mawdudi viewed the Islamic state as a democracy not because it would accommodate and incorporate diverse social interests, but because in such a state there would be no divisive socio-political issues.

It was obvious to Mawdudi that the Islamic state would not be able to reconcile the rigid demands of Islamic law and the ideals of democracy unless the population would willingly abide by the demands of Islamic law. The Islamic state should not be the enforcer of the Shari'a but the implementor of the will of the people. Ideally, popular will should demand implementation of the Shari'a, unburdening the state and legitimizing its rule. Hence, the shape of the state hinges as much on the character of its population as on its mode of operation.

Mawdudi's approach is perhaps best reflected in his treatment of the controversial *hudud* punishments (punishments for deeds proscribed in Islamic law). Mawdudi argued that the *hudud* punishments could be implemented only if a society was thoroughly Islamized – so that the population would be fully aware of the teachings of Islam and would have no excuse for not following the Shari'a – an argument which clearly parts ways with General Muhammad Ziau'l-Haq or Ayatollah Khomeini's implementation of these punishments in as yet unislamized societies in Pakistan and Iran. It followed that the *hudud* punishments would never be implemented; for they would not be implemented in societies that have not undergone islamization, and in the Islamic state in which society is islamized the population would never engage in activities that would necessitate their implementation. In practice, therefore, there would be no need for compulsion in religion or enforcement of the most coercive aspects of Islamic law by the state in the utopian Islamic order.[31]

With the agenda for the Islamic state in mind, Mawdudi advocated a view of Islam which mobilized the faith according to the needs of political action. He rationalized Islam into a stringent belief system, predicated upon absolute obedience to the will of God, amounting to a command structure which aimed to transform society and politics. By reinterpreting such key concepts as divinity (*ilah*), god/lord (*rabb*), worship ('*ibadah*), and religion (*din*), he recast the meaning of the Muslim faith such that social action became the logical end of religious piety, and religion itself became the vehicle of social action.[32] Despite the radicalism of his vision, and his polemic on Islamic revolution, throughout his career, Mawdudi's approach to politics remained irenic. He continued to believe that social change would result not from violent toppling of existing order by mobilizing the masses, but by taking over the centres of political power and effecting large scale reforms from the top down.[33] In Mawdudi's conception, Islamic revolution was to unfold within the existing state structures rather than with the aim of overthrowing them.[34] He discouraged the use of violence in promoting the cause of Islam and defined the ideal Islamic state as a 'theodemocracy' or a 'democratic caliphate'.[35] Moreover, education rather than revolutionary action constituted the crux of his approach to Islamic activism.[36] In this regard Mawdudi's position, as manifested in Jama'at's politics, stands in contrast to Ayatollah Khomeini's example, and has provided Islamic revivalism with an alternative paradigm for social action, one which may prevail among revivalists in the years to come.

In defining the shape and character of the Islamic state, Mawdudi has addressed such areas of concern as women's rights, the rights of minorities, and the conduct of economic matters. He dwelt less on socio-economic problems such as population growth, economic inequalities, and social justice. He believed that these problems were not real issues of concern, for they were symptoms of the absence of an Islamic order and reflections of the failure of western ideologies. They would disappear once the state and society were islamized, so Muslims were best advised not to dwell on these issues but to focus on establishing and managing the Islamic state. It was this approach that led Mawdudi to oppose land reform in Pakistan. He believed that in an Islamic state the issue of economic justice would not surface, and until there was an Islamic state there was no point in violating Islamic decrees which permit the holding of private property to reform and prolong a system which was un-islamic at its foundations. He preferred adherence to the teachings of Islam – a necessary prerequisite for establishing the Islamic state – rather than succumb to short-run political imperatives.[37] In sharp contrast to the populist rhetoric of Shi'i revolutionaries in Iran, Mawdudi avoided populism. In 1951 he openly opposed the land reform bill proposed by the Pakistan government, and throughout the 1970s he clamoured against Prime Minister Bhutto's nationalization of industries and land reform proposals. He never promised Pakistanis material gains or redistribution of wealth and resources.

Mawdudi's teachings on economics were therefore politically conservative and amounted to enumeration of the assorted teachings of the Shari'a on social transactions.[38] Mawdudi never sought to develop a science of economics based on the Islamic world view. Rather, he viewed Islamic economics as primarily the implementation of Islamic laws on such issues as usury, inheritance, and the rights of labour. Second, Islamic economics were the economic policies of the Islamic state. Since the Islamic state would be a utopian order, its economic system too would be an ideal type model. Mawdudi was therefore not concerned with the working or scientific bases of Islamic economics, but with its potential. Its viability rested not in its technical or operational features but in its ethical assumptions and the promise of the Islamic state.

Mawdudi also dealt with the role of women and minorities in the Islamic state. He argued that Islamic law was clear on these issues and as a result the Islamic state did not have to devise a way of accommodating them, but merely to implement what the Shari'a has enjoined. The question of minorities, he argued, was covered by the discussion of the *zimmis* (non-Muslim minorities) in Islamic law,[39] and that of women by various strictures which decide the modesty of dress and rights of women in an Islamic society.[40]

Mawdudi was aware of the fact that his teachings on the question of the rights of minorities and women would lead to criticism and cast a shadow on his claim to the democratic nature of the Islamic state. Yet he remained unapologetic. He argued that the Islamic state was an ideological one, and the preservation of its ideological purity was therefore the condition *sine qua non* for its survival and development. Extended rights for minorities would undermine the Islamic state as they would diffuse its ideological vigilance. Therefore limiting their rights to those of *zimmis* in Islamic law was a matter of national security and self-preservation. Mawdudi went further in his explanation by questioning the validity of criticisms of the Islamic state on account of protection of the rights of its minorities, arguing that the restriction of their rights in the

Islamic state pales before abuses of human rights in secular states, implying that western criticisms of the Islamic state on this account were unreasonable if not hypocritical.[41]

Mawdudi was not opposed altogether to a social role for women. In fact the Jama'at-i Islami has a women's division, and Jama'at-i Islami women have served on such state institutions as the Council of Islamic Ideology which advises the president of Pakistan on legislative issues, and as members of national and provincial parliaments. Mawdudi did not, however, accord women a socio-political role equal to that of men. More important, he believed their social role should be governed by the strictures of the Shari'a and its practical manifestations in Indo-Muslim life, the most contentious of which is the issue of *purdah* (the sartorial and procedural codes and rules which separate women from men in South Asia). In justifying the *purdah* Mawdudi parts with his usual line of argument wherein every teaching of Islam has a functional utility in advancing society, and asserts that the *purdah* is an instrument for preservation of the Islamic state. He implies that greater rights for women, and especially greater social interaction of the sexes, would lead to immorality which would undo the Islamic state just as it had caused the fall of many empires and civilizations in the West as well as the East.[42] As a result there is no positive contribution in *purdah*, but rather it prevents calamity for the Islamic state.

Mawdudi's arguments are weakest here, and in fact lose their underlying logic to become abstract, polemical, and apologetic. Moreover, he comes close to characterizing women as an insidious force whose activities ought to be regulated and restricted before they could wreak havoc. Mawdudi's views on women, more than any other aspect of his thought, reveal the influence of deep-seated conservative cultural attitudes.

All this said, again unlike many of his cohorts and successors, Mawdudi did not view the issue of women or minorities as central to his discussion of the Islamic state. They were issues of secondary importance, which he never became preoccupied with, believing that they would cease to be bones of contention in the utopian Islamic state. His discourse was never focused on morality, but on politics – not on women or social values but on the state.

Mawdudi's lectures and written works constituted only one aspect of his ideological corpus. The politics of the Jama'at-i Islami from 1941 onwards presented concrete socio-political issues which pushed the boundaries of his political ideas and reading of Islam further.

Jama'at-i Islami

The Jama'at-i Islami, the party which embodies Mawdudi's ideological vision, is one of the oldest Islamic religio-political movements of its kind, and has in its own right been influential in the development of Islamic revivalism across the Muslim world in general, and in South Asia in particular.[43] The party was established on 26 August 1941 in Lahore. Mawdudi had been involved in Muslim politics since 1938 with the aim of protecting Muslim interests. As mentioned earlier, he had opposed accommodating the Congress Party, believing that its secular pretensions were conveniently obfuscating its promise of Hindu rule, which would spell the end of Islam in India. Mawdudi had also been equally if not more ardently opposed to the Muslim League, which he believed to be a secularist entity, completely ill-equipped to respond to the imperatives before the Muslim homeland.[44] Jama'at-i Islami was primarily founded to rival the Muslim League for the leadership of the Pakistan movement, especially so after the Lahore Resolution of 1940 committed the League to creating a separate Muslim state.

Mawdudi's plans for a new Muslim organization, one which he believed would resolve the problems facing Muslims, was first propagated in *Tarjumanu'l-Qur'an*. It found support among a number of Muslim activists and young ulama. They joined Mawdudi in Lahore in August 1941 to form the new organization. The most notable of the young ulama who supported Mawdudi's project were Mawlanas Sayyid Abu'l-Hasan 'Ali Nadwi who in later years became rector of Nadwatu'l-'Ulama, and Muhammad Manzur Nu'mani who is today a prominent Deobandi *'alim*.[45] Mawdudi was elected the Jama'at's first titular head, Amir (president), by the seventy-five who gathered in Lahore to create the Jama'at, and led the Jama'at for the following thirty-one- years until 1972. The party's constitution was also ratified in that opening session.

Soon after, the party established its headquarters in Pathankot, away from the tumult of Lahore which Mawdudi was afraid would overwhelm the nascent organization. The isolation of Pathankot allowed the party to consolidate, and to exist as a community (*ummah*), an ideal which had been imbedded in Mawdudi's conception of the Jama'at.[46] Still, between 1941 and 1947, the Jama'at spread its message across India through its widely-distributed literature, rallies, conventions, and public sessions.[47]

Jama'at's Structure

Since its creation the Jama'at has closely followed Mawdudi's teachings and views. The party promises to create a utopian order to be constructed in the temporal realm, and encourages Muslims to embark upon an Islamic revolution, thus shaping society and politics in accordance with the precepts of the faith as interpreted by Mawdudi.[48] In the short run its aim is to preserve the interests of Islam in the political arena and to prevent secular forces from consolidating power.

The Jama'at's organizational structure was outlined in the party's founding constitution, which has been revised and amended on a number of occasions since 1941. The party consists officially of members (*arkan*, sing. *rukn*) and sympathizers (*muttafiqs* and *hamdards*), all of whom provide it with a cadre of workers (*karkun*).[49] Members alone, however, may hold office in the party. In 1947 Jama'at-i Islami of Pakistan had 385 members; in 1992 this figure stood at 7,861, and the party also boasted 357,229 official sympathizers.[50] The affairs of the Jama'at are managed by the Amir in consultation with the Majlis-i Shura' (consultative assembly). The administrative affairs of the party are supervised by the office of the Qayyim (Secretary-General). As the Jama'at grew, its organizational reach was extended, and this structure was reproduced at all levels of the party, from the national level to that of a village, thus creating an all-encompassing pyramidal structure of authority. The party has since the 1960s also developed a women's wing, and semi-autonomous organizations such as publication houses and various white-collar, blue-collar and peasant unions, and the student unions Islami Jami'at Tulabah (Islamic Society of Students), Jami'at-i Tulabah-i 'Arabiyyah (Society of Arabic Students), and Islami Jami'at-i Talibat (Islamic Society of Female Students) to extend the purview of its activities.[51]

The Jama'at from inception had viewed itself as an *ummah*, a virtuous Muslim community. Its creation was intended to signal both the renaissance of Islam, and provide Indian Muslims with an organizational model to emulate in asserting their political rights and cultural demands. To safeguard the party's particular aims and image discipline has always been rigorous and it is expected that members reform all aspects of their lives to conform to standards set by the party. There has therefore been an emphasis on calibre and quality rather than numbers. The Jama'at has not been a mass party, but a community of devoted Muslims who hope to take over society as a whole. The Jama'at has sought to do this by compelling society to change in accordance with Mawdudi's teachings. In political terms, the Jama'at's organizational model has performed the function of a vanguard party in the struggle for Islamic revolution.

Jama'at's History and Politics

Following the partition of India the Jama'at abandoned the relative isolationism of its Pathankot days and became fully immersed in Pakistani politics. The vagaries of Pakistani politics, meanwhile, provided the Jama'at with opportunities to articulate and implement its political programme. The party found a niche in the political arena, developed a social base, and grew in prominence over time. Pakistan was carved out of India as a new state which sought to embody the Muslim culture of the subcontinent, tying together diverse social and ethnic groups who shared little other than their religious confession. Pakistan has therefore had a particularly arduous experience in nation-building and consolidation of the state, which continues to this day. The state has not tamed the deep-seated cleavages in the polity as the country has fallen victim to military rule, social conflict, and a civil war, which led to the secession of the province with the majority of the country's population in 1971. All this has made the emotive power of Islam increasingly more appealing, providing Islamic parties with a say in national issues.

The Jama'at's agenda all along has been one of using the susceptibility to religious activism to push Pakistan towards islamization. It has sought to preserve the place of Islam in society and politics while it trains a vanguard Islamic elite to oversee the revival of Islam on a national level. The party's tightly-knit and well-structured network of activists and sympathizers has not only propagated Mawdudi's views, but has also enabled the party to project power in the political arena. Since 1941 the Jama'at has put forth a religio-political platform, wherein political realities and social concerns found meaning in the context of the Jama'at's greater concern for the renewal and reform of Islam.

While antagonistic towards traditional Islam, following the creation of Pakistan, Mawdudi and the Jama'at quickly closed ranks with the ulama and other Islamic parties in demanding an Islamic constitution.[52] The Jama'at's ideas and policy positions defined the demands of the Islamic alliance, and as such featured prominently in the ongoing debates between the government and the ulama and religious parties from 1947 to 1956. For instance, Mawdudi's demands, voiced by ulama, were clearly reflected in the Objectives Resolution of 1949, which outlined the government's aim with regard to the constitution. Jama'at's activism in these years eventually culminated in an open confrontation with the government over the role of religion in politics.

Soon after Pakistan's independence the Jama'at forbade Pakistanis to take an oath of allegiance to the state unless it became Islamic, arguing that a Muslim can in clear conscience render his or her allegiance to God alone. The government was troubled by Jama'at's challenge to its legitimacy, all the more so when such challenges involved foreign relations. In 1948, while observing a cease-fire with India, Pakistan had resumed support for insurgency in Kashmir, which by and large was spear-headed by armed paramilitary units dispatched from Pakistan. The government had organized the fighters by characterizing their struggle as a *jihad*. Mawdudi undermined the government's efforts by arguing that vigilante groups, organized by the government to conduct a covert war in Kashmir, could not be fighting a *jihad*, nor could the government surreptitiously support a *jihad* when observing a cease-fire. *Jihad* had to be properly declared by central government in justifying a legitimate and ongoing war (*jihad*, he argued, could not be declared in circumstances of 'hypocrisy'). Mawdudi thus asserted that the government should either formally go to war with India over Kashmir, or abide by the terms of the cease-fire to which it had agreed; covert war and diplomatic sleight of hand were not acceptable in Islam. The government did not take kindly to Mawdudi's position and accused the Jama'at of pro-Indian sympathies and anti-Pakistan activities. Several Jama'at leaders, including Mawdudi, were jailed and the party was charged with sedition, a charge previously levelled only against communist organizations.[53]

Despite the government's reaction, Mawdudi's arguments

placed it on the defensive. While the government sought to turn the tables on the Jama'at, it was clear that Mawdudi had damaged its position at a more fundamental level by questioning the wisdom of its policy of cessation of conflict with India over Kashmir, as well as revealing its susceptibility to criticism from the religious quarter. The entire episode, moreover, acted to confirm the Jama'at's place in Pakistan's politics and the ongoing constitutional debates in Karachi, and to increase the government's sensitivity to religious activism.

The government's clamp-down did not dismantle the Jama'at, nor did it diminish Islam's role in Pakistan's politics. Even while in prison, Mawdudi continued his activities by mobilizing the ulama and various other religious groups to press the Constituent Assembly to move Pakistan in the direction of islamization.

Jama'at's activities were further intensified when Mawdudi was released from prison in 1950. The party successfully reinforced the Islamic alliance, further anchoring constitutional debates in Islam. In 1951, the Jama'at became directly active in politics by taking part in the Punjab provincial elections, but it did not do well. The party was more successful in promoting its cause on the streets, which continued to create tensions with the government. These came to a head in the anti-Ahmadiyyah agitations in Punjab in 1953–54. In 1953, agitators, organized and led by the ulama and religious activists, demanded the dismissal of Zafaru'llah Khan, Pakistan's Ahmadi Foreign Minister, and the declaration of the Ahmadiyyah as a non-Muslim minority.[54] Such measures, it was argued, would serve as a litmus test for the government's commitment to Islam. While the agitations were led by the ulama and religious groups such as the Anjuman-i Ahrar-i Islam (Society of Free Muslims), the Jama'at's role in providing convincing justification for them, especially in the book *Qadiyani Mas'alah* ('The Ahmadiyyah Question'), had proved critical. In fact, the government viewed the Jama'at's support for the agitations with greater alarm and as more invidious than the provocative activities of the Ahrar. As a result, once the government clamped down, Mawdudi and a number of prominent Jama'at leaders were apprehended and put on trial. Mawdudi was charged with sedition and subsequently sentenced to death. That sentence was later commuted, and was eventually reversed by the country's Supreme Court in 1955.

By pitting the Jama'at against the state over a popular cause, the anti-Ahmadiyyah issue enhanced the party's political standing and following. Moreover, it placed Islam more squarely at the centre of the constitutional debates regarding the nature of the Pakistani state, all to the Jama'at's advantage. As a result, the Jama'at became more directly involved in politics, using its growing power to exert renewed pressure on the government, this time around the question of the Constitution of 1956.

By the time the anti-Ahmadiyyah issue was over it had become clear that despite the government's swift reactions the Jama'at had successfully anchored national politics in the concern for the islamicity of the state. This trend was reflected in the ongoing constitutional debates, culminating in the promulgation of the Constitution of 1956, which accommodated many of the demands of the Jama'at and its allies. Mawdudi and the ulama lost no time in claiming victory, and accepted the new constitution as Islamic, preparing themselves to now concentrate their energies on pushing for islamization of state institutions.[55]

The acceptance of the constitution as Islamic paved the way for the Jama'at to become even more directly involved in politics. For instance, in 1957, despite reservations in some quarters within the party, Mawdudi directed the Jama'at to recognize the legitimacy of the state by declaring that it would participate in the national elections of 1958 as a full-fledged party. The constitutional victory was, however, short-lived. For the armed forces of Pakistan, under the command of General Muhammad Ayub Khan (d. 1969), and with a modernizing agenda which opposed the encroachment of religion into politics, assumed power in 1958.

Over the course of the following decade, the political establishment became dominated by an authoritarian and bureaucratic elite who actively promoted Islamic modernism as a way of undermining the Jama'at and its allies, appropriating the right to interpret Islam, and slow the drive for the islamization of the country. Advocates of Islamic revivalism and an Islamic state were increasingly pressed into retreat. The Jama'at's offices were closed down, its leaders excoriated in government-sponsored publications, and its activities, networks and operations restricted. Mawdudi himself was imprisoned twice during Ayub Khan's rule, in 1964 and 1967. The government had launched an offensive against religio-political activism with the hope of freeing Pakistan and General Ayub's modernization schemes of the clamour for islamicity.

Unable to freely advocate the cause of Islam in the political arena, the Jama'at became more concerned with the removal of Ayub Khan and the restoration of a political climate more conducive to religio-political activism. Moreover, the Jama'at's experiences with the Ayub Khan government forced the movement to look for new allies outside the circle of Islamic revivalists. Consequently, the Jama'at joined an alliance of political parties that advocated restoration of democracy and an end to Ayub Khan's rule in Pakistan. The party went so far as to support the candidacy of Fatimah Jinnah in the presidential elections of 1965.

Ayub Khan was not, however, entirely successful in marginal-izing the Jama'at; on the contrary, he was on occasion even compelled to temper his opposition to Islamic activism. As Pakistan faced numerous national crises it turned more and more to Islam, and at times found itself beholden to those like Mawdudi who mobilized Islamic symbols, making them avail-able to the state. For instance, Ayub Khan, who had proved to be one of Jama'at's most determined enemies, in 1965 publicly appealed to Mawdudi for support in his war effort against India by declaring a *jihad*.[56] However, instances of government conciliation were rare, and for the most part the Jama'at was kept under pressure. As a result, the Ayub era politicized the Jama'at further, transforming it, more definitively, into a consummate political party.

The result of this transformation was clear in the Jama'at's policies in the post-Ayub period. In 1970 it participated in national elections with the aim of capturing power. Those hopes were dashed when the party won only four seats in the National Assembly, and four in the various provincial assemblies. In 1971, the Jama'at responded to the advent of civil war in East Pakistan by mobilizing its resources in defence of Pakistan, and by joining the conflict to prevent East Pakistan from becoming Bangladesh.

The secession of East Pakistan, and the rise of Zulfiqar 'Ali Bhutto (d. 1979) to power in 1971, intensified the Jama'at's political activism. The socialist content of the Pakistan Peoples' Party's political programme was particularly instrumental in prompting the Jama'at into action. Viewing Bhutto's populism as a direct challenge to the Islamic basis of Pakistan, and to its place in the country's political order, the party directly confront-ed the government on numerous political issues, most notably during the non-recognition of Bangladesh movement of 1972–74 and renewed anti-Ahmadiyyah disturbances of 1974.[57]

Throughout the Bhutto years the Jama'at spearheaded a

political movement which consciously appealed to religious sentiments with a view to weakening the Bhutto regime.[58] While opposition to Ayub had brought Islamic groups into an alliance for democracy, opposition to Bhutto brought disparate parties, secular as well as Islamic, under the banner of Islam. The Jama'at's religio-political programme proved instrumental in giving shape to this alliance – the Nizam-i Mustafa (order of the Prophet) movement – and in managing its nation-wide activities. The struggle against Bhutto bolstered the Jama'at's popular standing greatly. In the election of 1977, widely believed to have been rigged to favour Bhutto, the opposition gained thirty-six seats, nine of which were won by Jama'at candidates. During the subsequent anti-government protests, the party's popularity soared further.[59] It was the Jama'at and the movement which it led that eventually undermined the Bhutto government, and in July 1977 provoked a military coup. Mawdudi played an important role in that opposition movement. He had stepped down as the Amir of the Jama'at in 1972. But in 1977 with the Jama'at's Amir at the time in prison and Pakistan in the throes of a national crisis, Mawdudi returned to centre stage. He became the de facto leader of the opposition to the premiership of Zulfiqar 'Ali Bhutto.

Islamic symbolisms proved so efficacious in galvanizing the opposition to Bhutto that they became the basis for the programme of the new regime. The cause of the opposition, now enjoying large scale popularity, could not be ignored by the martial law administration of General Muhammad Ziau'l-Haq (d. 1988), who in his search for legitimacy was quick to appease the Nizam-i Mustafa movement. Zia accorded Mawdudi the status of senior statesman, one whose advice was sought by the new leadership of the country and whose words adorned the front pages of the printed media. Mawdudi retained his new-found stature until his death in Buffalo, New York on 22 September 1979. His funeral later that month in Lahore drew a crowd of over a million. He was buried in his house, in the Ichhrah neighbourhood of Lahore.

Zia's eleven year rule, from 1977 to 1988, was therefore a period of unprecedented success and political influence for the Jama'at.[60] During this period, the Jama'at became a major political and ideological force close to the centre of power. Jama'at leaders held important government offices, including cabinet portfolios, and the party's views were reflected in government programmes. The party played a direct role in the islamization of the country, as well as in articulating state policy, especially concerning the Afghan war and the government's reaction to provincialist and ethnic tendencies.[61]

The rise in the fortunes of the Jama'at during the Zia period, however, turned out to be a pyrrhic victory; for despite its influence at the top, the party failed to expand its social base, and was unable to exercise political influence outside of the channels provided by the government. As a result, in the national elections of 1985, it won only ten seats to the National Assembly and thirteen seats to the various provincial assemblies. Unable to utilize its newfound prominence to advance its own political position, or to distinguish its programme from that of the government, the Jama'at became an instrument of government policy-making and was, therefore, effectively co-opted by the Zia regime.

The Jama'at's experience with the Zia regime not only dealt a blow to the party's morale and prestige, but placed it in a position of great political vulnerability. As Zia gradually fell out of favour with the masses, so too did the Jama'at witness a turn in its political fortunes. The party's predicament manifested itself in its modest showing in Pakistan's national elections of 1988 and 1990, in which it participated as part of the Islami Jumhuri Ittihad (Islamic Democratic Alliance, IJI), a coalition of Islamic and right-of-centre parties which emerged in the wake of Zia's death to challenge Benazir Bhutto and the Pakistan Peoples' Party. In the elections of 1988 the Jama'at won eight seats to the national assembly and thirteen seats to the various provincial assemblies. In the elections of 1990 the Jama'at's tally of seats stood at eight and twenty respectively. The Jama'at's electoral share took a turn for the worse in the 1993 elections, when it participated outside the framework of any coalition. In these elections it won three seats to the National Assembly and six to various provincial assemblies.

Yet despite its limited electoral showings, by the end of the Zia period it was apparent that the Jama'at had become a powerful political force with significant social and cultural influence, mainly derived from its organizational structure and influence over the religious factor in Pakistan's political balance. The party's ability to project power disproportionate to its size off-set the handicap of its electoral showings. While unable to increase its influence in the Pakistani parliament, the Jama'at remains an important political party capable of influencing the course of politics through the use of its organizational muscle.

The Jama'at's political stature is reflected in the power that it wielded in the IJI between 1988 and 1992.

Continuity and Change in the Jama'at's Structure

During the course of its five decades of existence, the Jama'at has undergone important internal changes, which have influenced its vision and politics. The party has gone through a number of purges and reorganizations, as well as periods of uncertainty and redirection, none more significant than the transition from one leader to another. Since its creation, the Jama'at has been led by three Amirs, and gone through two succession periods, from Mawdudi (1941–72) to Mian Tufayl Muhammad (1972–87) to Qazi Husain Ahmad (1987-present), each of which has engendered a reorientation of the party.

Of equal importance are changes in the social base of the Jama'at. The party has, at one point or another, been associated with a definite social class or ethnic group; most notably, the urban middle classes, the petit-bourgeoisie, the Muhajirs (Urdu-speaking migrants who moved from India to urban centres of Sind following the partition of the subcontinent), the Punjabis, and more recently, the Pathans – ethnic groups with vested interests in the unity of Pakistan and dedicated to the idea of a Muslim homeland. In its concern for the islamization of the state, the party has eschewed populist politics, and instead sought to establish a base among the intelligentsia. As such, it has failed to inculcate support among any one social class, or to gain a large following. The Jama'at has remained small, relying on the power of discipline and organization rather than the power of numbers.

It has, however, compensated for its constricted social base by developing ties with students – Pakistan's future politicians, bureaucrats, and intellectual leaders. It is the party's following among students that best explains its gradual penetration of the bureaucracy, compensating somewhat for its limited social base. Mawdudi's following among the students is the best example of his doctrine of islamizing the state from within, and from above – revolution through education – at work.

The development of Islamic revivalism in Mawdudi's works and in Jama'at politics provides important insights into the origins and working of Islamic ideology and overall strategy. Although Mawdudi's views and the Jama'at's agenda differ sufficiently from other manifestations of Islamic revivalism so as to present a different model from those advocated in Iran or more recently in Egypt, they nevertheless best elucidate the nature of Islamic revivalism. And as Islamic parties from Algeria to Malaysia are opting for participation in elections over revolution, the Jama'at's example is likely to find more parallels across the Muslim world.

Notes

1. On the impact of Mawdudi's thought on Islamic movements in the Arab World, Afghanistan, Iran and Malaysia see John L. Esposito, *The Islamic Threat: Myth or Reality?*, New York, Oxford University Press, 1992, pp. 154–5; Emmanuel Sivan, *Radical Islam; Medieval Theology and Modern Politics*, New Haven, Yale University Press, 1985; Saad Eddin Ibrahim, 'Islamic Militancy as a Social Movement: The Case of Two Groups in Egypt,' in Ali E. Hillal Dessouki, ed., *Islamic Resurgence in the Arab World*, New York, Praeger, 1982, p. 125; Abdel Azim Ramadan, 'Fundamentalist Influence in Egypt: the Strategies of the Muslim Brotherhood and the Takfir Groups,' in Martin E. Marty and R. Scott Appelby, eds., *Fundamentalisms and the State: Remaking Polities, Economies, and Militance*, Chicago, University of Chicago Press, 1993, pp. 156 and 161; Abdelwahab El-Affendi, 'The Long March From Lahore to Khartoum: Beyond the "Muslim Reformation" ', *British Society for Middle Eastern Studies Bulletin*, vol. 17, no. 2, 1990, pp. 138–9; Said Amir Arjomand, *The Turban for the Crown: The Islamic Revolution in Iran*, New York, Oxford University Press, 1988; Olivier Roy, *Islam and Resistance in Afghanistan*, New York, Cambridge University Press, 1990, pp. 68–70 and 80; and Zainah Anwar, *Islamic Fundamentalism in Malaysia*, Kuala Lumpur, Peladunk Publishers, 1989.

2. On Jama'at-i Islamis of India and Bangladesh see Violette Graff, 'La Jamaat-i-Islami en Inde', in Oliver Carré and Paul Dumont, eds., *Radicalismes Islamiques*, vol. 2, Paris, L'Hartmann, 1986, pp. 59–72; and Mumtaz Ahmad, 'Islamic Fundamentalism in South Asia: The Jamaat-i-Islami and the Tablighi Jamaat,' in Martin E. Marty and R. Scott Appleby, eds., *Fundamentalisms Observed*, Chicago, University of Chicago Press, 1991, pp. 502–4.

3. Chaudhri 'Abdu'l-Rahman 'Abd, *Mufakkir-i Islam: Sayyid Abu'l-A'la Mawdudi* ('Thinker of Islam: Sayyid Abu'l-A'la Mawdudi'), Lahore: Islamic Publications, 1971, pp. 46–7; also see, Sayyid Abu'l-A'la Mawdudi, *Watha'iq-i Mawdudi* ('Mawdudi's Documents'), Lahore: Idarah-i Ma'arif-i Islami, 1984, p. 97.

4. Abu Mahmud Mawdudi, 'Himara Khandan' ('Our Family') in Ahmad Munir, *Mawlana Abu'l-A'la Mawdudi*, Lahore: Atashfishan Publications, 1986, p. 11.

5. 'Abd, *Mufakkir-i Islam*, p. 47.

6. Sayyid Abu'l-A'la Mawdudi, 'Khud Nivisht' ('Autobiography'), in Muhammad Yusuf Buhtah, *Mawlana Mawdudi: Apni awr Dusrun ki Nazar Main* ('Mawlana Mawdudi: In His Own and Others' View'), Lahore: Idarah-i Ma'arif-i Islami, 1984, p. 27.

7. Sayyid Asad Gilana, *Maududi; Thought and Movement*, Lahore: Islamic

Publications, 1984, pp. 25–8.

8. Mawdudi, 'Khud Nivisht,' p. 30.

9. *Ibid.*, p. 38; 'Abd, *Mufakkir-i Islam*, p. 59. Abad Shahpuri, *Tarikh-i Jama'at-i Islami* (History of Jama'at-i Islami), Lahore: Idarah-i Ma'arif-i Islami, 1989, vol. 1, p. 189.

10. Mawdudi, 'Khud Nivisht', pp. 31–2.

11. *Ibid.*

12. For more on this movement see Gail Minault, *The Khilafat Movement: Religious Symbolisms and Political Mobilization in India*, New York: Columbia University Press, 1982.

13. Sayyid Abu'l-A'la Mawdudi, *Da'wah Awr 'Amal* ('Call and Action'), Lahore, n.d., p. 3.

14. Khurshid Ahmad and Zafar Ishaq Ansari, 'Mawlana Sayyid Abul A'la Mawdudi: An Introduction to His Vision of Islam and Islamic Revival', in Khurshid Ahmad and Zafar Ishaq Ansari, eds., *Islamic Perspectives: Studies in Honour of Mawlana Sayyid Abul A'la Mawdudi*, Leicester: The Islamic Foundation, 1979. p. 361.

15. Mawdudi, 'Khud Nivisht,' p. 35.

16. Shahpuri, *Tarikh*, vol. 1, pp. 197–9.

17. In a sermon at Delhi's Jami' mosque Muhammad 'Ali, which Mawdudi attended, the Khilafat invited Muslims to clarify Islam's position on the use of violence before its critics; cited in Muhammad Salahu'ddin, 'Tajziah' ('Analysis'), in *Takbir* (Karachi), 28 September 1989, p. 31; and Mahmud Ahmad Allahwala, 'Mard-i Haqq Agah' ('The Man Who Was Aware of the Truth'), in *ibid*, pp. 41–3.

18. 'Abdu'l-Ghani Faruqi, 'Hayat-i Javidan' ('Eternal Life'), *Haftrozah Zindagi*, Lahore, Mawdudi Number, 29 September–5 October 1989, p. 23.

19. On Mawdudi's activities in Hyderabad see Seyyed Vali Reza Nasr, 'The Politics of an Islamic Movement: The Jama'at-i Islami of Pakistan', Ph.D. Dissertation, Department of Political Science, Massachusetts Institute of Technology, 1991, pp. 107–8.

20. The clearest version of this demand was spelled out in *Tarjumanu'l-Qur'an* (Hyderabad), November–December 1938.

21. *Tarjumanu'l-Qur'an* (Hyderabad), October–December 1938.

22. On the Daru'l-Islam project see Nasr, 'The Politics of an Islamic Movement', pp. 136–54.

23. 'Abd, *Mufakkir-i Islam*, pp. 152–64; and Manzuru'l-Haq, 'Mawdudi Hami-Pahlu Shakhsiyat' ('Mawdudi: the Multi-Dimensional Personality'), in Jalil Ahmad Rana and Salim Mansur Khalid, eds., *Tazkirah-i Sayyid Mawdudi* ('Biography of Sayyid Mawdudi'), Lahore: Idarah-i Ma'arif-i Islami, 1986, p. 107.

24. Nasr, 'The Politics of an Islamic Movement', pp. 156–67.

25. For more on Mawdudi's ideology see Charles J. Adams, 'The Ideology of Mawlana Mawdudi', in Donald E. Smith, ed., *South Asian Politics and Religion*, Princeton: Princeton University Press, 1966, pp. 371–97; *idem*, 'Mawdudi and the Islamic State', in John L. Esposito, ed., *Voices of Resurgent Islam*, New York: Oxford University Press, 1983, pp. 99–133; and Erwin I.J. Rosenthal, *Islam in the Modern Nation State*, Cambridge: Cambridge University Press, 1965.

26. See for instance, Sayyid Abu'l-A'la Mawdudi, *Tanqihat* ('Inquiries'), 22nd ed., Lahore: Islamic Publications, 1989; *idem, Capitalism, Socialism and Islam*, Sharif Ahmad Khan, trans., Lahore: Islamic Book Publishers, 1977; and *idem*, 'Economic and Political Teachings of the Qur'an', in M.M. Sharif, ed., *A History of Muslim Philosophy*, Wiesbaden: Otto Harrasowitz, 1963, vol. 1, pp. 178–98.

27. For a discussion of the equivalent process in Iran see Hamid Dabashi, 'Islamic Ideology: The Perils and Promises of a Neologism' in Hooshang Amirahmadi and Manouchehr Parvin, eds., *Post-Revolutionary Iran*, London: Westview Press, 1988, pp. 11–22.

28. Mawdudi, *Tanqihat; idem, The Process of Islamic Revolution*, 8th ed., Lahore: Islamic Publications, 1980; and *idem, Islami Hukumat Kis Tarah Qa'im Huta Hey* ('How Is the Islamic State Established'), Lahore, n.d.

29. 'Asim Nu'mani, *Tasawwuf Awr Ta'mir-i Sirat* ('Sufism and the Building of the Prophetic Way'), Lahore: Islamic Publications, 1972; Mawlana Shaikh Ahmad, *Mawlana Mawdudi Awr Tasawwuf* ('Mawlana Mawdudi and Sufism'), Deoband: Maktabah-i Tajalli, 1966; and Mawdudi, *Watha'iq*, p. 82.

30. Sayyid Abu'l-A'la Mawdudi, *Islamic Law and Constitution*, Khurshid Ahmad, ed., Karachi: Jamaat-e-Islami Publications, 1955.

31. *Ibid.*, p. 24; and *idem, Human Rights in Islam*, Khurshid Ahmad and Ahmad Said Khan, trans., Leicester: The Islamic Foundation, 1976.

32. Sayyid Abu'l-A'la Mawdudi, *Qur'an Ki Char Buniadi Istilahain: Ilah, Rabb, 'Ibadat, Din* ('Qur'an's Four Basic Terms: Divinity, Lord, Worship, Religion'), reprint, Lahore: Islamic Publications, 1988; and Christian W. Troll, 'The Meaning of Din: Recent Views of Three Eminent Indian Ulama', in Christian W. Troll, ed., *Islam in India: Studies and Commentaries*, Delhi: Vikas Publishing House, 1982, vol. 1, pp. 168–77.

33. Mawdudi, *The Process of Islamic Revolution.*

34. Sayyid Abu'l-A'la Mawdudi, *Islam Ka Nazriyah Siyasi* ('Islam's Political Views'), Delhi, 1967.

35. *Ibid.*; and *idem, Islami Riyasat*, Lahore: Islamic Publications, 1969.

36. *Ibid*; and *idem, The Process of Islamic Revolution.*

37. Sayyid Abu'l-A'la Mawdudi, *Malikiyat-i Zamin Mas'alah* ('Question of Land Ownership'), Lahore: Islamic Publications, 1982.

38. Sayyid Abu'l-A'la Mawdudi, *Economic System of Islam*, Khurshid Ahmad, ed., Riaz Husain, trans., reprint, Lahore: Islamic Publications, 1984; *idem, Islamic Economic System: Principles and Objectives*, reprint, Delhi: Markazi Maktabah Islami, 1980; *idem*, 'Economic and Political Teachings of the Qur'an,' pp. 178–98.

39. Sayyid Abu'l-A'la Mawdudi, *Islami Riyasat Main Zimmiun ki Huquq* ('The Rights of Minorities in the Islamic State'), Lahore, 1954.

40. *Idem, Purdah and the Status of Women in Islam*, reprint, Lahore: Islamic Publications, 1972.

41. *Idem, Human Rights in Islam*, Khurshid Ahmad and Ahmad Said Khan, trans., Leicester, The Islamic Foundation, 1976.

42. *Idem, Purdah.*

43. For Jama'at's accounts of its own history see Shahpuri, *Tarikh*, vol. 1; Sayyid Abu'l-A'la Mawdudi, *Jama'at-i Islami; Tarikh, Maqsad, Awr La'ihah-i 'Amal* ('Jama'at-i Islami; History, Aims, and Plan of Action'), reprint, Lahore:

Islamic Publications, 1963; and *idem, Jama'at-i Islami ki Untis Sal* ('Twenty-Nine Years of Jama'at-i Islami'), Lahore: Shu'bah-i Nashr'u Isha'at-i Jama'at-i Islami, Pakistan, 1970.

44.   Seyyed Vali Reza Nasr, *The Vanguard of the Islamic Revolution: The Jama'at-i Islami of Pakistan*, Berkeley: University of California Press, 1994.

45.   Mawlana Muhammad Manzur Nu'mani, *Mawlana Mawdudi Miri Sath Rifaqat Ki Sarguzasht Awr Ab Mira Mauqaf* ('The Story of My Friendship with Mawlana Mawdudi, and My Position Now'), Lahore: Quaraishi Book Agency, 1980.

46.   *Ibid.*

47.   *Rudad-i Jama'at-i Islami* ('Proceedings of Jama'at-i Islami'), Lahore, 1939–91, vols. 1–5.

48.   Ahmad, 'Islamic Fundamentalism in South Asia.'

49.   For more on the party's organizational structure, see Nasr, 'The Politics of an Islamic Movement', ch. 8.

50.   The figures have been provided by the central offices of the Jama'at in Lahore.

51.   On the Jama'at's student union see Seyyed Vali Reza Nasr, 'Students, Islam, and Politics: Islami Jami'at-i Tulaba in Pakistan', *The Middle East Journal*, vol. 46, no. 1, winter 1992, pp. 59–76.

52.   On Jama'at's activities on behalf of the Islamic constitution and in opposition to the new state see Leonard Binder, *Religion and Politics in Pakistan*, Berkeley: University of California Press, 1961; and Seyyed Vali Reza Nasr, *The Vanguard of the Islamic Revolution: The Jama'at-i Islami of Pakistan*, forthcoming from the University of California Press, 1994, ch. 6.

53.   For details of these events, see Nasr, *The Vanguard*, ch. 6.

54.   See *ibid.* and Ayesha Jalal, *The State of Martial Rule: The Origins of Pakistan's Political Economy of Defence*, Cambridge: Cambridge University Press, 1990, pp. 144–51.

55.   *Tarjumanu'l-Qur'an* (Lahore), January–February 1956, pp. 2–8.

56.   Altaf Gauhar, 'Pakistan, Ayub Khan, Awr Mawlana Mawdudi, *Tafhimu'l-Qur'an* Awr Main' ('Pakistan, Ayub Khan, Mawlana Mawdudi, *Tafhimu'l-Qur'an* and I'), *Haftrozah Zindagi* (Lahore), Mawdudi Number, 29 September–5 October 1989, pp. 41–5.

57.   *Ijtima'Se Ijtima'Tak (1963–1974); Rudad-i of Jama'at-i Islami, Pakistan* ('From Convention to Convention [1963–1974]; Proceedings of Jama'at-i Islami of Pakistan'), Lahore: Jama'at-i Islami, 1989.

58.   Kausar Niazi, *Zulfiqar Ali Bhutto of Pakistan: The Last Days*, New Delhi: Vikas Publishing House, 1992.

59.   'Abdu'l-Ghafur Ahmad, *Pher Martial Law A-Giya* ('Then Came the Martial Law'), Lahore: Jang Publications, 1988; and Kawthar Nyazi, *Awr Line Kat Ga'i* ('And the Line was Cut'), Lahore: Jang Publications, 1987.

60.   On relations between the Zia regime and the Jama'at see Seyyed Vali Reza Nasr, 'Islamic Opposition to the Islamic State: The Jama'at-i Islami 1977–1988', *International Journal of Middle East Studies*, vol. 25, no. 2, May 1993, pp. 261–83.

61.   Seyyed Vali Reza Nasr, 'Pakistan; Islamic State, Ethnic Polity', *The Fletcher Forum of World Affairs*, vol. 16, no. 2, summer 1992, pp. 81–90.

6

Hasan al-Banna
(1906–1949)

David Commins

In 1928, a 22-year-old schoolteacher named Hasan al-Banna founded the Society of Muslim Brothers, the twentieth-century's most influential movement for reorienting Muslim societies to a pure Islamic order. Until that time the call for religious reform and restoring Islam to a central place in society had enjoyed limited appeal among educated Muslims but had not developed into a mass movement. Banna transformed an elite intellectual fashion into a popular phenomenon that would profoundly influence the interaction between religion and politics not only in Egypt but throughout the Arab and Muslim worlds. In the early 1990s, movements inspired by Banna's vision contend for political power in Algeria, Tunisia, Egypt, Jordan, Sudan, and among Palestinians. Banna's impact derives less from original contributions to modern Islamic thought than from popularizing current ideas, devising an organizational platform to sustain them, and providing charismatic leadership that inspired thousands of Egyptians to act on his programme with deep faith in his sincerity and devotion.

Historical Background

During the nineteenth century, Egypt's political and economic fortunes became increasingly connected to its relations with Europe. During the early 1800s Egypt exported cotton to Europe in large quantities, and cotton eventually became Egypt's principal crop. In order to facilitate the growing trade between Egypt and Europe, foreign investors supported projects to develop a modern transportation and communications infrastructure. Railroads, ports, canals, telegraph lines, and dams rapidly expanded. The most significant project was the construction of the Suez Canal, completed in 1869. While these projects modernized Egypt's economy, they also pushed the Egyptian treasury deep into debt to European creditors.

The widespread commercial and financial penetration by foreigners and their vastly increased presence throughout Egypt led to the country's rulers and wealthy elite adopting European manners and customs. This cultural dimension of imperialism further irritated Egyptian sensibilities and nurtured anti-European sentiment and a desire to curtail foreign influence. In 1881 there erupted a movement to resist European political, economic, and cultural domination, but by appearing to threaten foreign investments, this movement triggered a British invasion in September 1882. Although the British claimed they would leave once foreign interests were safeguarded, they remained on Egyptian soil well into the twentieth century.

The British occupiers instituted a system of indirect rule whereby a British Resident and his advisors worked with the hereditary dynasty that had emerged earlier in the century but never completely broke away from Ottoman suzerainty. For most of the period before the First World War, the British Resident and the Egyptian ruler, known as the khedive or viceroy, co-operated in governing Egypt. In the early 1900s, however, a new nationalist movement appeared and agitated for Egyptian independence. By the outbreak of the First World War the nationalist movement had peaked and begun to decline. When the Ottoman empire entered the war against Britain, the British formally separated Egypt from it and declared a protectorate over Egypt. At the end of the war, in 1919, a popular nationalist movement for Egyptian independence emerged. Hasan al-Banna, just thirteen years old, participated in demonstrations demanding British evacuation.[1] The British rode out the storm of nationalist protest and eventually made a unilateral declaration of Egyptian independence (with significant reservations) in 1922. Thus, the political climate surrounding Banna's early years of social awareness was marked by foreign domination and resistance to it.

Britain established a political regime that provided for a constitutional monarchy with a parliament, elections, and political parties. There soon developed a political struggle among the royal palace, political parties, and the British. This struggle centred on two issues: modifying the limitations on Egypt's independence, and the balance of power between the palace and the nationalist parties, particularly the most influential party of the era, the Wafd, and its popular leader Saad Zaghlul. During the 1920s the conduct of all three elements in the political struggle discredited the parliamentary system as each one violated its democratic spirit to suit its own interests. Consequently, by the late 1930s, many Egyptians considered the political system corrupt and dominated by selfish interests.

In addition to Britain's continued role in politics, foreign interests remained dominant in the Egyptian economy. This was particularly the case in finance, industry, commerce, and infrastructural development. Egyptian economic relations were marked by acute inequality between a few thousand families possessing tremendous wealth, primarily in land producing crops for export, and millions of poor Egyptians labouring on the land and in the cities. Because of the dominant role of foreigners in the economy, nationalist sentiment became concerned with economic as well as political independence.

Egyptian society underwent substantial transformation in the first decades of the twentieth century. Improvements in public hygiene contributed to population growth. This combined with increasing landlessness among the peasantry to spur migration from villages to cities, thereby raising the proportion of Egyptians living in urban centres. Cities witnessed in addition to quantitative growth certain changes in character toward a more complex society. The traditional urban groups of tradesmen, artisans, and poor labourers continued to exist alongside a growing modern middle class of government civil servants and professionals, and industrial workers.

Europe's political and economic domination was accompanied by a corresponding cultural domination manifest in the tendency among Egypt's elite to adopt western ways and ideas at the expense of customary practices and beliefs associated with Islam. Already in the last decades of the nineteenth century, Muslims had articulated an Islamic response to cultural westernization by calling for a return to 'true' Islam untainted by centuries of historical accretion. Proponents of this view held that Islam, when properly understood, perfectly accorded with reason and science, and therefore Muslims could adapt to modern conditions while retaining faith in their religion.

Muhammad 'Abduh led this school of thought, and his disciple Rashid Rida amplified it in his journal *al-Manar*, published from 1898 until 1935. Yet neither 'Abduh nor Rida succeeded in converting many Egyptians to their vision of Islam. Most Egyptians continued to observe their faith by following the conservative scholars of al-Azhar or by attending the ceremonies of Sufi orders and crediting the orders' living and dead saints with miraculous powers.

During the 1920s Egypt's political and intellectual elite espoused a secular modernist ideology more than ever before. European political and cultural ideas permeated the pages of Egyptian newspapers, magazines, and books. Cairo and Alexandria had developed westernized neighbourhoods in which Egyptians could lead a European style of life by frequenting restaurants, night clubs, cinemas, and theatres. In this context, Egyptian writers elaborated a secular Egyptian national identity that looked to the pre-Islamic pharaonic legacy for inspiration. This secular Egyptian nationalism reduced Islam to a matter of personal conscience and devotion separate from public life. While this cultural orientation satisfied the educated urban elite, it was irrelevant, if not offensive, to most Egyptians' cultural values and mores.

Egypt's secular modernists believed in the superiority of European culture and sought to promote elements of that culture. Naturally, they applauded Mustafa Kemal's abolition of the caliphate in Turkey in 1924 as a major achievement for the struggle to separate religion from political authority. Beyond the political realm they argued that Muslims had to accept the scientific culture of the age as well, hence their embrace of Darwin's theory of evolution. In addition, secularists favoured changes in the status of women such as removing the veil. As if this secularist assault were not enough to alarm pious Muslims, the western missionary presence continued to increase and gain confidence to the extent that missionary authors publicly criticized Islam in lectures and writings. Thus, an observer of Egyptian society during the 1920s might have concluded that the tide of western secular culture would soon sweep away Egypt's Muslim culture.

Hasan al-Banna

Hasan al-Banna grew up in the Egyptian delta town Mahmudiya. His father combined a trade as a watch repairman with religious scholarship. As was customary in Egyptian society, Hasan followed in his father's footsteps, learning to repair watches and acquiring an elementary religious education. At the age of twelve, however, he enrolled in a state primary school and at the same time he continued to pursue a religious vocation by joining an Islamic group called the Society for Moral Behaviour. This society held its members to a strict code of Islamic morality, imposing fines on those who violated the code, by cursing for instance. He later participated in a similar group called the Society for Preventing the Forbidden. This society put pressure on fellow townsmen to observe Islamic rituals and morality to the full and sent threatening letters to those they detected violating Islamic standards.[2]

Banna's most influential early association was with the Hasafiya Sufi order, which he joined when he was thirteen. This Shari'a-minded order appealed to him because it strictly observed scripture in rituals and ceremonies. The Hasafiya forbade men to wear gold, encouraged women to dress modestly, and restricted conduct at tomb visits to acts and words sanctioned by scripture. Banna served as secretary for the order's charitable society, which strove to reform public morality and combat the influence that Christian missionaries attained by assisting orphans. As a youth, Banna actively strove personally to uphold Islamic standards and to impose them on others. He combined his personal commitment with a tendency to join groups that shared his sentiment.[3]

Banna's attachment to a Sufi order imbued him with a strong sense of the importance of the relationship between leader and follower. In his memoirs he described how one of his first teachers taught him to value the spiritual and emotional bonds that can grow between teacher and student. He also retained from his early Sufi affiliations a lifelong appreciation of Islamic mysticism as long as it did not incorporate innovations (bid'a) and heresies, which according to scripturalist Muslims often marred Sufi practices and beliefs. Banna never condemned Sufism per se, rather he called for the reform of misguided Sufis and for cleansing Sufi writings of religious impurities.[4]

In 1923 Banna left his Delta home for Cairo to attend Dar al-Ulum, Egypt's teacher training college. On arriving in Egypt's capital, he joined the local branch of the Hasafiya order, which provided him a familiar setting. During his five years in Cairo, he witnessed Egypt's lively, contentious political climate with its constant bickering between the two leading political parties. Of even greater significance, though, he directly experienced Egypt's cultural westernization, which he equated with atheism and immorality. Like many Muslims, he reacted with alarm to Mustafa Kemal Ataturk's abolition of the caliphate and his programme to secularize Turkey. The movement in Egypt to set up a secular state university in 1925, in Banna's eyes, would probably be the first step down the road to Turkish-style abandonment of Islam. He also viewed with apprehension the flood of newspaper articles and books that promoted secular western values. [5]

Banna sought and found likeminded men at Dar al-Ulum, al-Azhar, the Law College and the Salafiya library. Among his new acquaintances was an Azhari scholar, Shaykh Yusuf al-Dijwi, who had founded a society devoted to Islamic revival. According to Banna's memoirs, Dijwi acknowledged that his society had failed and that al-Azhar's ulama had proved ineffective in stemming the tide of western culture. He told Banna that one could only hope for individual salvation by adhering to Islam. The young man rejected this posture of resignation and urged Dijwi to draw on the power of the Muslim masses. [6]

Banna's first idea for a programme of action involved the formation of societies under the leadership of religious authorities who would inspire an Islamic revival. He found a sympathetic response from Muhibb al-Din al-Khatib, the Syrian Islamic reformer who ran the Salafiya library, published a weekly journal devoted to Islamic reform called *al-Fath*, and contributed to the establishment of the Young Men's Muslim Association (YMMA). This religious association, formally established in November 1927, clearly illustrates the new type of reformist movement which Banna would emulate several months later when he founded the Muslim Brothers. [7]

The YMMA sought to revive Muslim society through a return to true Islam as it is found in the Qur'an. This meant adhering to Islamic morality, striving for Muslim solidarity, and assimilating modern science. To pursue this agenda, the YMMA established schools to teach the Qur'an and sponsored lectures on the Prophetic Traditions and Muhammad's life. It called for the application of religious laws banning alcohol, gambling, and prostitution. The Association also opposed the spread of western culture, particularly lax morals and missionaries' criticisms of Islam. It favoured modest dress for women, supervision of public behaviour at summer resorts, and restrictions on the genders intermingling. As a long term goal, the YMMA wanted to restore the caliphate.[8] These ideas would become part of the Muslim Brothers' programme.

The YMMA also foreshadowed Banna's organization and activities. Regulations were formulated to govern the YMMA's internal structure. They provided for a general assembly that would elect a twelve member Board of Directors. To spread its views the YMMA set up branches in other Egyptian cities, Palestine, Syria, and Iraq. It also issued weekly and monthly publications. The Association encouraged the creation of Muslim Boy Scouts to promote physical fitness and athletics as signs of renewed Muslim strength. Finally, it envisioned contributing to Muslim economic development by planning Islamic banks and co-operatives. In all these respects, the YMMA reflected the growing mobilization of voluntary religious associations in the later 1920s. The Muslim Brothers would build upon foundations laid down by the YMMA and other activist religious groups.[9]

Toward the end of his stay in Cairo, in 1927 Banna composed his senior essay, in which he compared the social roles of school teachers and Sufi shaykhs. While he expressed appreciation of Sufis' sincerity, discipline, and devotion, he stated that their withdrawal from society limited their influence. Teachers, on the other hand, associate with people on a daily basis, thus allowing them to influence society through the educational system. This engagement with society makes teachers, in Banna's view, superior to Sufi shaykhs and better able to attack the fundamental malady afflicting Egyptian youth: their straying from Islam because of western influences. He declared that his goal was to steer Egyptians back to true Islam through teaching children during the day and holding classes, giving lectures, and preaching at night.[10]

This essay clearly illustrates Banna's sense of facing a choice between a lay vocation as a schoolteacher and a religious path in a Sufi order. He made the criterion of his choice their respective social utility. Even though he left reformist Sufism's institutional framework, he later infused select elements of Sufism into the Muslim Brothers: obedience to the shaykh, mindfulness of God; and conscientious observance of religious duties. Banna did not reject Sufism's pursuit of a personal relationship with God, rather he invented a new organizational framework for that pursuit.

After Banna graduated from Dar al-Ulum in 1927, the

ministry of education appointed him Arabic language teacher at a primary school in Ismailiya, located on the Suez Canal and site of the Suez Canal Company's headquarters. Foreign domination was starkly evident in Ismailiya, where European managers of the Suez Canal Company resided in luxurious bungalows while Egyptians lived in miserable huts. The Company provided the city's essential services like water, sanitation, and health. In addition, a British military camp was located nearby, another reminder of foreign power.[11]

Banna wanted to impart his reformist vision of Islam to the people of Ismailiya, but he did not wish to become entangled in local religious factions. Therefore he avoided speaking in mosques and resolved instead to preach at the town's three main coffeehouses, which he regularly visited to deliver brief religious sermons. He noted in his memoirs that at first people greeted his talks with surprise but that they eventually grew accustomed to him. He soon attracted a regular audience, and some followers asked him to lead discussions in a smaller, more private setting.[12]

In March 1928 Banna founded the Muslim Brothers with the purpose of promoting true Islam and launching a struggle against foreign domination. During the next four years, Banna founded branches in other Canal Zone towns and in the Egyptian delta. When the Ministry of Education transferred him to Cairo in 1932, the Muslim Brothers were poised to grow into a nationwide movement.[13] The centre of Muslim Brother activity moved with Banna to Cairo and spread from there throughout Egypt. The Society grew in numbers and developed an administrative structure that allowed Banna to exercise firm control. During the next ten years the Brothers established their own press, periodicals, and cultural programmes.[14]

The size and influence of the Brothers as well as Banna's ambitious public mission led to his involvement in national politics. In 1936 he published a letter to the king, prime minister, and other Arab rulers encouraging them to promote an Islamic order. Two years later Banna called on the king to dissolve Egypt's political parties because of their corruption and divisive impact on the country. After the war the Brothers played a prominent role in the violent campaign waged by various Egyptian groups against the British occupation. They also engaged in increasingly fierce tactics against their Egyptian adversaries. In December 1948, a Muslim Brother assassinated the prime minister. The Egyptian authorities struck back when members of the secret police assassinated Hasan al-Banna on 12 February 1949.[15]

Hasan al-Banna's Thought

Banna shared with earlier Muslim reformers like Jamal al-Din al-Afghani and Muhammad Abduh the belief that Muslim weakness and vulnerability to European domination stemmed from Muslims' deviation from 'true' Islam. In order to revive Egypt, Muslims had to recommit themselves to understanding and living according to Islam as defined by its scripture, the Qur'an and the Sunnah, and as exemplified by the first generations of Muslims, the *salaf*. The seventh-century Islamic state under the Prophet Muhammad and the early caliphs represented the concrete historical manifestation of a comprehensive Islamic order. Under subsequent rulers the Muslim realm grew weaker as a result of several factors: struggles for power; religious divisions over secondary issues; rulers' indulgence in luxury; rule by non-Arab peoples like the Turks and Persians who never learned true Islam; a lack of interest in practical sciences; and blind obedience to authority. By the thirteenth century these factors rendered the Muslim world vulnerable to the Mongol invasions and the Crusades. While a period of revival followed under the Mamluks and the Ottomans, Muslims remained uninterested in affairs beyond their realm and therefore neglected Europe's achievements in science and politics, which paved the way for its global hegemony in the modern age. By the early twentieth century the Muslim world from North Africa to Indonesia had come under European domination.[16]

The Muslim world's political subordination rendered it susceptible to European cultural influence. Banna believed that European civilization consisted of atheism, immorality, individual and class selfishness, and usury. He characterized European culture as a materialistic one that offered Muslims loans in order to gain control of Muslim economies. European vices imported into Egypt included liquor, dance halls, and immodest dress for women. Furthermore, Europeans founded schools that inculcated adulation of the West among Muslim elites and depicted Islam as defective.[17]

To compound the harmful effects of European culture, most Muslims misunderstood their own religion. They thought it consisted only of the rituals of worship and the moral and spiritual aspects of life.[18] Banna held that the scholars of al-Azhar bore a share of responsibility for Muslims' incorrect notions of their religion. He regarded Azhari ulama as men anchored to irrelevant interpretations of Islam, steeped in the concerns and methods of a bygone age.[19]

The solution to Egypt's political, economic, and cultural problems lay in a return to Islam as a comprehensive order for all aspects of human existence. Banna believed that religion is but a part of Islam, which also defines human conduct in everyday life.[20] Even though Islam was over 1,300 years old, its general principles are sufficiently flexible for adaptation to any place or time. In fact, Islam offers the only path to happiness and fulfilment.[21] Because it is God's way for all people, Muslims must not only strive to adhere to its teachings but to spread its blessings to all humanity, that is, ultimately to convert the entire world to Islam.[22]

According to Banna a true understanding of Islam requires familiarity with the Qur'an and the Sunnah, the authoritative sources for deriving Islam's rules for every circumstance. Muslims devote themselves to studying scripture in order to base their conformity with Islam on understanding rather than obedience to religious authorities. He admitted that individuals would often disagree on minor points of law, but he argued that such differences would not necessarily lead to enmity among Muslims. To minimize disagreement Muslims should avoid discussion of speculative issues and hypothetical questions because they have no practical significance.[23]

Banna's conception of true Islam required the purification of existing religious beliefs and practices. Muslims had to ground their worship in scripture and abandon superstitious beliefs in the efficacy of amulets, charms, soothsaying, and fortune-telling. In general they must combat any innovation in religious practice. With reference to the popular veneration of saints, Banna believed it proper to respect and praise righteous individuals for their good deeds, but he denied that such individuals possessed any spiritual power that could benefit or harm others. Likewise, he viewed visits to tombs as allowable, but he regarded popular practices associated with such visits as forbidden. For instance, Muslims could not seek the intercession of the entombed saint or decorate and illuminate tombs.[24]

On the issue of faith, Banna held that anyone is a Muslim who professes belief in God and Muhammad's prophecy, acts according to that belief, and performs the religious duties. He considered unbelief to consist of open declaration of apostasy, denial of beliefs or practices commonly known to be part of Islam, and deliberate distortion of the Qur'an's meaning. On the traditionally sensitive theological question of how to conceive of God, Banna held that Muslims must profess God's unity and utter unlikeness to any created being, and that Muslims should not interpret Qur'anic verses describing God's attributes. [25]

The reformer emphasized Islam's mundane relevance, noting that it encourages active engagement in the world, including any scientific investigation of nature that leads to technological advances. Banna believed that Islam's teachings could not conflict with the conclusions of science because religion and science deal with different spheres of reality. This position represented a continuation of nineteenth-century reformist thought. [26]

Banna's writings on religion and politics represent a transition from earlier Islamic reformers' insistence on their inseparability to a more detailed elaboration of an Islamic polity's functions and underlying principles. Living in an era when constitutional government, parliament, and elections had the support of politically-minded Muslims in Egypt and elsewhere, Banna asserted the applicability of Islamic principles to widely accepted beliefs about politics and political institutions. He wrote that Islam requires the establishment of a government to prevent anarchy but does not stipulate any particular form of government. Rather, it lays down three basic principles. First, the ruler is responsible to God and the people, indeed he is considered a servant of the people. Second, the Muslim nation must act in a unified manner because brotherhood among believers is a principle of faith. Third, the Muslim nation has the right to monitor the ruler's actions, to give advice to the ruler, and to ensure that its will is respected. Since these are such broad principles, Islamic states can take many forms, including a constitutional parliamentary democracy. [27] As a long-term goal, Banna advocated reviving the caliphate. He remarked that that task required complete co-operation among all Muslims through treaties, alliances, and ultimately an Islamic League of Nations. [28]

Banna considered Egypt's constitution of 1923 valid because it stated that all legislation had to conform with Islamic principles. Indeed, he even stated that constitutional government was the closest of all existing political systems to Islamic government. He appreciated the constitution's guarantees for personal freedom, the principle of consultation, and the ruler's responsibility to the people. On the other hand, Banna believed that certain articles of the constitution needed revision in order to ensure implementation of Islamic law. For Banna, the fundamental flaw in Egypt's political order was that its laws deviated from Islam, and this made them unconstitutional. For instance, he asserted that Egyptian law did not strictly forbid matters prohibited in Islam like alcohol, prostitution, gambling, and usury. Beyond such moral issues, Banna criticized the adoption of foreign law codes for commerce because Islam possessed ample regulations for all matters.[29]

While admitting that Islam validates parliamentary democracy, Banna rejected any role for a multiparty system in an Islamic state. He observed that a parliamentary system may have one, two, or several parties. Egypt's experience had shown that a multiparty system violates the fundamental Islamic value of national unity by sowing divisiveness. Indeed, Banna regarded Egypt's political parties as factions based on differences among prominent personalities. He called for the dissolution of all parties and the formation of a single party to unify the nation, lead it to independence, and strive for internal reform.[30]

Elections could ascertain the will of the nation, but Egypt's electoral system needed reform. Direct elections under the 1923 law and two-stage elections in 1930 had failed to elect the right people; instead they raised to office an unrepresentative group from Egypt's elite. To remedy the matter, Banna proposed that new election laws define qualifications for eligibility to run for office. He wished to restrict candidacy to experts in religious law and public affairs, and to society's 'natural' leaders: heads of tribes, families, and organizations. In addition, Banna wanted to restrict election campaign propaganda, specifically prohibiting personal attacks.[31]

Banna fitted his vision of an Islamic polity to Egypt's existing political system. Moreover, his desire to avoid confrontation with the state inclined him to articulate his views in general terms. This reluctance to give specific content to his envisioned Islamic state led Banna to describe it differently at various times. On one occasion he wrote that a government is Islamic as long as its members are Muslims who perform their religious duties and implement Islamic teachings. The duties of an Islamic government include providing security, enforcing the law, spreading education, promoting public welfare, strengthening morality, protecting property and wealth, defending the Muslim nation, and disseminating the call to Islam. When a government falls short in fulfilling its duties, the people should offer advice and guidance. If that does not bring results, then the people must dismiss the government, for Muslims cannot obey an authority that violates God's will. Banna did not explain how to get rid of such a government.[32]

Given the wide contours of his Islamic state, Banna did not call for the overthrow of Egypt's current political order, rather he sought to reform it. He once addressed a letter to Egypt's leaders detailing how they could work to instil a proper Islamic spirit in the existing structure of power. The leaders should spread an Islamic spirit in government so that civil servants would adhere to Islamic teachings. To further enhance religious sentiment within the state, authorities should offer graduates of al-Azhar positions in the armed forces and civil bureaucracy.[33]

Banna's advocacy of an Islamic state contradicted the predominant Egyptian nationalist sentiment of the time, so he discussed the Muslim Brothers' conception of patriotism and nationalism. He claimed to devote himself to strengthening Egypt as a Muslim country and expressed appreciation for Egyptian patriotism as a manifestation of Muslims' love for their homeland. He wrote that Islam endorses such sentiment in order to realize Muslim lands' freedom and power, to promote communal unity, and to spread the Islamic mission. Banna approved of nationalism when it sought to instil a people's pride in their history or solidarity among citizens. In these instances, nationalism contributes to a collective discipline that encourages the people to strive toward a common goal. On the other hand, Banna considered reprehensible any nationalism that sought to revive the customs of the pagan pre-Islamic age. He had in mind Pharaonism in Egypt, Phoenicianism in Lebanon, and Syrian nationalism. Banna also condemned aggressive nationalism in which one nation seeks to dominate others; here he intended the expansionist nationalism of fascist Germany and Italy. While Banna gave his qualified approval to patriotism and nationalism, he argued that religious belief offers a superior basis for social solidarity.[34]

Banna realized that secular critics would point out that religion is as divisive as any other basis of political identity. He admitted that disagreement in matters of religion is inevitable because of differences in Muslims' degree of knowledge and the influence of their particular situations on their views of religion.

Consequently, Muslims could not attain unanimity on points of detail. But they do agree on the core beliefs and practices, among which are some that call on Muslims to develop fraternal relations and preserve their unity.[35]

Just as Banna departed from earlier reformers in his ideas about Islam and politics, he also broke new ground when he made economic and social issues part of the Islamic reform programme. Such issues were becoming part of Egyptian public discourse in the 1930s, particularly with the growing influence of trade unions and socialism. Banna's address to the Brothers' Sixth Congress in 1941 vividly illustrates his incorporation of economic development concerns into his discourse. He noted that four million Egyptian peasants had no land at all, and another one million peasants owned less than one-half of a feddan. Egypt's urban workers suffered high unemployment, low wages, and dangerous conditions. Foreign-owned mono- polies controlled water, electric lighting, salt, and public transport. Altogether, 320 foreign companies were making exorbitant profits at Egyptians' expense. Banna also described Egypt's abysmal public health by referring to the high incidence of bilharzia, hookworm, and ophthalmia.[36]

Banna was acutely aware of the challenges to Islam from western ideologies on the question of social issues. Indeed, he believed that the Muslim world was in the midst of a battle among competing economic systems: capitalism, communism, and Nazism. Their proponents were urging Muslims to adopt their system, each of which contained benefits and flaws. He admired the Nazis' emphasis on discipline and obedience, but condemned their racism. As for the communists, Banna appreciated their vision of universal brotherhood and a society free of class struggle (though he did not believe in a classless society). On the other hand, he abhorred communism's antagonism toward religion and private property.[37] With respect to capitalism, he argued that it allowed people to manipulate principles of democracy and individual freedom to justify social disruption and immorality.[38] Banna asserted that Muslims did not need to borrow from foreign ideologies because they already had a perfect system in Islam.[39]

An Islamic state would provide jobs and the means of livelihood for anyone able to work. In addition, the state would raise the productivity of industrial workers and peasants. Workers' rights would include a guaranteed job with sufficient wages, limits on the number of work hours per week, health insurance, and a ban on child labour. To combat unemployment, the state would encourage a revival in household handicrafts producing cloth, soap, perfume, and processed foods such as preserves. By such means, women and children would participate in the economy and increase household income.[40]

An Islamic state would also strive to reduce glaring inequalities between rich and poor. The wealthy themselves should change their ways by giving up some luxuries and satisfying themselves with necessities. They would thereby act as a model for the rest of society, and there would be less resentment of disparities in wealth. Official authority must prohibit unlawful means of obtaining a livelihood, such as selling wine, pork, and narcotics. The state should also promote exploration and exploitation of natural resources. The only legitimate tax would be the *zakat* (religious tax on wealth), which has the advantages of preventing hoarding, recirculating wealth, and sparing the poor the burden of taxation. Revenues from the *zakat* would accrue to the armed forces, the poor, and orphans. Regarding the middle classes, Banna favoured an increase in salaries for lower level civil servants and salary reductions for senior civil servants.[41]

Islam protects wealth and property provided they are gained through legitimate means and properly managed and invested. Small property owners should enjoy special incentives whereas restrictions on large property would prevent hoarding and monopolies. The main limitation on private property is that its use not infringe on the public welfare. As for financial institutions, they must observe Islamic principles of fairness and forbid usury. In an Islamic economy, Muslims would spend for socially beneficial purposes and donate to charities.[42] To illustrate this principle, the Brothers regularly collected alms during Ramadan and distributed money and food to the needy. They also set up cemeteries for the poor and took care of orphans.[43]

Banna's vision of an Islamic economy contained an element of economic nationalism. Egypt would break with the British sterling bloc and issue its own currency based on the gold standard. Proper management of the currency would bring Egypt's high inflation under control and create more favourable conditions for her foreign trade balance. Another aspect of economic nationalism encouraged by Banna was the Egyptianization of private firms in real estate, transport, and utilities.[44]

To give substance to this vision of an Islamic economy, the Brothers established a Spinning and Weaving Company, a Commercial and Engineering Works company, and an Islamic Press. While these activities enjoyed only modest success, they demonstrated the harmony between economic activity and religious idealism.[45]

Banna's Islamic state would establish a truly Muslim cultural order as well. The idea of a ruler guaranteeing public morality long predated modern reform movements. For centuries Muslim authorities had assumed the task of safeguarding and enforcing Islamic morality, as in the ancient office of the *muhtasib*. On the other hand, some of Banna's concerns reflected Egyptian Muslims' adoption of western customs. The state would instil respect for public morality and inflict severe penalties on offenders. Prostitution and alcohol would be banned, fornicators punished with flogging, and dance halls closed. Schools would provide separate facilities and devise distinctive curricula for boys and girls. The state should also exercise the power to censor songs, lectures, films, plays, and books.[46]

Correct observance of religious practices also comes under government authority. Illegitimate innovations surrounding the celebration of weddings, births, and holidays must be curbed. To spread a correct understanding of Islam, religious instruction should be a part of education from primary school to university. Such instruction would include memorization of the Qur'an, Arabic grammar, and Islamic history. Civics classes would instil a strong sentiment of patriotism and morality. In general the state should encourage Egyptians to abandon western customs and return to Egyptian ones in their homes and in public.[47]

Banna did not pin all his hopes for an Islamic order on the government. In fact, his early enthusiasm for Sufism found its way into his prescriptions for the formation of an Islamic personality in individual Muslim Brothers. He expected that by converting Muslims to true Islam and reshaping their personalities, eventually a purely Muslim society would develop and then transform the state.[48] In this latter regard, Banna sought to convey his sense of the proper Muslim life and mind, a sense steeped in the ethos of Shari'a-minded Sufism's conscientious adherence to the Prophet's model as reflected in the thousands of *hadiths* that comprise the Sunnah.

In one essay Banna described how a Muslim could strengthen his faith and adherence to Islamic teachings. The fundamental principle is to practise *dhikr*, mindfulness of God, and to follow the example of the Prophet in doing so. When properly practised, *dhikr* creates a state of mind that inclines one to obedience to God, the very core of Islam, which means submission to God's will. When one practises *dhikr*, one should do so in a low voice and mentally focus on the meaning of the words being recited. When one performs *dhikr* in a group, the individuals should recite the litany in unison to create a sense of harmony and solidarity. Participants in group *dhikr* should keep good hygiene in their dress and surroundings. Properly performed, group *dhikr* strengthens the bond among believers. It is a useful way to spend one's spare time, and it can impart knowledge of Islam to less educated Muslims. On the other hand, group *dhikr* is reprehensible if it disturbs a Muslim in prayer, or when it is accompanied by laughter, or when the prescribed litanies are altered. Banna recommended group *dhikr* for the Muslim Brothers at their headquarters or in a mosque before going to work in the morning and on returning home in the evening.[49]

In addition to *dhikr*, the Muslim attains great merit through daily recitation of a portion of the Qur'an. The pious forefathers, the *salaf*, realized this, and by frequently reciting the Qur'an they made it the fountainhead of their lives for which God rewarded them with dominion in the world. In later centuries Muslims neglected the Qur'an, and as a result they became weak. Therefore, a Muslim revival depends in part on daily recitation of the Qur'an. How large a portion of the Qur'an one recites each day depends on the Brother's circumstances. One should not recite it in fewer than three days or more than a month. The middle way is to complete the Qur'an in one week, if circumstances permit. Illiterate Muslims are exempt from the requirement to read the Qur'an each day, but they should make an effort to listen to another Muslim reciting it or to memorize parts of it and recite them. When one recites the Qur'an, one should strive for complete concentration on its meaning. Banna encouraged group meetings at which members would listen to the Qur'an's recitation while they observed silence, pondered its meaning, and adopted a humble attitude before God.[50]

Banna mined the Prophetic Traditions for prayers suitable to all aspects of a Muslim's daily life. These included prayers to recite when one awakens in the morning, dresses or undresses, leaves or enters the home, walks to, enters, or leaves a mosque, and suffers from insomnia or experiences a nightmare. Other prayers could be recited for a particular need, for God's guidance, or during a thunderstorm.[51]

Finally, Banna recommended a daily litany for Muslim Brothers. They were to recite a prayer seeking God's forgiveness one hundred times; they were also to recite the formula 'There is no god but God' one hundred times. These were to be performed after the morning prayer and after one of the two evening prayers. In another prayer for brotherhood among his disciples, to be recited at sunset every evening, one would create a mental image of a Brother, feel a spiritual bond with a Brother one does not know well, and pray for him. When one gets ready to go to sleep, one should recite a prayer that involves scrutinizing one's actions that day.[52]

To enhance one's religious experience, a Muslim should strive always to be mindful of God, behaving in a manner intended to win God's pleasure. One can grow closer to God through performing supererogatory acts of worship like praying at night, fasting three days each month, and frequently doing *dhikr*. A Muslim can improve his purity by remaining in a state of ablution as often as possible. Of course, Muslims should try to be consistent in performing the obligatory prayers, seeking to perform them in a group and in a mosque as often as possible.[53]

Banna enumerated the duties of the Muslim Brothers in their personal lives. The Brother must recite a portion of the Qur'an each day, memorize at least forty Prophetic Traditions, study the Prophet's life, early Islamic history, and the basic principles of Islamic law. The Brother must take care of his health, regularly undergo physical exams, and build up his physical strength. He should avoid excessive consumption of coffee and tea, and he must abstain from tobacco altogether. Attention to personal hygiene and cleanliness at home and the workplace is required. The Muslim Brother has a duty to develop his intellect through wide reading, especially in the Society's essays, newspapers, and magazines. Each Brother should build up a private library, no matter how modest, and develop a specialized knowledge or technical skill.[54]

In personal conduct, one should be wary of committing small sins as well as the obvious major ones. The best way to discipline oneself is to engage in a *jihad* against one's self, to make the instincts yield to one's will and redirect them to permitted things. A Muslim should not keep company with people who drink alcohol or have immoral character; this includes corrupt family relations and friends. Banna added that one should not waste time, because time is life. Therefore, one should manage to spend all one's time in beneficial activities.[55] In dealings with others, the Brother must always be truthful and keep his promises. He must speak the truth frankly, admit mistakes, and control himself when he becomes angry. Further, he must maintain a dignified manner without taking himself so seriously that he cannot enjoy humour. The Brother should actively seek to serve others and to derive joy from helping the ill and the needy or consoling those in grief. In general, he should have a merciful, gentle heart for people and animals.[56]

No matter how wealthy, the Brother must continue to work for his livelihood. He should not pursue a government position, but he should accept such a position if it is offered and it does not prevent him from working for the Brothers' mission. In general, one should devote oneself wholeheartedly to one's occupation. The Brother should also contribute a portion of his wealth to support the mission and save a portion for emergencies. Muslims can serve their religion by eating, wearing, and buying only products made in Muslim lands. Banna urges his followers to boycott civil courts because they enforce unislamic laws. Likewise, they should boycott unislamic newspapers, schools, clubs, and associations.[57]

Banna's ideas about the role of women were strictly traditional, although he couched his conservative vision in terms claiming a natural basis and benevolent purpose. In his essay on the Muslim woman, he wrote that Islam gives women complete personal and political rights. But men and women have different roles in society based on natural, biological differences; therefore, Islam provides guidance for women to fulfil their God-given natural roles, which for Banna stem from their reproductive functions. In other words, a woman's place is the home, and her primary roles are mother, wife, and housekeeper. Muslim girls, then, should be prepared for their later adult responsibilities with education in reading, writing, arithmetic, religion, early Islamic history, hygiene, child-rearing, and home-making. Women have no need to learn law, foreign languages, or technical sciences because their place is in the home.[58]

A second principle governing women's conduct stems from a common Muslim notion that sexual attraction is the fundamental feature of relations between men and women. In order to protect men and women from their instinctive urges, Islam prohibits social mixing between genders. Otherwise, morals would be corrupted and adultery would occur, thereby ruining marriages and violating families' honour. To prevent that, Islam forbids a woman to be alone with a stranger and encourages women to stay at home as much as possible. When women go out, they must dress modestly and avoid eye contact with men. All this means that Banna regarded as alien to Islam mixing of genders in schools and public places. Banna cited a number of Prophetic Traditions to support his position. One Tradition forbids a woman from travelling for three days or longer without a male guardian. Another states that when a woman appears in public she may expose only her face and hands. Banna even cited a Tradition that urges women to pray at home instead of at the mosque.[59]

Hasan al-Banna: Organizer and Activist

Banna's chief innovations for modern Islamic movements lay in the practical realms of organization and action. One lesson he drew from his first years in Cairo as a student at Dar al-Ulum was that earlier reformers had the right intentions but had not developed effective means. He resolved to rectify this by creating an activist organization to implement the Islamic reform mission.[60] In developing a structure for the Society, he introduced principles of bureaucratic organization, which had spread from state and military institutions more broadly into Egyptian society. Banna was himself a member of the education bureaucracy, and he naturally brought a number of institutionalized rules and procedures to his creation.

Because the Muslim Brotherhood grew gradually in its early phase, Banna did not devise an organized framework until his transfer to Cairo in 1932, although the previous year he had drawn up a set of regulations to govern the Society's operations. In Cairo he developed a headquarters with a fulltime administrative staff to communicate directly with the numerous provincial branches, each of which had its own administrative council and general assembly. The headquarters provided a schedule of activities for the branches to follow and monitored their adherence to it.[61]

Banna approached the task of organizing the Brothers in a pragmatic fashion, developing new institutions to exercise control over growing numbers of members and experimenting with different structures. By 1946, he had formulated a chain of command designed to secure his authority over all units within the Society. He stood at the apex as General Guide, an office he would hold for life. A General Guidance Council of twelve assisted in executing the General Guide's policy. The closest body to a party congress was the Consultative Assembly, which had between 100 and 150 members. The Assembly held annual meetings, conducted by Banna, and it elected the members of the General Guidance Council.[62]

In addition to a core of leading bodies, Banna devised a hierarchy of units of descending size from district to branch to cells, known as families. He supplemented this vertical model with committees responsible for the Society's financial, legal, and welfare functions. Finally, a third type of organizational framework, called sections, roughly corresponded to a corporate division of Egyptian society into urban workers, peasants, students, and professionals. Other sections dealt with physical education, the press, and spreading the Society's teachings to other Muslim countries.[63]

Banna paid close attention to the functions of each component in the Society's organization. With respect to the 'family' (al-usrah), the smallest unit, he wrote that it had three pillars. The first was mutual acquaintance, which would ensure the unity of its members. Second, family members had to achieve mutual understanding by giving and accepting advice. Finally, they would exhibit their solidarity by helping each other. They would come together at weekly meetings at which each member related such daily problems as illness and financial needs. The family would discuss ways to solve the Brother's particular problem in an atmosphere of sincerity and trust. Members also discussed general Islamic affairs and directives from the central leadership. Banna strongly discouraged quarrels. In the event of disagreement, the head of the family would refer the issue to the leadership for clarification. Weekly meetings also provided an occasion for studying useful books.[64]

In addition to weekly meetings, family members could strengthen their solidarity with occasional outings for cultural or athletic purposes. Banna specifically mentioned canoe trips, hikes in the mountains and the desert, and bicycle rides. He also encouraged family members to regularly join in religious observances by meeting to perform the dawn prayer at a mosque at least once a week or by fasting together one day every week or two. In Banna's mind then, the family would provide a microcosm of the ideal Muslim society in which believers treated each other as brothers and shared in the endeavour to heighten religious, social, and cultural aspects of their lives.[65]

Banna's interest in physical education found expression in the Muslim Brothers' scouts, or rovers. This section resembled youth groups established by the Wafd party and Young Egypt. All three emphasized discipline, martial spirit, and solidarity. The rovers' activities included participation in sports like wrestling, boxing, basketball, and football. They also went on camping trips and performed acts of public service in the realms of education, health, and sanitation.[66] Banna instructed Muslim Brothers belonging to the rovers' battalions to become thoroughly acquainted with each other by faithfully attending meetings. They must abandon any group or organization whose principles did not accord with the Brothers' mission.[67]

The rovers' ethos recalls European militarism of the 1930s, but Banna held that while fascism and Nazism represented pure militarism, the rovers were only one component of an Islamic system which regulates the military aspect.[68] Nonetheless, the rovers did resemble Europe's militarist youth organizations in their stress on absolute obedience to the leader and the cause, and in their declared readiness to resort to force in pursuit of the mission. The rovers also provided a recruiting ground for another of Banna's creations, the Special Apparatus.[69]

Brothers who demonstrated a high degree of commitment to the mission could join the Special Apparatus. Its members vowed to observe a more disciplined daily regime that involved keeping a record of all their efforts toward memorizing the Qur'an and reciting various portions of it. They also had to undergo fitness examinations to verify their adherence to a regimen of exercise. Banna organized special courses in religion, law, first aid, and weaponry. These shock troops for Islam had to be prepared spiritually and physically to engage in *jihad* for the mission. The oath of allegiance symbolized this commitment. It took place in a darkened room where the initiate would swear to secrecy on a Qur'an and a pistol. To inspire these most militant and devoted Brothers, Banna invoked *jihad*, martyrdom, and 'the art of death,' which he sanctioned with reference to a Qur'anic verse urging believers to love death more than life.[70]

Banna considered organization necessary, but by itself insufficient to realize the Brothers' aims. He always stressed that a spirit of activism in all fields of life was absolutely essential in order to give practical expression to his vision of Islam as a total framework for individual and collective human action. He personally exemplified this activism with a zeal for his mission that captivated his followers. For example, when he was in Ismailiya he set out to establish a branch of the Brothers in another town. He walked through the streets looking at people in the shops and cafés until he found a shopkeeper who looked like a receptive individual and successfully recruited him.[71] Banna conducted hundreds of such trips, travelling throughout the country by train, automobile, and cart. He would pray in the village mosque and then talk with people about religion. He thereby constructed a vast network of personal relationships, which were the foundation of his special leadership, for literally thousands of Egyptians believed he was their friend.[72] Banna also personified an activist ethos in his daily routine when he lived in Cairo. Typically, he would go to the headquarters in the morning, then teach at elementary school. Afterwards he would return to the headquarters, then return home to rest during the afternoon. In the evening he gave lectures at the headquarters on the Qur'an and its relevance to everyday life.[73]

Banna imparted his activism to the Muslim Brothers and directed them to demonstrate Islam's comprehensiveness in the variety of their endeavours. In an essay published in 1934, Banna described the Brothers' activities in various parts of Egypt. These included setting up schools for boys, girls, and workers; building mosques and a textile factory; forming charitable clubs to assist the needy; preaching at coffee houses, public places, parties, and wakes; volunteering to repair mosques, clean streets, and instal street lighting in villages; combating corrupt habits and superstitions; collecting surplus grain as a form of *zakat* and distributing it to the needy; providing shelter for the poor; and publishing a newspaper to combat missionary influences.[74]

The Brothers' central purpose was to spread the call to true Islam, and this entailed education. Banna the schoolteacher tirelessly toured the country to give lectures and preach his message. At the Brothers' first branch in Ismailiya Banna collected donations to build a mosque and a school. The mosque-school complex became a ubiquitous feature of the Brothers' branches. For the school in Ismailiya Banna instructed pupils to wear a uniform consisting of a long shirt and a coat of Egyptian fabric, a cap, and shoes. The curriculum he devised included religious education as well as industrial training.[75] In later years the Brothers established primary, secondary and technical schools. Separate schools for girls were also set up. Banna was a firm believer in adult education, so the Brothers ran night schools for workers and peasants to teach literacy and religion. The Brothers also conducted special courses for university students to help them pass examinations.[76]

Because of his abiding faith in ordinary Muslims, Banna conducted his lessons at a simple level, seeking to teach correct performance of ablution before prayer, the prayers themselves, and explaining their basis in the Sunnah. He intended his direct style and frequent anecdotes to capture his listeners' attention, and he preferred brief, fifteen minute talks to lengthy speeches. Part of his spellbinding manner was his ability to articulate ideas in an Islamic idiom that wrapped his speech in an aura of legitimacy. In his courses on Qur'anic recitation, Islamic history, and Islamic law he deliberately avoided controversial matters that often divided ulama formally trained at al-Azhar. Banna believed that most of these contested issues were trivial and that they detracted from his aim of nurturing Muslim unity.[77]

Banna paid close attention to public communication, developing not only his own splendid oratorical talents, but also purposefully selecting individuals to act as spokesmen on the basis of their public speaking ability. In his desire to reach ordinary Egyptians he recruited men from the popular classes who could speak the language and address the needs of the Egyptian masses. Finally, Banna organized special courses to provide instruction in public speaking.[78] Banna's approach to reaching the public extended beyond the spoken word to writing. He admitted that he had learned the utility of propaganda from European examples, and developed a propaganda apparatus for the Brothers that began with a newsletter, continued with a weekly journal, and culminated with a daily newspaper and a monthly periodical which was modelled on Rashid Rida's *al-Manar*.[79]

For all of Banna's devotion to organization and action, he seems to have intentionally left vague his vision of how to transform Egypt into an Islamic order. Yet he did describe the process in general terms. The first stage involved propagating the message through public lectures, speaking on ceremonial occasions, and publishing. In the second stage, the Brothers moved into action with groups like the rovers, who developed physical and martial skills in addition to further refining their religious discipline. The final stage would bring the Brothers' mission to fruition with the inauguration of an Islamic order.[80] He warned the Egyptian government that when all peaceful means had failed, the Brothers would resort to force and seize power to instal an Islamic regime. Banna stated that the Brothers did not choose violent upheaval, but a revolt would inevitably result from the pressure of circumstances burdening the Egyptian people. Even so, Banna also stated that the Brothers did not seek to rule the country, rather they wanted to assist a ruler who would act according to Islam. Banna never clearly described the conditions in which the Brothers would use force, rather he frequently reminded his more impatient followers that action required planning and patience. They must wait for the nation to be thoroughly islamized and properly prepared to support an Islamic regime.[81]

Hasan al-Banna in Historical Perspective

Hasan al-Banna approached the task of reforming Muslim society not as a systematic theoretician but as a pragmatic populist leader. It is difficult to obtain a clear, comprehensive image of his thought because he developed his ideas, for the most part, not from a detached philosophical perspective but in light of immediate events and circumstances. His writings consist of brief essays and articles rather than lengthy books that elaborate in detail the Islamic order he sought. Instead of viewing his intellectual modesty as a defect, we should see it as one aspect of his populist appeal. Muhammad Abduh and Rashid Rida had more elegantly formulated the intellectual and methodological underpinnings for Banna's simpler discourse, but they had not cultivated a mass audience for their ideas. Banna's seminal contribution to modern Islamic revival lay in the practical realm of organization and action. By founding and developing the Muslim Brothers, he created a model that Muslim revivalists would replicate throughout the Arab world and beyond.[82]

One source of Banna's divergence from earlier thinkers may have been his lay education in state schools; by contrast, Abduh and Rida had more traditional religious training. Banna's lay education and vocation became increasingly frequent traits of Islamist activists and thinkers in the second half of the twentieth century. He learned of psychology, philosophy, economics, and physical education, subjects that he would have neglected had he opted for the traditional route of an al-Azhar training. On his own he read in law, education, and political science.[83]

Perhaps as a result of this lay background, Banna's and other Islamist's insistence on scriptural authority as the criterion of truth and value is couched in a discourse distinctly modern in its definition of problems and categories of analysis. Muslim societies are seen as backward, a notion that is sensible only in the context of western domination. This backwardness permeates politics, economy, and culture, themselves modern categories of analysis. Banna pondered the problem of Muslim backwardness by examining both the collective, social level, thereby introducing a sociology of Muslims, and the individual level, thereby devising a psychology of Muslims.[84] His discourse would have been inconceivable fifty years earlier, before the diffusion of modern western categories of analysis.

There remained a powerful tradition at work in Banna's discourse, namely Shari'a-minded Sufism. Indeed, he perpetuated this tradition with his instructions to Muslim Brothers to frequently perform *dhikr* and recite litanies. Likewise, he called on his followers to be ever mindful of God in all their doings, to observe all religious duties, to scrutinize their conduct, and to measure their social interactions by Islamic norms. Banna gave new form to an old tradition by infusing it with an activist engagement in political struggle and by devising a novel organizational framework for the realization of Muslims' duty to command the good and prevent the forbidden (*amr al-ma'ruf wa nahy al-munkar*).

Banna also retained the Sufi order's spirit of authority by adopting the relationship of shaykh to disciple in which the latter owes complete obedience to the former. Banna's charismatic leadership, so frequently cited by followers and observers alike, is strongly reminiscent of that of Sufi shaykhs. Indeed, one contemporary observer of the Brothers in the early 1930s wrote that at first many considered them a new Sufi order.[85] A critical Egyptian biographer compared his followers' utter devotion to him to that of believers in a Sufi saint.[86] Banna's influence, then, cannot be reduced to the words he wrote or spoke, texts available to historians for analysis and interpretation. Rather, to understand his impact on modern Muslim history, one must try to imagine the magnetism of his personality, his ability to inspire and lead by example: qualities that are irreducible to words, but, like memories of and feelings for Muslim saints, they continue to resonate in Muslims' lives.

Notes

This chapter is dedicated to the memory of Richard P. Mitchell.

1. Hasan al-Banna, *Memoirs of Hasan al-Banna Shaheed*, Karachi: International Islamic Publishers, 1981, p. 84.

2. *Ibid.*, pp. 62–5; Richard P. Mitchell, *The Society of the Muslim Brothers*, London: Oxford University Press, 1969, pp. 1–2.

3. Banna, *Memoirs*, pp. 68–74.

4. *Ibid.*, pp. 59–61, 75–77.

5. *Ibid.*, pp. 102, 108–10.

6. *Ibid.*, pp. 111–13.

7. *Ibid.*, pp. 115–16.

8. G. Kampffmeyer, 'Egypt and Western Asia', in H.A.R. Gibb, *Whither Islam?*, London: Victor Gollancz Ltd., 1932, pp. 114–15, 121, 133–5, 137.

9. *Ibid.*, pp. 103–4, 109–110, 114, 133. On the variety of religious associations in Egypt at the time, see James Heyworth-Dunne, *Religious and Political Trends in Modern Egypt*, Washington: J. Heyworth-Dunne, 1950, pp. 29–30.

10. Banna, *Memoirs*, pp. 117–19.

11. *Ibid.*, pp. 112–26, 140–1.

12. *Ibid.*, pp. 127–9.

13. *Ibid.*, pp. 141–2, 155, 178–80, 224; 'Risalat al-mu'tamar al-khamis', in *Majmu'at rasa'il al-imam al-shahid Hasan al-Banna*, Beirut: Dar al-Andalus, 1965, pp. 264–5.

14. Mitchell, *Society*, pp. 13–34.

15. *Ibid.*, pp. 35–71; Rif'at Sa'id, *Hasan al-Banna: Mata wa kayfa wa li-madha*, Cairo: Madbuli, 1971, pp. 104–17.

16. Hasan al-Banna, 'Between Yesterday and Today,' in Charles Wendell, *Fives Tracts of Hasan al-Banna*, Berkeley: University of California Press, 1975, pp. 17–24.

17. *Ibid.*, pp. 26–8.

18. Hasan al-Banna, 'Risalat al-mu'tamar al-khamis,' pp. 242–3; *Hal nahnu qawm 'amaliyyun?*, Mansurah: Dar al-Wafa, 1980, pp. 38–9.

19. Banna, *Hal nahnu*, p. 64; Mitchell, *Society*, pp. 211–14.

20. Hasan al-Banna, 'Mushkilatuna fi daw' al-nizam al-islami,' in *Majmu'at rasail*, p. 341; 'Risalat al-mu'tamar al-khamis,' pp. 244–5; 'Risalat al-ta'alim,' in *Majmu'at rasa'il*, p. 7.

21. Banna, 'Risalat al-mu'tamar al-khamis', pp. 239, 244–50; 'Risalat al-ta'alim,' p. 7; 'Mushkilatuna,' pp. 341–2.

22. Hasan al-Banna, 'al-Ikhwan al-muslimun tahta rayat al-Qur'an,' in *Majmu'at rasa'il*, pp. 308–11; 'To What Do We Summon Mankind?' in *Five Tracts*, pp. 72, 80; 'On Jihad,' in *Five Tracts*, p. 151.

23. Banna, 'Risalat al-ta'alim', pp. 7–9; 'Risalat al-mu'tamar al-khamis,' p. 252.

24. 'Risalat al-ta'alim', pp. 8–10.

25. *Ibid.*, pp. 9, 11.

26. *Ibid.*, p. 11; 'Toward the Light', in *Five Tracts*, pp. 115–16.

27. Banna, 'Mushkilatuna', pp. 358–9, 366.

28. Banna, 'Risalat al-mu'tamar al-khamis', pp. 284–5.
29. *Ibid.*, pp. 274–8; 'To What Do We Summon Mankind?' pp. 88–90.
30. Banna, 'Risalat al-mu'tamar al-khamis', pp. 287–8; 'Mushkilatuna', pp. 374–6.
31. Banna, 'Mushkilatuna', pp. 377–80.
32. Banna, 'Risalat al-ta'alim', p. 13.
33. Banna, 'Toward the Light', in *Five Tracts*, p. 126.
34. Hasan al-Banna, 'Our mission', in *Five Tracts*, pp. 48–56.
35. *Ibid.*, pp. 56–9; 'Risalat al-ta'alim', p. 9.
36. Hasan al-Banna, *Risalat al-mu'tamar al-sadis* (al-Wafa', 1941), pp. 16–21; for similar remarks, see 'Between Yesterday and Today', pp. 31–3.
37. Banna, 'Mushkilatuna', p. 389; I.M. Husayni, *The Moslem Brethren*, Beirut: Khayats, 1956, p. 93.
38. Banna, *Memoirs*, p. 208.
39. Banna, 'Mushkilatuna', p. 389.
40. Banna, 'Toward the Light', p. 130; 'Mushkilatuna', pp. 391, 406; Husayni, *The Moslem Brethren*, pp. 57–8.
41. Banna, 'Mushkilatuna', pp. 395, 404–05; 'Toward the Light', p. 130.
42. Banna, 'Mushkilatuna', pp. 391–2, 404; 'Toward the Light', p. 130.
43. Husayni, *The Moslem Brethren*, pp. 52–3.
44. Banna, 'Mushkilatuna', pp. 399–400; 'Risalat al-ta'alim', p. 23.
45. Husayni, *The Moslem Brethren*, p. 56.
46. Banna, 'Toward the Light', pp. 127–8.
47. *Ibid.*, pp. 128–9.
48. Banna, 'Between Yesterday and Today', p. 33; 'Our Mission', pp. 63–4.
49. Hasan al-Banna, *al-Ma'thurat*, Kuwait: Maktabat al-Manar, 1950, pp. 6–12.
50. *Ibid.*, pp. 38–53.
51. *Ibid.*, pp. 55–98.
52. *Ibid.*, pp. 99–101.
53. Banna, 'Risalat al-ta'alim', pp. 11–12, 23–4.
54. *Ibid.*, pp. 20–2.
55. *Ibid.*, p. 24.
56. *Ibid.*, p. 20–1.
57. *Ibid.*, pp. 23–4.
58. Hasan al-Banna, *al-Mar'ah al-muslimah*, Cairo: Dar al-kutub al-salafiyyah, 1983, pp. 9–14, 25.
59. *Ibid.*, pp. 10, 14–22.
60. Banna, *Memoirs*, pp. 113–15; 'Risalat al-mu'tamar al-khamis', p. 240.
61. Mitchell, *Society*, pp. 13, 163–70, 175–80.
62. *Ibid.*, pp. 165–9.
63. *Ibid.*, pp. 170–82.
64. Hasan al-Banna, 'al-Usrah', in *Majmu'at rasa'il*, pp. 28–31.
65. *Ibid.*, p. 32.
66. Sa'id, *Hasan al-Banna*, p. 70.
67. Banna, 'Risalat al-mu'tamar al-khamis', p. 255; Mitchell, *Society*, pp. 202–5; Husayni, *The Moslem Brethren*, pp. 58–9.
68. Banna, 'Toward the Light', pp. 111–13.

69. Mitchell, *Society*, pp. 30, 203–5; Sa'id, *Hasan al-Banna*, p. 127.
70. Mitchell, *Society*, pp. 205–8.
71. Banna, *Memoirs*, pp. 176–8.
72. Sa'id, *Hasan al-Banna*, pp. 47–8.
73. Mitchell, *Society*, p. 12.
74. Banna, *Hal nahnu*, pp. 15–17.
75. Banna, *Memoirs*, pp. 142–3, 151–8, 171.
76. Husayni, *The Moslem Brethren*, pp. 13, 52.
77. Banna, *Memoirs*, pp. 127–33; Sa'id, *Hasan al-Banna*, p. 54.
78. Mitchell, *Society*, p. 190.
79. Banna, 'Our Mission', pp. 45–6,; Mitchell, *Society*, pp. 185–6.
80. Banna, 'Risalat al-mu'tamar al-khamis', pp. 255–8.
81. *Ibid.*, pp. 268–73; *Risalat al-mu'tamar al-sadis*, pp. 27–8; Mitchell, *Society*, pp. 15, 103.
82. For a group in Pakistan that consciously followed the Muslim Brothers' example, see Seyyid Vali Reza Nasr, 'Students, Islam, and Politics: Islami Jami'at-i Tulaba in Pakistan', *Middle East Journal* 46, no. 1, Winter 1992, p. 61.
83. Husayni, *The Moslem Brethren*, pp. 25–31.
84. Banna, *Hal nahnu*, pp. 4–7.
85. Heyworth-Dunne, *Religious and Political Trends*, p. 33.
86. Sa'id, *Hasan al-Banna*, p. 46; see also Mitchell, *Society*, pp. 297–9.

7

Sayyid Qutb:
The Political Vision

Charles Tripp

Introduction

There is a strong temptation to relate Sayyid Qutb's life experiences straightforwardly to his writings, as a way of explaining their orientation and their development. This applies both to his literary output, as well as to his later works on Islam, society and politics. Qutb himself appears to have encouraged such an association, through his semi-autobiographical writings. More seriously, his own approach to Islam was not only unashamedly subjective, at times almost mystical, but this was also the basis of the method which he advocated to others as the one most likely to bring them to a true understanding of God's commands. Furthermore, the case against him at his trial by the Egyptian authorities was based almost entirely upon the writings which had defined his life and were now to be used to justify the ending of it.

Sayyid Qutb's experience can, indeed, be read into his writings, since he is one of the more confessional of contemporary Muslim writers: his awakening aesthetic appreciation of the Qur'an; his growing disgust with the society around him in Egypt, as well as his direct experience of what he came to regard as the source of its corruption during his two-year stay in the United States; his self-described 'conversion' to Islam; the optimism of the years which followed, coinciding as they did with a new regime in Egypt; his growing disillusionment and the pain and bitterness of his eleven-year imprisonment, as well as the consolation which he found during those years in the text of the Qur'an. All of these experiences can plausibly be used to understand the direction taken by his thinking about society, about politics and about the place of Islam in the world.

However, beyond the autobiographical, one should also examine the structure and logic of his thought, the categories which he used and the ways in which he sought to resolve the problems and contradictions therein. This is particularly necessary since Sayyid Qutb was writing from a self-consciously Islamic standpoint which led him finally to advocate the rejection of *jahili* – that is, un-Islamic – concerns and modes of reasoning. Yet he himself was writing as an intellectual of the mid-twentieth century, unavoidably influenced by the very intellectual and moral forces which he sought to reject. This resulted in an interesting tension in his writings – a tension which has been evident to a large degree among those who have been inspired by him. Qutb was adamant in insisting that his interpretation of the nature of Islamic obligation should not be taken as an intellectual exercise only, but should become the basis of effective practice as well. Some have taken him at his word, but, in seeking to attach power to the vision of the good life, have demonstrated some of the ambiguities on which that vision rests.

Life, Career and Writings

Sayyid Qutb lived in Egypt during a period in which the diversity of thought and debate under the monarchy was to give way to the monologue of Nasserism. His formative years witnessed the vicissitudes of the movement for independence from British control, as well as the spirited debates and conflicts among the Egyptians themselves about the future of their country.

Born in 1906 to a middling family of rural Upper Egypt, Qutb moved to Cairo in the 1920s to complete his education. He was eventually to become a teacher and inspector for the Ministry of Education, serving as an official of that ministry until he resigned in 1953. At the same time, he gained some prominence as a literary critic and writer, under the initial guidance and influence of figures such as Abbas al-Aqqad. A minor, but nevertheless active, participant in the literary circles of Cairo during the 1930s and 1940s, Qutb was party to the debates of the time.[1]

Some of these revolved around the perennial question of the social, as opposed to the aesthetic, responsibility of the artist – a common enough theme where people are seeking to assert their identity and their independence as a national community. In Egypt, it was to raise the key question of the nature of that communal identity. 'Egypt for the Egyptians' had been the slogan of the nationalist movement since the 1880s, as a means of assertion chiefly against outside, European powers. With the achievement of a progressively greater degree of independence from those powers, it was becoming important for many Egyptians that they should understand what it meant to assert their identity as Egyptians, since that would clearly affect the distinctive kind of political and social order which would emerge.

For a number of the more prominent intellectuals of the day, it seemed that this act of collective re-imagination required that priority should be accorded to the Islamic heritage in Egyptian history and society. There were clear differences concerning the practical implications of such a position: some saw this as a kind of cultural 'gloss' which would in no way alter the political structure of the state or compromise the status of non-Muslim Egyptians; others suggested that the inescapable obligation upon those who accepted the distinctively Islamic nature of the Egyptian community was the establishment of an Islamic political order, founded on the Shari'a alone; for others, again, the very nature of the Islamic vision required a different aesthetic, based on criteria that were specifically not derived from the western tradition which had shaped so much of the intellectual life of the country.

Qutb was, therefore, immersed in the spirited and, in some respects, optimistic discussions of the time. For many, it was the very plight of the Egyptians, whether on social, economic, political or indeed cultural levels, which made it so urgent that a better, more rewarding way forward be found. Nevertheless, in much of the writing of the 1930s and 1940s, however desperate the portrayal of existing conditions, there is a certain optimism about the capacity of the Egyptians themselves to remedy their situation. This might require political upheaval or revolution, but the improvement of the people's lot in a redefined and re-ordered society was frequently depicted as attainable, if not necessarily easy. As always in such debates, whether in Egypt or elsewhere, much of the discussion revolved around the question of what exactly needed to be changed in order to bring about the required improvements.

Sayyid Qutb appeared to enter this debate as a moralist. He decried what he saw as a moral decline in the behaviour of those around him and sought both to understand the reasons for this laxity, and to urge a greater awareness of those ethical norms which he seemed to associate with a good life. At the same time, he appeared to be influenced by the general trend towards a re-examination of Islamic themes which was then evident in the literary circles of Egypt. His examination of the imagery used in the Qur'an, hardly broke new aesthetic ground, nor did it propose a different principle of aesthetic or literary merit to those which he had absorbed in his largely western-shaped education. Nevertheless, it represents, in his own field, an endeavour to return to the Islamic heritage in an explicit way – moreover, in a way which clearly had an effect upon his ethical, as well as his aesthetic sensibilities.[2]

Increasingly, therefore, during the 1940s, Sayyid Qutb's moralizing was grounded in an Islamic ethic. That is, the criteria of moral probity by which he judged the behaviour of others were founded upon a conception of social obligation and of human nature which had as reference point his understanding of Islam. At this stage, he appeared to be anxious to interpret the ethical obligations of Islam in the light of the understanding of the individual which appeared so dominant, not simply in the structure of the surrounding organization of society, but also in the structures of thought that had helped to shape his own conception of the world, his sensibilities and his approach to language. In short, there is evidence in Qutb's writings during this period that he was making an effort to reconcile a liberal understanding of the individual's needs and interests with a growing appreciation of the importance and indeed uniqueness of the Islamic community.

The more he thought of the definition of this distinctively Islamic community and the foundations, as well as particularities of its ethical system, the more he differentiated it from others. Thus, from a position in which he had been primarily a moralist, concerned about the conduct of individuals and the reform of that conduct, Sayyid Qutb became increasingly concerned with the security and the probity of the community. Equally, the more he saw this as a question of communitarian stability, the more he identified other systems, other collective forms of organization, as essentially inimical to the Islamic design.[3]

As an Egyptian whose country had been for most of his life under British control, he had little difficulty in identifying the specific enemy. However, it appears that his experience of living in the United States, where he was sent by the Ministry of Education during the years 1948-1950, caused him to see the enemy as a more generic and, in some respects, more intrusive one. British imperialism was characterized merely as one aspect of a more wide-ranging and sinister form of collective enmity – that of the secular, materialist, individualist and capitalist West. It was not surprising, therefore, that, on his return from the United States, his writings should take on a more explicitly communitarian tone, rather than one of mere individual, moral exhortation.

Sayyid Qutb's return to Egypt in 1950 coincided with the growing crisis of Egyptian politics which was to lead to the military coup of July 1952. It was during this period that Qutb's writings became more obviously characterized by social critique and political polemic. He had evidently found, in Islam, the fixed vantage point from which he could not only confidently diagnose the ills of contemporary Egyptian society, but also, with equal confidence, prescribe the cure for its maladies (given his view of society and state, the medical metaphor is an apt one). Thenceforward, his understanding of the Islamic vision and his interpretations of Islamic obligation were to form the axis around which his writings were to develop. Books such as *Al-'Adalah al-Ijtima'iyyah fi al-Islam* ('Social Justice in Islam') (1949), *Ma'arakat al-Islam wa-l-Ra'smaliyyah* ('The Struggle between Islam and Capitalism') (1951), and *Al-Salam al-'Alami wa-l-Islam* ('World Peace and Islam') (1951) were both affirmations of the capacity of Islam to act as an appropriate and desirable ideology for the world of the mid-twentieth century, and testimony to Qutb's own discovery of the wholly satisfying nature of this ideology. In his view, Islam seemed to have an answer to all current social and political problems, as he defined them at the time. It also held out the possibility of establishing a harmonious and wholly integrated community.

It was scarcely surprising that, with his concerns and his gift for spirited polemic, he should have drawn closer to the Muslim Brotherhood. He saw it both as an organization dedicated to the refounding and the protection of a specifically Islamic political community, and as a group of people willing to do something about their beliefs. Their activism, both in the Palestine war and in the attacks on British military installations in the Suez Canal

Zone, clearly impressed Sayyid Qutb and led him to believe that the Muslim Brotherhood combined the virtues that he was to extol at length in his later writings: a true Islamic vision, combined with an intent and a capacity to make that vision a practical reality in the world.[4]

His close association with a number of figures prominent in the Muslim Brotherhood of the time, as well as the tenor of his writings, makes the date of his actual adherence to the organization itself a matter of some conjecture. Nevertheless, it appears that he was inscribed officially as a member in 1952 and was almost immediately placed in charge of the Muslim Brotherhood's Section for the Propagation of the Call and Publishing. Given Qutb's gifts and interests, this was clearly an appropriate appointment. It was also important for the Muslim Brotherhood to have someone of Qutb's stature in charge of this crucial area of its activities at a time when the other, violent activities of the Brotherhood were threatening to subvert and take over the organization as a whole, both in the eyes of the authorities, and in reality, through the Secret Apparatus.[5]

After the July 1952 coup d'état, it has been alleged that the early relationship between the Free Officers and Sayyid Qutb was so close that Nasser approached Qutb with the proposal that he should be the Secretary-General of the newly formed Liberation Rally.[6] It is certainly true that Nasser and his associates shared many of the Muslim Brotherhood's views on the need for greater social justice and for 'reform', even if they did not ground them explicitly in a specifically Islamic rationale. Equally, the Free Officers were well aware of the scale of the Muslim Brotherhood's organization and its capacity for violence. They appear to have been somewhat wary of the Brotherhood and willing to placate it in the early years of the new regime. It is not inconceivable, therefore, that Nasser should initially have seen Qutb as a useful ally.[7] Whatever the truth of the matter, it appears that it was not long before Qutb shared the general disillusionment of the Brotherhood with the new regime.

The banning of the Muslim Brotherhood in early 1954 led to the temporary arrest of Sayyid Qutb and other Brotherhood figures. Their release from gaol in February/March 1954 was due to the temporary ascendancy within the Revolutionary Command Council of those officers who feared Nasser's growing power and ambition. Wittingly or not, therefore, the Brotherhood had become associated with one faction within the regime. When that faction was in turn outmanoeuvred by Nasser, its perceived allies were to suffer accordingly.[8]

The pretext for action was the assassination attempt against Nasser in October 1954. This allowed Nasser not only to act directly to break the organization and power of the Muslim Brotherhood, but also to implicate other political enemies in the alleged conspiracy against him and the Egyptian state. Sayyid Qutb was arrested in November 1954, as part of the general round-up of Muslim Brotherhood leaders. He was not tried with the senior leadership, nor was he one of those charged in connection with the alleged activities of the Secret Apparatus (which led to the execution of six of the leading figures of the Muslim Brotherhood). However, in 1955 he was charged with subversive activity, in the form of anti-government agitation, pamphleteering etc., and was sentenced to fifteen years' hard labour.[9]

Qutb had reportedly been tortured during the interrogations of 1954 and this made his already fragile state of health worse. Prison conditions were to cause it to deteriorate still further and he was to spend a good deal of the time until his release in 1964 in the prison hospital. However, it was during this period of confinement and hardship that Sayyid Qutb was to write most of the works for which he subsequently became famous. Possibly because of previous links with some of the Free Officers, Sayyid Qutb was, rather surprisingly, allowed to write and to publish during his time in prison. It is true that a special censorship committee was established by the authorities to vet his output, but this did not prevent him from developing his ideas about the need for a thoroughgoing revolution, not simply in people's attitudes, but in the very structure of the state. It is during this period, therefore, that the logic of Sayyid Qutb's earlier conceptions of a specifically Islamic polity was to play itself out. The full implications of this were to become apparent in his final work, *Ma'alim fi al-Tariq* ('Signposts on the Road') (1964). This was the book which the Egyptian authorities allowed to be published and reprinted five times, only to ban it the following year and then to use it as the main item of evidence in the trial of Sayyid Qutb for conspiracy to overthrow the regime.

Ma'alim fi al-Tariq was, however, in part composed of extracts from the much more extensive and substantial work that Sayyid Qutb completed while in prison: *Fi Zilal al-Qur'an* ('In the Shade of the Qur'an') (1952–1965). This is a Qur'anic commentary which eschews the traditional methods of *tafsir*, with their constant cross referencing to previous accepted commentaries and other established authorities. Instead, Qutb gives the reader his personal and spontaneous, if considered reactions to the Qur'anic verses. In doing so, he does make reference to other Islamic writers, but these are as likely to be twentieth-century figures such as Abu'l-A'la al-Mawdudi, Abu al-Hasan Ali al-Nadawi, Abbas al-Aqqad or Abd al-Qadir Awda, as classical authorities. During the ten years of his imprisonment, the instalments of this extensive Qur'anic commentary were to appear regularly, representing, over time, the development of Qutb's thoughts about Islam.[10]

More specifically, the commentary allowed him to explore the ways in which the original message of Islam, conveyed in the Qur'an, could become the foundation for an all-embracing ideology. It was a faith which would not only change the way in which the individual perceived and apprehended the world, but would simultaneously provide a programme of conduct which was, of moral necessity, a programme of political action. Sayyid Qutb was to say that the Qur'an had given mankind the means whereby it could re-invent itself in the mould intended by the Prophet and, through him, by God.[11] His commentary, therefore, laid considerable stress on the need for people to approach the faith intuitively, directly, in a way which need not, indeed perhaps could not, be rationalized or explained with reference to any known canon of philosophical criteria. At the same time, there was an obligation to carry this knowledge of the faith, through direct action, into the life, not simply of the individual, but also of the social and political order. The intention was no less than the recreation of the 'Qur'anic generation'. That is, Qutb urged emulation of the founders of the Islamic community who had embraced Islam as a transforming personal experience in Mecca and had then proceeded to establish the Islamic order in Medina. This development had harnessed power-in-the-world to the Islamic idea and had thereby created the ideal community, under the leadership of the Prophet and the rightly guided Caliphs.

The implications of this procedure for the existing structures of society and state were understandably radical. Qutb was to use extensively the mobilizing analogy of the days of Muhammad, when the latter had to meet the challenge of the *jahiliyya*, that is, the challenge of the surrounding society of Arabia which remained wilfully ignorant of the message he had to convey. Armed with the same message, the contemporary Muslim had a duty to struggle against the forces of the *jahiliyya* in the twentieth century in order to re-establish the perfect community and, more ambitiously, to elevate Islam to its rightful position as the dominant universal creed. Above all, this meant restoring God to his place as the only rightful sovereign and ensuring that the divine law, the Shari'a, was the only law governing the community. Inevitably, this meant the abolition of what Qutb called 'man-made' laws and the removal of the political systems which enforced them.[12]

In developing these ideas of contemporary *jahiliyya*, of the indivisible sovereignty of God and the duty of *jihad* (struggle) to restore the Shari'a to its rightful place in society, there is little doubt that Qutb had been influenced by the writings of Mawdudi and Nadawi. Indeed he had openly acknowledged their influence and had been instrumental in ensuring the publication of their works in Egypt in the early 1950s.[13] In prison, however, Qutb seemed to be trying to come to terms with the particular fate that had befallen him and his Brotherhood colleagues, as well as to understand the reasons for the disappointing behaviour of the new regime in Egypt. As far as he was concerned, it had developed into an oppressive, nationalist tyranny, the brutality of its effects felt only too sharply by Qutb and his imprisoned colleagues. Yet the rulers and their minions professed to be Muslims, as did the mass of the population who did nothing to rid themselves of the regime. For Qutb, the answer was that neither the rulers of Egypt nor its inhabitants could legitimately be called Muslim. They were, in fact, disguised representatives of the very *jahiliyya* which the Islamic message was intended to disperse.[14]

The determination to differentiate that which was truly Islamic from that which was *jahili* became the hallmark of the other works that Sayyid Qutb wrote while in prison. Precisely because he believed that he had come across a truth which had not only eluded others, but ignorance of which continued to delude many, he saw it as imperative that he should alert people to the fact that not everything was as it seemed. The significance of this was, of course, that he was thinking of his own society primarily – the government of Egypt, the prison staff, the security forces, but also, beyond them, the society of Egyptians, the vast majority of whom undoubtedly saw themselves as Muslim. Writing from the relative isolation of prison, Qutb seems to have seen his mission as one of communicating these vital truths to the world beyond. On one level, this was to be achieved by the continuing commentary of *Fi Zilal al-Qur'an*, in which he could share his own subjective appreciation of this fundamental text, as well as point out the implications of its pronouncements for those who sincerely believed it to be the word of God.

Against the background of this continuing interpretative endeavour, he also published a series of works which appear to have been intended both to assert the distinctiveness and superiority of Islam as a system of belief and conduct, and to demonstrate the ways in which it corresponded more closely to 'human needs' than all other faiths and other 'man-made' systems of belief and of laws. These are themes which he returned to again and again, with differing degrees of emphasis, in the books *Hadha al-Din* ('This Religion') (1955), *Al-Mustaqbal li-hadha al-Din* ('The Future Belongs to this Religion') (1956), *Khasa'is al-Tasawwur al-Islami wa-Muqawwamatuhu* ('The Characteristics and the Values of the Islamic Vision') (1960) and *Al-Islam wa-Mushkhilat al-Hadarah* ('Islam and the Problems of Civilization') (1960).

These books represent Qutb's rather characteristic mixture of apologetics, polemic and naturalistic reasoning. Thus, he not only dwells upon the inimitable and sublime nature of Islam, he also suggests that in its comprehensive reach and its total conception of human life it is both unique and uniquely compelling. In this respect, as in others, he is careful to distinguish Islam from all other systems of belief. However, it is noticeable that he is not content simply to assert the correctness of the Islamic vision and the Islamic ethic as being the path decreed by God. While he certainly repeats this assertion, he seems to feel impelled to state, in addition, that only the Islamic prescription for human behaviour corresponds with the natural order of things and, in particular, with the essential requirements of human nature.

In part, this may have been due to his constant determination to impress upon his readers the fact that Islam is not simply a system of belief concerned with matters of the spirit, but is also a system for the organization of human life on earth. In Qutb's view, it is the practical nature of Islam which has been forgotten and, with it, the duty of Muslims to ensure that it alone is the guide and foundation of their social existence. In this respect, he contrasts it with the fallible, unreliable and, finally, blasphemous systems of law which men have devised, independent and ignorant of the will of God. These, he declares, are the obstacles not merely to true belief, but also to the true practice of Islam. It is, therefore, incumbemt upon all sincere believers to establish this as the dominant practice of their societies. They have a duty to struggle, not simply to understand the full implications of the Islamic message and to internalize its commands, but also to execute those commands in the world at large. Whatever the obstacles in their way and however impressive the edifice of the other, *jahili* forms of power, the Muslim must work to ensure that God's law, as revealed through the Qur'an, becomes the only law governing human conduct and commanding obedience. These were the concerns, expressed with considerable force, in Sayyid Qutb's final book, *Ma'alim fi al-Tariq.*

This book can be seen as an attempt to restore the flagging spirits of the Muslim Brothers: many of them had been in gaol since the mid 1950s; Nasser was at the apogee of his power, confident not only of the security apparatus at his command, but also of the dominance of Nasserism, his blend of nationalism, socialism and non-alignment which had captured the imagination of many in Egypt and beyond; Islam, in the shape of the ideological output of Al-Azhar and of a large number of Egyptian writers, some of them former members of the Muslim Brotherhood, had also been successfully pressed into the service of Nasserism.

It is not surprising that Qutb's message of hope and his stirring call for struggle should have created considerable enthusiasm. It cheered many of the despondent adherents of the disbanded Muslim Brotherhood. At the same time, it seems to have appealed to those who had already taken active, if necessarily clandestine steps to reconstitute an organization of Brotherhood sympathizers. In the tradition of the Muslim Brotherhood, this appears to have taken shape initially during the years 1959-1962, in the formation of study groups, where like-minded individuals could discuss the principles of their faith. Among these people, Sayyid Qutb's *Ma'alim fi al-Tariq* acted as a support and an encouragement. It expressed in vivid language their sensed dissatisfaction with the status quo. It also gave them the hope that they would be the vanguard to successfully challenge the dominant ideology of Nasserism and lay the foundations for a truly Islamic community in Egypt.

It was at this point – in May 1964 – that Sayyid Qutb himself was released from prison, ostensibly on grounds of ill health, but possibly also at the intercession of the Iraqi president, Abd al-Salam Arif, who was on a state visit to Egypt at the time. Whatever the reasons, Qutb was able to establish regular contact with larger circles of Muslim Brotherhood sympathizers, including many who had been impressed by his writings. One such group, headed by a member of the Muslim Brotherhood, Abd al-Fatah Ismail, asked Sayyid Qutb to become their advisor on questions of the faith and to lead discussions arising from his writings. Qutb agreed and became closely associated with the members of this group.[15]

In the summer of 1965, the arrests of Muslim Brotherhood members and sympathizers began. In August, Sayyid Qutb was arrested, as were virtually all the members of the group with which he had been associated, and by September the Egyptian authorities had made out their case. They alleged the existence of a massive conspiracy, organized by a new Secret Apparatus of the Muslim Brotherhood, and aimed at the assassination of President Nasser, the creation of general chaos and, ultimately, the seizure of power.

In the hands of the State Prosecutor, the exhortations and polemics characteristic of *Ma'alim fi al-Tariq* took on a sinister aspect and were used to build the state's case against Sayyid Qutb. His trial by special Military Tribunal began on 12 April 1966. Largely on the basis of his writings, but also on the 'confessions' of others, he was charged with attempting to overthrow the Egyptian government by force. On 21 August 1966, Sayyid Qutb, together with Abd al-Fatah Ismail and Sayyid Qutb's former cell-mate Muhammad Yusuf Hawwash, were found guilty and sentenced to death. The sentence was carried out on 29 August 1966, when Sayyid Qutb and his two companions were hanged.[16]

The Political vision from *Al-'Adalah al-Ijtima'iyyah fi al-Islam* to *Ma'alim fi al-Tariq*

In the light of these developments, it is useful to look more closely at Sayyid Qutb's conception of the political and the ways in which the ideas, proposals or exhortations associated with that conception developed. It is evident from his earliest socio-political writings that Qutb began his diagnosis of and prescription for the ills of his society from a position which echoed the concerns of many – namely, that the impact of the West's systems of power had shattered the indigenous community. Existing communitarian values, ethics and norms had been challenged not simply by the new ideas, but, even more insidiously, by the systems of power which appeared to make those ideas credible, persuasive and seductive.

In common with many communitarian thinkers, Qutb was dissatisfied with the utilitarian philosophy of hedonistic egoism. Although it had apparently contributed to the material success on which the power of the West was founded, he believed not only that it led to deplorable moral conduct, but also that the conception of society which underpinned it was, in the final analysis, a soulless, rootless and empty one. At the heart of the moral system founded on such a belief lay a void, in Qutb's view. He was, therefore, searching for something that would meaningfully fill that void: a lost harmony and an implicit faith in which this could be securely grounded. He found these qualities in God and Islam.[17] Having made this personal discovery, he devoted his energies to exploring and advocating the ways in which the values of the harmonious community could be restored. In doing so, he faced the problems that other communitarian thinkers have also encountered: how to reconcile human agency and human volition with the structures, moral and collective, of the community as a whole.

In the book *Al-'Adalah al-Ijtima'iyyah fi al-Islam* (1949), broadly liberal concerns were combined with the preoccupations of someone anxious about the condition of the Islamic community. However, in his later writing, Qutb moved increasingly towards a position in which the constitution of the latter and the authority which sanctioned its existence took precedence over all other considerations. Under the logic of his own argument, by the time he came to write *Ma'alim fi al-Tariq*, Qutb had abandoned the notion of the individual with which he had first begun and moved increasingly towards a position in which the community, as a theistically imagined and sanctioned abstraction, became logically and ethically prior to all those individuals who constituted it.

The implications of this for his vision of politics were twofold: first, politics was now about nothing less than the creation of divine harmony in this world; secondly, the pursuit of politics was to consist in the intuitive apprehension of the knowledge of this absolute truth, its patterns and its harmonies, followed by the radical reshaping of human society to accord with its rhythms. Stable, reassuring and morally fulfilling community would thereby be restored and all manifestations of the politics of individual choice, with its implied egoism and conflicts of interest, would be eradicated. It is scarcely surprising that this was a powerful vision for those who felt themselves to be simultaneously alienated from their surrounding societies, as well as helpless before the complexities and compromises that piecemeal reform might require. Simpler and purer was the idea of refounding the community on a divinely sanctioned basis, even if this meant radically reconstructing the individuals who were intended to comprise it.

There are, consequently, two major themes running through Sayyid Qutb's political writings. The first concerns the ends of politics, that is, the nature of the Islamic community and its relationship to the individual. The second addresses the means of bringing about those ends and thus examines the question of power and authority. Both themes weave in and out of Qutb's writings and are handled by him in rather different ways, at different stages of his development. In the earlier work, his thoughts have clearly been influenced by western liberalism, to some extent by socialism, or at least by the ways in which other Islamic reformers had responded to the assumptions underlying these modes of thought. In his later writing, he has made a conscious effort to rid his thought of precisely such influences and, in doing so, seeks to provide a distinctively Islamic rationale for the vision of politics which he wishes to advance. The result appears to be a clear antithesis between the Islamic polity and all other forms of political organization. However, a possibly unforeseen consequence of this approach is its strong flavour of mystical salvationism. Ironically, this tends to make specifically political concerns of secondary importance in the larger scheme of things.

As far as the question of the ends of politics are concerned, *Social Justice in Islam* deals extensively with the form of the ideal Islamic community, the establishment of which should be the proper goal of all political endeavour. In representing such a community, as well as the relationships among the individuals which constitute it. Qutb appears to use two different criteria of desirability. One is aesthetic, almost Platonic, and stresses the unity, the perfection and the comprehensiveness of God's creation. Mankind is portrayed as essentially the same and men should be working to shed their diversity, thereby restoring a lost harmony between earth and heaven. Politics is, therefore, about the achievement of a community of uniformity, placing worldly power in the service of divine harmony. This might be called the strong, theistic communitarian thesis: politics should be about maintaining the community, and the maintenance of the community requires unanimity among men in conformity with the will of God. Political activity must, therefore, be directed towards ascertaining the will of God, putting it into practice and ensuring that dissenting practice does not rupture the harmony thereby established.[18]

There is, however, another theme evident in this book. It seems to owe more to the concerns of contemporary liberals and communitarians who have sought to reconcile the claims of the community with the rights of the individual. Qutb appears to vacillate, as many others have done before and since, between assigning priority now to the community, now to the individual. In the end, however, he seems to settle for some form of calculus of social benefit, founded on social responsibility, which leaves room for 'fruitful individualism', while not allowing 'that individualism to become a harmful egoism'.[19] Although it seems clear that Qutb comes down on the communitarian side of the argument, his apparent concern for 'the rights of the individual, to give him freedom in his desires and inclinations' would suggest a liberal individualist influence.[20]

His discussion of the power of the ruler in an Islamic state and the limits to that power demonstrates a similar tension between competing claims. This is not wholly disguised by Qutb's insistence on the perfection of the Islamic political order. Qutb's reliance on the corporeal or organicist analogy appears to perform the same function for him in explicating the relationship of the ruler to the community, as it had earlier in seeking to explain the relationship of the individual to the community. Thus, Qutb asserts that 'someone becomes the ruler by the complete choice of the Muslims, acting in absolute freedom', but derives his authority from his continual enforcement of the divine law. Should he fail in this respect, the ruler can be deposed when the Muslim community is no longer satisfied with him.[21] There is a suggestion here that the 'community' can rid itself of a ruler who no longer fulfils his function, as if the members of the community would automatically be in accord about the matter. As he remarks earlier on, 'The whole Islamic community is one body.'[22] The presumption, of course, is that the body cannot disagree with itself about the function of one of its parts.

Yet, in seeking to outline what those functions are, Qutb vacillates between the desirability of the ruler having limited powers and the need for his powers to be unlimited. On the one hand, he states that if the ruler 'maintains the divine ordinances and ensures that the religious duties are carried out, that is as far as he may go; his power over the people will have reached its limits and God will protect them from his power'. A little further on, however, he claims that the ruler should have the greatest possible powers in dealing with matters relating to the welfare of the community. Indeed, the ruler should have the power to take whatever decisions he believes are necessary to achieve the general goals of the religion, as well as the welfare of the individual, the society and humanity as a whole.[23] Just as in the case of the relationship between the individual and the community, there seems to be a number of different and contrasting influences at work in Qutb's thinking about the relationship of the ruler to the community.

By the time he came to write *Signposts on the Road*, Sayyid Qutb appeared to have resolved some of these contradictions or tensions in a characteristic way. In the first place, the identity between the natural order and the political order had become absolute: 'Obedience to God's Shari'a is a requirement of the complete harmony between human life and the life of the universe and between the natural law which governs both human nature and the universe; thus there is a necessity for conformity between this general natural law and the law which governs human life.'[24] The aim of politics is thereby wholly geared to the creation of harmony and the removal of discord: '[Islam] intends by this rightly guided leadership, the good and the well-being of humanity. The good which comes from the return of humanity to its creator, and the well-being which comes from harmony between all human activities.'[25] This can only be achieved by total submission to God alone and, clearly, in such a dispensation there can be no room for individual choices and preferences: 'Islam did not come to condone people's desires, as represented in their imaginings, their organizations, their practices, their habits or their customs ...'[26]

The implications of this for Sayyid Qutb's earlier concern with voluntarist, liberal, social welfare criteria become clear when he states: 'If it is asked "Should not the interest of individuals shape their existence?", then we must refer once again to the question and answer at the heart of Islam: "Do you know or does God know?" "God knows and you do not know." The interest of the individual is included in the law of God, as God handed it down and the Prophet announced it. If people imagine one day that their welfare is different from that which God has decreed, then they are deluded, first of all, and, secondly, they are unbelievers.'[27] Clearly, in such a scheme of things, the requirements of divine order supersede anything individuals may think that they want. Since one of these requirements is that all mankind should follow the laws laid down by God for the universe as a whole, the community takes on truly global proportions and it is the sole duty of each individual to act in harmony with it. In this way, Qutb has evidently resolved to his own satisfaction any potential conflict that might have existed between the interests or rights of the individual and the good of the community.

At the same time, it would appear that, in such a community, there is no need for a ruler and, consequently, questions about the limits on the ruler's powers simply do not arise. Or, rather, as *Signposts* repeatedly asserts, there can be only one ruler, one judge, one sovereign in such a community: God. There is a notable absence in *Signposts* of any discussion of command or rule, except insofar as all forms of earthly rule, of the domination of man over man are vehemently condemned. Qutb does not even talk about the attributes of the ideal Islamic ruler, leaving one with the impression that, as far as he is concerned, only God can possess such attributes. This has significant implications not simply for the notion of the political order, but also for the means whereby the goal of establishing and maintaining that order is to be achieved.

In keeping, perhaps, with the greater optimism of the time when he wrote it, *Social Justice in Islam* does not dwell at length on how power can be harnessed to Qutb's vision of the desirable Islamic order. There seems to exist a belief that if the desirability of the Islamic order can be convincingly established by rational means, people will accept it as the preferred programme for their lives. This is evident in Qutb's eagerness to argue the case for his vision of the ideal political order, not simply on the grounds that God desires it, but also on grounds of social utility, based on individualist assumptions about human rights and needs. In the same vein, his advocacy of methods of interpreting God's command such as *sadd al-dhara'i* and *masalih mursalah*, as well as his particular gloss on these methods, suggest a strong inclination to provide reasons for acting, based on an appeal to liberal and largely secular beliefs about human welfare and volition.[28] Implicitly and explicitly at this stage in the development of his socio-political thought, Qutb acknowledged the need to justify his claims for the superiority of the

Islamic order. The importance of persuasion and of reasoning in convincing others of the desirability of accepting the Islamic revelation was, after all, the motive for writing the book in the first place, as well as the *raison d'être* for Qutb's own existence as moralist, publicist and propagandist.

By contrast, *Signposts on the Road* is a rousing call to action, explicitly written for 'the vanguard that is resolute and which must take the road, through the vast extent of *jahiliyya* in this world'.[29] In some respects, therefore, it is written for those who need no convincing, but who must now take on the rest of the world. In directing his call to them, Qutb has narrowed the range of those whom he considers worthy to be addressed. He urges them to discover the power of direct action and exhorts them to non-discursive practices in their interaction with the unregenerate, *jahili* world: 'Setting up the kingdom of God on earth, and eliminating the kingdom of man, means taking power from the hands of its human usurpers and restoring it to God alone ... and [establishing] the supremacy of the Shari'a alone and the repeal of all man-made laws. ... This general call to liberate mankind on earth from all power that is not the power of God ... was not a theoretical, philosophical or passive one ... it was a dynamic, active, positive call'.[30] Sayyid Qutb also pours scorn on what he calls 'philosophical reasoning' and calls for more direct, more spontaneous and more intuitive ways both of apprehending the commands of God and of ensuring that they become the law for all mankind. Thus, *Signposts* is about how to harness power to the vision of perfect order, how to create harmony out of discord and how to bring this about in the world.

Precisely because Qutb wishes to make a clear-cut distinction not only between the particular beliefs of Islam and of the *jahiliyya*, but also between their very forms of imagination and reasoning, he sees little need to justify his claims in the light of mutually agreed criteria. As he makes plain towards the end of *Signposts*: 'There is an abyss [between *jahiliyya* and Islam] which is not spanned by a bridge to allow for a meeting half-way between the two, but to allow for the people of the *jahiliyya* to come over to Islam.'[31] In effect, Qutb wishes to separate Islam from the *jahiliyya*, its methods and influences, in the hope that, unsullied, Islam will eventually banish it from the world, establishing an ideological hegemony which he obviously regards as only proper: 'Islam did not come to condone people's desires ... rather, it has come to eliminate these completely ...

and to found human existence on a particular basis. It came to organize life once and for all. To construct a life which will spring wholly from [Islam] and which will be firmly united with the very core of Islam itself.'[32] Islam is to be presented to the people of the *jahiliyya* in simple and straightforward terms. There must be no question of seeking to placate them or to come to terms with them. Rather, they must be told: 'This state of *jahiliyya* in which you are living is squalid and God wants to purify you.'[33]

In *Signposts*, therefore, Qutb appears to have abandoned the idea of rational exchange or argument as the chief means of spreading the truth of Islam. Faced with the ineffable beauty and startling truth of the vision of the good life vouchsafed by God to Muhammad, Qutb seems to advocate an end to reasoned – 'philosophical' – argument. Instead, faith seems to be all that is required. The apprehension of the truth of that faith is more likely to come about subjectively through a direct appreciation of the beauty and inevitability of the Islamic way than through intellectual conviction, let alone philosophical speculation.[34] In many respects, this development appears to be connected with Qutb's pessimism and growing mistrust of human reason. His confidence in the powers of the 'human heart' may be equated with his frequent recourse to the notion of human nature: he found that he could generalize incontrovertibly about these putative aspects of human existence, reading into them those moral features which he favoured and thereby giving his speculations an apparent foundation in 'natural fact', in the 'order of the universe'. Consequently, just as with the very idea of God, these 'facts' could allegedly be known – it was claimed that they had an objective existence which could be apprehended as knowledge of the truth, thereby validating the ethical order with which they were associated.

The faculty of human reason, however, was a rather different matter, more problematic and more questioning. Not only is it in many respects defined by its very individuality, but it demands consensus on the rules of justification, as well as compliance with those rules if the interlocutor's claims are to be taken seriously. This seems to have presented Qutb with a particular problem. Qutb had used the dismissive term *jahili* to refer not simply to the obvious non-Muslim societies, but also to those Muslims whom he judged to have become tainted by ways of thought and action which he regarded as un-Islamic. It was, therefore, going to be difficult to establish rules whereby reasoned debate might take place, not simply with the adherents of avowedly non-Muslim creeds, but also with much of the Muslim intellectual world. In pronouncing so wide-ranging and exclusive a condemnation, Qutb had apparently cut himself off from all those whom he regarded as unworthy targets of reasoned argumentation. For someone who had a message to convey, this left him with few options, should he seriously wish to communicate that message. Fundamentally, he seemed to be demanding that agreement should precede discussion. Thus, he appeared to exclude the possibility that there could be any disagreement between sincere Muslims – all would agree with each other (and, of course, with him) and, if they did not, it meant that they were insincere. Having developed such an attitude, it was not surprising that he was wary of the powers of human reason.

Instead, he extolled the virtues of direct, non-philosophical apprehension of the truth, of 'dynamic' *fiqh* and of the privileged understanding of the 'activist'. It is here that many have read into his work elements for a revolutionary manifesto, calling for direct action, in the political sense of a violent attack on the structures and personnel of the existing state. There are certainly grounds for such an interpretation in the pages of *Signposts*. Nor is there any reason to suppose that Qutb harboured particularly charitable thoughts towards the organizations of the Egyptian state which had been responsible not only for his own incarceration and torture, but also for the entrenchment of *jahili* practices, as he saw them, in Egyptian society. Nevertheless, one might also read into the methods and the goals that Qutb advocates in *Signposts* a distinctly mystical subtext. That, at least, could be said to be one of the implications of his writings.

There need not be any contradiction between the two readings. It has been said that Qutb's ideal was the militant Sufi – that is, someone who had achieved complete harmony and understanding in himself and who sought to convey the message to others, to open up their hearts to a similar understanding of God and of God's commands. For Qutb, with his preoccupation with the ubiquity and danger of the *jahiliyya*, there was something reassuringly self-sufficient about the mystical reconstruction of the self: 'There is no doubt that we suffer under the social pressures, images, customs and leadership of the *jahiliyya* ... especially within ourselves. We must not be seduced by this *jahili* society, nor should we give it our loyalty. ... Rather, it is our task first to change ourselves, in order then to change society.'[35] In many respects, the thrust of much of Qutb's writing, as well as the method of such works as *Fi Zilal al-Qur'an*, were highly subjective endeavours. He appeared to be advocating, by example as much as by direct exhortation, a similar individual 'rediscovery' of Islam for all those who wished to reform themselves into the new 'generation of the Qur'an'.

Such an approach would appear to have resolved, within his own understanding, a number of problems or potentially conflicting themes. In the first place, the idea of mystical, subjective communication with God and direct intuitive understanding of God's commands would appear to reconcile the key concepts of faith and reason. In this understanding, the latter now becomes the means of knowing the perfect truth and, as such, can avoid the antithesis which would appear to be suggested by the social, consensual rules of reason, as well as its discursive, critical and demanding intent. Secondly, the idea of a mystic communion of reformed souls, each linked individually to the divine and forming, both individually and as a whole, a harmonious entity, at one with the laws of the universe, could be seen as an attempt to reconcile the individualist and the communitarian values that inform much of Qutb's writing.

The vacillation between faith and reason, as well as that between individual and communal values which were evident in *Social Justice*, have been replaced, in the pages of *Signposts*, by the amalgamation of all these elements into the divine harmony which characterizes Qutb's portrayal of Islam. In this conception, there can be no room, indeed no grounds, for discord or disagreement. Faith and reason, individual and community, human freedom and servitude to God would all work in concord towards the same harmonious end. Qutb had thereby provided a vision of Utopia in which the human and the divine are reconciled: not only would conflict cease between individuals, but also humanity could rest secure in the knowledge that the path they had chosen was that favoured by God. Harmony and stability would have been restored to the universe in its entirety, including, of course, human society.

In addition, Qutb appeared to prescribe the means by which this utopia could be achieved: individual faith and social, political action. Thus, the building block was to be the faith of individuals, guiding their beliefs and the conduct of their lives: 'When the number of believers reaches three, then the faith itself says to them: "You are now a society, an independent Islamic society, separated from the *jahili* society" ... In this way, the Islamic society comes into being.'[36] The apparently comprehensive, aesthetically pleasing and emotionally satisfying nature of this vision made it a potent focus for many who were dissatisfied with the piecemeal, disordered and often oppressive reality of everyday life. The advocacy of subjective effort, whether of interpretation or action, as well as the promise that such effort would bear significant fruit, appear to have been encouraging for many. Taken in conjunction with the assertion that such individual activity, even if it were to begin in a small way, had the potential to transform society, the state and indeed the world, this was to be a powerful incentive for those who shared Qutb's concerns about the disintegration of their community.

Influence

It is often difficult to ascertain, with any degree of certainty, the influence that any particular writer has over subsequent events. On the one hand, it can always be argued that similar developments or arguments might have occurred in any case, and that, therefore, the influence of a particular writer was relatively slight. On the other hand, the many acts of reinterpretation to which the writings of any author are subjected, particularly after the author's death, may lead to a diffusion of influence, or at least to some uncertainty about the area in which the chief legacy is to be found. This is no less the case with Sayyid Qutb, despite the fact that in the past twenty years or so, groups have emerged in Egypt which have been labelled – by others, it should be noted, rather than by themselves – as '*qutbiyyun*' ['Qutbists'].

Evidently, the influence of Sayyid Qutb and of his writings was sufficient by 1964 to cause Abd al-Fatah Ismail to look to him as the leader of their 'study group', once Qutb was released from prison. The text of *Ma'alim* had circulated in various forms and, as Qutb intended, had inspired a number of former members and sympathizers of the Muslim Brotherhood to see themselves as the vanguard to whom it was addressed. Furthermore, the regular publication of *Fi Zilal al-Qur'an* had reached a large audience and had undoubtedly left a mark on the way in which many people may have approached the Qur'an. Equally importantly, at a time of domination by Nasser's regime of all forms of public expression and of the very obvious subordination to the government of the Egyptian Islamic 'establishment' at al-Azhar, it was exciting and stimulating for Egyptians to read the thoughts of someone who was clearly no creature of the regime.

The immediate consequences of Qutb's influence with one particular group were to be fatal, since the prosecution was to use his work as evidence that he was both advocating and masterminding the violent overthrow of the Egyptian government. Undoubtedly, Qutb's death on the gallows helped to strengthen his influence among some, since his martyrdom now conferred a particular poignancy and significance on his writings. It also tended graphically to bear out his thesis that the existing regime was irremediably hostile to the Islamic call (as outlined by Qutb and his admirers). It also undoubtedly led to the belief that the state's violence could only be met by counter-force to defend the Islamic ideal and to dismantle the oppressive structures of the *jahili* state.

However, for some, the freedom of interpretation, the rejection of many of the traditionally accepted Islamic authorities and the dogmatism of Qutb's assertions were all redolent of the spirit of *kharijism*.[37] For others, it was not simply theoretical or methodological unease which troubled them, but the practical concern about the consequences if people began to take books such as *Ma'alim* as a manifesto for violent political action. Memories of the ill-fated Secret Apparatus of the Muslim Brotherhood in the late 1940s and early 1950s, as well as of the reaction which this had provoked from the government authorities, had convinced many that this was not the way to proceed with the promotion of the Islamic call. Equally, for many of the Muslim Brothers and their sympathizers, the idea that the vast majority of other Muslims should be declared to be unbelievers simply because they did not conform with one particular, controversial interpretation of Islamic obligation was evidently an abhorrent one. Misgivings of precisely this kind informed the book by the Supreme Guide of the Muslim Brotherhood, Hassan al-Hudaybi, *Du'ah, La Qudah* ('Preachers, not Judges'), written soon after Qutb's execution, but not published until 1977.[38]

Nevertheless, not everyone accepted that Qutb's writings had the inflammatory and subversive political implications which both the authorities and some of the Muslim Brotherhood leadership seemed to fear. Most notably, and perhaps unsurprisingly, Sayyid Qutb's brother, Muhammad Qutb, became a leading interpreter of his brother's works.[39] He sought to explain that Qutb had not intended physical violence in his calls for action, but had rather meant to exhort Muslims to make a conscious effort to defend and promote their faith. That is, while he acknowledged that Sayyid Qutb had written often and in an impassioned way about the need for *jihad* to combat the forces of the *jahiliyya*, what he was really attacking was a mentality, an attitude. Thus, the favoured strategy of the *jihad* was to be, first, an inner effort to build a sound basis for the faith in the believer and, second, the communication of that faith to the rest of society through preaching and persuasion. Like any good exegete, Muhammad Qutb could, of course, find passages in his brother's works to support such an interpretation: 'Neither follow the *jahiliyya*, nor cut yourselves off from it ... but use discrimination when mingling with it, give and take with discernment, come out with the truth openly and with love and explain the superiority of the faith with due modesty.'[40]

Muhammad Qutb and those who have followed his lead, have, therefore, tended to emphasize the intellectual and moral aspects of Sayyid Qutb's call to make Islam a dynamic practice. For such authors, Qutb's influence lies in his powerful call for spiritual regeneration and reconstruction, for the attention which each individual must pay both to the soundness of his or her beliefs and to the correspondence between those beliefs and the conduct of their lives. The vision of harmony which they derive from Qutb is not the unforgiving political harmony of the neo-Platonic ideal, but rather individuals' discovery of God and, through God, the discovery of the divine pattern in their common humanity.

As with many creeds, this more subjective, moralistic and non-political interpretation of Sayyid Qutb's exhortations may be the one which is adhered to by the majority of Muslims who find inspiration in his writings. There is, of course, no way of telling whether or not this is the case. More evident and more eye-catching have been those groups which have taken Sayyid Qutb's vision and his call to action and have used them as justification for seeking to force their own urgent agendas upon the world. This tendency has been particularly noticeable in Egypt, with the emergence of Islamic protest groups during the past twenty years or so.

Members of Al-Jama'at al-Islamiyya [the Islamic societies]

which began to appear on the campuses of Egypt's universities and then developed into underground organizations beyond the campuses, felt strongly about the economic and social dislocations of the 1970s. They were also troubled by the degree to which secular and western values appeared to have displaced Islam as the primary cultural referent of most Egyptians. Nor was there any doubt in their minds that the chief blame for this lay with the unrepresentative and authoritarian Egyptian regime. At the same time, they were clearly impatient both with the leadership of the Egyptian Islamic establishment at al-Azhar and with the leadership of the Muslim Brotherhood: the former they regarded as servants of the government, and the latter they believed were so preoccupied with the reconstitution of their organization that they would not dare confront the government in any effective way.

In many respects, therefore, the writings of Sayyid Qutb appeared to strike a chord of recognition with members of these groups: here was someone concerned about the same kinds of social and political problems as they themselves, and for much the same reasons. The inadmissability of any sovereignty other than that of God, the ignorance and blindness of surrounding *jahili* society, the need for *jihad* to combat the forces of *jahiliyya* and the need for a small vanguard which would proceed to enlighten and free the society were themes stressed by Qutb in his later writings. They provided many members of these groups with the language in which they could express their own indictment of Egyptian society. Furthermore, Qutb's exhortation to act, to interpret Islamic obligations in a dynamic way, as well as his assurance that this would lead, as in the days of the Prophet, to the inevitable triumph of Islam, provided these groups with some of the encouragement they needed to take action against the apparently overwhelming forces of the Egyptian state.

There have been differences of interpretation among such groups about the most effective strategies to be pursued, as well as about the meaning of some of Qutb's own exhortations. Nevertheless, the call to reestablish the rule of the Shari'a by first becoming re-acquainted directly with the text of the Qur'an, eschewing the difficult and distracting body of traditional *fiqh*, and then by proceeding to take on the structures of state and society, with the intention of dismantling them, has been inspiring and encouraging for those who were already profoundly dissatisfied with the status quo. The attack on the

Egyptian Military Academy in 1974 by a group calling itself the Islamic Liberation Organization (*Tanzim al-Tahrir al-Islami*), the kidnap and murder of the former Minister of Awqaf in 1977 by a group labelled by the press and the security authorities *Al-Takfir wa'l-Hijra* and, most spectacularly, the assassination of President Sadat in 1981 by members of the *Jihad* organization have been the most dramatic of the acts carried out by the groups that others have labelled 'Qutbists'.

There is no doubt that members of these groups had been acquainted with Sayyid Qutb's writings and had taken from them encouragement and inspiration. As far as the *Jihad* organization was concerned, it was noticeable that the tract *Al-Faridah al-Gha'ibah* ('The Absent Duty') by one of its chief ideologues, Abd al-Salam Faraj, made a number of explicit references to Sayyid Qutb's writings and cited those passages in which he encouraged people to fulfil their duty of *jihad* on behalf of God.[41] The extensive coverage which this tract received during the trial of Faraj for his part in the conspiracy to assassinate President Sadat, as well as the continuing use of Qutb's language and writings by Islamic protest groups to justify their activities, have made it seem that his influence is paramount.

However, it might be more helpful to see Qutb himself as representative of a continuing trend in the Islamic world, of which the protest groups are also a part. The members of these groups, like Qutb, are evidently disturbed by the material and moral dislocation of their societies, by the unresponsive and authoritarian regimes to which they are subject and by the continuing denial of power to ordinary people to shape their lives as they would prefer. In facing the kinds of problems which they have identified, they, like Qutb, have found many of the established authorities of the Islamic tradition to be unhelpful, remote or incomprehensible. They clearly found the idea of renewed and largely individual *ijtihad*, in order to determine the obligations of the faith, more promising, even if the results have been as diffuse as any such multiple, individual endeavours were bound to be. Qutb also enjoyed the liberating effects of this exercise for his own thoughts and writing. However, it is in the nature of this very process that it could not provide the basis for a more general certainty, beyond the individual conviction which Qutb appears to have found for himself.

Conclusion

Sayyid Qutb's vision of the political was a vision of perfection, of the possibility of restoring harmony between heaven and earth, between humanity and the universe, between individuals and between man and his creator. On one level, this was to be a task of inner reconstruction, since each individual was urged to acquaint themself, as he had done, with the word of God and thus with the sublime beauty of the divine language of command. In assigning priority to this task, there was always a possibility of encouraging a drift to mysticism, in which the individual no longer stood in need of social ties. Whether the community was one of reason or of faith, the individual, finally, had the responsibility of seeing to his or her own soul and of developing a direct understanding of the divine, stripped of intermediaries. A tendency in this direction is certainly evident in Qutb's writing. However, he sought consciously to hold it in check by asserting that this was but the first step towards a more obviously political end in which power would be used to make all of mankind conform with the divine law.

In this respect, he sought to make his vision of perfection realizable. He urged people to abandon mere contemplation and to throw themselves into the active application of the divine injunctions which they had directly and vividly apprehended. The 'activist' tenor of some of his writings may be seen, in one respect, as an understandable attempt to suggest to people that their beliefs have real consequences. Furthermore, Qutb was also seeking to impress upon people the fact that their actions count, that they contain within them the seeds of revolutionary possibility. However, in order to do so, Qutb increasingly stressed the 'dynamic principle', as he was to call it. That is, he seemed to suggest that 'action' was a simple, straightforward and uncomplicated matter, the antithesis of philosophy, theory and other intellectualizing activities. Although he claimed that this was intended to restore a fractured unity between thought and deed, the effect was to refocus attention on this distinction, reintroducing thereby a dualism which he had already decried.

Qutb sought to reduce the significance of the apparent contradiction in this position, as well as of other tensions in his work, by resorting to strategies of apologetics and of polemic in which he tried to redefine the terms of reference. Indeed, his relegation of the faculty of reason – and thus of the rules of justification and of exchange, associated with reasoning – to an insignificant position, compared to that of faith, was a symptom of the direction in which his writing was going. It was also, perhaps, a symptom of the curious, but by no means unique position in which he found himself: as a Muslim intellectual whose concerns, categories and very methods had been shaped as much by western traditions of thought, as by the intellectual traditions of Islam. The problem for Qutb was that he was advocating the rejection of all that could not be specifically appropriated for a – redefined – Islamic tradition. His stress on dynamism, activism and the importance of unquestioning faith seemed to provide a means of escape from this dilemma, insofar as all doubts and apparent contradictions could be met by the affirmation of faith.

Intellectually, this escape is only temporary and may simply be illusory. It is perhaps not surprising, therefore, that Qutb's writings should have had their greatest impact among those who have been predisposed either to see them as the key to a personal and intensely private salvation, or to find in them inspiration and encouragement for their unforgiving indictment of the political status quo. Qutb succeeded well in giving voice to the attitude of many who were seeking to come to terms with the undeniable, but often abhorrent power of western forms of organization, western modes of thought and western values. The very dilemmas and ambiguities within his own position contribute, in some measure, to the appeal of his writings for those who find themselves in similar positions. Whether they derive from those works a vision of harmony and communion which is primarily mystical or socio-political in nature, it is clear that Qutb's re-affirmation of the faith will continue to strike a chord of recognition among many Muslims in the late twentieth century.

Notes

1.   The principal sources used for information on the life of Sayyid Qutb are: Majdi Fadl Allah, *Ma' Sayyid Qutb fi Fikrihi al-Siyasi wal-Dini*, Beirut, Mu'assasat al-Risalah, 1979; Muhammad Tawfiq Barakat, *Sayyid Qutb*, Beirut, Dar al-Da'wa, n.d.; A.A. Musallam, *The Formative Stages of Sayyid Qutb's Intellectual Career and his Emergence as an Islamic Da'iyan 1906-1952*, PhD thesis, 1983, University of Michigan, Ann Arbor, U.M.I., 1983.

2.   Sayyid Qutb, 'Al-Taswir al-Fanni fi al-Qur'an al-Karim', *Al-Muqtataf* 94/2, 1 February 1939, pp. 206-11 and *Al-Muqtataf* 94/3, 1 March 1939, pp. 313-18; Musallam, *Formative Stages*, pp. 96, 130-2; S. Haim 'Sayyid Qutb', *Asian and African Studies*, 16, 1982, pp. 148-9.

3. Musallam, *Formative Stages*, pp. 181-8.

4. Musallam, *Formative Stages*, pp. 224-33.

5. Musallam, *Formative Stages*, pp. 232-7; Mahmud Abd al-Halim, *Al-Ikhwan al-Muslimun: Ahdath Sana'at al-Ta'rikh*, Part 3, 1952-1971, Alexandria, Dar al-Da'wa, 1985, pp. 63-9, 201-2.

6. Fadl Allah, *Sayyid Qutb*, pp. 90-1; O. Carré, *Mystique et Politique: lecture révolutionnaire du Coran par Sayyid Qutb, frère musulman radical*, Paris, Presses de la FNSP et Editions du Cerf, 1984, p. 14.

7. G. Kepel, *The Prophet and Pharaoh*, London, Al Saqi Books, 1985, pp. 40-1.

8. Musallam, *Formative Stages*, pp. 257-60.

9. Musallam, *Formative Stages*, pp. 268-9.

10. Carré, *Mystique et Politique*, pp. 24-38; S. Qutb, *Fi Zilal al-Qur'an*, Beirut, Dar Ihya' al-Turath al-'Arabi, 1967, Part I, pp. 3-12.

11. See particularly the Chapter 'Jil Qur'ani Farid' ('A Unique Qur'anic Generation') in Sayyid Qutb, *Ma'alim fi al-Tariq*, Cairo, Dar al-Shuruq, 1988, pp. 14-23.

12. On aspects of the *jahiliyya* and of the need for *jihad* to combat its insidious effects, see, for instance, S. Qutb, *Fi Zilal*, Part III, pp. 70-9, Part IV, pp. 19-32, Part V, pp. 148-50 and 195-202.

13. Y.M. Choueiri, *Islamic Fundamentalism*, London, Pinter Publishers, 1990, p. 95.

14. Y.Y. Haddad, 'Sayyid Qutb: Ideologue of Islamic Revival', Ch. 4 in J. Esposito (ed.), *Voices of Resurgent Islam*, Oxford, O.U.P., 1983, pp. 85-7.

15. Farid Abd al-Khaliq, *Al-Ikhwan al-Muslimun – fi Mizan al-Haqq*, Cairo, Dar al-Sahwa li-l-Nashr wa-l-Tawzi', 1987, pp. 113-16; O. Carré & G. Michaud, *Les Frères Musulmans (1928-1982)*, Paris, Editions Gallimard/Julliard, 1983, pp. 75-6.

16. Carré & Michaud, *Frères Musulmans*, pp. 76-81.

17. S. Qutb, *Ma'arakat al-Islam wa-l-Ra'smaliyyah*, Cairo, Dar al-Shuruq, 1979, pp. 29-34, 55-62.

18. S. Qutb, *Al-'Adalah al-Ijtima'iyyah fi al-Islam*, Cairo, Dar al-Shuruq, 1980, pp. 74, 103-4.

19. Sayed Kotb (sic), *Social Justice in Islam*, tr. J.B. Hardie, American Council of Learned Societies, Near East Translation Program, New York, Octagon Books, 1970, p. 276.

20. Kotb, *Social Justice*, p. 26.

21. Qutb, *'Adalah*, pp. 106-7.

22. *Ibid.*, p. 77.

23. *Ibid.*, p. 110.

24. Qutb, *Ma'alim*, pp. 114-15.

25. Qutb, *Ma'alim*, p. 165.

26. *Ibid.*

27. *Ibid.*, pp. 106-7.

28. Kotb, *Social Justice*, pp. 260-7. It is interesting that this section – which consists principally of a long quotation from Muhammad Abu Zahra's work on Imam Malik – is not to be found in the Arabic edition. This may possibly be because Qutb, who saw and approved this English translation, felt that these terms were largely familiar to his Egyptian readers.

29. Qutb, *Ma'alim*, pp. 12-13.

30. *Ibid.*, p. 68.

31. *Ibid.*, p. 177.

32. *Ibid.*, pp. 165-6.

33. *Ibid.*, p. 168.

34. L. Binder, *Islamic Liberalism*, Chicago, University of Chicago Press, 1988, pp. 194-5.

35. Qutb, *Ma'alim*, p. 22.

36. *Ibid.*, p. 129.

37. Binder, *Islamic Liberalism*, p. 174; Kepel, *Prophet and Pharaoh*, pp. 58-61.

38. Hasan al-Hudaybi, *Du'ah, La Qudah*, Cairo, Dar al-Da'wa, 1977.

39. Kepel, *Prophet and Pharaoh*, pp. 64-7.

40. Qutb, *Ma'alim*, p. 176.

41. J.J.G. Jansen, *The Neglected Duty*, New York, Macmillan, 1986, pp. 30, 226.

8

Musa al-Sadr

Augustus Richard Norton

Shi'i Islam burst into western consciousness with the toppling of the Shah of Iran in 1979. Thereafter, Iran came to be viewed as the epicentre of a tempest that threatened to engulf neighbouring lands. If western observers magnified the challenge and misunderstood the appeal of the new revolutionary exemplar, they were not alone. The victors in Tehran, and in Qum, made parallel miscalculations, generalizing Iranian sociopolitical realities to the *ummah* while exaggerating the appeal of their revolutionary model for Arab Shi'i Muslims and Sunni Muslims alike.

Victory in revolution naturally inspires hyperbole, intellectual intoxication and zealotry, clouding the minds of participants and observers. Predictably, the Arab Shi'i populations of Bahrain, Iraq, Lebanon and Saudi Arabia appeared as outposts of the so-called 'Islamic revolution', to both advocates and adversaries of the revolution. It was as though these disparate communities – which, for the most part, predate the introduction of Shi'ism to Persia – had no history, no ideas, no importance, no politics, until the reign of the *wilayat al-faqih* (the rule of the jurisconsult) and the advent of the Islamic Republic of Iran.

This skewing of evidence is nowhere clearer than in Lebanon where dramatic social change and widespread political mobilization among the Shi'i were markers of the 1960s and 1970s, well before the fall of the Pahlavis and the rise of Ayatollah Ruhollah Khomeini. If this were all just a detail, a scholarly dotting of an 'i' or a pedantic crossing of a 't', there would be nothing more to say. There is more to say, however, because what was happening in Lebanon, well before the revolution in Iran, was an experiment in political reform led by a charismatic political figure, a Shi'i cleric, who literally disappeared, half a year before the denouement in Tehran. Al-Sayyid Musa al-Sadr, an Iranian by birth but a Lebanese by descent, spent two decades in Lebanon during which he made an indelible mark on the Lebanese political scene. Arguably, his impact upon Lebanese politics has been even greater since his physical disappearance from the scene, in 1978. If history is, by definition, one contingent piled upon another, then it is interesting to ponder how the survival of this remarkable man might have affected the course of events in Lebanon, and, for that matter, within Iran as well.

Peripheral Arabs

It is tempting – especially for venerable Orientalists – to explain the complaints and the anger of the Shi'i by reference to the enduring weight of early schisms within Islam. The very term Shi'i, standing as it does for the partisans of Ali, signifies the importance of these long-past events. Yet, the contemporary reality of the Arab Shi'i is often trivilized by such explanations. In order to understand the Arab Shi'i it is necessary to come to grips with the social, political and, often, economic marginality which reflects contemporary patterns of discrimination and alienation, and then to see how such realities resonate within the mystical and symbolic richness of Shi'ism.

If the Shi'i militants see themselves under the domination of the establishment, it is an establishment dominated by Sunni Muslims. During the Ottoman empire, the Shi'i were treated derisively by the Sunni rulers, and were often denied access to education, military training and government office because their links to rival Persia made their loyalty suspect. A similar pattern of discrimination and suspicion continues in the Arab states and only reinforces Shi'i dogma that emphasizes the division of the world into those who dominate and those who are dominated. Thus, the distinction rings true when leading Shi'i clerics dichotomize humanity between the *mustazifen* (oppressed) and the *mustakberin* (oppressors).

There are obvious risks in characterizing a community's ethos, but there is little doubt that the Shi'i of the Arab world see themselves as members of a persecuted, underprivileged community victimized by the ruling establishment. There is an objective basis for this perception. As a rule of thumb, we may state that wherever they are found in the Arab world the Shi'i, although they are predominalty ethnic Arabs, are likely to be disadvantaged vis-à-vis non-Shi'i Arabs. This is not to say that all Shi'i are mired in poverty. In addition to the traditional notables (al-'ayan), there are certainly a number of Shi'i families in Bahrain, Kuwait and Lebanon who have amassed considerable wealth in commerce or in the professions; however, even wealthy Shi'i often emphasize – if somewhat ironically – their sense of membership of a disadvantaged, persecuted minority. Centuries of impoverishment and discrimination are not easily erased, and deeply ingrained biases among ruling elites are difficult to expunge. In some isolated cases serious efforts were made by governments to bring the Shi'i into the mainstream of economic and political life. Noteworthy in this respect, in Lebanon, is the presidency of Fuad Chehab (1958-64), whose prescient insights and ambitious development programmes did not survive his tenure, to the great misfortune of the country.[1]

Shi'ism has often proved to be a potent symbol with which to mobilize political action precisely because an individual's status as a Shi'i often corresponds with lower economic and social standing and political subordination. Just as the convergence of socio-economic class and race has proved a potent mixture for mobilizing minority groups in the West, so the coincidence of objective deprivation with sectarian identity in the Middle East has proved to be an explosive context for inspiring collective action among the Shi'i.

Of course, excepting Iran there is no country in the world where Shi'i Muslims dominate a political system. In the Arab world, the closest they have come to doing so in modern times was in Iraq, in 1920, when Britain quashed a revolt in which Shi'i tribes, rural notables and Shi'i ulama were heavily involved. In Lebanon, as in the larger Arab world, the Shi'i have been typically kept at arm's length from political power. Even in the 1990s, when the status of the Lebanese Shi'i as the single largest confessional group in the country was no longer in dispute (they now constitute a third or more of the total population), the forces aligned to check Shi'i power remained most impressive. In recent years, some writers, more impressed by the weight of numbers than the realities of political power, have predicted that the Shi'i would become the dominant political force in Lebanon. Thus, it was asserted the Shi'i would supplant the Maronite Catholics who have been dominant politically since the mid-nineteenth century. Yet, these predictions do not take sufficient account of the countervailing internal forces that enjoy important regional, and international support. Although no confessional group constitutes a majority of the population in Lebanon, there is a working majority of non-Shi'i groups prepared to align – tacitly, if not otherwise – to check Shi'i power. Simultaneously, the Lebanese Shi'i remained hobbled by intra-communal conflict and an unenviable global reputation for malevolence.

Significantly, the 1989 al-Ta'if agreement, which provided the framework for ending Lebanon's civil war, only accorded the Shi'i equal treatment with the second and third largest sects, the Sunnis and the Maronites.[2] As the godfather of the Ta'if accord, Shi'i-phobic Saudi Arabia was transparently intent on tempering Shi'i claims through the persistence of Sunni Muslim influence in Lebanon. (Saudi Arabia's small but sometimes restive Shi'i population arouses deep suspicion in official Saudi circles, not only because many puritanical Wahhabis view Shi'ism as heretical, but because much of the Saudi Shi'i minority – perhaps 5 per cent of the population – sits atop the oil-rich Eastern Province.)

Historical Roots of Shi'ism

Just as sectarian divisions separate Christians into adherents of Orthodoxy, Catholicism and an array of Protestant denominations, Islam is divided into an admixture of sects, and schools of religious law. The most important division in Islam stems from the seventh and eighth centuries A.D., when the Shi'i Muslims emerged as an organized sect within the *ummah* or world community of Muslims.

The event that gave rise to Shi'ism was the debate over succession that followed the death of the Prophet Muhammad in 632. The basic disagreement on the succession issue led to the most significant and enduring schism within Islam. Muhammad could not be replaced *qua* prophet. He was and is viewed by Muslims everywhere as the 'Seal of the Prophets', the last and final prophet selected by Allah through the Angel Gabriel, in 610.

Muhammad was not only a prophet, but a statesman as well. He was the head of the nascent Islamic state created in the city of Medina and thereby the leader of all Muslims on Earth. At the time of his death, the majority of his followers held that the prophet had not designated a successor, therefore leaving the community free to elect a successor to Muhammad; however, some Muslims disagreed. They argued that the successor should come from the *ahl al-beit* (the House of the Prophet). Because this minority argued for the succession of Ali, Muhammad's cousin and the husband of his daughter, Fatima, they came to be called Shi'it Ali (literally, the partisans of Ali), the derivation of 'Shi'i'. According to Shi'i accounts, on at least two occasions Muhammad designated Ali as his successor.

The majority did not share this view and Abu Bakr, the brother-in-law of Muhammad, was named *khalifa* (literally: successor) to the Prophet. This exercise of communal consensus, *ijma*, is characteristic of Sunni Islam, in contrast to Shi'ism with its emphasis on the imamate and the associated doctrine of an authoritative clerical hierarchy. This is one reason that the laity has played a much more active role in leading Sunni religious movements than in Shi'i ones.

The Shi'i persist in claiming that only members of the *ahl al-beit* were legitimate successors to the Prophet. Thus, the first three caliphs, Abu Bakr, 'Umar and 'Uthman, are viewed as usurpers of the role which should rightly have gone to Ali. In Shi'i terminology, the legitimate successors to the Prophet are called 'Imams' (the noun 'Imam' means simply the one who stands in front of a group at prayer).

After the deaths of the first three caliphs, Ali was finally named caliph in 656. Caliph Ali led a Muslim army from Medina against the rival claimant to the caliphate, Mu'awiya, who was the nephew of 'Uthman and the governor of Syria. Although his army held the upper hand on the battlefield, Imam Ali – as he is called by the Shi'i – was assassinated in 660 by a group of his own followers who were angered at his unwillingness to press his military advantage against Mu'awiya. To the dismay of his killers, Imam Ali, who is revered as a man of justice and wisdom, had agreed to arbitration in order to settle the rival leadership claim between himself and Mu'awiya. So ended the last and only time that a member of the *ahl al-beit* was accepted as the leader of the *ummah*, encompassing the community of all Muslims.

Mu'awiya, the successful rival of Ali, established the Umayyad dynasty in Damascus, but the Shi'i argued that the rightful successors to Ali were his sons, Hasan and Husain. Hasan abdicated the imamate, and he died soon afterwards (the

Shi'i claim that he was poisoned, but experts disagree about the cause of his death). Shi'i accounts usually insist that all of their imams, except the twelfth or 'hidden imam' (al-imam al-ghaib), came to a brutal end, emphasizing the persecution that the Shi'i have often suffered throughout their history. All the Shi'i sects share a belief in the 'Mahdi' (the expected One), who will return before the Day of Judgement. The Mahdi will lead the victorious final battle against the forces of evil. The earth will then be filled with justice. The Mahdi will then rule for a period of time, numbered in years. In Twelver Shi'ism the Mahdi is the Twelfth Imam who did not die, but disappeared into ghaiba (occultation) in the ninth century. The Twelfth Imam is ever present but unseen by mortals.

The imams lived under very difficult conditions, and in many cases they were put under virtual house arrest by rulers who feared their potential influence. Thus, it is not hard to understand that the doctrine of occultation evolved as a means of protection.[3] Nor, under the oppressive circumstances in which many Shi'i were forced to live, is it strange that the doctrine of taqiyya emerged. Taqiyya permits a Shi'i when faced with danger or imminent harm to pretend to adhere to another religion as a measure of self-defence. The legitimate employment of taqiyya has been radically circumscribed in recent years, especially by Ayatollah Khomeini who viewed the doctrine as a rationale for inaction. Khomeini's recurrent boast that he was 'Husain not Hasan' evoked the memory of the Prophet's grandsons and their contrasting choices of political submission versus political activism. By rejecting Hasan's example, Khomeini was rejecting the quietism that is associated not only with the taqiyya doctrine but also with the Sunni Muslim establishment.

The Martyrdom of Imam Husain

The most famous death in Shi'ism is undoubtedly that of Imam Husain, who came to the fore after the abdication of his brother Hasan. Shi'ism is alive with rich and powerful myths, but the central and defining myth of Shi'ism stems from 680 A.D. when Husain, the grandson of the prophet Muhammad, was martyred on the desolate plain of Karbala, in what is modern-day Iraq.[4] Imam Husain is a figure of stirring bravery, and in many ways his importance for the Shi'i is surpassed only by that of the Prophet Muhammad. In particular, it is the martyrdom of

Husain that has captured the imagination of many modern Shi'i.

Husain took to the field with a small force of 72 men to meet the armies of Yazid, who had replaced his father Mu'awiya as caliph. Husain warned his followers that the likely outcome of their expedition was death. At Karbala they were badly outnumbered and Husain's prediction proved correct. Surrounded, lacking food and water, and after days of arduous siege, Husain was slaughtered with his followers. His decapitated body was left on the sands, and his severed head was carried in triumph to Damascus. Husain was succeeded by his son Ali Zain al-'Abidin, the only son of Husain to survive the Karbala massacre. He was captured by Yazid's army and later allowed to retire to Medina.

The events at Karbala occurred on the tenth day, *'ashura*, of the month of Muharram in the Islamic lunar calendar. Traditionally *'ashura* was the occasion for Shi'i Muslims to show their piety or to pray for the intercession of Imam Husain. *'Ashura* lives on in the hearts of many Shi'i who commemorate Husain's martyrdom annually, often in the form of ritual processions, as well as folk dramas (the general term is *ta'ziyeh*, but the drama often has unique vernacular names like *shabih* in Lebanon) which recreate the noble tragedy. The public staging of *'ashura* ceremonies is still proscribed in Saudi Arabia; until the 1940s, in the Beirut suburbs *'ashura* was only observed out of public view in order to avoid offending inter-sectarian harmony. When it was publicly staged in the Beirut suburb of Ghobiere in the early 1940s, *'ashura* was used by aspiring political leaders as a means of building a social base among the new immigrants.[5]

In recent years *'ashura* has become a revolutionary statement. Yet, for centuries the Shi'i were quietist and subdued. It is widely argued that the Shi'i display a marked tendency toward resistance and rebellion stemming from their beliefs that leadership was usurped and that temporal rulers were, therefore, illegitimate. But observations of this sort obscure the long centuries of quiescence that have marked the Shi'i. Throughout the history of the Shi'i *'ashura* has had opposing aspects: it exemplifies the need to acquiesce in the suffering inherent in the temporal, but also serves as a model of the imperative to take a stand.

The recent recasting of *'ashura*, emphasizing its heroic essence, has helped to foster political consciousness and to engender assertiveness.[6] Contemporary Shi'i leaders have used the martyrdom of Husain with great effect to remind their followers of the bravery and the sacrifice that is their heritage.

To borrow a thought from the anthropologist Clifford Geertz, a truly powerful religious ritual fuses the ethos and world view of a people, evoking a broad range of moods and motivations on the one hand, and metaphysical conceptions on the other.[7] 'Ashura sums up the spiritual consciousness of the Shi'i, their dichotomous world view in which the corrupted powerful sit atop the deprived and the tormented, and their ethos of sacrifice, courage and tolerable pain. Powerful rituals are not enactments of the past, but reminders of the present. They are events staged in the historical present, in the time which is no time.[8]

The genius of men like al-Sayyid Musa al-Sadr was to refashion the familiar myth of 'ashura and to give it new political meaning, to 'repoliticize' Islam.[9] What had been a lesson in submission became an exemplar for political activism and for sacrifice.

Islamic Populism and the Shi'i Movements

The emergence of Shi'i movements, such as Amal and Hizballah in Lebanon, is a reflection of a broader pattern of activism which we may label the Islamist phenomenon, or, even more accurately, Islamic populism. The phenomenon defies easy generalization. In terms of socio-economic class, the Islamist movements recruit across the spectrum. Many draw their memberships from relatively well-educated middle and lower middle classes as well as the lower classes. Hopes born of education, urban migration and other facets of social mobilization are often thwarted by ineffective, corrupt or unresponsive government. Thereby fostering a ripe opportunity for populist ideologues to mobilize support.

Islam, not the Islam of the establishment, but a fresh, pristine Islam unsullied by power and compromise, offers a culturally authentic and familiar banner. Among many of the more radical Sunni groups, as in Egypt, the enemies are the apostates, the 'nominal' Muslims of their own society. In contrast, the Shi'i ulama play a leading role in Shi'i movements, although only a fraction of Sunni associations and protest movements are led by ulama. In fact, a number of groups are avowedly anti-clerical, reflecting the view that the ulama are mere minions of the government. This reveals an important point of contrast between the Shi'i and the Sunni Muslims. Whereas, many Sunni groups are led by the laity, the mode for Shi'i groups is clerical leadership.

The Renovation of Shi'ism as a Political Ideology

Traditionally, Sunni Muslims have believed that revelation stopped with the death of the Prophet and that the 'gates of *ijtihad*' (independent interpretation) closed in the tenth century. Thus, Sunni religious scholars are constrained to avoid independent deduction or extrapolation of the Shari'a (religious law). The Shi'i reject these views and argue that for every age there is an infallible imam who would establish truth through his interpretation of the word of Allah as embodied in the holy book of Islam, the Qur'an.[10] While the imam is in occultation, i.e. present but unseen, the role of independently interpreting religious truth devolves to the learned men of Islam, the 'doctors' of law who in Shi'ism are called *mujtahids*.

In Islam there is no concept of formal membership in a specific parish or a congregation. Whether defined by piety or conspiracy, and there are certainly far more Muslims in the former category, Islamic groups tend to be loosely clustered around a leader who maintains his following by espousing a version of Islam which his followers find credible and compelling. Common Islamic institutions have provided a locus for political action for both Shi'is and Sunnis, even – or especially – where the right of free political association has been limited or proscribed by the governing authority. Islamic groups often have been able to organize in the mosque relatively free from the government's intrusive gaze.

The *husainiyya* is an important rallying point for political action for Shi'i Muslims. Constructed specifically to commemorate 'ashura, the *husainiyya* is used, typically, as a community religious centre, where both religious ceremonies and political meetings may be held. In the early 1980s, this writer attended politically-laden memorial services (*thikrs*) for Shi'i martyrs (*shuhada*) conducted in village *husainiyyas* in southern Lebanon where one lay-speaker after another would deliver a variety of political messages and appeals, all laced liberally with a refashioned Shi'i idiom in which adversaries wear the clothes of Yazid and fallen heroes follow the example of Husain.

In the contemporary Sunni movements clerical leadership is atypical, since there is no doctrinal requirement for the leaders to be clerics.[11] In contrast, the Shi'i ulama are so tightly bound up with religion that an anti-clerical Shi'i movement would arguably be a contradiction in terms. This distinguishes most Shi'i groups from their Sunni counterparts. Only a *mujtahid* has acquired the mastery of *fiqh* necessary to authoritatively interpret religious responsibilities (i.e., to perform *ijtihad*), so a Shi'i who spurned all *mujtahids* would scarcely be a Shi'i.

Thus, Shi'i *mujtahids* have a much more central, directive and organic role than the Sunni ulama. But, in contrast to Shi'i and Sunni clerics elsewhere, the Shi'i clerical establishment in Iran has historically evolved to enjoy an unusual degree of social and political influence. Their power is grounded not only in their monopoly exercise of *ijtihad*, but in the financial resources that allow them autonomy from state control. All Muslims accept *zakat* (or alms-giving) as a duty, but in Iran the alms were often paid directly to the *mujtahids*, providing Shi'i institutions a substantial economic base. Unlike Iran, where the religious establishment constituted an autonomous professional class unto itself, the Shi'i ulama in the Arab states are typically dependent upon the patronage of the state or individual benefactors. In the Arab lands, the *awqaf* (religious trusts) are typically under state supervision, if not control, in marked contrast to Iran where the mullahs have long controlled a network of trusts, benevolent societies, and foundations. For example, in Ba'thist Iraq the Shi'i upper classes have been decimated by government nationalization policies and the traditional middle class, based largely in the bazaar, has suffered economically as well, thereby undermining any hope of an independent financial base for the ulama.

The phenomenon of activist Shi'ism is largely a manifestation of the radicalization of the Shi'i ulama. The intellectual roots of the resurgence of Shi'ism run to the shrine cities of Iraq and especially Najaf, where a remarkable collection of Shi'i scholars was gathered in the 1960s.[12] These clerics formed an important inner fraternity which has played a central role in mobilizing the Shi'i for political action. Of course, not all of the ulama succumbed. The quietist perspective was personified by Ayatollah Abu al-Qasim al-Khu'i (1899-1992), the distinguished Najaf ayatollah, who specifically questioned the validity of the concept of guardianship as employed by Khomeini. Al-Khu'i argued that guardianship is usually taken to apply to the context of welfare, such as the care of orphans, cripples and the like, rather than guardianship of the state as construed by Khomeini's innovative doctrine of *al-wilayat al-faqih*.

Najaf was the breeding ground for the ideas that motivate many of the leaders of the Shi'i movements in the Arab world today. The personalities who gathered in Najaf were a virtual who's who of contemporary Shi'i personalities. Until his death in 1970, the Ayatollah Muhsin al-Hakim, whose ancestral roots ran to Jabal 'Amil, the heartland of Arab Shi'ism, was a central figure in Najaf. His surviving sons (three were executed in Iraq and one assassinated while in Khartoum, probably by Saddam Hussain's agents) are active leaders of the Tehran-based Shi'i opposition to the Ba'thist regime in Baghdad.

These personalities included Ayatollahs Muhsin al-Hakim and Muhammad Baqr al-Sadr, who, provoked by the appeal of communism for Iraqi youth, including the children of Shi'i *mujtahids*, set about rejuvenating Shi'ism.[13] They were joined in 1965 by Ayatollah Khomeini, who delivered a series of seminal lectures on Islamic government in 1970. Others were Baqr al-Sadr's Iranian-born cousin Musa al-Sadr, Muhammad Mahdi Shams al-Din and Muhammad Husain Fadlallah who later would step out of Musa's shadow to become a major political presence in Lebanon, particularly in the Hizballah (or Party of God).[14] In many ways, the most remarkable among them was Muhammad Baqr al-Sadr, an intellectual who is often compared favourably by his admirers with Khomeini.[15] Baqr al-Sadr's erudite studies include a number of influential books revered by educated Shi'i.[16] While Ayatollah Khomeini signified hope and political success, it was Baqr al-Sadr who provided the intellectual underpinning to the revolution. When this writer asked Shi'i leaders in Lebanon to identify the greatest modern thinker among the Shi'i it was the name of Baqr al-Sadr not Khomeini which was uttered, although Khomeini was and is deeply revered. Baqr al-Sadr's role in the creation of the radical groups al-Da'wa and al-Mujahidun remains murky, but there is no gainsaying his seminal role in elaborating the theory of the Islamic state.

Najaf also hosted a score of younger, more militant clerics such as Raghib Harb, Hasan Nasrallah, Ibrahim al-Amin, 'Abbas Musawi, and Subhi Tufayli, all of whom made their way back to Lebanon in the 1970s and early 1980s. Many of the senior members of the circle were linked by marriage and often blood. For instance, the mother of 'Abd al-'Aziz Muhsin, the youngest son of the ayatollah, was from the Lebanese al-Bazzi family in Bint Jbail, an important Shi'i town in the south. Fadlallah's mother was the sister of Ali al-Bazzi, a prominent member of parliament. Musa al-Sadr married a sister of Baqr al-Sadr, and Musa's sister Rabaab married into the prominent Sharaf al-Din family of Tyre.

Musa al-Sadr

Al-Sayyid Musa al-Sadr is one of the most intriguing and fascinating political personalities to have appeared in the modern Middle East. If the Lebanese Shi'i admired Baqr al-Sadr's intellect, and saw Khomeini as the hero of the age, they reserved their love for Sayyid Musa. He was an ambitious but tolerant man, whose controversial career had an enormous impact on the Shi'i Muslim community of Lebanon. His admirers describe him as a man of vision, political acumen and profound compassion, while his detractors remember him as a deceitful, manipulative political chameleon. In a society all too marked by pettiness, greed and political cowardice, Musa al-Sadr was a towering presence (literally as well as figuratively – he was well over six feet tall). Though he disappeared in 1978, he remains a vibrant presence in Lebanon, still inspiring his followers and dogging his enemies.

Musa was born in Qum, Iran, in 1928, the son of Ayatullah Sadr al-Din Sadr, an important Shi'i Muslim *mujtahid* (a Shi'i jurisprudent qualified to make independent interpretations of law and theology). In Qum he attended primary and secondary school, and a Shi'i seminary, and then he went on to Tehran University where he matriculated from the School of Political Economy and Law of Tehran University; the first *mujtahid* to do so. He did not intend to pursue a career as a cleric, but upon the urging of his father he discarded his secular ambitions and agreed to continue an education in Islamic jurisprudence (*fiqh*). One year after his father's death in 1953, he moved to Najaf, Iraq, where he studied under Ayatollahs Muhsin al-Hakim and 'Abdul Qasim Khu'i.

He first visited Lebanon, which was his ancestral home, in 1957. During this visit he made a strong and positive impression on the Lebanese Shi'i, including his relative al-Sayyid 'Abdul Husain Sharaf al-Din, the Shi'i religious leader of the southern Lebanese coastal city of Tyre. Following the death of Sharaf al-Din in 1957, Musa was invited to become the senior Shi'i religious authority in Tyre. Initially he spurned the invitation, but the urgings of his mentor Ayatollah al-Sayyid Muhsin al-Hakim proved persuasive. In 1960 he moved to Tyre. In 1963 he was granted Lebanese citizenship, an early mark of his looming influence in Lebanon. Although he was a man of Qum, he understood Lebanon and the fundamental need for compromise in a land of sects, insecurity and long memories. He emphasized ecumenicalism, and his was an assertiveness laced with empathy.

One of his first significant acts was the establishment of a vocational institute in the southern town of Burj al-Shimali (near Tyre), where Shi'i youths could gain the training that would allow them to escape the privation that marked their community. The institute was constructed at a cost of half a million Lebanese pounds (about $165,000) with money provided by Shi'i benefactors, the Ministry of Education of Lebanon, and bank loans. The institute would become an important symbol of Musa al-Sadr's leadership; it is still in operation – now bearing his name – providing vocational training for about five hundred orphans under the supervision of Musa's sister Rabaab.

A man of keen intelligence, widely noted personal charm and enormous energy – one of his former assistants told this writer that he frequently worked twenty hours a day – al-Sadr attracted a wide array of supporters, ranging from Shi'i merchants in West Africa to petit-bourgeois youth. The Shi'i who had fled the poverty of Lebanon to seek their fortunes in West Africa, proved to be an important source of financial support for Musa al-Sadr. Many of these men were attracted to a man who promised to challenge the old system which had humiliated them and denied them a political voice. If there is an Arabic equivalent to the word 'charisma' it is *haiba*. This word captures the dignified presence and allure of this man from faraway Qum and Najaf.

Imam Musa – as he came to be called by his followers – set out to establish himself as the paramount leader of the Shi'i community in Lebanon, which was most noteworthy at the time for its poverty and general underdevelopment. He helped to fill a yawning leadership void which resulted from the growing inability of the *za'ims* (traditional political bosses) to meet the cascading needs of their clients. From the 1960s on, the Shi'i had experienced rapid social change and economic disruption, and the old village-based patronage system, which presumed the underdevelopment and the apathy of its clients, was proving an anachronism. Patronage is an inextricable component of Mediterranean societies, but the Shi'i *za'ims* in Lebanon were overwhelmed by burgeoning demands.

One informed scholar argues that the appointment of al-Sayyid Musa al-Sadr, in preference to the distinguished *mujtahid* Imad Mughniyya, a more qualified son of Jabal 'Amil, actually bought the Shi'i establishment time. He argues that until his disappearance in 1978, al-Sadr never clashed directly with his benefactors.[17] In terms of al-Sadr's popular image this is irrelevant, and he is widely credited with confronting the interests of the traditional Shi'i *'ayan* and *zu'uma* (notables and political Imams).

Musa al-Sadr could see beyond the villages, the patronage networks and the clans of the Shi'i. He was able to stand above a fragmented and often victimized community and see it as a whole. Through his organizational innovations, his speeches, and his personal example, he succeeded in giving many Shi'i an inclusive communal identity. Furthermore, he reminded his followers that their deprivation should not be fatalistically accepted, for so long as they could speak out through their religion they could overcome their condition. As he once observed, 'whenever the poor involve themselves in a social revolution it is a confirmation that injustice is not predestined.'[18]

Musa al-Sadr recognized that his power lay in part in his role as a custodian of religious symbols, and shrewdly used the central myths of Shi'ism, especially the martyrdom of Iman Husain at Karbala thirteen centuries before, to spur his followers.

Referring, on the occasion of *'ashura* in 1974, to the Shi'i revolutionary model of Imam Husain who rejected quietism for action, al-Sadr noted: 'This revolution did not die in the sands of Karbala, it flowed into the life stream of the Islamic world, and passed from generation to generation, even to our day. It is a deposit placed in our hands so that we may profit from it, that we may extract from it a new source of reform, a new position, a new movement, a new revolution, to repel the darkness, to stop tyranny and to pulverize evil.'[19] He exhorted: 'Brothers, line up in the row of your choice: that of tyranny or that of Husain. I am certain that you will not choose anything but the row of revolution and martyrdom for the realization of justice and the destruction of injustice.'[20]

Political Style

Imam Musa was not averse to hedging his bets. The record of

his political alliances shows that he was – above all – a prag-
matist. It is both a tribute to his political skill and a commentary
on his tactics that well-informed Lebanese should have
commented that nobody knew where Imam Musa stood.
According to reliable reports, Musa was friendly with both
King Husain of Jordan and President Anwar Sadat of Egypt,
and he travelled regularly throughout the Arab world and
Europe. He was hardly a provincial figure.

His followers today often characterize him as a vociferous
critic of the Shah of Iran, but it was only after the October War
of 1973, when Iran supported Israel against the Arabs, that his
relations with the Shah deteriorated. From the autumn of 1973 he
became a vehement critic of the Shah, accusing him of
suppressing religion in Iran, denouncing him for his pro-Israel
stance, and describing him as an 'imperialist stooge'. As his
relations with Iran deteriorated, to the point where his Iranian
citizenship was revoked, he improved his relations with Iraq
from which he may have received significant funding in early
1974. However, for more than a decade he had maintained
close, even cordial ties with the Pahlavi regime, and during his
visits to Tehran in the 1960s and early 1970s he was warmly
received by the Shah. It seems that the Shah of Iran provided
financial subsidies to Musa al-Sadr, and his Iraqi cousin, the
learned Muhammad Baqr al-Sadr. In the first instance, the
Shah's motives may have been simply to keep a hand in
Lebanon, while in the latter case he was clearly interested in
causing difficulties for rival Ba'thist Iraq.[21]

Musa al-Sadr was a strong supporter of Ayatollah Ruhollah
Khomeini, indeed, the last article he published was a polemic in
Le Monde (23 August 1978), castigating the Shah of Iran and
praising Khomeini. However, al-Sadr's vision of Shi'ism was
more moderate, more humanistic than Khomeini's. He was a
friend of Ali Shariati (who died in 1977), the writer who
propounded a liberal, modernist Shi'ism and thereby inspired
many opponents of the Shah (including, the Mujahidin
al-Khalq, the organization that has proved to be the staunchest
opponent of the government of the Islamic Republic). Musa
al-Sadr's admiration for Shariati stemmed from his intellectual
commitment to confront tyranny and injustice through the
renovation of Shi'ism, rather than through the rejection of faith.
In Iran, Shariati's ideological message, with its stress on
humanism, anti-imperialism and self-reliance, appealed to the
educated classes; while his emphasis on the martyrdom of

Husain as a revolutionary exemplar appealed across socio-economic lines.[22] Absent from Shariati's writings and lectures was the vengefulness, anger and intolerance that marked Iran's post-Shah rulers. Many observers suspect that al-Sadr would have moderated the course of the revolution in Iran, were he not consumed by it. While Musa al-Sadr was not an original thinker of the quality of Muhammad Baqr al-Sadr, he could claim a venerable genealogical heritage in modern Shi'ism. Had he lived, he may well have become a serious rival to Khomeini himself.

Like the Maronite Christians, the Shi'i are a minority in a predominantly Sunni Muslim Arab world, and for both sects Lebanon is a refuge in which sectarian identity and security can be preserved. Al-Sadr's message to the Maronites in the period before the civil war of 1975-76 was a combination of muted threat and impassioned egalitarianism. In his ecumenical sermons to Christian congregations he won many admirers among his listeners. He is said to have been the first Shi'i *mujtahid* to visit the Maronite patriach in his bastion at Bkerke. Many Maronites, not surprisingly, saw a natural ally in Imam Musa. He was a reformer, not a revolutionary. He sought the betterment of the Shi'i in a Lebanese context. He often noted, 'For us Lebanon is one definitive homeland.' The convenant or pact of the Movement of the Deprived, which al-Sadr authored in 1974, emphasizes that the movement 'adheres to the principles of national sovereignty, the indivisibility of the motherland, and the integrity of her soil'.[23]

Musa al-Sadr recognized the insecurity of the Maronites, and he acknowledged their need to maintain their monopoly hold on the presidency. Yet he was critical of the Maronites for their arrogant stance toward the Muslims, and particularly the Shi'i. He argued that the Maronite-dominated government had neglected the South, where as many as 50 per cent of the Shi'i lived since independence, and had made the Shi'i into a disinherited class in Lebanon. Quoting from the Qur'an, he reminded his listeners: 'He who sleeps while having a needy neighbour is not considered a believer.'

Musa al-Sadr was anti-communist, one suspects not only on principled grounds but because the various communist organizations were among his prime competitors for Shi'i recruits. He claimed to reject ideologies of the right and the left, noting that 'we are neither of the right nor the left, but we follow the path of the just' (*al-sirat al-mustaqim*).'[24] Yet when the two branches of the Ba'th party (pro-Iraqi and pro-Syrian) were making significant inroads among the Shi'i of the south and the Beirut suburbs he appropriated their pan-Arab slogans.

Although the movement he founded, Harakat al-Muhrumin (or the Movement of the Deprived), was aligned with the Lebanese National Movement (LNM) in the early stages of the Lebanese civil war (1957-76), al-Sadr found its Druze leader, Kamal al-Jumblatt, irresponsible and exploitative of the Shi'i. As he noted, the LNM was willing 'to combat the Christians to the last Shi'i'. He imputed to Jumblatt the prolongation of the war: 'Without him the war in Lebanon would have been terminated in two months. Because of him, it has been prolonged two years and only God knows how long the encore will last.'

Thus, it was hardly inconsistent with al-Sadr's political stance that he should have deserted the LNM in May 1976, when Syria intervened in Lebanon on the side of the Maronite militias and against the LNM and its Palestinian allies. He was a friend and confidant of Syrian President Hafez al-Asad, yet he mistrusted Syrian motives in Lebanon. It was, in Imam Musa's view, only the indigestibility of Lebanon that protected it from being engulfed by Syria. Nonetheless, the Syrians were an essential card in Musa's serious game with the Palestinian resistance.

Musa al-Sadr pledged his support for the Palestine resistance movement, but his relations with the PLO were tense and uneasy at best. During the 1973 clashes between the PLO and the Lebanese army, he reproached the Sunni Muslims for their support for the guerrillas. On the one hand he chastised the government for failing to defend the south from Israeli aggression, but on the other he criticized the PLO for shelling Israel from the south and hence provoking Israeli retaliation. He consistently expressed sympathy for Palestinian aspirations, but was unwilling to countenance actions that exposed Lebanese citizens, and especially Shi'i citizens of the south, to additional suffering. In Musa al-Sadr's view Israel was an 'absolute evil', yet he was realistic enough to understand the overwhelming dominance of Israeli military power. Thus, his ambition vis-à-vis Israel was not to destroy it, but to see it respect the 1949 armistice line that substituted for a border between Israel and Lebanon.

After the 1970 PLO defeat in Jordan, most PLO fighters relocated to south Lebanon where they proceeded to supplant the legitimate authorities. Imam Musa prophetically warned the PLO that it was not in its interests to establish a state within a state in Lebanon. It was the organization's failure to heed this warning that helped to spawn the alienation of their 'natural allies' – the Shi'i – who, only a few years later, actively resisted the Palestinian fighters in their midst. After he was gone, Shi'i militiamen invoking his memory fought pitched battles with the PLO and its Lebanese allies, applauded the *fida'i* defeat at the hands of Israel in 1982, laid siege to their camps in 1985, and pledged never to permit the recreation of the Palestinian state-within-a-state in Lebanon. For their part, some PLO officials believed that Musa al-Sadr was a creation of the Army's Deuxième Bureau (the Second – or Intelligence – Bureau), of the CIA.

But Musa's unremitting opponent was Kamil al-As'ad, the powerful Shi'i political boss from the south, who accurately saw al-Sadr as a serious threat to his political power base and opposed him at almost every move. For Imam Musa and his followers, al-As'ad was the epitome of the *za'im* system.

In 1967 the Chamber of Deputies (the Lebanese parliament) passed a law establishing a Supreme Islamic Shi'i Council (SISC), which would for the first time provide a representative body for the Shi'i independent of the Sunni Muslims. The council actually came into existence in 1969, with Imam Musa as its chairman for a six-year term – a clear confirmation of his status as the leading Shi'i cleric in the country. The council quickly made itself heard by its demands in the military, social, economic, and political realms, including: improved measures for the defence of the south, the provision of development funds, construction and improvement of schools and hospitals, and an increase in the number of Shi'i appointed to senior government positions. The SISC quickly became a locus of the Shi'i intelligentsia, the emerging middle class, as well as many of the traditional elites.

One year after the formation of the SISC, and following a string of bloody Israeli incursions and bombardments, Musa al-Sadr organized a general strike 'to emphasize to the government the plight of the population of southern Lebanon vis-à-vis the Israeli military threat'. Shortly thereafter, the government created the Council of the South (*Majlis al-Janub*) which was capitalized at 30 million Lebanese pounds and was chartered to support the development of the region. Unfortunately, the *Majlis al-Janub* became more famous as a cockpit of corruption than as a font of worthwhile projects. The creation of the council was a victory for al-Sadr, but it was the formidable Kamil al-As'ad who dominated its operation.

By the early 1970s, the existing social and economic problems of the Shi'i were compounded by a rapidly deteriorating security situation in the south. While the SISC seemed a useful vehicle for the promotion of the community's interests (as mediated by Musa al-Sadr of course), the council was ineffectual in a milieu that was quickly becoming dominated by militias and extra-legal parties. On 17 March 1974, the 'arbain, the fortieth day after 'ashura – Musa al-Sadr was to be found in the Bekaa Valley city of Ba'albak at a well-attended rally. Standing before a crowd estimated at 75,000, Imam Musa declared the launching of a popular mass movement, the Harakat al-Mahrumin (the Movement of the Deprived). He ranged over Shi'i grievances – poor schools, non-existent public services, governmental neglect – and vowed to struggle relentlessly until the social grievances of the deprived were satisfactorily addressed by the government. He recalled that a Kufan judge had accused Imam Husain of straying from his grandfather's way, but he refused to relegate himself to a life of quiet scholarship and prayer.

> The rulers say that the men of religion must only pray and not meddle in other things. They exhort us to fast and to pray for them so that the foundations of their reign will not be shaken, while they move away from religion and exploit it to hold on to their seats of power. Do not think that men in power who proclaim their opposition to communism are opposed to atheism ... They are the infidel of the infidels and the most atheist of the atheists. They want us to give ourselves up to them.[25]

Just one year later, al-Sadr's efforts were overtaken by the onset of civil war in Lebanon. By July 1975 it became known that a militia adjunct to Harakat al-Mahrumin had been formed. The militia, *Afwaj al-Muqawama al Lubnaniya* (the Lebanese Resistance Detachments), better known by the acronym AMAL (which also means 'hope'), was initially trained by al-Fatah (the largest organization in the PLO) and it played a minor role in the fighting of 1975 and 1976. Musa al-Sadr's movement was affiliated with the LNM and its PLO allies during the first year of the civil war, but it had broken with its erstwhile allies when the Syrians intervened in June 1976 to prevent the defeat of the Maronite-dominated Lebanese Front.

Four months before the Syrian intervention President Sulaiman Franjiya accepted a 'Constitutional Document' that Imam Musa indicated was a satisfactory basis for implementing political reform. The document – which called for an increase in the proportion of parliamentary seats allocated to the Muslims, as well as some restrictions on the prerogatives of the Maronite President – seemed to offer a basis for restoring equilibrium to Lebanon. When it was combined with the prospect of bringing the PLO under control through the Syrian intervention, there appeared to be a prospect for a new beginning. Unfortunately, the opportunity to stop the carnage was more apparent than real. While the pace of fighting had decreased by the end of 1976, the violence continued. (Incidentally, even a cursory review of the 1989 al-Ta'if accord, which ended the decade-and-a-half of civil war in Lebanon, will confirm that the 1976 and 1989 reform formulas are basically the same; that is, both establish Christian-Muslim political parity while preserving the confessional distribution of privilege, notwithstanding the integral stipulations for de-confessionalizing Lebanese politics.)

The growing influence of Musa al-Sadr prior to the civil war was certainly a bellwether of the increased political importance of the Shi'i; however, it bears emphasizing that Imam Musa led only a fraction of his politically affiliated coreligionists. Impressive though he was, it is important not to exaggerate his impact in terms of the political mobilization of the Shi'i. For instance, in Fouad Ajami's finely styled and powerful account, *The Vanished Imam*,[26] the reader might infer that the hero of the piece had succeeded in mobilizing all of the Shi'i. However, this was not true.

The multi-confessional parties and militias attracted the majority of Shi'i recruits and many more Shi'i carried arms under their colours than under those of AMAL. And even in war the Shi'i suffered disproportionately; by a large measure they incurred more casualties than any other sect in Lebanon. Perhaps the single most important success achieved by al-Sadr was the reduction of the authority and the influence of the traditional Shi'i elites, but it was the civil war, and the associated growth of extra-legal organizations, that rendered these personalities increasingly irrelevant in the Lebanese political system.

Whatever he may have been and despite his occasionally vehement histrionics. Musa al-Sadr was hardly a man of war. (He seems to have played only an indirect role in directing the military actions of the AMAL militia.) In a poignant effort to curtail the onslaught he declared a hunger strike, but the combination of visceral fury and frustration, government impotence and the strength of the emerging warlords dwarfed the gesture. His weapons were words, and as a result his political efforts were short-circuited by the war. He seemed to be eclipsed by the violence that engulfed Lebanon. In the months preceding the outbreak of mayhem, Musa al-Sadr's star was still rising, but his political fortunes plummeted by 1976.

Imam al-Ghaib

Ironically, it was the still mysterious disappearance of Musa al-Sadr in 1978 that helped to retrieve the promise of his earlier efforts. In August 1978 he visited Libya with two companions, Sheikh Muhammad Shahhadih Ya'qub and the journalist 'Abbas Badr al-Din. The party has not been heard from since. While Musa's fate is not known, it is widely suspected that he was killed by henchmen of the Libyan leader, Colonel Mu'ammar Qaddafi for reasons that remain obscure. The Libyans did attempt a clumsy cover-up, sending a trio of impersonators, armed with doctored passports and the luggage of the ill-fated group, to Rome, although some evidence suggests the group never left Libya. What is clear is that the disappearance of Musa al-Sadr has been of enormous importance to the Shi'i of Lebanon. (The anniversary of his disappearance, the thirty-first of August, is celebrated annually with a national strike in Lebanon.)

Musa al-Sadr has become a hero to his followers, who revere his memory and take inspiration from his words and his suffering. The symbol of a missing imam – reminiscent as it is of the central dogma of Shi'ism – is hard to assail, and even Musa's blood enemies are now heard to utter words of praise. The movement he founded, now simply called AMAL, has – since his disappearance – become the largest Shi'i organization in Lebanon and one of the most powerful. Simultaneously, the more militant Hizballah claims the Imam al-Gha'ib (or the Hidden Imam) as its forebear.[27]

Though hope for his safe return naturally has faded with the passage of time, he remained formal head of the SISC until his sixty-fifth birthday in 1993, when the vice president, Muhammad Mahdi Shams al-Din, was elected to replace him as president of the SISC. Even now his successors cling to the thin hope that he survives in a Libyan gaol cell.

Many of Musa's key followers and associates are now dead: the Iranian engineer Mustafa Chamran died in 1980 while serving as chairman of Iran's Supreme Defence Council. He had been heavily implicated in the formation of the AMAL militia, as well as the training of anti-Shah militants; Khalil Jaradi and Muhammad Sa'ad, revered leaders of the post-1982 resistance to Israel's occupation, were blown up – ironically in Musa's ancestral home village of Marakeh – in 1985; Sadeq Ghotbzadeh, confidant to Khomeini and friend of Musa al-Sadr, was executed in 1982 for plotting to execute the Ayatollah; and, Daoud Sulaiman Daoud, devoted aide to Imam Musa and later the dynamic leader of AMAL in the south, was killed on 22 September 1988, by an anti-tank rocket fired at his motorcade (the trigger men were reputedly Shi'is, who were apprehended, but their employers are still unknown – publicly at least). Others remain active on the political scene, especially Nabih Berri who has headed AMAL since 1980 and Husain al-Husaini, former general-secretary of AMAL and speaker of the Lebanese parliament from 1984 until 1992, when he relinquished the post to his rival Berri. Hasan Hashim, a schoolteacher from the Zahrani district of Sidon, in the south, was an early follower of Musa al-Sadr, and attained local fame for his courage in directing the anti-Israeli resistance following the 1982 invasion. Following a clumsy and unsuccessful lunge at a leading position within AMAL, he retreated into obscurity.

The competition for supremacy in Lebanon among the Shi'i is in large measure over who is the rightful heir to the legacy of Musa al-Sadr. On the one side is Hizballah, under the strong influence of Muhammad Husain Fadlallah, which emerged after the Israeli invasion of Lebanon and was deeply engaged in the kidnapppings of foreigners.[28] On the other side is AMAL, still a reform movement, but now struggling to maintain its bearings in a Lebanon at peace. Both groups are now represented in the Lebanese parliament, where the Shi'i enjoy an unaccustomed voice.

The fall of the Shah in 1979 provided an exemplar for the dissatisfied, of what pious, well-organized Muslims can accomplish in the face of seemingly insurmountable odds. Even those many Islamic groups that do not seek to emulate the form of the revolution in Iran, derive inspiration from the success of their Muslim colleagues there. The revolution was an object lesson that deprivation or second-class citizenship did not have to be passively accepted. In fact, it was precisely that lesson which was driven home in one speech after another by Shi'i leaders like Musa al-Sadr prior to the revolution. The message retains it power today.

Notes

1. For an assessment of the socio-economic standing of the Shi'i in Lebanon, especially in the period preceding the civil war, see Augustus Richard Norton, *Amal and the Shi'i: Struggle for the Soul of Lebanon*, Austin, University of Texas Press, 1987, chapter 2.

2. See Augustus Richard Norton, 'Lebanon after Ta'if: Is the Civil War Over?' *Middle East Journal*, Summer 1991, pp. 457-73.

3. As Moojan Momem explains: 'The occurrence of the Occultation is considered to have been due to the hostility of the Imam's enemies and the danger to his life. He remains in occultation because of the continuance of this threat. The severance of communication with the Hidden Imam is not considered to contradict the dictum that the "earth is not left without an Imam", for, say the Shi'i writers, the sun still gives light and warmth to the earth even when hidden behind a cloud.' See his excellent *An Introduction to Shi'i Islam: The History and Doctrines of Twelver Islam*, New Haven, Yale University Press, 1984, p. 165.

4. 'Myth' is used here in the anthropological sense and is not meant to imply that the event did not occur, only that the patina of time and culture has enriched and enlivened the event.

5. Fuad I. Khuri, *From Village to Suburb: Order and Change in Greater Beirut*, Chicago, University of Chicago Press, 1975, esp. pp. 181-6.

6. The Granada TV 1987 documentary 'The Sword of Islam' contains extraordinary pictures of '*ashura* as commemorated in Nabatiya.

7. Clifford Geertz, 'Religion as a Cultural System', in *The Interpretation of Cultures*, idem., New York, Basic Books, 1973, p. 113.

8. I borrow this formulation from Peter J. Chelkowski of New York University.

9. The term 're-politicize Islam' was coined by Bassam Tibi. See his *Islam and the Cultural Accommodation of Social Change*, Boulder, Westview Press, 1990.

10. Accuracy requires that the reader note that among the Sunni Islamist thinkers there is a trend toward commending the adoption of *ijtihad*.

11. Sa'ad al-Din Ibrahim, 'Anatomy of Egypt's Militant Islamic Groups: Methodological Note and Preliminary Findings', *International Journal of Middle East Studies*, vol. 12, no. 4, December 1989, pp. 423-53.

12. A dated, but still noteworthy account of Najaf is Fadil Jamali, 'The Theological Colleges of Najaf ', *Muslim World*, vol. 50, no. 1, 1960, pp. 15-22.

13. See the rich articles of Chibli Mallat, 'Muhammad Baqer as-Sadr and the Islamic Opposition in Contemporary Iraq', *Third World Quarterly*, vol. 10, no. 2, April 1988, pp. 699-729; and 'Iraq', in Hunter, ed., *Politics of Islamic Revivalism*, pp. 71-87.

14. Fadlallah's most widely read book is *Islam wa manataq al-quwa* (or Islam

and the Logic of Force), Beirut, al-dar al-Islamiyya, second ed., 1981.

15. Hanna Batatu, 'Shi'i Organizations in Iraq: Al-Da'wah al-Islamiyah and al-Mujahidin', in Shi'ism and Social Protest, Juan R.I. Cole and Nikki Keddie, eds., New Haven, Yale University Press, 1986, pp. 179-200, esp. p. 182.

16. Notably, Falsafatuna (Our Philosophy), 1959; Iqtisaduna (Our Economy), 1960; and Al-bank al-la-ribawi fi al-Islam (the Non-usurious Bank in Islam), 1973.

17. Chibli Mallat, Shi'i Thought from the South of Lebanon, Oxford, Centre for Lebanese Studies, Papers on Lebanon, no. 7, 1988, p. 17.

18. In Norton, Amal and the Shi'i, p. 40.

19. Al-Hayat, 1 February 1974, quoted in Norton, Amal and the Shi'i, pp. 40-1.

20. Ibid.

21. See Norton, Amal and the Shi'i, pp. 52-4; and, Batatu, 'Shi'i Organizations in Iraq', p. 192.

22. Here I draw on Mary Elaine Hegland, 'Islamic Revival or Political and Cultural Revolution? An Iranian Case Study', in Religious Resurgence: Contemporary Cases in Islam, Christianity, and Judaism, Richard T. Antoun and Mary Elaine Hegland, eds., Syracuse, Syracuse University Press, 1987, pp. 194-219, esp. pp. 211-12.

23. For the complete text, see Norton, Amal and the Shi'i, pp. 144-66.

24. Thom Sicking and Shereen Khairallah, 'The Shi'i Awakening in Lebanon: A Search for Radical Change in a Traditional Way,' in Vision and Revision in Arab Society, 1974, Beirut, Dar al-Mashreq, CEMAN Reports 2, 1975, pp. 97-130, esp. p. 111.

25. An-Nahar, 18 March 1974, as translated in Fouad Ajami, The Vanished Imam: Musa Al Sadr and the Shia of Lebanon, Ithaca, Cornell University Press, 1986, p. 147.

26. Ithaca, Cornell University Press, 1986.

27. A 1986 Hizballah calendar, in the author's possession, features pictures of: 'the Hidden Imam, Musa al-Sadr'; 'Deputy Islamic Imam, the Imam Khomeini'; 'the Distinguished Mujtahid al-Sayyid 'Abd al-Husain Sharaf al-Din'; 'the Joyous Martyr al-Sayyid Muhammad Baqr al-Sadr'; 'the Joyous Martyr al-Sayyid 'Abd al-Latif al-Amin'; and, 'the Joyous Martyr the Shaykh Raghib al-Harb'.

28. See Augustus Richard Norton, 'Lebanon: The Internal Conflict and the Iranian Connection', in John L. Esposito, ed., The Iranian Revolution: Its Global Impact, Miami, Florida International University Press, 1990, pp. 116-37.

9

Ali Shariati:
Teacher, Preacher, Rebel

Ali Rahnema

Family Background

Ali Shariati came from a long-standing professional religious family in Iran. Akund Mulla Qurban-Ali, better known as Akhund-e Hakim, Ali Shariati's great-grandfather, was originally invited to live in Mazinan as the principal religious authority of the region. Mazinan was at the time a small village built on the edge of the desert in the Khorasan province. Locally, the family had a reputation for piety, social service and asceticism.[1]

Muhammad-Taqi Mazinani (Shariati), Ali Shariati's father, came to the holy city of Mashhad between 1927 and 1928 to pursue his religious studies at the Mashhad Seminary School, which in terms of academic status in Iran was second only to the Qum Seminary School. Upon the completion of his introductory (*moqadamat*) theological studies and having started his intermediate (*sath*) studies, Muhammad-Taqi left the religious establishment to become a teacher in the national educational system.[2] He believed that the educated youth who would constitute the responsible citizenry of the future had to be exposed to an Islamic teaching compatible with the requirements of modern times. Thus Muhammad-Taqi broke two long-standing family traditions. First, upon the termination of his studies he did not return to Mazinan, the traditional abode of the family. Second, even though he was equipped to become a cleric, as his forefathers had been, he replaced his religious garb with a western suit and wore the typical western *chapeau* instead of the turban. Muhammad-Taqi took it upon himself to educate what he believed to be the future agents of change or the young Islamic intellectuals. For this purpose he needed to study the literature which attracted them, employ their language and adopt their dress code. In the words of Mughniya, the Lebanese Shi'ite intellectual cleric, Muhammad-Taqi wore the *chapeau* to protect thousands of bearded and turbaned clergy from the ridicule of the new generation.[3]

After the forced abdication of Reza Shah in 1941, public political and religious activities, which had been totally curbed until that time, were resumed. On the one hand, the activities of the Tudeh Party, which had not called itself the Communist Party of Iran to avoid offending the religious sensitivities of the people, expanded. On the other hand, Ahmad Kasravi, an ex-cleric, questioned the fundamental bases of Shi'ism and considered it an aberration of Islam.[4]

Under such circumstances, in 1941, Muhammad-Taqi Shariati started a one-man campaign to propagate what he believed was the progressive spirit of Islam. In 1944, the Centre for the Propagation of Islamic Truths (Kanoun-e Nashr-e Haqayeq-e Eslami) was officially opened in Mashhad.[5] Its primary objective was that of blocking and rolling-back the influence of atheism propagated by the communists. It also wished to win back those Muslim intellectuals whose aversion to the clergy's obscurantism and uncritical acceptance of all old dogmas had pushed them into the arms of the Kasravists. The Centre's Islamic modernist tendency, however, ultimately brought it into conflict with the well-entrenched powerful Shi'ite establishment of Mashhad. In the words of Ali Shariati, in the tumultuous years after 1941, intellectuals had Marxist tendencies, while religionists had reactionary tendencies. Religious intellectuals found themselves baseless, and forlorn. Muhammad-Taqi Shariati opened a third road between these two.[6]

After the 1953 American-staged coup against the nationalist government of Mosaddeq and until its first closure in the summer of 1957, the Centre became the hub of pro-Mossadeqist activities in Mashhad. Once the National Resistance Movement (NRM), which was dedicated to the continuation of Mossadeq's policies, was established in 1953, the members of the Centre joined the NRM. At this time, members of a Muslim–Socialist group originally called Nehzat-e Khoda Parastan-e Socialist or the Movement of God-Worshipping Socialists (MGWS), founded by Muhammad Nakhshab and active in Mashhad, also joined the NRM. Among the joining members of MGWS who were also very closely affiliated with the Centre, was

Muhammad-Taqi Shariati's twenty-year-old son, Ali.

Childhood and Adolescence

Ali Shariati, the first child of Muhammad-Taqi and Zahra was born on 24 November 1933. This corresponds to the period when his father was completing his preliminary religious studies and teaching in a primary school, Sherafat. Ali was born into a modest family, where even though religious rites and rituals were strictly observed, Islam was conceived by the father of the house more as a social and philosophical doctrine of modern relevance than a privatized and introverted creed of the past.

In 1941, Ali entered the first grade of the Ibn Yamin private school, where his father was employed. At school, Ali had two distinct types of behaviour. He was quiet, unorganized and studious. He was considered a loner, who lived in his own cocoon, protected from the outside world and indifferent to it. He, therefore, seemed unsociable. According to one of his classmates, he neither mingled much with his classmates nor did he play football, the customary group sport of the boys of his age. In class, it is said that he gazed out of the window, oblivious to the world around him. Shariati was later to recall that grown-ups would remind him of the fact that he was very different from other children of his age.[7] Even though Ali used to stay up with his father, reading late into the night and sometimes, into the early morning hours, he never read what he was assigned at school, nor did he do his homework. While at primary school he read the Persian translation of Victor Hugo's *Les Misérables* along with books on such disparate topics as vitamins and the history of the cinema.[8]

Shariati was initiated to philosophy and mysticism during his first years at high-school.[9] During these years, preferring to study at home, he immersed himself in his father's 2,000 volume library which he had first become acquainted with in his primary school years.[10] It is said that while Muhammad-Taqi Shariati's Centre for the Propagation of Islamic Truths attracted large numbers of young Islamic students and intellectuals, some of whom were Ali's classmates, Ali was so busy with what he was learning at home that he seldom attended these lectures and discussions. It is felt that the discussions at the Centre did not quench his intellectual thirst and curiosity.[11] According to Shariati, his father was instrumental in shaping his soul and spirit. It was he, who taught him the 'art' of reflection and the 'technique' of being a human being. It was also his father who first exposed him to the taste of 'freedom', 'dignity', 'magnanimity' and 'faith'.[12]

But in view of his unforthcoming and solitary conduct during this period, one could argue that Ali's self-education at home rendered him too self-sufficient to join and enjoy the crowd. Later he would say, immodestly, that during this period, in each of his classes he was 100 lessons ahead of the rest of the class and 99 ahead of his teachers.[13] What is known about his interests during this period of his life indicates that he was more attracted to literature, poetry and humanities than to the social sciences or religious studies. Even though he studied Arabic at home with his father, he focused mainly on the study of philosophy and the works of modern Iranian and foreign poets and writers. He is said to have studied and been inspired by the works of Saddeq-e Hedayat, the famous Iranian nihilistic novelist; Nima Yousheej, the father of modern Iranian poetry; Akhavan-e Saless, the famous contemporary Iranian poet and Maurice Maeterlinck, the Belgian writer whose works combined mysticism with symbolism. Shariati remembers that his interest in philosophy was kindled by a line from Maeterlinck which reads: 'When we blow out a candle, where does its flame go?'[14]

Ali, however, was not the typical studious, anti-social loner who avoided the crowds because he had nothing to say to them nor anything in common with them. When he was in the right mood, Shariati became sociable, extroverted and lively. He became the mischievous brat who participated in the usual student plots in class to ridicule the teacher.[15] Shariati's serious and premature philosophical behaviour should be understood along with his sense of fun-making, sarcasm and satire. He was well known among his friends for his sense of humour, quick wit, gags, jests and pleasantries; qualities which later became important and lethal weapons in his arsenal against intellectual opponents and enemies.

According to his own account, Shariati experienced his first serious personality crisis between the years 1946 and 1950.[16] At the age of thirteen, adolescents in the West enter the care-free period of 'teenage' life. In the Iran of the late 1940s, comics and detective or romance stories for adolescents were unheard of. The most important pastime for this age group in educated middle-class urban families was the study of the books and literature that were read by their fathers. It is therefore not surprising to learn that during his period of adolescence, Shariati was reading the works of Maurice Maeterlinck, Arthur Schopenhauer, Franz Kafka and Saddeq-e Hedayat. Under their influence, Shariati recalled that his religious convictions were shaken to the foundation.[17] The reassuring comfort and certainty of God's existence gave way to the anxiety of doubt. For Shariati, the thought of existence without God was so awesome, lonely and alien that life itself became a bleak and futile exercise. His long hours of study and reflection had ushered a deep crisis in his faith. He found himself at a philosophical dead end, the outcome of which, he thought could only be suicide or insanity.[18] On a cold winter's night he toyed with the idea of suicide at the romantic sight of the *Estakhr-e Koohsangi* in Mashhad. Whereas Occidental philosophy confused him, rendering his path towards cognition and consciousness ever more slippery, he found consolation, meaning and security in Mowlavi's Masnavi; the eternal spiritual repository of Oriental philosophy. On that particular night, it was finally the words and the thoughts of Mullana that saved him from self-destruction. Mowlavi's mysticism left an indelible mark on the young Shariati.[19] Later he would characterize mysticism along with equality and freedom as man's three main historical quests and the fundamental dimensions of the ideal man.[20]

In 1950, having completed his ninth grade, Shariati left the *Ferdowsi* high-school and entered Mashhad's Teacher Training College as a boarder. At the time he was torn between contradictory conceptions of the meaning and objective of life, the modes of attaining those objectives and man's role and responsibility on earth. In 1952 he graduated from Mashhad's Teacher Training College. At this time it seemed as if he had settled a number of teleological issues that had preoccupied him for a number of years. The volcano and rage of his cognitive agnosticism, mercurial certitudes, philosophical dilemmas, growing uncertainties and persisting half-beliefs characteristic of his years of adolescence and youth came to a temporary rest. Incertitude and anxiety were replaced by a momentary firm belief in the fact that he had attained the first summit of certainty. He had uncovered Islam as the epistemological medium of recognizing and defining the ideal life and society. Furthermore, he had identified the ideal role model or agent for attaining the ideal Islamic society in the character of Abu Zar. For Shariati, life was hence meaningful.

Shariati's newly found peace and equilibrium are well

reflected in his first serious works, *Tarikh-e Takamol-e Falsafe* (A History of the Development of Philosophy), generally known as *Maktab-e Vaseteh-e Islam* (The Median School of Islam) and *Abu Zar-e Ghifari*, written between 1953 and 1956. Both of these important works attempted to distinguish Islam from other philosophical, political and socio-economic schools of thought, thus providing an Islamic interpretation for modern socio-economic and political concepts, and modernizing, actualizing and politicizing traditionally neutral Islamic concepts. Furthermore, Shariati presented a functional and purposive description of a committed Muslim and his socio-political role and responsibility in life. These two works reflected the important influence of the arguments and views of those affiliated with the *Nehzat-e Khoda Parastan-e Socialist*, with which Shariati had come into close contact.[21]

Abu Zar-e Ghifari is based on the Arabic text of the contemporary Egyptian writer Abdul-Hamid Jowdat al-Sahar. Even though the text was called a translation, Shariati admitted that he freely added his own reflections, research and commentary, rendering the distinction between Shariati's and Jowdat al-Sahar's ideas impossible.[22] In *Abu Zar-e Ghifari*, Shariati created a hero, a model and a symbol, who defied wealth, power and even religious authority to save the 'authentic' Islam of the poor, the oppressed and the socially conscious. One man against the mighty ruler of the Islamic empire.

Abu Zar is Shariati's first symbolic creation, his first 'meaning sign' for those who later became members of the initiated circle around him and his works. Abu Zar is the signal, code or allegory for the committed, defiant, revolutionary Muslim who preaches equality, fraternity, justice and liberation. Whether the book is a factual historical account of Abu Zar's life is of secondary importance. The purpose of the book, as is clearly reflected in Shariati's future references to it, was a means of remembrance and a straightforward lesson in what he believed to be the proper Islamic conduct in an age of anti-values and anti-heroes. Furthermore, Shariati's discovery of Abu Zar convinced him that concepts, such as social justice, equality, liberation and socialism, which had reached Iran through western intellectuals, were integral parts of the Islamic heritage. Shariati could, therefore, proudly claim: 'Abu Zar is the forefather of all post French Revolution egalitarian schools.'[23]

It would be fair to say that from the age of twenty until his death, Shariati's youthful hero-worship of Abu Zar developed into a deeply felt reverence. He thus tried to remain as sincere as he could to the image of Abu Zar, as he had outlined in his book: the righteous and responsible Muslim who resisted all deviations from the egalitarian and fraternal Islam of the Prophet. Later in his life, Shariati openly admitted that he was a follower of Abu Zar and that his Islam, Shi'ism, ideals, wants and rage, were those of Abu Zar.[24] Shariati felt so close to Abu Zar that he may have considered himself something like his reincarnation. For example, he described himself, his position and situation in life in terms similar to those which he had employed in describing Abu Zar.[25] Interestingly enough, in the late 1960s, once Shariati's sharp criticism turned against the official clergy as the custodians of oppression and exploitation, his clerical enemies also chose to discredit him by attacking Abu Zar. Haji Ashraf, a prominent Tehran preacher, claimed that Abu Zar was a common thief, who turned to Islam only after it had become widespread and that he challenged Othman, simply because he too wanted a share of the wealth that Othman was distributing among his friends.[26] After Shariati's death, many called him 'the Abu Zar of his time'.[27] What the Prophet was supposed to have said about Abu Zar, was repeated by Shariati's supporters in Iran in reference to him: 'He lives alone, he dies alone and he shall be resurrected alone.'[28]

Shariati's Political Heritage

Shariati recalled that, in the years 1950 and 1951, 'suddenly a hurricane approached and disturbed the world's peace. Gusts of struggle erupted from every corner and I too was jolted from my peaceful seat of isolation and ... the story started.'[29] The hurricane that Shariati spoke of was Dr Mosaddeq's nationalist movement. Like all nationalist intellectuals of his time, Shariati participated in pro-Mosaddeq demonstrations and rallies, party meetings and discussions.

In Mashhad, sixteen young modernist Islamic nationalists, closely affiliated with Muhammad-Taqi's Centre had joined the Movement of God-Worshipping Socialists. These included Ali Shariati, Kazem Sami, Mehdi Momken, Kazem Ahmadzadeh and Ibrahim Harati.[30] The God-Worshipping Socialists blended Islam with socialism and maintained that Islam's socio-economic system was that of scientific socialism based on

monotheism. Their newspaper called for the overthrow of
feudalism and capitalism, depicting the Prophet and Imam Ali
as the forefathers of both socialism and democracy.[31] Keeping
steadfast to its philosophical positions, the Movement of
God-Worshipping Socialists merged with the Iran Party
(Hezb-e Iran) which was a member of the Mosaddeqist National
Front, on 21 May 1951.[32] During the summer of 1952 Shariati
frequented the headquarters of the party in Mashhad.[33] By 16
February 1953, the Movement of God-Worshipping Socialists
had splintered from the Iran Party to found a new organization
called the League for the Freedom of the Iranian People
(Jam'iyat Azadi-e Mardom-e Iran). Shariati remained a member
of this League and his name appeared under a circular addressed
to the people of Khorasan and published in the organization's
newspaper.[34] After the coup in 1953, the League for the
Freedom of the Iranian People maintained its Islamic socialist
principles, yet changed its name and called itself the Party of the
Iranian People (Hezb-e Mardom-e Iran). Whether Shariati was a
member of this party is not clear. One of his close friends recalls
that Shariati had categorically denied having ever been a
member of the Party of the Iranian People, while a few key
members of the party maintain that he had close ties with it and
even paid his membership fee, of one toman.

After the fall of Mosaddeq's nationalist government in
August 1953, the anti-imperialist and nationalist aspirations of
the youth that had participated in the popular movement were
stunted and stifled. All attempts at resistance were swiftly and
systematically dealt with. The end of a short-lived parliamentary democracy turned all hopes for an independent and
prosperous Iran which had been pinned on the Popular
Movement to remorse, frustration and despair. This prevalent
national mood is well reflected in Shariati's second personality
crisis, which could be characterized more as an identity crisis.
Between 1956 and 1958, Shariati was essentially preoccupied
with an inner self-evaluation and a soul-searching process. He
sought to find an answer to the question 'Who am I?'[35]

Deeply influenced by Mosaddeq and grieved by the failure of
his movement, later in his life Shariati developed a
contradictory stand towards freedom and democracy. On the
one hand, love and affection for freedom and Mosaddeq as its
personification; on the other hand, hate and loathing for
parliamentary democracy as a weak political system unfit for
developing countries.[36] In 1975, twenty-two years after the fall

of Mosaddeq, Shariati wrote a poetic and symbolical allegory eulogizing freedom. In it, he referred to Mosaddeq as his guide and leader (*pishva*), who constantly lamented for freedom during the seventy years of his life.[37]

The coup against Mosaddeq revealed the alliance of a trinity which became the target of disdain in the heart of that segment of Iran's young who had actively participated in the Popular Movement. The role played by the United States, the monarchy and its military allies and, finally, an important segment of the clergy represented by Ayatollahs Behbahani and Kashani induced a large majority of Iran's politicized youth to look upon revolutionary communism as a viable alternative. As an ideology it provided a historical explanation for the behaviour of imperialism, monarchical dictatorship and clerical collaboration. It provided Mosaddeq's young partisans with the necessary intellectual nourishment to combat the trinity which had come to be viewed as the source of Iran's misfortunes.

Marked by the forces that led to the downfall of Mosaddeq, later, Shariati coined and popularized his evil trinity of gold or wealth, coercion and deceit (*Zar-o Zoor-o Tazvir*), which due to its alliteration became a catch phrase in Persian. This was one of Shariati's many catchy simple formulas, through the symbolic use of which he communicated his subversive socio-political messages. According to Shariati, the wealthy, the oppressors and their apologetic accomplices or the official clergy have, throughout history, been the source of all evil.[38] Shariati's construction symbolized capitalism (wealth), dictatorship and imperialism (coercion), and the role of the official clergy (deceit).

In the aftermath of the 1953 coup, Shariati joined the Mashhad branch of the post-coup clandestine organization of the National Resistance Movement (NRM) which was a Mosaddeqist organization with strong religious tendencies. He recalled that during this period, he was involved in organizing and planning strikes and rallies. He was also instrumental in the clandestine publication of books and leaflets.[39] On 28 February 1954, Shariati and a friend of his, Mr Falsafi, who were organizing a demonstration in commemoration of Mosaddeq's return to power in 1952, were arrested on the charge of pro-Mosaddeqist agitation and imprisoned for seventeen days. Shariati had been teaching at the Ketabpour primary school in Ahmadabad close to Mashhad. After the coup, he started preparing himself for his twelfth grade diploma examinations.

In June 1954, in the midst of all his other activities, Shariati passed his exams and obtained his diploma with a specialization in literature. At this time he continued his collaboration with the NRM, and also joined the editorial board of a newspaper called *Khorasan*. As a contributor to *Khorasan*, Shariati developed his literary and poetic talents, his allegorical style and the use of symbolism and similes, which he used widely and effectively in his later speeches and writings.

Shariati's University Years

In 1955, Shariati entered the newly inaugurated Faculty of Literature at the University of Mashhad. During his university years, despite the administrative problems that he had because of his official job as a full-time teacher, Shariati ranked at the top of his class. His flair, knowledge and passion for literature made him popular among his fellow students. At this time, Shariati was gaining some fame among Mashhad's political and intellectual circles. He had not only manifested his literary talent in his poems, but had also grappled with the identification and outline of a non-conventional, progressive and modernist exposition of Islam.

In 1957, all across Iran, the branches of the NRM came under attack. Fourteen key members of the NRM's Mashhad branch were arrested and flown to Tehran in an army plane and subsequently imprisoned at *Qezel Qal'eh*. Muhammad-Taqi Shariati and Ali Shariati were among them. Ali Shariati was the youngest in the group. The group was accused of having 'followed Mossadeq's doctrine.'[40] Ali Shariati was released after a month.

At university, Shariati met Pouran-e Shariat Razavi, also a student in the literature faculty. Bibi-Fatemeh, known as Pouran, was the daughter of Haji Ali-Akbar and Pari. One of Pouran's brothers, Ali-Asghar (Toofan), had been killed in action, defending Iran during the 1941 Soviet occupation of Azerbaijan. Another brother, Azar, had become a national hero in university circles. On 7 December 1953, less than four months after the coup, students at Tehran University demonstrated against the visit of the US vice-president, Richard Nixon, to Iran. On that day the army fired on the students and three were shot to death. Azar Shariat-Razavi, Naser Qandchi and Mostafa Bozorgh-Nia, all students of the prestigious faculty of engineering (Daneshkadeh-e Fanni) of Tehran University became the first post-coup martyrs of the student movement against the Shah.

Pouran and Ali were married in Mashhad on 15 July 1958. Five months after his marriage, Shariati obtained his BA degree in Persian literature. For his outstanding academic performance at the university he was awarded a scholarship to continue his education abroad. In April 1959, Shariati went to Paris alone. His wife and his newborn son, Ehsan, joined him a year later.

Shariati's Paris

Shariati's experience in Paris was both enlightening and agonizing. Paris threatened, educated and overwhelmed him. Shariati had very mixed feelings about Paris. He hated certain aspects of it and yet adored other aspects. On the one hand, he despised the mesmerizing Paris of social evil and moral degeneration, reflected in its women of the streets, cabarets, gambling houses and night clubs.[41] In this vein, Shariati depicted Europe as a pitiless iron monster, which swallowed everyone despite their different cultures and identities. It digested them, stripped them of their spirituality and converted them into amoral, licentious, and hedonistic materialists, content with their consumerist life.[42] Shariati, the sensitive provincial student, writhed at the thought of losing his faith, spirituality, ethical values and divine ideals in the belly of this 'evil behemoth'. On the other hand, he had great reverence for the Paris of social awakening and intellectual enlightenment, reflected in the humble luminaries of its educational institutions. Shariati later recalled how the wisdom and intellectual talents of his French teachers and mentors took him by the hand and guided him to the summits of human reflection, spiritual illumination and social thought.[43] Without them he would have had an impoverished soul, a shrivelled heart, a mediocre mind and an infantile view of life, the thought of which made Shariati shudder.[44]

In Paris, Shariati found that blinded by western moderniz-ation, material achievements, individual liberties and parlia-mentary democracy, third-world intellectuals came to place their faith entirely in the western bourgeois way of thought and life. Subsequently, on their return home, they embarked on developing their country on the basis of the western model. From Shariati's point of view, however, such intellectuals became the Trojan horse of colonialism and imperialism, further cementing the dependence and underdevelopment of third-world countries.[45]

Acknowledging the dual capacity of western civilization to educate or to stupefy, Shariati later identified two types of western-educated or influenced third-world intellectuals. First, the *assimile*, who completely abandoned their historical and cultural heritage, aped the values and ideals of the West and thus became completely assimilated.[46] The *assimile* were European-oids, whom Shariati called 'humanoids' and thus excluded them from his own definition of intellectuals. They were convinced of the utter uselessness and inadequacy of their cultural heritage and viewed their traditional mode of thought and life as the most fundamental barrier to modernity and civilization.[47] For the Iranian *assimile*, therefore, the Islamic tradition was a remnant of the past and also a significant if not the principal cause of their country's backwardness. Shariati's numerous references to his intense dislike for Sayyed Hassan Taqi-Zadeh, who is quoted as having said: 'we should detonate the bomb of surrender to foreigners in this country and eventually become foreign from head to toe,' should be understood in this context.[48]

Second, the real intellectuals, who according to Shariati carried the mantle of the prophets after the end of the age of 'revelations' and followed in their tradition of bringing consciousness to the people during the age of 'reason'.[49] Real intellectuals, according to Shariati, had a social responsibility and mission to communicate the objective abject conditions of the masses to the masses, until they attained a level of consciousness that would lead them to revolt.[50] The effective process of communication with the masses and the estab-lishment of common goals and ideals, to which the intellectual should invite the masses, required a common language and a common experience with them. The attainment of such common grounds necessitated a deep understanding of their belief system.[51] As such, Ali Shariati was his own model of the Muslim intellectual.

Islam in the eyes of the modern intellectual was, however, associated with superstition, resignation, inertia, justification of the status quo, dissimulation (*taqiyeh*), irrelevance and the reactionary power of the clergy as its interpreters and custodians. It represented all those characteristics which were anti-developmental and change-resistant. Shariati had to demonstrate that Islam was a progressive tool for action. He identified the real message of Islam as an outlook deeply concerned with liberation, freedom, equality and spiritualism, and distinguished it from the reactionary Islam which cohabited with and justified political oppression and economic exploitation.

Given the anti-imperialist and anti-western mood of the 1960s, which at times boarded on xenophobia among third-world intellectuals, Shariati, the Iranian prototype of a Muslim intellectual, never denied his intellectual and Islamic indebtedness to his western educators. From them he learnt a highly critical perspective of their own society and a rigorous methodology to present and defend their theories. Shariati's western education also opened his eyes to the scholarly works and interpretation of non-Shi'ites on Shi'ism. Subsequently, his Shi'ism became very different from that of its official custodians in Iran. He was more concerned with the socio-political content, message and implications of what was being written on Islamic issues than the Shi'ite credentials of those who were writing them.

As a reformer, he preferred the analysis of those islamologists who presented an egalitarian, humanitarian, mystical and defiant image of Islam. His non-dogmatic use of sources which were not widely used by Shi'ite scholars and jurists led some of his clerical critics to accuse him of being a Sunni and a Wahabi.[52] In an iconoclastic statement he prayed for the day when religious awareness and consciousness in Iran would reach a stage when official Shi'ite spokesmen would present Fatemah in the manner in which Sulaiman Katani, the Christian doctor, had portrayed her; Ali as George Jordaq, the Christian doctor, has written about him; the *ahl-e beyt* (descendants of the Prophet through Imam Ali) as Massignon has depicted them in his research; Abu Zar through the eyes of Jowdat al-Sahar; the Qur'an through the translation of the Christian Priest Régis Blachere; and the Prophet through the eyes of Maxime Rodinson, the Jewish academic.[53] Shariati's unabashed preference for the works of non-Shi'ite, and especially non-Muslim, scholars on Islamic issues infuriated the Iranian clergy. To them Shariati was suggesting that they ought to learn their Islam not only from non-Shi'ites, but from non-Muslims.

In a highly controversial article entitled 'My Idols', which was later used against him by his clerical enemies, Shariati eulogized his western teachers. He sanctified Louis Massignon, the famous French Catholic islamologist, and called him a genius, a perfect human being, a most beautiful spiritual figure, the absolute good and a pure and overwhelming spirit.[54] According to Shariati, between 1960 and 1962 he worked as Massignon's research assistant. Shariati's autobiography indicates that in Massignon's company and under his influence he underwent a significant inner transformation. On his arrival in Paris, Shariati had asked for Mullana's Masnavi to give him the necessary spiritual support and force to face the materialism and hedonism of western society.[55] His discovery of Massignon seems to have provided him with a western substitute. Just as Mullana had changed his vision and view in early adulthood, so had Massignon in his early maturity. Referring to him, Shariati wrote: 'He taught me the art of "seeing".'[56] In Paris, Shariati started translating Massignon's book on Salman Farsi.

After Massignon, Shariati owed his western intellectual formation to the prominent sociologist George Gurvitch, whose lectures Shariati attended conscientiously and regularly during his five-year stay in Paris. He venerated the lifestyle and sociological theories of this militant Russian émigré, who had fallen out with Stalin and had escaped both the Fascists and the Stalinists. Gurvitch was not only Shariati's sociological mentor and guru, but his life-long record of different crusades against injustice further endeared him to Shariati.[57] In a sense, Shariati had discovered a western Abu-Zar. Later, in 1972, when Shariati came under considerable attack from the traditional clergy, he wrote a defiant if not sacrilegious letter to his father, in which he differentiated between the essence and form of Shi'ism. In a provocative style, he posited that Gurvitch, the Jewish ex-communist, who had spent all his life fighting against Fascism, Stalinist dictatorship and French colonialism in Algeria was closer to the spirit of Shi'ism than Ayatollah Milani, one of Iran's principal sources of imitation (maraj'e taqlid), who had never engaged himself in any just struggle.[58]

During his stay in Paris, Shariati was exposed to new and illuminating works and ideas which influenced his perception of life and world outlook. He attended the lectures of academics, philosophers, poets and militants, read their works, sometimes exchanged ideas with them and observed the works of artists and sculptors. From each he learnt something and later acknowledged his debt to them. Frantz Fanon taught him third-world solidarity and internationalism, the rejection of the European model of development and the need for the third world to create 'a new man' based on 'a new idea' and 'a new history'.[59] Shariati translated Fanon's *A Dying Colonialism* and asked him to write a preface to it, which never materialized. Fanon and Shariati did, however, correspond and exchange ideas over the role of Islam in the broad anti-colonial war which Fanon promoted as the point of departure of the third world for its battle to regain its identity and independence. Shariati himself refers to three letters between the two men in which Fanon expressed his misgivings over the schismatic role of religion in the broad anti-colonial front.[60] In his later writings and speeches, Shariati made numerous references to the conclusion of Fanon's *Wretched of the Earth*, which he had translated in Paris.[61]

From Jacques Berque's classes he attained a sociological view of religion.[62] From Sartre's works he learnt the principle of man's freedom and subsequently man's responsibility to rebel against all types of oppression.[63] Jean Cocteau showed him the extent to which the human spirit could develop and blossom.[64] Alexis Carrel's works demonstrated to him the compatibility of science with faith. Carrel's reputation as a Nobel Prize winner in medicine gave substance to Shariati's predisposition that one could be scientific, yet believe in metaphysical powers which even science could not explain. Carrel's scientific background and his faith were, for Shariati, sufficient evidence to demonstrate the fallacy of association between religious belief on the one hand and superstitious and reactionary thought on the other. Carrel facilitated Shariati's task of convincing other intellectuals that the ideal man would be one who understands and appreciates the beauty of this material world as well as the beauty of God.[65] Soon after his arrival in Paris, in 1959, Shariati found Carrel's book *Prayers* and translated it into Persian.[66] Later Shariati used examples such as Carrel and Max Planck to demonstrate a tendency among scientists towards spiritualism and the search for a deeper understanding of faith in God.[67]

Shariati's life in Paris was not only confined to his studies. He led an active political life both in the Mosaddeqist circle of Iranian students abroad and that of Algerians sympathetic to the FLN (National Liberation Front), which was fighting French colonialism in Algeria. Shariati participated in the debates of the Iranian students in France on what was to be done in Iran. He joined the Confederation of Iranian Students, maintained his organizational ties with the National Front and became closely attached to Bazargan's Iran Freedom Movement (IFM). Mehdi Mozaffari, the official IFM representative in Paris during those years, explained that even though Shariati was close to the IFM and a good number of his close friends in Paris were members of the IFM, he never became an official member.[68] Even though membership of both organizations was not uncommon at the time, Shariati is said to have believed that by simply remaining a member of the National Front he could be more useful to the cause of the IFM.

He wrote regularly and prolifically for Mosaddeqist opposition publications. His writings included translations of prose and poetry and analytical articles concerned with Iran and its social, political and cultural problems. In the Journal of the Organization of Iranian Students in France Associated with the National Front (JOISFANF) his articles appeared under different names. The pen-name of *Sham'*, which in Persian means candle, was one that he often used. *Sham'* is composed of the first letters of his own name: *Sh* stood for Shariati, *m* for Mazinani and *ayn(')* for Ali. On the basis of his pen-name, Shariati created a fictive personality, whom he called Chandel, similar to the French word for candle. Chandel is introduced as an outstanding thinker and a mujtahid.[69] His words of wisdom support Shariati's arguments and discourse in virtually every volume of his collected works. Shariati was the ventriloquist behind Professor Chandel's words.

After the First Congress of the National Front in Europe, held at Wiesbaden in Germany, Shariati was made editor of the Front's organ, *Iran-e Azad* (Free Iran). The first issue of *Iran-e Azad* appeared on 15 November 1962. Most of its editorials, in addition to a column called 'events and perceptions' (*ruydadha va bineshha*), were written by Shariati. He also wrote for *Name-ye Parsi* (The Persian Letter), the quarterly journal of the Iranian Students' Confederation and *Andishe-ye Jebhe* (Thoughts of the Front), the monthly organ of the National Front in the United States. In *Name-ye Parsi* he wrote under the name of Ali Shariati and *ayn* Mazinani, while in JOISFANF, he also wrote under the pen-name *Nam*.[70]

Between 1962 and 1963, Shariati's time seemed to be totally consumed by his political and journalistic activities against the Iranian regime. Inspired by the strategy and tactics of the FLN and the success of its military wing, the ALN (The National Liberation Army), Shariati became convinced of the necessity of military action by a small group of highly dedicated, well-trained, professional, organizationally independent and clandestine revolutionaries. In a letter to Ibrahim Yazdi, a prominent member of the IFM in the United States, Shariati called for the creation of a 'special cadre', to topple the Shah's regime through armed struggle.[71] The members of the 'special cadre' would comprise militant Iranian intellectuals overseas. In the tradition of the FLN, which in 1954 had called upon all Algerian students in Paris, Brussels, London and Cairo to cease their studies immediately, return to the mountains in Algeria and pick up arms, Shariati asked his friends to inform him of the date at which they would be prepared to be dispatched to their revolutionary training camps.[72] The task of laying the revolutionary groundwork and preparing the 'means of revolutionary work' by the 'workers, peasants, students and intellectuals' was given to this 'special cadre'.[73] The success of Shariati's proposal of forming an intellectual revolutionary vanguard hinged on the willingness of Iranian intellectuals to join the 'special cadre' and for a revolutionary government in the region to provide them with the necessary military training. However, neither condition was fulfilled. Later, confronted with the social, cultural and economic realities of Iran, Shariati abandoned his voluntaristic view of the existence of 'objective' revolutionary conditions in his country.

During the June 1963 riots in Tehran, which brought Khomeini, as the leading religious opposition figure, to the forefront of Iranian politics, Shariati was in Paris. He supported the Islamic movement for its defiance of the regime and its Islamic nature. He is said to have submitted for publication an editorial entitled 'Mosaddeq, the national leader; Khomeini, the religious leader', which the executive committee of the National Front abroad, in Lausanne, is said to have rejected, arguing that Mosaddeq was the sole leader of the National Movement.[74] In the titleless editorial that was finally published in the June 1963 issue of *Iran-e Azad*, Khomeini's name was not mentioned, but the events in Tehran were referred to as a revolution with a signficant impact on Iran's National Movement.[75]

If Shariati had come to Paris to obtain a formal education and excel in his studies as he had done in Iran, his stay between 1959 and 1964 must be considered unsuccessful. In 1963, Shariati defended his doctoral thesis, 'Les Mérites de Balkh' (The Merits of Balkh). His thesis was a 155-page translation into French of the third chapter of a thirteenth-century document by Safi-eddin-e Balkhi. His Doctorate (*Doctorat d'Université*) was written under the direction of Professor Gilbert Lazard, for the *Faculté des Lettres* of the University of Paris at the Sorbonne.[76] Shariati's dissertation was barely accepted with a grade of *passable*, the lowest passing grade possible. Some have mistakenly written that he received a doctorate in sociology or history of religions or both.[77] On the basis of his thesis some have argued that he studied philology, the historical or comparative science of languages.[78] On his official diploma it is stated that his doctorate is in History of Medieval Islam *Histoire de l'Islam Médiéval (Hagiographie Persane)*. The Iranian embassy in Paris recognized his degree as a doctorate in literature. Shariati, however, studied one thing and translated a text, as his doctoral thesis, which was in no direct way related to his studies. The courses he took and the lectures he attended were mostly in the field of sociology, history, philosophy, comparative religion and Islamology. It seems as if his dissertation had a purely functional purpose. The possession of a doctorate from the Sorbonne would have facilitated his access to a university teaching position in Iran.

The Return to Iran

In September 1964, Shariati and his family returned to Iran by land. At the border between Turkey and Iran, Ali Shariati was arrested and sent to Khoy prison in Azarbayejan. Shariati was later transferred to the Qezel Qal'eh prison close to Tehran. He was released after some one and a half months and went to Mashhad, where he hoped to find employment at the university. This was the beginning of a life of total dedication to the cause of articulating, formulating and propagating a radical Islamic ideology which he hoped would lead to a radical Islamic political movement among the Iranian youth. Shariati was to live in Iran for a little less than thirteen years. He left Iran on 16 May 1977 for Belgium and then England. He never returned to his country and met his fate on 19 June 1977 in England. Shariati's stay in Iran may be divided into five distinct periods.

Bewilderment and Disappointment
The first period, between November 1964 and September 1967 is characterized by desperation and disillusion. To realize his social and political projects, Shariati had to be in contact with potential intellectuals and therefore needed to be in a university atmosphere. His message was targeted at the discontented, change-oriented, potentially revolutionary youth. His language, symbolism, allegories and parables demanded some formal educational background and familiarity with selected

western philosophical, sociological, psychological and historical concepts. At first, his writings and speeches were too controversial, militant and also esoteric, for the general public. Without a university audience, Shariati spoke into a vacuum.

Shariati shuttled between Mashhad and Tehran to obtain a new equivalence to the doctorate that he had earned in Paris. The bureaucracy took some time and Shariati was growing impatient. He was caught up in the bureaucratic process of finding a university position, which did not seem to be forthcoming in the immediate future. As an employee of the Ministry of Education he was given three high-school positions at three different locations in and around Mashhad. At these schools, he was supposed to teach Persian grammar, literature, spelling and composition. Even though Shariati proved highly gifted in lecturing on whatever he felt appropriate, irrespective of the assigned topic or subject matter, teaching at three relatively small and parochial high-schools was not the most conducive place for him to launch his Islamic consciousness-raising campaign. In 1965, he was transferred to the Ministry of Education's research centre in Tehran, where he wrote a tourist handbook 'The Guide to Khorasan'.

The absence of national and especially international political awareness and involvement among Iranians, further astounded and depressed Shariati. He lamented to a friend how politically involved the French had become over the issue of Algeria's independence, while in Iran no one seemed to care.[79] Shariati was clearly feeling initial withdrawal symptoms, as a politicized intellectual away from the hub of political debate and activity.

During this period, however, Shariati completed the translation of Massignon's study on Salman, one of the Prophet's close Companions, and also a Persian. His book *Kavir* (The Desert), which is essentially a literary autobiography, is also the product of this period. Some of the most important pieces in the book recount Shariati's mental struggle to come to terms with his true self and his relation with God. Even though Shariati refers to his inspirations and theosophical experiences in 1957, *Kavir* represents the gnosticism that fundamentally shaped his life between late 1964 and late 1969. *Kavir* is written in a poetic and highly figurative literary style. It is an honest, bold and revealing psychological, philosophical and personal self-assessment. This mystical-theosophical literary work throws light on Shariati's travel through the traditional stations of a Sufi in search of inner knowledge or *ma'rifah*. This path

would take the initiated through the station of a union of his
soul with the divine after which he would become extinct and
annihilated in the Eternal. *Kavir* is more than a therapeutic
exercise, it is an important document, explaining Shariati's
deeply rooted belief that he was a twentieth-century Messiah.[80]
In the age of imperialism and colonialism, his perceived mission
was to deliver and liberate all the culturally, politically and
economically oppressed people of his country. During a period
of despair, which characterized the first period of his return to
Iran, Shariati had to turn weakness into strength, pessimism
into optimism and irresoluteness into a messianic mission. His
tool was his own version of Sufism. While *Kavir* reflects
anguish, loneliness, emptiness, turbulence, confusion and even
obscurity, it shows the light at the end of the tunnel. On more
than one occasion, Shariati recounts a miraculous firework of
erupting colourful stars brightening and livening the dead black
sky, until darkness catches fire, punctuating the age-old lull of
the barren desert.[81] *Kavir* was Shariati's definitive source of
mystical and spiritual power. It not only legitimized his
revolutionary mission, but assured him of success. Later,
Shariati was to acknowledge that if he were to choose his two
favourite works among the multitude that he had written or
spoken, he would have chosen *Kavir*, for himself and
Eslamshenasi (Islamology) for the people.[82]

A New Islamic Discourse
The second period, between 1967 and 1971, is characterized by
Shariati's entrance on the university scene, contact with
students, the popularity of his message and his rising
prominence.

In Spring 1967, Shariati was offered a post at the
University of Mashhad to teach the history of Islam at the
College of Literature. At the dull and relatively eventless
university of Mashhad, Shariati's classes soon became an
event. He established a reputation as an Islamic intellectual
who was masterfully capable of weaving topics from half a
dozen different disciplines in the social sciences to present his
argument and prove his point. In his presentations he
synthesized ideas pertaining to different intellectual schools
within each discipline. Shariati's knowledge of western
academic jargon gave him the stature and appearance of a
super-teacher who knew it all and, curiously enough, sought to
explain political and socio-economic problems in Islamic terms

and provide Islamically based solutions for them. The content and form of his teaching represented a real break with the teaching methods of the traditional academic dons. Reinforcing the thought-provoking and defiant content of his lectures, Shariati's captivating oratory bewitched his audience. His many idiosyncrasies endeared him to his students. The Shariati model of absent-minded, defiant, philosophical, chain-smoking young men looking afar abounded.

During this period, Shariati set out to attain the objectives of the first stage of his design: that of attracting potential Islamic intellectuals. Shariati had to demonstrate the superiority and effectiveness of the Islamic intellectual in bridging the gap between the intellectuals, as the revolutionary vanguard, and the masses. He set out to show that irrespective of their faith in religion, militant intellectuals who sought social and political change in Iran were obliged to learn their religious heritage and speak its language.[83] As socially responsible and politically conscious agents of change, they would be incapable of communicating socio-political problems and their solution to the masses, if they failed to understand the history, culture and common language they shared with those masses. The common culture, history and language of the Iranian people, Shariati argued, was rooted in Islam. The pre-Islamic heritage, he argued, had been a glorious one, but it was long dead, buried and forgotten by the masses. He argued, that the authentic Iranian identity, therefore, remained Islamic and Shi'ite. The successful militant intellectual would be obliged to use the language, symbols, codes and heroes and eventually the ideology of Islam, as the primary medium of interlocution. The substance of Islamic ideology, however, had to be cleansed of its impurities and transformed from an introverted doctrine of quietism and resignation relevant only to the Hereafter, into an insurgent and rebellious school of thought concerned with both this world and the Hereafter. This transformation called for an Islamic renaissance, which Shariati planned to launch gradually.

In January 1969, Shariati published a book, *Eslamshenasi*, or Islamology. The book was essentially a compilation of his lectures on the history of Islam, which he had given at the University of Mashhad. *Eslamshenasi* contained the germs of many of Shariati's ideas, on which he focused and elaborated at length later in life. First, Shariati lashed out at westernized or assimilated intellectuals, whom he accused of thinking, judging and writing only based on translations from foreign sources.[84]

He accused them of being incapable of independent and endogenous analysis and intellectual production. Having ascertained that Iranian society was a religious one, he did not wish to affront the sense of nationalism of his audience and therefore argued that one learnt about 'the true spirit of Iran's history', through an understanding of Islam.[85]

Having settled scores with assimilated westernized intellectuals, Shariati then confronted the clergy, claiming that *Eslamshenasi* is 'the first step, in Persian, towards a scientific and analytical understanding of Islam'.[86] In *Eslamshenasi*, Shariati enumerates fourteen essential characteristics of the 'original Islam', which he readily dissociates from actually existing Islam.[87] It is important to point out that Shariati's free interpretation of what constitutes the 'original Islam' is based on primary Islamic sources. Later, however, he was sharply criticized by the clergy for his use of non-Shi'ite sources.[88] On each characteristic, Shariati refers to one or a combination of the following sources: the Qur'an, the Tradition of the Prophet and that of the Shi'ite imams along with the accounts of the first four caliphs. *Eslamshenasi* is one of the few, if not the only, academic and well-documented book written by Shariati. It reflects Shariati's initial concern with and emphasis on academic research.[89] Shortly after *Eslamshenasi*, he succumbed to the demands of his young and eager audience for more intellectual output from their 'great teacher'. Shariati, too, was impressed by the reception he was getting and became so preoccupied with propagating his message and politicizing the young that he abandoned academic research in favour of speeches, whose content was usually arousing and electrifying. At one point, Shariati even ridiculed those who prompted him to employ a scientific approach, based on research, in his speeches and writings. In his own defence, Shariati argued that applying the scientific approach to the pressing social problems would take too long and would therefore effectively be a waste of time.[90] Looking at his writings from 1976, seven years after *Eslamshenasi*, one finds the same references and quotes that he used in *Eslamshenasi* to prove a point. During these years, Shariati was so actively engaged in spreading the message that he had effectively no time to do significant research.

Eslamshenasi served a triple purpose. First, it presented a modern, egalitarian and democratic Islam as the ideal and original form of Islam. Second, it identified the obstacles to the realization of the ideal Islam. Third, it showed why it was incumbent upon Muslims, as true believers in the most fundamental aspect of their religion, namely monotheism (*tawhid*), to challenge and overcome these obstacles.

Shariati's first objective in *Eslamshenasi* was to obliterate the traditional charges of conservatism and anti-modernism against Islam by showing not only that Islam was compatible with certain modern concepts and concerns, but that these concepts have for long constituted an integral component of it. For example, he referred to the Prophet to argue that, according to Islam, reason and religion were identical. He argued that the Qur'an explained various notions of evolution and therefore, contrary to the view of the clergy, Darwin's concept was defensible from an Islamic perspective.[91] At the political level, he argued that Islam was based on democracy, expressed in *shura* and *ijma'* along with the freedom of thought and expression canonized in the concept of *ijtihad* and finally the freedom of religion.[92] He believed that the ideal Islamic economy was and should be based on equality, the prohibition of exploitation, the prevention of the emergence of a class society and the implementation of an economic system based on perfect equality in consumption.[93] The Qur'anic concept of man's common lineage, according to Shariati, indicated that all were created equal and therefore 'individual freedom and independence could be deduced from this position'.[94] On the issue of men and women, Shariati limited himself to the statement 'They were of the same origin and kind'.[95] Later in the book, Shariati acknowledges that Islam does not believe in the equality (*mosavat*) of men and women, but wishes to place each in their 'natural position'.[96] On the philosophy of Islam, Shariati argued that man is both free and constrained. He is capable of voluntarism and subjected to determinism.[97] The deterministic framework is the general law governing the process of social and historical development, which in a Hegelian fashion, tends towards the progressive unfolding of the absolute or ideal.[98] This Shariati later called 'the progression of history towards the awakening of God in Man'.[99] For Shariati, the dialectical transformation process held the key to social and historical development. He accepted the dialectical method, whereby thesis, anti-thesis and synthesis could be used to explain the general nature of historical development.[100] In this sense, he employed the Marxian scheme of historical stages and considered people (*nas*) as the generators and the real force behind historical developments.[101]

Shariati was thus presenting an Islamic *Weltanschauung* in embryo; a world outlook which seemed inconsistent and contradictory, since it blended religious idealism based on faith in God and revelation with materialism based on reason and scientific inquiry. Shariati's eclecticism, which had its roots in the early ideas of the God-Worshipping Socialists, enraged both the official custodians of materialism and the religious establishment in Iran. Later, Shariati developed his conception of an Islamic ideology and formulated the 'geometrical form' of the Islamic doctrine as a complete belief system.[102]

The second objective of *Eslamshenasi* was to identify and expose those who contradicted the rule of God and obstructed the peoples' right to attain perfection. Here Shariati singles out his main targets of attack: the monarchy and the institutionalized or formal clergy. He claims that polytheism does not refer only to the formal rejection of God. Its modern manifestation can be found in those cases where individuals perform those acts which are the monopoly of God, thus substituting themselves for God. The cult of personality, character worship or any human relationship in which one individual depends on, blindly follows, obediently complies with or is subservient to another individual, is a case of idolatry. Shariati wrote: 'Anyone who ... imposes his will on the people and rules according to his own whim, has made a claim to being God and whoever accepts such a claim is a polytheist, since absolutist rule, will, power, dominance and ownership is only in God's monopoly.'[103] Even though Shariati did not attack the monarchy by name, his subtle and sometimes explicit references to absolutist rule was clear and direct. On the issue of the clergy, Shariati was much more direct: 'If one praises a religious jurist and has genuine respect for him to the extent of accepting everything he says, and every judgment he makes and every order he gives and follows every one of his ideas, such a person would become a polytheist and I would call this [Muslim] follower a "religious idolater".'[104] Shariati also argued that Islam did not allow for a centralized and institutionalized clerical organization, mediating between God and man, since God's relation with man was a direct one. He, therefore, maintained that institutionalized religion would ultimately lead to reaction and dogmatism, perpetrating 'religious and clerical despotism'.[105]

Shariati's third objective in *Eslamshenasi* was to show why true Muslims should oppose polytheism which he defined as the rule and authority of those who wished to substitute themselves for God. Having established the people as catalysts of change, Shariati set out to shed the peoples' fear of challenging unjust authority. On the surface, Shariati made a rather naive generalization by singling out the evil trinity of ignorance, fear and acquisitiveness as the source of all deviations, sins, crimes, vileness, baseness, vice, and even underdevelopment.[106] The *movahed*, or monotheistic individual, Shariati argued, was immune to the evil trinity. His behaviour was governed not by expediency, but by the awareness of the fact that only God was to be feared and respected unconditionally and all others were impotent before Him. Shariati endowed the *movahhed* with those characteristics that would make an ideal Islamic revolutionary. The *movahhed* was an 'independent, fearless, selfless, dependable and wantless' individual, who bowed to no other authority than to God.[107] Shariati's naive generalization becomes a galvanising political invitation to reject, resist and combat all sources of polytheistic power, including dictatorship, the capitalist system and the official clergy. Shariati also wished to credit Muslims as the only social agents who could rise to this historic and revolutionary occasion, since as monotheists, they could not coexist with polytheism. The polytheistic world outlook was based on and nurtured contradictions. Monotheism as a world outlook had the objective of eradicating contradictions. It was an invitation to 'rebel' against all false gods.[108]

With the publication of *Eslamshenasi* in 1969, Shariati became involved in a virulent rhetorical feud with certain factions of the clergy. In his works, he attacked the reactionary clergy for misrepresenting the genuine essence of Islam, which in his opinion was primarily concerned with social objectives and ideals rather than individual and private rites.[109] Shariati criticized the clerical institution (*ruhaniyat*) for its pacifying socio-political role and its historical record of collaboration with forces of political oppression and economic exploitation. Shariati held that all ruling classes were composed of three distinct and interdependent elements: the political, the economic and the religious.[110] He thus distinguished two types of Islam. First, a static and hidebound Islam of the ruling classes, which he called 'institutionalized Islam' and assailed at every occasion. Second, a militant Islam, the goal of which was challenging all injustices. This he called the 'dynamic Islam'.[111] Shariati accused the clerical institution of retaining the masses in a state of ignorance and obscurantism.[112] Finally, Shariati argued that since the livelihood and economic sustenance of Shi'ite Islamic jurists (*fuqaha*) was based on the *sahm-e emam*, or a share of the believers' earnings, the clerical institution became dependent upon and the protector of the property owning classes.[113]

It was, therefore, not surprising that Shariati's work was attacked and criticized as erroneous, nonsensical, derogatory, non-Shi'ite and even heretical by some of the clergy. Shariati was denounced and his works were subjected to abuse, vilification and sometimes scholarly criticism by different types of religious and clerical figures.[114] The reputable monthly Islamic journal *Dars-ha'y az Maktab Eslam* reviewed Shariati's *Eslamshenasi* and concluded that his arguments were baseless, incorrect and alien to the debates among Islamic experts.[115] One of his staunchest clerical enemies, Shaykh Muhammad-Ali Ansari wrote: 'We warn the Royal government of Iran, the Iranian people and the Iranian clergy that during the past 1,000 years, the history of Islam and Shi'ite Islam has never encountered a more dangerous, dreadful and bolder enemy than Ali Shariati.'[116]

Insurrectionary Discourse

The third period of Shariati's stay in Iran is characterized by a shift in his discourse from consciousness raising to one of invitation to political action and rebellion. This radical shift in his public addresses and writings begins at the end of October 1971 and continues until the closure of the Hosseiniyeh Ershad, on 19 November 1972.

From June 1971, Shariati was denied his teaching position at the University of Mashhad and was sent to Tehran. During this period, he spent all his time and energy at the Hosseiniyeh Ershad, which he tried to transform into a radical and modernist 'Islamic University'. Political events in Iran in 1971 played an important role in shaping and directing the orientation and activities of the Hosseiniyeh Ershad which became ever more militant and subsequently more popular among the young.

In the political history of contemporary Iran, the year 1971 constitutes an important landmark. The Shah who exercized full control over the reins of power decided to demonstrate and publicize his absolute authority and military might both to his own people and to foreign powers. The pompous celebrations of Iran's 2,500 years of monarchy before scores of foreign heads of states and dignitaries at Persepolis served this very purpose. The Shah's message was clear: if Iran was a politically stable country on the road to rapid modernization, its achievements were due only to the Pahlavi dynasty which was the true heir to the long line of Persian monarchies. However, armed opposition to the Pahlavi rule was similarly intent on proving the fallibility, precariousness and unpopularity of the Shah's regime.

On 8 February 1971, nine heavily armed members of the Marxist-Leninist People's Fadai'an of Iran attacked and overcame a gendarmerie outpost in the village of Siahkal, situated in the mountainous and wooded northern region of Gilan.[117] After nineteen days of encirclement by government forces, Ali-Akbar Safai'-Farahani, the commander of the Siahkal operation, along with Jalil Enferadi, and Houshang Nayeri were captured by the local people and handed over to the military authorities.[118] The rest of the group were killed or captured. Even before the attack on the Siahkal outpost, a number of active members of the Fadai'an organization were rounded up by the security forces in Tehran and Gilan. On 16 March 1971, the government issued the names of thirteen men who had faced the firing squad on the charge of participating in the Siahkal insurgency.[119] This marked the beginning and end of an armed insurgency movement aimed at inducing the rural masses to revolt against the Pahlavi regime. As bold as the attack may have been, its dramatic failure demonstrated the futility of applying Cuban or Chinese revolutionary tactics to the social conditions of Iran.

The military activities of the Islamic and radical Peoples' Mojahedin of Iran followed the Siahkal operation. The Mojahedin launched a series of daring attacks on sensitive targets such as dams and electricity plants to sabotage the celebrations. During late summer and the early autumn of 1971, SAVAK, the Shah's secret police, rounded up some 105 people suspected of membership in an urban guerrilla organization, the name, ideology and objectives of which was not quite clear to them at the time. Among those arrested, sixty-nine were put on trial during the spring of 1972. Muhammad Hanifnejad, Saeed Mohsen, Ali-Asghar Badi'zadegan, the founders of the Peoples' Mojahedin, along with six other members of the organization's Central Committee (*Cadr-e Markazi*) were executed in April and May of 1972.

The wave of guerrilla activities and the repression and executions that ensued affected Shariati's discourse. Shariati disagreed with the voluntaristic revolutionary vanguard theory and concomitant acts of terrorism and sabotage by a professional revolutionary elite, which had become popular among Iranian guerrilla organizations of different convictions.[120] A firm believer in his own special type of historical determinism, Shariati did not consider the subjective social conditions ripe for a social revolution.[121] He could not, however, remain indifferent to the armed struggle that was being waged against the Pahlavi regime, which he had opposed ever since his youth. Urban skirmishes and their regular reports in the national media were sensitizing the people and raising their social awareness. Furthermore, among those who were imprisoned, executed or slain in gunfights with the Iranian security forces, were some who were Shariati's acquaintances if not friends. Shariati had known Massoud Ahmadzadeh, and Amir-Parviz Pouyan, two of the founders of the Peoples' Fadai'an, both of whom were from Mashhad. Ahmadzadeh faced the firing squad on 8 March 1972 and Pouyan committed suicide in the summer of 1971 after a long battle with the security forces who had surrounded his 'safe-house'.[122] Ahmadzadeh and Pouyan had debated, corresponded and disagreed with Shariati on the proper solution to the pressing social problems of Iran.[123] At the University of Mashhad, Shariati had met and once again discussed and disagreed on the mode of social analysis and struggle with other members of the Peoples' Fadai'an such as Hamid Tavakoli and Saeed Ariyan.[124] Both Tavakoli and Ariyan were also killed by the security forces, in the winter of 1971/72.[125] It is said that Shariati had discussed strategy and tactics with the founders of the Mojahedin and had tried to convince them not to engage in guerilla activities before a radical and revolutionary Islamic ideology was thoroughly and completely articulated. As the wave of repression, characteristic of those years, took its toll among Shariati's friends, students and fellow anti-Shah activists, his speeches became ever more fiery, militant and provocative.

In 1971, the Shah celebrated 2,500 years of glorious monarchical rule in Iran, at the tomb of Cyrus the Great in Persepolis where he repeatedly trumpeted his grandiose idea of leading Iran to the 'gates of the Great Civilization'. At the Hosseinieh Ershad, Shariati spoke of 5,000 years of 'deprivation, injustice, class discrimination and repression'.[126] In public, Shariati referred to those who were building the 'Great Civilization' and defiantly lamented that 'he [the Shah] who had played no role other than oppressing the people and uttering a few forceful words' was taking all the credit for everything that was being done in Iran, without uttering a single word about the real toilers and workers.[127] In the same speech Shariati called for the necessity of a leader and a Messiah such as Imam Ali, who would free the people with his sword and once again establish a just system based on unity and the true Islamic school of thought.[128]

On 13 November 1971, in his well-known speech 'The Responsibility of being a Shi'ite', Shariati enumerated the responsibilities of true or revolutionary Shi'ites, whom he had labelled 'Alawi Shi'ites' or the followers of Imam Ali. According to Shariati 'Alawi Shi'ites' were obliged to confront and defy injustice, even at the cost of their lives; assure that the ruler was 'an honest and just leader'; struggle against repression, exploitation, despotism, injustice, class rule, pragmatism, ignorance and fear.[129] In defining the responsibilities of Shi'ites in the above terms, Shariati was defiantly calling for the overthrow of the economic and political system at the apex of which stood the Shah. In the same speech, Shariati reminded his audience of the just cause for which Imam Hossein had chosen to sacrifice his life by fighting, against enormous odds, Yazid whose rule epitomized the reign of evil and injustice. In symbolic terms Shariati hammered his famous slogan that 'every month of the year is *moharram*, every day of the month is *ashura* and every piece of land is *karbala*'.[130] To anyone even remotely familiar with Shi'ite culture, Shariati's analogy and his message was clear. He publicly declared that the time had come for every man to wage a holy war against the Shah and the political, social and economic system that he perpetrated. He called on Iran to become the arena of a historical struggle between justice and injustice, sacred and profane, good and bad. Invoking *moharram, ashura* and *karbala* as the prevailing socio-historical condition of every day and everywhere in Iran was an open invitation to armed struggle. Eight years later, during the Iranian revolution, the sound of millions of voices chanting this very slogan all across the country filled the air. But on 19 November 1972, three weeks after Shariati openly discussed 'armed struggle' as one of Shi'ite Islam's suitable strategies, the security forces closed down the Hosseiniyeh Ershad and silenced his rebellious, subversive and defiant voice.[131]

The closure of the Hosseiniyeh Ershad removed one of the most significant threats to the clergy's monopoly over the interpretation of religious thought in contemporary Iran. No fewer than ten books were written by religious figures denouncing and repudiating Shariati and the Hosseiniyeh Ershad. They charged Shariati with misleading and deceiving the young on the true teachings of Islam. Certain sources of imitation (*maraj'-e taqlid*) such as Ayatollah Kho'e, Milani, Rouhani and Tabatab'i had even issued authoritative pronouncements (*fatwa*) against the purchase, sale and reading of Shariati's writings. They also called upon their followers not to attend the lectures at the Hosseiniyeh Ershad. It is even said that the Hosseiniyeh Ershad was closed after the Shah's visit to Shiraz in October 1972. Certain influential members of the clergy, it is said, gave Shariati's speech *Tashayo' Alavi va Tashayo' Safavi* (Alawi Shi'ism and Safavid Shi'ism) to the Shah and asked him to silence its author.[132]

Silence and Imprisonment

The fourth stage of Shariati's life in Iran, after his return from Paris, starts with the closure of the Hosseiniyeh Ershad. Without his pulpit and his ever-growing devoted audience Shariati was essentially cut off from his roots and forced into silence and socio-political isolation. In the meantime a growing number of people who regularly attended lectures at the Hosseiniyeh Ershad were arrested or killed in gun battles with the security forces. Due to the large attendance of members or sympathizers of the Mojahedin at Shariati's lectures, the regime was erroneously convinced that Shariati maintained some sort of organizational ties with the Peoples' Mojahedin. If the regime had allowed Shariati and the Hosseiniyeh Ershad to operate relatively freely, it would perhaps have weakened the influence of Marxist, socialist and revolutionary thoughts among the young. However, the government finally came to realize that it had dramatically miscalculated the power of Shariati's radical and revolutionary message. The fact that Shariati's message was based on Islam, made the regime's task of neutralizing and countering it far more difficult. After the closure of the Hosseiniyeh Ershad, the regime seemed convinced that to stop the social tide that Shariati's 'rebellious literature' had created, he had to be imprisoned and forced to repent.

Conscious of greater surveillance by the ever watchful eyes of the Iranian security forces, Shariati felt the danger and went into hiding. Forced to change his hideout, he moved from the house of one relative or friend to another. In August 1973,

Muhammad-Taqi Shariati, Ali's father and Reza Shariat-Razavi, Ali's brother-in-law were arrested. When the security forces came to arrest Ali Shariati at his home, they told his family that the two men close to Ali were arrested as hostages and would remain in prison until Ali surrendered. After a month of lengthy discussions and debates, with relatives and close friends, on the best course of action, Shariati surrendered to the security forces, in September 1973. After he had been interrogated on his political activities, objectives and connections with the Mojahedin, Shariati spent the greatest part of his eighteen months of imprisonment in solitary confinement at the Komiteh prison.

The notorious Komiteh prison was usually used for newly arrested political prisoners. It was essentially a temporary prison used for intensive and violent interrogations, breaking-in suspects, extracting confessions and building a 'sound' case against the detainees before they were put on trial. Clearly, Shariati was no ordinary prisoner. He was a well known public figure with a considerable following among the young. According to his fellow inmates, compared to others, Shariati's living conditions were rather privileged. He was allowed to read and write, was provided with cigarettes and utensils such as a fork. One could argue that since the Komiteh prison had become his permanent detention quarters, he was allowed certain rights usually granted to those in regular prisons. As was the case with all authoritarian regimes at the time, intellectual dissidents and political activists were forced to repent publicly in a well-orchestrated interview on national television. In spite of considerable pressure on Shariati to make such an appearance, he refused.

Isolation and reflection
The fifth and last period in Shariati's life in Iran began with his freedom from prison. It was not until March 1975, that Shariati was released, without ever having been put on trial. It is said that at the 1975 OPEC meeting in Algiers, Abdel-aziz Bouteflika, the Algerian minister of foreign affairs at the time, who had known Shariati from his Paris days of involvement with the FLN, had requested Shariati's release.[133] Even though he was freed, Shariati was placed under tight surveillance.

By this time, Shariati's books had been banned and anyone possessing them could have been arrested. The ban on his books further increased their readership, as is the natural reaction in all dictatorships. Shariati's imprisonment had also enhanced his reputation and bolstered his militant stature among his supporters and even those revolutionary activists who had maintained that he was more of a romantic reformist than a real revolutionary. Shariati's refusal publicly to recant constituted a considerable setback for the security forces, who considered their laborious efforts as incomplete and fruitless. They, therefore, tried to discredit him by demonstrating that even though he would not participate in any act of public self-condemnation, he had given up his socialist ideals and become an anti-Marxist and an anti-revolutionary before leaving prison. To this end, one of Shariati's early (1967) and relatively unknown lectures, *Ensan, Eslam va Maktabha-ye Maqrebzamin* (Man, Islam and Western Schools of Thought), was serialized in the popular afternoon newspaper *Keyhan*. When the first part of what seemed to be an article appeared, no reference was made to the date at which it was spoken or written, giving the impression that it was written in prison and willingly submitted to *Keyhan*. Hardly anyone knew that the article was the transcription of an old lecture and that it was being published without Shariati's consent or even knowledge.[134] The fact that Shariati was permitted to have books and to write in prison made it seem even more plausible that this was in fact what he had been writing there.

In this article, like many others, Shariati hammered at the inability of 'western liberalism', and 'eastern communism' to provide conducive conditions for the 'free development of human nature'.[135] But in this piece he had taken his arguments to extremes by arguing that both Marxism and Islam were integrated, complete and perfect ideologies, in contradiction and at odds with one another. Shariati had further argued that neither could be decomposed or deconstructed and reconstructed with features of the other ideology. Therefore if one construction borrowed an aspect of another and applied it to its own, such a reconstruction would lead to the complete breakdown of that ideology.[136] The impression that the regime wished to convey was that in prison Shariati had 'matured' and abandoned his attempt at reconciling revolutionary socialism with Islam; opting for the traditional Islam of private rites and quietism. The sub-title 'Marxism against Islam', which was added to the original title, by the security forces, clearly demonstrated the object of the sudden and unprecedented publication of one of Shariati's works in a semi-official newspaper. The stunt worked to a large extent because Shariati could neither deny having made the speech nor publicly declare that in spite of the ideas he had expressed in 1967, he continued to believe that socialism and revolution were integral parts of his conception of Islam.

Shariati responded to his government imposed isolation and the intellectual smear campaign conducted against him in the only way available to him. Once again, he started to write and talk to small groups of friends, old students and relatives. Weary of being under permanent surveillance, once out of prison, Shariati usually slept during the day and worked through the night. After long hours of writing, discussions or monologues during the night, Shariati walked the quiet and empty streets of Tehran in the early hours of the morning.

Between March 1975, when he was released from prison, and May 1977, when he left Iran, Shariati was freed from the hectic tempo of the Hosseiniyeh Ershad period. His post-prison life constituted a period of reflection and stock-taking. On 10 January 1977, in an interesting conversation with the future Islamic Republic's second spiritual leader, Ayatollah Khamenei, its ideologue, Ayatollah Motahhari and one of its renowned figures, Fakhreddin-e Hejazi, and in the presence of a group of students, Shariati explained the pressing issues of this period. He argued that given the achievements of the recent Islamic movement, it was necessary to address the issue of sustaining the movement and protecting individual Muslims in it from the constant attack of two hostile camps. He maintained that Islam was posing a threat to other ideologies since it had adopted a clear anti-imperialist, anti-dictatorial and anti-capitalist orientation. According to Shariati, Islam's contradiction with imperialism and capitalism was of an antagonistic nature, incapable of reconciliation, whereas Islam's contradiction with Marxism was of a non-antagonistic nature. For Shariati the imperialist camp constituted an enemy, while the Marxist camp constituted a rival.[137] Under these conditions, Shariati called for the development and presentation of an 'Islamic manifesto' based on an Islamic ideology, the components of which he believed to be available.[138] He placed the preparation and presentation of a 'reconstituted Islamic world outlook' on the agenda of the day.[139] It was essentially to this task that he turned his attention during the rest of his life.

Shariati's writings during this period were clearly marked by his growing concern and preoccupation with three important themes. He argued that if one were to analyse all movements, ideologies, philosophies, religions and revolutions in the history of mankind, one would identify three primary currents: 1) love and mysticism; 2) freedom; and 3) the quest for social justice.[140] Shariati presented this trinity also under the title: mysticism, freedom and equality.

Mysticism, he argued, was a natural manifestation of the human essence. Man's curiosity condemned him to reflect on what was not materially existent in this world. Mysticism allowed him to reach out into the metaphysical. It guided the individual beyond the mundane and enabled him to develop towards divine spiritual perfection.[141]

After his imprisonment, Shariati came to appreciate freedom and eulogized it in his poetic narrative 'Freedom, blessed Freedom'.[142] In the tradition of classical anarchists, he wrote: 'O freedom, I despise governments, I despise bondage, I despise chains, I despise prisons, I despise governments, I despise dictation, I despise whatever and whomever enchains you.'[143] Despite his adoration for political freedom, Shariati's concept of individual freedom continued to remain rigid and non-liberal. He upheld freedom only in contrast to dictatorship, imperialism and exploitation and rejected 'freedom without criteria or orientation'. Remaining a prisoner of his original notion of 'directed democracy', he believed that freedom had to be 'planned and goal oriented'.[144] Freedom needed socio-political prerequisites. To prepare for the perfect stage of freedom, awareness and political maturity, Shariati remained loyal to the Leninist concept of the revolutionary leadership. To free society from 'ignorance and injustice', Shariati expected the ideal revolutionary leader to engage in 'the revolutionary purification of his environment and the revolutionary education of the people'.[145] Like all traditional Muslims he argued that individual liberty constituted partial freedom, while goal-oriented Islamic freedom secured felicity (falah) or total emancipation from all possible bonds.[146]

Shariati's later writings expressed his open disdain and animosity towards capitalism and the bourgeois values and mores that accompanied it. For Shariati, capitalism had to be destroyed. Capitalism was not only unjust, inequitable and exploitative, but it was immoral, destroying all real values and perverting the vicegerents of God on earth. According to Shariati, capitalism prevented man from becoming God-like.[147] The system which could deliver equality and social justice in his opinion was socialism. Shariati's socialism, however, was primarily an ethical one. Socialism was laudable because it freed man, 'the retainer of God's spirit,' from the bondage of exploitative private property ownership and 'infested bourgeois' values.[148] Shariati maintained that if a classless post-capitalist society were to usher in the socialization of moral decadence and corruption, through the spread of 'pornographic magazines and films, night clubs, discotheques, brothels and immoral television programmes', he would support the system of private property ownership and the class society that had prevented the widespread dissemination of such decadent bourgeois values.[149] Shariati's ideal society is founded on a socialist economic system governed by ethical and spiritual values firmly based on the Islamic belief in God.[150]

Hejira and Death

On 16 May 1977, Shariati left Iran. Once Shariati's absence from home became prolonged, SAVAK became suspicious. On 6 June, knowing that he would not be allowed to leave the country under the name of Ali Shariati, SAVAK officially requested the Ministry of Foreign Affairs to check whether someone under the name of Muhammad Ali Mazinani had left Iran during May.[151] Some three weeks after his departure, assuming that he must have fled the country, the Iranian security service was still guessing, incorrectly, at the precise date. On 8 June 1977, SAVAK issued a circular to its agents abroad, informing them that Shariati had illegally fled the country and that he was to be located and placed under close surveillance.[152]

Shariati's wife, Pouran, had applied for a passport for Ali Mazinani, which was the surname indicated in Shariati's birth certificate. At the Mehrabad airport, the authorities failed to make the association and Shariati fled the country. He went to Brussels and from there to London. On 18 June of the same year, Pouran accompanied by her three daughters, Soosan, Sara and Mona, was to join Ali Shariati in London. This time, the authorities caught on and refused Pouran and six-year-old Mona, who shared her mother's passport under the name of Shariat-Razavi, permission to leave the country. Soosan and Sara were allowed to leave. Pouran immediately called Shariati and informed him of the new development.

One can only speculate as to what went on in Shariati's mind.

His bitter previous experience must have immediately dawned upon him. When the security forces arrested his father and brother-in-law as hostages to coerce him into surrendering himself, the plot proved to be effective. This time, Shariati had no reason to doubt that the authorities would exert as much pressure as possible on his wife, who remained trapped in Iran, to get him back. The agonizing and awesome thought of Pouran, under pressure, in the Komiteh prison and the probability of his own return to the same prison must have caused him a great deal of anguish. The possibility of physical damage resulting from such a psychological shock cannot be ruled out. Once Soosan and Sara arrived at Heathrow, Shariati accompanied them to a house that he had rented in Southampton. The next day, early in the morning of June the nineteenth, Shariati's body was found dead on the floor.

The sudden and mysterious death of Shariati at the age of forty-four, made the Iranian security services the prime suspect. It was argued that the Shah's regime was the prime beneficiary of the silence of a prolific and charismatic speaker, who had become an idol of the Islamic Iranian youth. If the trauma of the events of 18 June is considered to be the prime cause of his death, then the Iranian government of the time should be held responsible. Otherwise, one would have to accept the coroner's report, issued on 21 June in England, that Shariati died as the result of a heart attack.[153]

On 26 June 1977, Shariati's body was flown to Damascus, where he was buried close to the shrine of Zeinab, Imam Hossein's daughter. In a bold and defiant speech, at the peak of his confrontation with the Shah's regime, Shariati had argued that every revolution had two apsects: blood and the message. Imam Hossein was the symbol of martyrdom and blood, while the grave responsibility of communicating and disseminating Imam Hossein's revolutionary message, after his martyrdom, was left to Zeinab. Without the preacher of the message, history would have forgotten the blood and the sacrifice.[154] Shariati's role was thus similar to that of Zeinab. He was not the man of blood, he was the teacher and the preacher.

The ceremonies of the fortieth day of his death (chelleh) were held at the Ameliat high school in Beirut. At the ceremony, which resembled a mini-summit of liberation organizations, Yasser Arafat said: 'Dr Shariati is not only an Iranian combatant nor one limited to this region. He is a Palestinian, Lebanese, Arab and also an international fighter.'[155] The list of the

ceremony's host organizations reflected Arafat's contention.
They included: The Palestine Liberation Organization (Fatah);
Harakat al-Mahrumin of Lebanon; Lebanese Resistance
Detachments (AMAL); Peoples' Front for the Liberation of
Eritrea; Front for the Liberation of Eritrea; Iran Freedom
Movement, The Militant Clergy of Iran; The Organization of
Iranian Muslim Students in Europe, America and Canada; The
National Liberation Movement of Zanzibar; The National
Movement for the Freedom of Zimbabwe and The National
Movement for the Freedom of Southern Philippines.[156]

Shariati's death sparked a series of political activities by the
Islamic Association of Students (IAS) and the Union of the
Islamic Associations of Students (UIAS) overseas. The
memorial day, which was organized by Shariati's family,
friends, the IAS and the UIAS, turned out to be a successful
anti-Shah political event. It attracted a large crowd from all over
the world. Huge pictures of Shariati, Khomeini, Mosaddeq,
Taleqani and Montazeri along with those of the founders of the
Mojahedin were carried by participants in the procession. At
Imam Mussa Sadr's home, after the ceremonies at Ameliat
high-school, the Iranian participants who included Sadeq
Tabataba'i, Qotbzadeh, Chamran, Qarazi, Do'a'i and
Muhammad Montazeri, decided to maintain the political
momentum that had been created by the events following
Shariati's death. A hunger strike was planned by the Militant
Clergy in Paris, demanding the release of political prisoners in
Iran. The strike attracted considerable publicity in France and
was even reported in the Iranian press. In Rey, close to Tehran,
a group of 120 people demonstrated in the Hazrat-e Abdulaziz
mosque. They sympathized with the hunger strike in Paris,
demanding the release of Islamic militants in prison.[157] The
chain of events overlapped. On 10 October 1977, Iranian
intellectuals gathered at the Goethe Institut in Tehran and
inaugurated an unprecedented series of ten nights of speeches
and poetry reading by the cream of Iran's intellectuals. The
content of what was said was targeted against the regime's
policy of censorship and repression of artistic and intellectual
freedom. The intellectuals fired the first effective volley at the
Shah's regime. On the fifth night, Baqer Mo'meni, speaking on
the topic of 'censorship and its consequences', referred to those
writers, poets and artists who in the past fifty years had passed
away in the middle of their lives, in pursuit of freedom of
expression in Iran. He asked the huge crowd to observe a

minute of silence for Nima Yousheej, Saddeq-e Hedayat, Samad Behranghi, Jallal al-Ahmad, and Ali Shariati.[158] Thus Shariati, the exclusively Islamic intellectual in the group, was given a special position of prominence among Iran's leading modern intellectuals.

It would be safe to say that in all the broad-based, oppositional and confrontational events of the Iranian revolution, the portrait of Shariati loomed large and his catchy slogans chanted by hundreds, thousands and sometimes hundreds of thousands filled the air all across Iran. Shariati's Shi'ite sub-system was undoubtedly a seminal force in mobilizing the people and especially the youth for revolutionary action. His most important role, however, was that of articulating a radical Islamic ideology and convincing non-religious social groups of the compatibility of Islam with other revolutionary ideologies. Even in post-revolutionary Iran, where Shariati's protagonists and antagonists continue to battle over his Islamic interpretations, with the exception of Khomeini, all prominent clerical leaders of Iran, past and present, have hailed him as a 'pioneer', 'an outstanding contributor to the Islamic revolution' and 'he who transformed a people'.[159]

Notes

* This article would not have been possible without the encouragement, co-operation and generous help of many, including those who wish to remain anonymous, who agreed to talk to me and provide me with important documents. In particular, I would like to thank Ehsan Shariati, Sara Shariati and Dr Pouran Shariat-Razavi Shariati who shared with me their memories, reflections and detailed insights. The opinions and shortcomings are mine.

1. *Keyhan-e Farhangi*, Bahman, 1363.
2. *Pajoom*, 1370, p. 53.
3. *Ibid.*, p. 371.
4. *Kasravi*, 1989, pp. 141-71.
5. *Pajoom*, 1370, pp. 40, 53.
6. *Ibid.*, p. 66.
7. Shariati, *Collected Works*, vol. 33 (*C.W.* 33), Part 1, p. 6.
8. *Ibid.*, p. 8.
9. *Ibid.*, p. 7.
10. Shariati, *C.W.* 13, p. 326.
11. M. Momken, Private Interview, Paris, 1991.
12. Shariati, *C.W.* 13, p. 325.
13. *Ibid.*
14. Shariati, *C.W.* 33, Part 1, p. 7.
15. Shariati, *C.W.* 13, pp. 237-8.
16. Shariati, *C.W.* 34, p. 293; *C.W.* 1, p. 99.

17. Shariati, *C.W.* 30, p. 69.
18. Shariati, *C.W.* 1, p. 99; *C.W.* 34, p. 293.
19. Shariati, *C.W.* 34, pp. 295-6.
20. Shariati, *C.W.* 2, p. 42.
21. See *Ganj-e Shayegan*, Year One, No. 1-3, Khordad, Tir, Mordad, 1332.
22. Shariati, *C.W.* 3, p. 7.
23. *Ibid.*, p. 19.
24. Shariati, *C.W.* 20, p. 249.
25. Shariati, *C.W.* 1, p. 146.
26. Shariati, *C.W.* 33, Part 2, p. 25.
27. *Nehzat-e Azadi-e Iran*, 1356, pp. 101, 107.
28. Shariati, *C.W.* 3, p. 112; *Nehzat-e Azadi-e Iran*, 1356, p. 75.
29. Shariati, *C.W.* 33, Part 1, p. 9.
30. M. Momken, Private Interview, 1991, Paris.
31. *Mardom-e Iran*, nos. 20, 22, 29.
32. H. Razi, Private Interview, 1992, Tehran.
33. F. Hejazi in *J. Saeedi*, 1370, p. 153.
34. *Mardom-e Iran*, Organ-e Jamiyat-e Azadi-e Mardom-e Iran (Khoda Parastan-e Sosialist), no. 22, Sunday 30 Farvardin 1332.
35. Shariati, *Nashriyeh-e Farhang-e Khorasan*, no.6. 1337; *C.W.* 13, p. 277; *C.W.* 30, p, 70
36. Shariati, *C.W.* 2, pp. 117-28; *C.W.* 26, pp. 600-62.
37. *Ibid.*, p. 128.
38. Shariati, *C.W.* 5, p. 188; *C.W.* 19, p. 45.
39. Shariati, *C.W.* 1, p. 49.
40. *Nehzat-e Azadi*, 1356, pp. 14-15.
41. Shariati, *C.W.* 34, pp. 59-60.
42. Shariati, *C.W.* 1, p. 100.
43. Shariati, *C.W.* 34, p. 60; *C.W.* 13, p. 325.
44. *Ibid.*
45. Shariati, *C.W.* 20, pp. 336-9.
46. Shariati, *C.W.* 4, p. 73.
47. *Ibid.*, p. 107.
48. Shariati, *C.W.* 4, pp. 41, 63, 129; *C.W.* 1, pp. 164, 245; *C.W.* 20, p. 338.
49. Shariati, *C.W.* 4, pp. 151, 155.
50. Shariati, *C.W.* 20, p. 280.
51. Shariati, *C.W.* 30, p. 4.
52. Shariati, *C.W.* 1, p. 165.
53. Shariati, *C.W.* 8, pp. 103-4.
54. Shariati, *C.W.* 13, pp. 315-21.
55. Shariati, *C.W.* 1, p. 100.
56. Shariati, *C.W.* 13, p. 335.
57. *Ibid.*, pp. 320-1, 327.
58. Shariati, *C.W.* 1, p. 13.
59. Shariati, *C.W.* 4, pp. 405-7.
60. Shariati, *C.W.* 17, p. 169.
61. This translation appeared for the first time in *Andishe-ye Jebhe*, Organ-e Jebh-e Melli dar Amreka, Zemestan-e 1342, 1964, nos. 5 and 6. A number of references to Shariati's translation of the whole book are completely erroneous.

See Shariati, *C.W.* 4, p. 420.
62. Shariati, *C.W.* 13, p. 327.
63. Shariati, *C.W.* 24, pp. 314, 327.
64. Shariati, *C.W.* 13, p. 327.
65. Shariati, *C.W.* 25, p. 226.
66. Shariati, *C.W.* 8, pp. 5-10.
67. Shariati, *C.W.* 24, p. 119.
68. M. Mozaffari, Private Interview, Paris 1992.
69. Shariati, *C.W.* 20, p. 143.
70. See: *Name-ye Parsi*, Dowreh-e Dovom, Shomareh-e Aval, December 1962. Azar 1340. *Nashriyeh-e Sazman-e Daneshjouyan-e Irani-e Moqim-e Farance Vabasteh be Jebheye Melli Iran*, no. 2, March 1962.
71. *Nehzat-e Azadi-e Iran*, 1356, p. 24.
72. *Nehzat-e Azadi-e Iran*, 1356, p. 24; Shariati, *C.W.* 5, p. 87.
73. *Nehzat-e Azadi-e Iran*, 1356, p. 26.
74. A. Shakeri, Private Interview, Paris, 1992.
75. *Iran Azad*, no. 10, June 1963.
76. Library of the University of Paris Pantheon. Ref: W Univ. 1963, 33.
77. Watt, 1988, p.133. Bakhtiar and Saleh, n.d., p. 12.
78. Abrahamian, 1989, p. 107.
79. N. Mirzazadeh (Azarm), Private Interview, Paris, 1992.
80. Shariati, *C.W.* 13, pp. 483, 535.
81. *Ibid.*, pp. 431-2, 446-7.
82. Shariati, *C.W.* 33, Part 2, p. 1262.
83. Shariati, *C.W.* 4, pp. 11-25.
84. Shariati, *C.W.* 30, p. 5.
85. *Ibid.*, p. 13.
86. *Ibid.*, p. 5.
87. *Ibid.*, p. 20.
88. See Ibrahim Ansari-e Zanjani, *Eslamshenasi dar Tarazoy-e Ilm va Aql*, Qum, Chape Hekmat, 1351, pp. 47-52.
89. Shariati, *C.W.* 31, p. 65.
90. Shariati, *C.W.* 7, pp. 1-14.
91. Shariati, *C.W.* 30, p. 58.
92. *Ibid.*, pp. 30-1, 54, 60.
93. *Ibid.*, pp. 26-9.
94. *Ibid.*, p. 27.
95. *Ibid.*, p. 28.
96. *Ibid.*, pp. 513-14.
97. *Ibid.*, p. 43.
98. *Ibid.*, p. 41.
99. Shariati, *C.W.* 10, p. 79.
100. Shariati, *C.W.* 30, p. 45.
101. *Ibid.*, p. 46.
102. Shariati, *C.W.* 16, p. 15.
103. Shariati, *C.W.* 30, p. 95.
104. *Ibid.*, pp. 93-4.
105. *Ibid.*, pp. 24-5.
106. *Ibid.*, p. 78.

248   PIONEERS OF ISLAMIC REVIVAL

107. *Ibid.*, p. 88.
108. Shariati, *C.W.* 16, p. 41.
109. Shariati, *C.W.* 7, pp. 23-8.
110. Shariati, *C.W.* 4, p. 381.
111. Shariati, *C.W.* 9, p. 37.
112. Shariati, *C.W.* 7, p. 116.
113. Shariati, *C.W.* 10, pp. 98-100.
114.   See: M.A. Ansari; *Defa' az Eslam va Ruhaniyat, Pasokh be Doctor Ali Shariati*, Qum, Chape Mehr-e Ostovar. 1351; Shaykh Qasem-e Islami, *Sokhani chand ba Aqay-e Ali Shariati*, Chape Heydari, Shaval-e 1392; M. Moqimi, *Harj o Marj*, Tehran, Chape Shams, 1351; H. Rowshani, *Barrasi va Naqd*, Tehran, Chape Etehad, 1351.
115.   *Darsha'y az Maktab Eslam*, no. 1, Bahman 1350.
116.   *Ansari*, 1351, p. 384.
117.   *19 Bahman* 1355, p. 16.
118.   *Ibid.*, p. 17.
119.   *Ibid.*, p. 18.
120.   Shariati, *C.W.* 9, p. 112; *C.W.* 22, pp. 205-6; *C.W.* 25, p. 357; *C.W.* 27, p. 258.
121.   Shariati, *C.W.* 27, p. 258.
122.   *Nabard-e Khalq*, 1353, p. 6.
123.   N. Mirzazadeh (Azarm), Private Interview, Paris, 1992.
124.   N. Mirzazadeh (Azarm), Private Interview, Paris, 1992.
125.   *Nabard-e Khalq*, 1353, p. 6.
126.   Shariati, *C.W.* 22, p. 191.
127.   *Ibid.*, p. 180.
128.   *Ibid.*, pp. 188-91.
129.   Shariati, *C.W.* 7, pp. 263-4.
130.   *Ibid.*
131.   *Ibid.*, p. 156.
132.   Shariati, *C.W.* 9, Introduction p.*j.*
133.   *Nehzat-e Azadi*, 1356, p. 51.
134.   Later, Shariati referred to the issue as the 'outrage of the likes of Keyhan' (Shariati, *C.W.* 1, p. 257).
135.   Shariati, *C.W.* 24, p. 37.
136.   *Ibid.*, pp. 123-4.
137.   Shariati, *C.W.* 2, pp. 16-20.
138.   *Ibid.*, p. 27.
139.   *Ibid.*, p. 28.
140.   Shariati, *C.W.* 2, pp. 42-7.
141.   *Ibid.*, pp. 62-6.
142.   Shariati, *C.W.* 2, p. 117.
143.   *Ibid.*, p. 118.
144.   *Ibid.*, p. 86.
145.   Shariati, *C.W.* 10, p. 83.
146.   Shariati, *C.W.* 2, p. 45.
147.   Shariati, *C.W.* 10, pp. 78-9.
148.   *Ibid.*, p. 79.
149.   *Ibid.*, p. 80.

150. Shariati, *C.W.* 2, p. 165.

151. An official letter dated 16/3/36 from SAVAK; the Prime Minister's Office, the third Bureau, (*Nakhostvaziri, Edareh-e Kol-e Sevom*) to The Ministry of Foreign Affairs (*Vezarate Omur-e Kharejeh*). Signed by Sabeti. The following numbers appear on the letter: 312-1780 and 17588.

152. An official letter dated 18/3/36 from SAVAK; the Prime Minister's Office, Center 337, to all agencies (*Koliyeh Namayandegiha*). Signed by Sabeti. From Dr Ali Shariati's file in the 312th Office.

153. *Nehzat-e Azadi-e Iran*, 1356, p. 69.

154. Shariati, *C.W.* 19, pp. 203-8.

155. *Bozorgdashte Dr Shariati dar Beirut*, n.d., p. 31.

156. *Ibid.*, p. 5.

157. *Keyhan*, 19 October 1977.

158. *Moazen*, 1357, p. 253.

159. Khamene, Hashemi-Rafsanjani, Taleqani in *Saeedi*, 1370, pp. 48, 57, 64.

Bibliography

Abrahamian, E., *Radical Islam*, London, I.B. Tauris, 1989.

Ansari, M.A., *Defa' az Eslam va Ruhaniyat, Pasokh be Doctor Ali Shariati*, Qum, Chape Mehr-e Ostovar, 1351.

Ansari-e Zanjani, I., *Eslamshenasi dar Tarazoy-e Ilm va Aql*, Qum, Chape Hekmat, 1351.

Bakhtiar, L. and Saleh, H., (Translators) Shariati: *Martyrdom*, Tehran, Abu Dharr Foundation, n.d.

Bozorgdashte Doctor Shariati dar Beirut, n.p., n.d.

Eslami, Q., *Sokhani chand ba Aqay-e Ali Shariati*, Tehran, Chape Heydari, Shaval-e 1392.

Kasravi, A., *Baha'egary, Shi'igary, Sufigary*, Köln, Mehr Verlag, 1989.

Moazen, *Dah Shab*, Tehran, Amir Kabir, 1357.

Moqimi, M., *Harj o Marj*, Tehran, Chape Shams, 1351.

Nehzat-e Azadi-e Iran, *Yad Nameh Shaheed-e Javeed Ali Shariati*, Ill. USA, n.p., 1356.

Pajoom, J., *Yadnameh-e Ostad Muhammad-Taqi Shariati Mazinani*, Qum, Nashr-e Khoram, 1370.

Rahnema, A. and Nomani, F., *The Secular Miracle: Religion, Politics and Economic Policy in Iran*, London, Zed Books, 1990.

Richard, Y., *L'islam Chi'ite*, Paris, Fayard, 1991.

Rowshami, H., *Barrasi va Naqd*, Tehran, Chape Etehad, 1351.

Saeedi, J. (Pajoom), *Doctor Ali Shariati as Didgah-e Shakhsiyat-ha*, Tehran, Nashr-e Eshraqiyeh, 1370.

Safai'-Farahani, A.A., *Anche Yek Enqelabi Bayad Bedanad*, Entesharate 19 Bahman, 1355.

Shariati, A., *Collected Works* 35 volumes.
Compiled and corrected by *Daftar-e Tadvin va Tanzim-e Majmo'e Asar-e Mo'aleme Shaheed Doctor Ali Shariati*. Volumes 13, 33 and 35 are in two different parts or books. The different volumes are printed by different

publishers in Iran and abroad but have the same pagination if published under the auspices of the Daftar.

Watt, W.M., *Islamic Fundamentalism and Modernity*, London, Routledge, 1988.

Newspapers and Periodicals

Darsha'y az Maktab Eslam, Shomareh Aval, Sale 13, Bahman 1350.

Ganj-e Shayegan, Sale 1, Shomareh-e 1-3, Khordad, Tir, Mordad, 1332.

Iran-e Azad, no. 10, June 1963.

Keyhan, 19 October 1977.

Keyhan-e Farhangi, Bahman-e 1363.

Mardom-e Iran, Organ-e Jamiyat-e Azadi-e Mardom-e Iran (Khoda Parastan-e Sosialist), no. 22. Sunday 30 Farvardin 1332.

Nabard-e Khalq (Zamimeh), Sazeman-e Cherikhay-e Fada'ie Khalq, Esfand 1353.

Name-ye Parsi, Dowreh-e Dovom, Shomareh-e Aval, December 1962, Azar 1340.

Nashriyeh-e Farhang-e Khorasan, Shomareh-e 6, Sale Dovom, 1337.

Nashriyeh-e Sazman-e Daneshjouyan-e Irani-e Moqim-e Farance Vabasteh be Jebheye Melli Iran, no. 2, March 1962.

10

Muhammad Baqer as-Sadr

Chibli Mallat

I

A decade ago, it would probably still have been necessary to defend the inclusion of an *'alim* who was completely unknown in the western world, and who, for a few scholars in the Middle East, merely evoked one book, *Iqtisaduna* ('Our Economic System'), and a tragic existence which ended in execution in obscure circumstances in Iraq.

The picture in the late 1980s has radically changed, as the reputation of Sadr, by now well established among his followers currently in exile (mostly in Iran), has crossed the Mediterranean towards Europe and the United States. In 1981, Hanna Batatu had already drawn attention in an article in the *Middle East Journal* in Washington to the importance of Sadr for the underground Shi'i movements in Iraq.[1] In 1984 *Iqtisaduna* was translated, in part, into German, with a long introduction on the Shi'i *'alim* by a young German orientalist.[2] It soon became impossible to ignore his importance in the revival of Islamic political movements, in Iraq, in the Shi'i world, and in the Muslim world at large. A comparative book on the Islamic movements put Sadr centrestage in relation to Iraq.[3] Then acknowledgement came in Israel,[4] and in France, where a well-informed new journal on the Middle Eastern scene dedicated a long dossier to Muhammad Baqer as-Sadr in 1987.[5]

The other famous resident of Najaf in the 1960s and 1970s was, of course, Ruhollah al-Khomeini, whose Najaf-based 'network'[6] would later offer leadership to the Iranian revolution. This network, however, was essentially Iranian.

251

The seclusion of the Khomeini supporters is not a coincidence. Since his arrival in Iraq in late 1964, and until the death of his main protector, Ayat Allah Muhsin al-Hakim, in June 1970, Khomeini was living under the shadow of the Arab *mujtahids* of the southern Holy Cities. But in 1968, the access to power of the Ba'th started the tension which culminated in the struggle to the death between Najaf and Baghdad. From then on, Khomeini needed to be extremely circumspect in terms of Iraqi politics. Any mistake would have seen him delivered to the Shah, and the two networks of *mujtahids* – Arab and Persian – became clearly separate after the death of Hakim. It was not until the access of Khomeini to power in 1979 that a more organic relationship was re-established. Organized in haste, it proved fatal to Muhammad Baqer as-Sadr.

But Sadr, like Khomeini, was not on his own. Several important figures in the intellectual and political movement, from all over the Shi'i world, were formed in Najaf. The political content of Muhammad Baqer as-Sadr and these companions will show the extent of the stakes at play.

II

As one of its most prominent thinkers, Muhammad Baqer as-Sadr epitomizes the intellectual renaissance which took place in Najaf between 1950 and 1980. The other striking feature of the renewal was its political dimension, and the close interplay between what happened in the obscure alleys and dusty colleges of Najaf, and the Middle East at large. When Sadr was executed, with his sister Bint al-Huda, probably on 8 April 1980, the event was a culminating point for the Islamic challenge in Iraq. With Sadr's death, Iraq lost its most important Islamic activist.[7]

The Islamic movement based in Iraq can be followed through the three stages of its intellectual and political development. Back in the late 1950s, the religious circles of Najaf were essentially reactive. When the first major opus of Sadr, *Falsafatuna* ('Our Philosophy'), was published in 1959, it coincided with the anxious calls by the Najaf ulama, including Muhsin al-Hakim and Sadr's uncle Murtada al Yasin, to reject the communist appeal.[8] The silence of the ulama until that date was itself a legacy of twentieth-century Iraqi history. The last time the ulama had exercised an active political opposition was in 1923-24, a few years after the great Iraqi revolt of 1920. Then the most famous leaders of Najaf and Karbala went into exile after their confrontation with King Faisal and the British representatives who ruled Iraq. Except for Shaykh Mahdi al-Khalisi, who died in Persian exile in 1925, most returned to Iraq a few years later, and paid the price of their reinsertion with silence. Political mutism remained for three decades, while Shi'i integration in the new nation state was proceeding slowly but surely. But in 1959, with the ulama's audience at an all-time low, the leaders of Najaf and Karbala faced the danger of complete marginalization as they were threatened into oblivion by the inroads of communism into the fabric of their followers. At the same time, their general perception of 'Abd al-Karim Qasem, the leader of Iraq between 1958 and 1963, who sometimes relied on the communist wave to strengthen his own power, was inimical. For the ulama, the combination of suspicion towards central rule and the spectre of communism turned direct involvement in politics into a condition for survival. In the reaction to communism and Qasem, Pandora's box was opened.

That first reactive phase of the late 1950s was followed by a period of hesitation and consolidation. Through the following decade of turbulent coups and rapid changes of régimes, an active wing of the ulama pursued its political course, both intellectually and organizationally. The competition between Najaf and Baghdad took many forms. Several documents and testimonies show the efforts in Najaf, Karbala, and Baghdad to heighten awareness of the ulama's assertive bid in the population at large.

In addition to their hostility to Qasem for being too soft on communists, the attempt of central rule to further diminish the *mujtahids'* sway on sensitive issues like matrimonial and family law by implementing an integrated Code of Personal Status was received in Najaf with dismay, even by the well-established and relatively apolitical ulama. The role of the old Muhsin al-Hakim in the opposition to Qasem's Code is paramount, and it took the form of a full-length critique of the 1959 Code by one of his close collaborators, who was himself the scion of an important family of scholars from Najaf.[9]

In the case of Muhammad Baqer as-Sadr, the publication of *Falsafatuna* and *Iqtidaduna* propelled him as the foremost theoretician of the Islamic renaissance. The philosophical and economic alternative system was to be completed by a social and institutional leg. In *Falsafatuna* and *Iqtisaduna*, a third important volume was promised, which was to be called, on the same pattern, *Mujtama'una* ('Our Islamic Society').[10] The book was never published, and it is doubtful whether it was ever written. Instead, we have a number of articles by Sadr on societal themes, which were published in *al-Adwa'*, a journal published at Najaf, and collected after his death as *Risalatuna* ('Our Message').[11]

The full series of the journal itself is not available, but Sadr's editorials in *Risalatuna* do not betray great originality, and his later articles of the time of the Iranian revolution proved to be of much greater significance. But the mere existence of an openly political journal like *al-Adwa'* in hitherto sedate Najaf was significant.

The reconstitution of the picture of collaborators to the journal is enlightening for the network of leaders which was then being formed in southern Iraq. It includes, along with Sadr's sister, who was in charge of the 'feminist' rubric, many of the young Iraqi ulama, as well as some Lebanese scholars who, like Muhammad Husayn Fadlallah, were to come to prominence twenty years on.

Al-Adwa' was discontinued around 1963–64, but the testimony of a collection entitled *Min Hadi an-Najaf* ('From the Guidance of Najaf'), which was published in the second half of the 1960s, shows how the network of militant ulama proceeded on the margins of the Najaf establishment.

The books of the collection extant include discussions on themes such as the political significance of pilgrimage, the misreading of the Qur'an by Orientalists, Islamic literature, the socio-political legacy of the revolt of Imam Husayn, and the importance of fasting as a symbolic stance against injustice and wrongdoing. These works were authored by scholars from Najaf who were destined to political leadership in the 1980s, such as Muhammad Mahdi Shamseddin (head of the Lebanese Higher Shi'i Council), Mahmud al-Hashimi and Muhammad Baqer al-Hakim (the leaders of the Tehran-based Supreme Council for the Islamic Revolution in Iraq).[12]

Yet the political involvement of the new generations of ulama was constrained by the wariness of older and better established figures, who had much sympathy for the new enthusiam, were grateful for its success in countering communist influence, but were also aware of the dangers of unbridled militancy. Testimonies from militant circles shed light on the hesitations of the older ulama (most prominent among whom is *Ayat Allah* Abul-Qasem al-Khu'i) who, as in Muhammad Husayn Fadlallah's recollections, succeeded in the mid 1960s in putting a curb on political activities. But as the central government was getting increasingly authoritarian and sectarian, hesitation slowly gave way to the ascendancy of activism.

Then came the third phase, which started when the Ba'th came to power in the summer of 1968. Now, there was open confrontation, which ended in the death of Sadr and the destruction of all forms of worldly activity in Najaf, while a series of strikes, demonstrations, arrests and repression increased the tension until breaking point. In the recollection of the protagonists, the first trigger came in the form of a confrontation between Najaf and Baghdad over the establishment of a university at Kufa. The university project had been part of the great expansion in Iraq of the educational system, and the active work towards the eradication of illiteracy and the development of higher education. The leaders of Najaf, who saw the establishment of a university in the neighbouring historic city of Kufa as a worthwhile opportunity, pressed the issue forward and were successful in raising the funds needed for the university from wealthy Shi'i businessmen.[13]

The Ba'th government saw otherwise. Administrative stalling on the Kufa project was accompanied by an increased curb on political activity throughout the country. In retrospect, it is clear that the central government of Ahmad Hasan al-Bakr and Saddam Hussein could not tolerate a project which rendered close control by the repressive apparatus difficult, but its rejection of the well-financed venture could not be plainly directed against an educational endeavour. The way for a repressive government, for whom the peripheral threat clearly consisted in a southern Shi'i and a northern Kurdish one, was to attack the circles of Najaf on the charge of an 'American-Zionist conspiracy'. Mahdi al-Hakim, the son of the Great *Ayat Allah* Muhsin, was the first target of the attack. With Muhammad Bahr al-'Ulum, another close collaborator of his father, a life of underground and exile was beginning. This took place in late 1968 and 1969.

Muhsin al-Hakim was understandably angry, and efforts to patch up the quarrel between him and the Ba'th proved useless. He was reportedly 'on strike' when the government chose to send to Lebanon in 1969 an *'alim* of the Kashif al-Ghita' family as 'Najaf representative', to the great dismay of some Lebanese

Shi'i circles.[14] The stage for the next two decades was set. Governmental packing of Najaf was one way, which continued well into the Iran-Iraq war with the same 'Ali Kashif al-Ghita' presiding over numerous 'Islamic popular meetings' in Baghdad. Dividing the south and the north was another successful strategy. There was great resentment in Najaf over the rapprochement between Saddam Hussein and the Kurdish leader Mulla Mustafa Barzani, which had culminated in the March 1970 agreement: Muhsin al-Hakim and other personalities had expressed dismay at the heavy-handed treatment of the Kurds by the central government in the preceding years, and the 1970 Agreement was perceived as an ungrateful let down at a time when the Ba'th and the ulama were at daggers drawn. When, in June 1970, crowds assembled in Najaf to mourn the death of Muhsin and to voice their disbelief to the accusation that Mahdi was an agent of the CIA,[15] Muhammad Bahr al-'Ulum and Mahdi al-Hakim were in exile and unable to return to Iraq for the mourning ceremonies.

From 1970 onwards troubles recurred yearly against the Iraqi government in Najaf. Muhammad Baqer as-Sadr was arrested several times, and subjected to interrogation and brutal treatment. In the last such instance, in June 1979, as he was preparing to head a delegation to greet *Ayat Allah* Khomeini in Tehran, he was detained and confined to house arrest. He remained under house arrest until his transfer to Baghdad on 5 April 1980. That date coincided with the second attack on high governmental officials within a week. On 1 April 1980, Tariq 'Aziz, who was then a prominent Ba'thist (but not yet foreign minister) was the target of a grenade attack on the occasion of a speech at Mustansariyya University in Baghdad. 'Aziz was wounded but survived. Students in the rally were not so lucky, and on the occasion of their mourning at the Baghdad Waziriyya University on 5 April, a grenade was again hurled into the crowd. This was for the government the signal to begin the final confrontation with what they considered the root of its problems. Najaf was invaded in the evening, and Muhammad Baqer as-Sadr transferred to Baghdad. Najaf lore recalls that Sadr escaped abduction and imprisonment back in June thanks to Bint al-Huda's rallying the mourners gathered at the *sahn* (Ali's mosque in Najaf) with the cry 'Your Imam is being kidnapped'. This time, the government secured the silence of Sadr's sister by taking her along to Baghdad, and by executing her with her brother. Muhammad Baqer's body was reported to have been buried at dawn on 9 April in the presence of relatives from Najaf. Thus the presumption of his death a day earlier. But many questions remain unanswered.

Thus ended the build-up of the confrontation inside Iraq between Najaf and Baghdad. The assassination was the focal point for a renewed struggle, which had now extended to the whole Middle Eastern stage. In Lebanon, Kuwait, Iran, Pakistan, India and Sudan in the following decade, there were to be many victims of the war between Muhammad Baqer as-Sadr's friends and Saddam Hussein's supporters.

At a more global level, the confrontation turned into Armageddon, as the Ba'th government's first *fuite en avant* came in the Iran–Iraq war, which had started with the invasion of Iran on 22 September 1980. Then came the invasion of Kuwait, and, in the wake of the Iraqi rout, the Iraqi *intifada* (revolt) of March 1991, where pictures of Sadr were paraded in the cities of the south during the brief period when they were freed from brutal rule.

Had history gone full circle? Only time will tell. But the emergence of the Islamic movement in Iran, Iraq and Lebanon cannot be understood without the network which originated and developed in the city of Najaf. A glance at the most prominent figures of the movement in the late 1970s and the 1980s will show that, without exception, they had studied, resided, or visited their colleagues in Najaf.

With such a complex web of personal and institutional relations as was woven in the Iraqi city, many developments in the Middle East since the access to power in Iran of the most famous Najaf resident, Ruhollah al-Khomeini, bore in a direct or indirect way the imprint of Najaf. The internal Iraqi, Lebanese, and Iranian developments, as well as the international developments which came in the wake of the establishment of the Islamic Republic, were influenced by the legacy of the network.

This, in a nutshell, is the political background of the renaissance in Najaf. There would, however, not have been a universal character to the Islamic political challenge started in Najaf without the peculiar intellectual and cultural dimension which it carries. In the midst of dramatic events which were increasingly assuming a global reach, it is important to bear in mind that the Najaf renaissance was an intellectual phenomenon, involving primarily jurists and legal production. This is the less known dimension of the turbulent Middle East, and the more lasting one.

At the centre of the cultural renewal and the shaping of the system was 'the Shi'i International', itself the product of the networks of Najaf. In Najaf, Muhammad Baqer as-Sadr, the prize of the universities as Ruhollah Khomeini called him posthumously, emerges as the founder of a new constitutional and economic system.

III

Muhammad Baqer as-Sadr was born, according to his Arab biographers,[16] in 25 Dhu al-Qi'da 1353/1 March 1935 in Kazimiyya, Iraq, to a family famous in the Shi'i world for its learning. His great grandfather Sadr ad-Din al-'Amili (d. 1264/1847), who was brought up in the southern Lebanese village of Ma'raka, emigrated to study in Isfahan and Najaf, where he was to be buried. His grandfather Isma'il was born in Isfahan in 1258/1842, moved in 1280/1863 to Najaf then Samarra', where he is said to have replaced al-Mujaddid ash-Shirazi in the local *hauza* (circle of Shi'i scholars). He died in Kazimiyya in 1338/1919. His son Haydar, the father of Muhammad Baqer as-Sadr, was born in Samarra' in 1309/1891, and studied under his father and under *Ayat Allah* al-Ha'iri al-Yazdi in Karbala. He died in Kazimiyya in 1356/1937, leaving a wife, two sons and a daughter. Though a relatively well-known *marja'*, he seems to have died penniless. 'The family, until more than a month after [his] death, was still unable to secure their daily bread, *kanu ha'irin fi luqmat al-'aysh.'*[17]

The 'international' scholarly background, and the relative poverty into which Sadr was born, are the two important elements which determined the context of Sadr's upbringing. The economic hardship that the family faced upon the early death of Haydar as-Sadr came to Muhammad Baqer when he was still an infant.[18] Other members of his family looked after his education, and he grew up under the supervision of his uncle on his mother's side, Murtada Al Yasin,[19] and of his older brother, Isma'il (1340/1921-1388/1968).[20]

In Kazimiyya, Muhammad Baqer went to the Muntada an-Nashr primary school, where, according to reports of schoolmates, he established himself early on as a subject of interest and curiosity to his teachers, 'so much so that some students took to imitating him in his walk, speech and manner of sitting in class.'[21]

Post mortem descriptions are often eulogistic, and must be taken with circumspection. Against such testimonies, there is unfortunately no material for contrast, since the government in Iraq does not even acknowledge the existence of Sadr, let alone his intellectual or political achievements. One is therefore limited to the texts themselves, and to the reminiscences of students and followers close to the deceased 'alim. However unlikely this may be, several reports mention, for example, that Sadr wrote a first treatise at the age of eleven. 'Abd al-Ghani al-Ardabili, quoted in Ha'iri's biography, refers to this book as a treatise on logic.[22] The earliest published work that can be traced dates however from 1955.[23] This study, an analysis on the episode of Fadak and its significance in Shi'i history, shows great maturity in the young scholar's thoughts in terms of method and substance. The content however betrays a sectarian Shi'i tone which soon disappeared from Sadr's language, until it came back to the fore at the time of the confrontation with the Ba'th in the late 1970s.[24]

In 1365/1945, the family moved to Najaf, where Sadr would remain for the rest of his life. The importance of Najaf had already been established in the 1920s as the city and its ulama emerged as the central focus of resistance against the British invasion.[25] A lull followed after a relative defeat against king Faisal in 1924, when major jurists took the route of exile, but most returned a few years later to resume their study and teaching away from political turmoil.

The picture changed radically in the 1950s, as the quietism of the *mujtahids*, instructed by their inability to stand up to the confrontation with Baghdad, received a serious challenge in the years leading to the 1958 revolution from an unsuspected quarter, the communists.[26]

Sadr found himself in the midst of a bitter intellectual confrontation between traditional Najaf and the communists, and his worldview was formed with this twofold intellectual background: a socialist-communist call prevailing in the whole of the Middle East, which permeated the concern in his writings with the 'social question';[27] and the traditional education of the ulama, including the relatively strict structure of their hierarchy.

The strict, more traditional dimension of Sadr's works appears in several publications which span his life. Most conspicuous are his books on the jurisprudential discipline of *usul al-fiqh*, of which two samples can be considered. One sample belongs to the early years in Najaf, where Sadr wrote an introduction to the history and main characteristics of the discipline, *al-Ma'alim al-Jadida fil-Usul*.[28] This book, which became widely used for introductory teaching at Najaf, was published in 1385/1965. It remains one of the more interesting and accessible works in the field.[29] Sadr himself authored more complicated *usul* works. In 1397/1977, the first of a series of four volumes on *'ilm* (the science of) *al-usul*, which were designed to prepare students for the higher degree of *bahth al-kharej* (graduate research), appeared in Beirut and Cairo.[30] Sadr suggests that he prepared these works to facilitate the task of students, who were otherwise subject to the 'pressure in the language'[31] of the four basic works in use for over half a century in Najaf.[32] *Al-Ma'alim al-Jadida* and the *Durus* series represent the didactic side of Sadr's interest in *usul al-fiqh*. They were intended for the apprentice *'alim* who would find the direct approach to the requirements necessary before *bahth al-kharej* too difficult, and to the lay person generally interested in the overview of the discipline. But Sadr also had published, sometimes posthumously, more advanced works in *usul*. Most of these were in the form of notes taken by his students. This is the case of Kazim al-Husayni al-Ha'iri, who compiled a first volume of *Mabaheth al-Usul* in 1407/1987,[33] and of one of Sadr's favourite disciples, Mahmud al-Hashimi, who assembled the section of Sadr's lectures on *Ta'arud al-Adilla ash-Shar'iyya* in a book published in 1977.[34]

The works on *usul* being traditionally student compilations of the lecturers' notes, there is little doubt that many of Sadr's classes must have been recorded, and there will probably appear more *usul* works by Sadr in the future. Biographical sources also mention a first volume in a series entitled *Ghayat al-Fikr fi 'Ilm al-Usul* ('The Highest Thought in the Science of *usul*'),[35] but it is doubtful whether the entire works of Sadr in this field, which he started teaching in Najaf on the higher *kharej* level in 1378/1958[36] will ever be completely recovered.

Akin to these difficult works are Sadr's more general investigations in jurisprudence (*fiqh*), and in logic and philosophy.

The interest in these two areas stems from various concerns. The interest in logic was part of the exercise in *usul*, with a more universal dimension which was meant to offer a response to the same discipline in the West. The main work in this domain is Sadr's *al-Usus al-Mantiqiyya lil-Istiqra'*.[37] Sadr tries to take on the field of logic on its own terms, and *al-Usus al-Mantiqiyya* is filled with references to Bertrand Russell. Sadr uses in this work numerous mathematical symbols and equations, leading up to the revelation of the 'true objective' of the work: 'to prove ... that the logical bases on which are built all the scientific conclusions derived from observation and experience are the very logical bases on which is built the conclusion on the evidence of a creator and organizer of this world ... This conclusion, as any other scientific conclusion, is inductive in its nature.'[38] This work is actually part of the larger system which Sadr was trying to construct on the basis of Islam, and the dabbling in logic with *al-Usus al-Mantiqiyya*, as well as with other smaller contributions,[39] was perhaps the least successful achievement of the system, for Sadr was not well equipped to take on such an arcane discipline. It must be noted nonetheless that the display of technical terms in Arabic is rather remarkable in a field where even terms-of-art are still in the making.

Sadr is better known for his work on philosophy, *Falsafatuna*, which has recently been translated into English.[40] How much the substance of *Falsafatuna* has enriched the philosophical debate in the Muslim world, and whether the work is up to par with the great philosophers in history, is doubtful. The book bears the imprint of the pressing conditions that produced it. Sadr is said to have completed the research and writing in less than a year.[41] In passages where the authentic Islamic tradition in philosophy surfaces, however, the book reveals the diversity and originality of Sadr's mind.

It is now well established that *Falsafatuna* was written in 1959 in reaction to the growing communist tide in Iraq, particularly among the more disenfranchised Shi'i.[42] Sadr's first purpose was to stem the tide by offering a better understanding and a closer look at Marxism's own system and terminology. *Falsafatuna* appears as a detailed critique, from an Islamic point of view, of the most sophisticated expression of materialist philosophy then available in the Arab world. An appendix to the first edition of the book reveals Sadr's Marxist sources.[43] For a Shi'i *mujtahid*, the effort is remarkable, but the longer-term prospects of a book based on a Stalinist-cum-Politzerian dialectical materialism were doomed. Reading *Falsafatuna* now gives a distinct flavour of a *dépassé* language.

Irrespective of whether the Islamic system proposed in the

book is valid, it may be said that its subject matter and first *raison d'être* is negative, and this underlying concern weakens the work, although it proved no doubt valuable to the opposition to communist ideology in the Iraq of the early 1960s. *Falsafatuna* is so obsessed with Marxist categories that its Islamic language becomes affected by it. In hindsight, of course, criticism is easy: Stalin, Politzer and even Engels's arguments have long become out of fashion in philosophical circles, and their decay has negatively affected Sadr's philosophical treatise itself, which accorded them an importance they do not deserve.

Falsafatuna remains a good example of Sadr's comprehensive efforts to build a full Islamic system of thought. As in the works of logic, the test of time has weakened the arguments, but both efforts remain a unique example of Sadr's diversity of thought. Little in them results from the *mujtahid* tradition, and this is perhaps why they do not appear to be as original and authentic as Sadr's other treatises, in which his professionalism emerges more forcefully.

In *fiqh* works by contrast, Sadr was producing what he was expected to produce, namely works of a general legal nature which represent his position as a *mujtahid*. It might be surprising to find Sadr to be different in this respect from other established *mujtahids*, who, unlike him, have tried to offer a comprehensive work of *fiqh* embracing their vast legal knowledge of Shi'i law.[44] The absence of such a *risala 'amaliyya* in his case is attributed to his young age. Sadr was not fifty when he was executed. But there are signs of a work of that nature in his commentary on Muhsin al-Hakim's two-volume *Minhaj as-Salihin* in 1976 and 1980,[45] which was probably completed in the early 1970s, as well as in his three volumes of comments on the nineteenth century classic by Muhammad Kazem at-Tabataba'i (d.1327/1919), *al-'Urwa al-Wuthqa*.[46] More importantly, Sadr published the first volume of a comprehensive work of *fiqh* of his own, *al-Fatawa al-Wadiha*, which he meant as a *risala 'amaliya*.[47] This book was the first in a series which was interrupted, and deals merely with the *'ibadat* section of *fiqh*.

The *fiqh* works may be said to depart little from the tradition, and one cannot see easily how much innovation could be developed in commentaries on works of such respected figures as Hakim and Tabataba'i. But the *Fatawa Wadiha* includes an interesting introductory chapter,[48] which reveals Sadr's readiness to depart from the tradition, even in such established schemes as the century-old dichotomy between *'ibadat* and *mu'amalat*.[49]

Sadr never completed *al-Fatawa al-Wadiha*, and Islamic law will probably remain bereft of an authority of his stature to affect and re-adapt traditional schemes. But his legal expertise was not confined to reordering the *usul* and *fiqh* disciplines. Where he was most innovative appears in two areas: the field of economics, including an important work on Islamic banking,[50] and the constitution.[51]

Before turning to the details of Sadr's contributions in this field, I shall mention several others works of his encyclopaedic output.

Muhammad Baqer as-Sadr worked on Qur'anic exegesis and on history, and some of his publications in this field are remarkably rich. This is the case of the lectures given in 1979-80 on the 'objective exegesis of the Qur'an', where a combination of historical, political, and methodological remarks on the text and significance of the Qur'an are at work.[52] Similarly, the more historical analyses of Sadr – from *Fadak fit-Tarikh* to his lectures on the Twelve Imams, the 1977 pamphlets on Shi'ism, the various articles on Islamic education, on the Qur'an, and on the political tasks at various stages of the development of the opposition at Najaf – all offer rich insights into the general system on which Sadr was working from his earlier days and into the Iraqi world of hopes and constraints.[53]

IV

The many remarkable contributions of Sadr to Islamic historical themes, *usul*, and philosophy notwithstanding, it is in the field of Islamic economics and constitutional law that Sadr's works are most innovative.

In Islamic economics, Sadr wrote several treatises of varying length. The two most important are *Iqtisaduna*, which is a general theory of 'Islamic economics', and *al-Bank al-la Ribawi fil-Islam*, which is a detailed text on the operation of an Islamic bank in an adversarial 'capitalist' context.

Two elements distinguish *Iqtisaduna* from the general literature on Islamic economics. In terms of structure and methodology, this is no doubt the most serious, and most widely respected contribution to the literature. The reason for the seriousness is twofold. In the first place, Sadr was clearly concerned to represent the rival ideologies, especially Marxism, in a serious manner. His criticism of Marxism may be flawed or insufficient, but it is a serious intellectual endeavour. As for capitalist theories, the research done was more limited, but this is due to the ascendancy of Marxism. At the time of *Iqtisaduna*, and until the late 1970s, the intellectual field of the 'social sciences' was dominated by the left. In *Iqtisaduna*, only thirty pages are devoted to a structural critique of capitalism, which is in any case much less thorough than the three hundred pages devoted to the refutation of Marxist theories.

All in all, however, this is not the main reason for the methodological importance of the book. With time, Sadr's reading of Marxism, which was in any case constrained by his reliance on Arabic translations, has become of secondary importance given the worldwide disillusionment with socialism. More significant is the methodology of Sadr in his presentation of the Islamic economic doctrine, where non-scientificity is acknowledged, and where the method itself rests on the most appropriate Islamic tradition: the legal tradition.

Nothing is more repetitive and disappointing than the mushrooming works on Islamic economics which dwell on obscure and irrelevant verses of the Qur'an by way of faulty and badly digested economic schemes derived from the field. With all its references to social relations and wealth, the Qur'an offers insufficient ground for grand economic theories. Nor is there any significant tradition which can be called 'economics' in Islamic thought.

The only serious and worthy point of departure in this field, therefore, is the law, and Sadr's work is based on the important and rich tradition to be found in *fiqh* books. They constitute the 'superstructure', as Sadr explains, and *Iqtisaduna* chiefly uses these sources to discover the underlying economic doctrine of Islam.

Fiqh, of course, is a vast and unruly field. Like the Qur'an, it allows for various and sometimes opposed interpretations. In comparing *Iqtisaduna* with later works, we find that some contradictions do surface at times in Sadr's system. But the bulk of the work is serious, and indicates a reading of the tradition which is essentially *dirigiste*, with a significant role for the state both in the pre-production and post-production phases identified by Sadr. Even beyond the discussion on the role of the state, the distribution of land, which is the focus of *Iqtisaduna*, is one where collective property is legally justified and further reinforced by 'the requirement' of constant labour.

These, in a nutshell, are *Iqtisaduna*'s distinguishing features: a distributionist and interventionist network and a reliance on the significant legal tradition of Islam.

The legal tradition is also important in *al-Bank al-la Ribawi fil-Islam*. With the flow of oil from the Arabian peninsula, plenitude of money has replaced scarcity. Sadr wrote a book in answer to a query put to him by the Kuwaiti Ministry of Awqaf: that Kuwaiti demand was not concerned with distribution or the role of the state. The question for Sadr was whether it was possible to design a bank working on Islamic principles in an adversarial context, i.e. in a world financial system dominated by the western concept of interest.

Sadr embarks on a full-fledged analysis of the structure and financial operations of such a set-up. As for structure, the question is about the legal triangle constituted by the depositors, the borrowers, and the bank itself. In recent 'Islamic banking' literature, this triangle is often described as a 'two-tier' *mudaraba*, where *mudaraba* is the key contract drawn from classical Islamic law. Sadr's definition of *mudaraba* in *al-Bank al-la Ribawi fil-Islam* is as good and precise as any. It is:

> a nominal [special, *khass*] contract between the owner of capital [lender, *mudarib*] and the investor-entrepreneur [borrower, *mustathmir*] to establish a trade [or enterprise] with the capital of the former and the labour of the latter, whereby they specify the share of each in the profit on a percentage basis. If the enterprise is profitable, they will share the profit according to the agreed percentage; if the capital remains as it was, the owner of capital will receive his capital back, and the worker will get nothing. If the enterprise makes a loss, and the capital is consequently diminished, the owner of capital only will bear the loss.[54]

The three parties to the *mudaraba* are therefore the depositor (*mudarib*), the entrepreneur-investor (*mudarab, mustathmir*) or agent (*'amel*), and the bank which is the intermediary between the despositor and the entrepreneur, as well as the agent (*wakil*) of the owner of capital deposited in its safes. Then Sadr proceeds, in some detail, with describing the rights and duties of the three parties.

Whilst the definition of *mudaraba* is not different from the one which can be found in the classical literature, it is noteworthy that Sadr, unlike most contemporary scholars in the field, does not see the system operating as a 'two-tier' *mudaraba*, i. e. as the bank contracting a *mudaraba* with the depositor, in a separate operation from a second *mudaraba* entered with the borrower-entrepreneur.

The other distinguishing feature of *al-Bank al-la Ribawi fil-Islam* is the remarkable analysis of the various operations (cheques, discounts, letters of credit, foreign currency transactions etc.) which are the subject of *fiqh* perusal by Sadr. Here, as early as 1969, he anticipates several practical problems faced by the welter of Islamic 'banks' that were established a few years later. It is surprising to see the accuracy and knowledge that Sadr displayed in his treatment of banking, even though several passages demonstrate some superficiality in the analysis. To date, *al-Bank al-la Ribawi fil-Islam* remains the most remarkable theoretical contribution to the literature on Islamic finance.

Alongside economics and finance, Sadr has also offered modern Islamic thought remarkable inroads into the renewal of the constitutional field. Though it may be a truism that the common denominator of all present political messages which call for the establishment of an Islamic state is that it be ruled by Islamic law, it is no less true that the diversity of Islamic law is matter for little common agreement.

In terms of the basic law of a state – a constitution – an answer was urgently needed for those revolutionaries in Iran who were confronted precisely with the definition of the Islamic state. With Khomeini's relatively imprecise and highly rhetorical expatiations in his 1970 Najaf lectures on *wilayat al-faqih* and Islamic government, those in the Shi'i world who were observing the rapidly changing scene of Iran in 1978/79 were eager for an answer. It came in a little work of Muhammad Baqer as-Sadr, which was written a few weeks before Khomeini went back to Iran to lead the revolution.

The work was an answer to a query from the Lebanese ulama, some of whom had graduated from Najaf,[55] who wrote to Sadr in acknowledgement of his status as the most innovative living thinker on the (Shi'i) Muslim scene.

Sadr's answer foreshadows, in the most striking way, the Iranian constitution which would come into being in late 1979. In both texts, the central feature is the combination of a western electoral process, which produces such representatives as popularly elected president and parliamentarians and the special role for the defence of Islamic law by the classical *mujtahids*. This is what is known in Iran, under Chapter 7 of the Constitution, as the 'Leadership'. Sadr uses the Arabic word *qa'ed* (leader), as the highest authority in the *marja'iyya*. The *marja'iyya* is none other than the clerical system known to Shi'i societies and popularly known under the denomination Ayatollahs.

In *Iqtisaduna*, Sadr tried to counter the communist appeal to redress the 'social balance' by an elaborate legal theory of property and distribution. In his work on banking, he was able to offer a blueprint for the now fashionable 'Islamic banks'. And in his constitutional works, the detailed arrangements at the heart of the Islamic Republic of Iran were presented. If only for these contributions, Sadr's thought is significant in the renewal of Islamic law. Insofar as the depth of his writings in 'new' fields is unmatched in modern Muslim societies, he will remain in the Shi'i, and more generally in the Islamic world, a unique source of inspiration and respect.

Notes

Chibli Mallat is Director of the Centre for Islamic and Middle Eastern Laws at SOAS. This chapter is adapted from his book on Sadr, published at Cambridge University Press in 1993, entitled *The Renewal of Islamic Law: Muhammad Baqer as-Sadr, Najaf and the Shi'i International*.

1. H. Batatu, 'Iraq's underground Shi'i movements: characteristics, causes and prospects', *Middle East Journal*, vol. 35, no. 4, spring 1981, pp. 577-94; published also with slight alterations as 'Shi'i organizations in Iraq: *al-da'wah al-islamiyya* and *al-mujahidin*', in J. Cole and N. Keddie eds., *Shi'ism and Social Protest*, New Haven, 1986, p. 182.

2. Muhammad Baqer as-Sadr, *Unsere Wirtschaft, Eine Gekürzte Kommentierte Übersetzung des Buches Iqtisaduna*, Translation and Comments by Andreas Rieck, Berlin, 1984.

3. R. Dekmejian, *Islam in Revolution*, Syracuse, 1985, pp. 127-36.

4. A. Bar'am, 'The shi'ite opposition in Iraq under the Ba'th, 1968-1984', in *Colloquium on Religious Radicalism and Politics in the Middle East*, Hebrew University, Jerusalem, 13-15 May 1985.

5. 'Dossier: Aux sources de l'islamisme chiite – Muhammad Baqer al-Sadr', *Cahiers de l'Orient*, issue 8-9, 1987-88, pp. 115-202.

6. As aptly described by Shaul Bakhash, *The Reign of the Ayatollahs*, London, 1985, pp. 40-4.

7. A fuller analysis of the political dimensions and implications of the Najaf renaissance can be found in various articles which I have published in recent years. The following topics related to the Najaf renaissance are addressed in some detail: the reaction of Najaf to the unification of personal status law by the government of 'Abd al-Karim Qasem ('Shi'ism and Sunnism in Iraq:

Revisiting the Codes', in Mallat and Connors eds., *Islamic Family Law*, London 1990, pp. 71-91); the causes of the Iran-Iraq war from the vantage-point of the Najaf-Tehran axis ('A l'Origine de la Guerre Iran-Irak: l'axe Najaf-Teheran', *Les Cahiers de l'Orient*, Paris, autumn 1986, pp. 119-36); the works of Muhammad Baqer as-Sadr in the mirror of the delicate Sunni-Shi'i controversy in Iraq ('Religious Militancy in Contemporary Iraq'); the general rise of political Islam and the role of Sadr and his companions, as well as the development of the Islamic movement after Sadr's death ('Iraq', in Shireen Hunter ed., *The Politics of Islamic Revivalism*, pp. 71-87. This is a shortened version of a fuller unpublished study, 'Political Islam and the Ulama in Iraq', Berkeley, October 1986); the worldview of Sadr's sister ('Le Féminisme Islamique de Bint al-Houdâ'); and the role in Lebanese politics of three graduates from Najaf, Muhammad Jawad Mughniyya, Muhammad Mahdi Shamseddin, and Muhammad Husayn Fadlallah ('Shi'i Thought from the South of Lebanon', Centre for Lebanese Studies Papers, Oxford, April 1988). The reader can also consult a recent study on the larger scene of the Iraqi opposition, of which the Islamic movement is of course part. (*The Iraqi Opposition: a Dossier*, SOAS, London, 1991. This includes a short article on 'Démocratie à Bagdad', *Le Monde*, 12 February 1991.) For a fuller bibliography on an increasingly well-documented phenomenon, the reader is referred to the works cited in these articles.

8. The *fatwa* of Muhsin al-Hakim, which was issued in February 1960, is reported in O. Spies, 'Urteil des Gross-Mujtahids über den Kommunismus', *Die Welt des Islam*, no. 6, 1959-61, pp. 264-5.

9. I discussed with the late Mahdi al-Hakim the rather unclear picture of the early confrontation between Najaf and Baghdad, but his assassination in February 1988 prevented the completion of fascinating interviews started in the summer of 1987. The present remarks are also the result of close collaboration with Muhammad Bahr al-'Ulum, who has tirelessly given me his time and documentation to lift the veil on obscure aspects of modern Iraqi history.

10. Muhammad Baqer as-Sadr, *Iqtisaduna*, p. 5; *Falsafatuna*, p. 400.

11. Muhammad Baqer as-Sadr, *Risalatuna* ('Our Message'), Tehran, 1982. Original said to have been published fourteen years earlier (1967-68).

12. For details on the collection *Min Hadi an-Najaf*, see my 'Religious militancy', pp. 719-23; for Hashimi and Hakim, 'Political Islam', pp. 23-40; for Shamseddin, 'Shi'i Thought', pp. 25ff.

13. Conversations with Dr Ahmad Chalabi, a prominent Iraqi businessman, now living in exile in London, and with Dr Muhammad Bahr al-'Ulum.

14. See Nizar az-Zein, *Hadith ash-Shahr* ('Talk of the Month'), *al-'Irfan* (Sidon), 57:6, October 1969, pp. 888-9; quoted in 'Shi'i Thought', p. 14.

15. Muhsin al-Hakim recalled the shouts of the mourners, '*Sayyed Mahdi mu jasus, isma' ya rayyes* (Sayyed Mahdi is no spy, listen oh President [Bakr])', and was still afflicted two decades later for not having been able to attend the funerals of his father. Conversations with Mahdi al-Hakim, London, summer 1987.

16. The most comprehensive and authoritative biography of Sadr appears in K. Ha'iri, *Tarjamat hayat as-sayyid ash-shahid* ('Life of the martyred sayyed [Sadr]'), in Muhammad Baqer as-Sadr, *Mabaheth al-Usul* (Studies in *usul*), Ha'iri ed., Qum, 1407/1987, pp. 11-168. The birthdate is mentioned at p. 33. Other biographies consulted include, by order of importance, Ghaleb Hasan

Abu 'Ammar, *Ash-Shahid as-Sadr Ra'ed ath-Thawra al-Islamiyya fil-'Iraq* ('Martyr as-Sadr, leader of the Islamic revolution in Iraq'), Tehran, 1401/1981 (published under the auspices of the Iranian Ministry of Islamic Guidance); *Al-imam ash-shahid as-sayyid Muhammad Baqer as-Sadr* ('the martyred imam Muhammad Baqer as-Sadr'), *Tariq al-Haqq* (London), 2:12, Feb. 1982, pp. 5-20. In European languages, the most comprehensive biography is Rieck's 'Introduction of the translator', in Sadr, *Unsere Wirtschaft*, pp. 39-68. See also the remarks of Batatu, 'Underground', pp. 578-81; P. Martin, 'Une grande figure de l'islamisme en Irak', *Cahiers de l'Orient*, 8-9, 1987-88, pp. 117-35. The birthdates vary between 1930 and 1934. The late Mahdi al-Hakim told me that Sadr, like his older brother Isma'il, died a year before reaching 50. If Sadr died at 49, he must have been born in 1931. Conversations with Mahdi al-Hakim, London, summer-autumn 1987. (Mahdi al-Hakim was assassinated in the Sudan in February 1988.)

17. Ha'iri, '*Tarjamat*', p. 28.

18. Muhammad Baqer as-Sadr was then three years old according to Ha'iri and Abu 'Ammar. His sister Bint al-Huda was his junior, born according to Ha'iri in 1356/1937, the year of their father's death.

19. The name of his mother is not mentioned in the sources. She was the daughter of Ayat Allah ask-Shaykh 'Abd al-Husayn Al Yasin, who is said to have been an important religious figure of Baghdad after the death of Murtada al-Ansari. Sadr's mother was the sister of Murtada Al Yasin.

20. Murtada was a well-established scholar when he issued a famous *fatwa* against the communists on 3 April 1960. The *fatwa* is reported in H. Batatu, *The Old Social Classes and the Revolutionary Movements of Iraq*, Princeton, 1978, p. 954. (This important work, along with Samir al-Khalil's *Republic of Fear*, London, 1989, provide the most challenging studies of twentieth-century Iraq. See further my article on 'Obstacles to democratization in Iraq', which is a critical reading of modern Iraqi history in the light of Batatu and Khalil's theses, published by University of Washington Press, Goldberg, et al, eds, 1993, pp. 224-47. Isma'il is said to have written several books, two of which, a commentary on Islamic penal legislation and a first volume of Qur'anic exegesis, were published. Ha'iri, '*Tarjamat*', p. 29.

21. Ha'iri, '*Tarjamat*', p. 44, relating a recollection by a classmate of Sadr, Muhammad 'Ali al-Khalili.

22. Ha'iri, '*Tarjamat*', p. 42; also Abu 'Ali, 'A glimpse of the life of the martyred imam Muhammad Baqer al-Sadr', n.p., n.d., p. 7.

23. Muhammad Baqer as-Sadr, *Fadak fit-Tarikh* (Fadak in history), 1st ed., Najaf, 1955. A reference to this first edition, which was published care of Muhammad Kazem al-Kubti, is mentioned s.v. in F. Abdulrazak ed., *Catalog of the Arabic Collection*, Harvard University, Boston, 1983. A second edition was published at al-Haydariyya Press, also in Najaf, in 1970. Several Beirut reprints followed, 'Dr Abu Ali' states that Sadr wrote *Fadak fir-Tarikh* when he was 17. 'A glimpse', p. 7. This is corroborated in Ha'iri, *Tarajamat*, p. 64.

24. See on Fadak within the Shi'i-Sunni communitarian background, my 'Religious militancy in contemporary Iraq: Muhammad Baqer as-Sadr and the Sunni-Shi'i paradigm', *Third World Quarterly*, 10:2, April 1988, pp. 714-15.

25. There is a large literature on the 1920 revolt and on the role of the ulama leadership. See e.g. R. al-Khattab, *Al-'Iraq bayna 1921 wa 1927* ('Iraq between

1921 and 1927'), Najaf, 1976; A. al-Fayyad, *Ath-Thawra al-'Iraqiyya al-Kubra* ('The great Iraqi revolt'), Baghdad, 1963. An excellent account is 'Ali al-Wardi, *Tarikh al-'Iraq al-Hadith* ('History of modern Iraq'), vol. 6, *Min 'Am 1920 ila 'Am 1924* ('From 1920 to 1924'), Baghdad, 1976, pp. 201-67. See also the telling testimony of Amine ar-Rihani, an eye-witness visitor, *Muluk al-'Arab* ('The Arab Kings'), Beirut, 2nd ed., 1929, vol. 2.

26. The 'communist threat' was in the 1950s a common phenomenon in the Middle East, particularly in Iran and Iraq. See generally Batatu, *The Old Social Classes*, Book Two, pp. 365-705.

27. Muhammad Baqer as-Sadr, *Falsafatuna* ('Our Philosophy'), 10th ed., Beirut, 1980, pp. 11-53.

28. Muhammad Baqer as-Sadr, *Al-Ma'alim al-Jadida fil-Usul* ('The new configuration of usul'), Beirut, 1385/1964.

29. *Usul al-fiqh* is the most arcane discipline in Islamic law. For a recent introduction in English, see M.H. Kamali, *Principles of Islamic Jurisprudence*, Malaysia, 1989, rpt. Cambridge, 1991. On classical Sunni *usul*, see recently W. Hallaq, 'The development of logical structure in Sunni legal theory', *Der Islam*, 64, 1987, pp. 42-67. On early Shi'i *usul*, R. Brunschvig, 'Les *usul al-fiqh* imamites à leur stade ancien', in *Le Shi'isme Imamite*, Paris, 1970, pp. 201-14.

30. Muhammad Baqer as-Sadr, *Durus fi 'Ilm al-Usul* ('Lessons in the discipline of usul'), 3 parts in 4 vols., Beirut, 1978-1980.

31. '*Daght fil-'ibara*', Sadr, *Durus*, I, p. 9.

32. The four Shi'i books mentioned are: the *Ma'alim* of ash-Shahid ath-Thani (d.966/1559), Qummi's (d.1231/1816) *Qawanin*, al-Khurasani's (d.1328/1910) *Kifaya*, and Ansari's (d.1329/1911) *Rasa'el*. See also Muhammad Baqer as-Sadr, *Durus*, Introduction, I, pp. 19-29; Muhammad Bahr al-'Ulum, '*Ad-dirasa wa tarikhuha fin-Najaf*' ('Teaching and its history in Najaf'), in J. Khalili ed., *Mausu'at al-'Atabat al-Muqaddasa, Qism an-Najaf* ('Encyclopaedia of the Holy places': section on Najaf), vol. 2, Beirut, 1964, pp. 95-6.

33. Sadr, *Mabaheth al-Usul*. According to Ha'iri, this book is only the compilation of Volume one of Part 2 in a series of lectures by Sadr.

34. Mahmud al-Hashimi, *Ta'arud al-Adilla ash-Shar'iyya Taqriran li-Abhath as-Sayyid Muhammad Baqer as-Sadr* ('Contradictions of legal evidence, a report on the research of Muhammad Baqer as-Sadr'), Beirut, 2nd ed., 1980. Introduction in Sadr's hand, dated 1394/1974.

35. Ha'iri, '*Tajribat*', p. 67. In his introduction to the translation of *Iqtisaduna*, p. 67, Rieck mentions ten volumes printed in Najaf since 1955.

36. Ha'iri, '*Tajribat*', p. 44.

37. Muhammad Baqer as-Sadr, *Al-Usus al-Mantiqiyya lil-Istiqra*' ('The logical bases of induction'), Beirut, 1972.

38. Sadr, *Al-Usus al-Mantiqiyya*, p. 507.

39. Muhammad Baqer as-Sadr, '*Al-yaqin ar-riyadi wal-mantiq al-wad'i*' ('Mathematical certainty and positive logic'), in *Ikhtarnalak* ('Choice of works'), Beirut, 1975, pp. 9-21.

40. Muhammad Baqer as-Sadr, *Falsafatuna*, 1st ed., Najaf, 1959. Translated by Shams Inati, London, 1987.

41. Ha'iri, *Tajribat*, p. 63. Conversations with Mahdi al-Hakim, summer 1987.

42. See Sadr's Introduction to *Falsafatuna*. Y. Muhammad, *Nazarat falsafiyya*

fir fikr ash-shahid as-Sadr ('Philosophical enquiries into the thought of martyr as-Sadr'), *Dirasat wa Buhuth* (Tehran), 2:6, 1983, p. 173. The debate has persisted to date. See H. Haidar, *Madha Ja'a Hawla Kitab Falsafatuna?* ('What has been written about *Falsafatuna?*'), Qum, 1403/1983.

43. The appendix was prepared by Muhammad Rida al-Ja'fari, *Falsafatuna*, 1st edition, pp. 348-9. It was omitted in later editions. The list includes classics in Arabic by Marx, Engels, Stalin, Mao Tse Tung, Plekhanov, a fair number of French communists popular in the 1950s, Henri Lefebvre, Roger Garaudy, Georges Politzer, as well as some 'local' Arab and Iranian Marxists such as Georges Hanna and Taqi Arani.

44. In contemporary Shi'i law, see e.g. the treatises of Muhsin al-Hakim (d.1970), *Minhaj as-Salihin* ('The path of the righteous'), 2 vols., Beirut, 1976, 1980; Ruhollah al-Khomeini (d.1989), *Tahrir al-Wasila* ('Clearing the way'), 2 vols., Beirut, 1985 [Original published in Najaf, 1387/1967]; Abul-Qasem al-Khu'i, *Minhaj as-Salihin*, 10th ed., Beirut, n.d., 2 vols.; summary in *al-Masa'el al-Muntakhaba* ('Chosen questions'), 22nd ed., Beirut, 1985.

45. Muhammad Baqer as-Sadr's comments on Muhsin al-Hakim's *Minhaj as-Salihin* appears in the edition mentioned in the previous note. They were written in 1974.

46. Muhammad Baqer as-Sadr, *Buhuth fi Sharh al-'Urwa al-Wuthqa* ('Studies on al-'Urwa al-Wuthqa'), 3 vols., Najaf, 1971ff. Another *fiqh* work is Muhammad Baqer as-Sadr, *Mujaz Ahkam al-Hajj* ('Compendium of Pilgrimage rules'), Beirut, n.d. (Introduction dated 1395/1975). Sadr also wrote an Introduction to the Shi'i Imam Zayn al-'Abidin's book of prayers *As-Sahifa as-Sajjadiyya*, Beirut, n.d.

47. Muhammad Baqer as-Sadr, *al-Fatawa* [or *Fatawi*, plural of *fatwa*] *al-Wadiha Wifqan li-Madhhab Ahl al-Bayt* ('The clear decrees according to the rite of the Household of the Prophet'), Beirut, 1976. But see a critique of the *risala* as genre in *al-Fatawa al-Wadiha*, pp. 11-12.

48. In the 1976 edition of *al-Fatawa al-Wadiha*, there is a separately paginated pamphlet, *al-Mursil, ar-Rasul, ar-Risala* ('The sender, the messenger, and the message'), which is not very original. It is independent from the proper chapter introducing *al-Fatawa al-Wadiha*, which, in contrast, includes interesting and novel remarks.

49. See Sadr, *al-Fatawa al-Wadiha*, pp. 46-7.

50. Muhammad Baqer as-Sadr, *al-Bank al-la Ribawi fil-Islam* ('The interest-free bank in Islam'), Kuwait, 1969.

51. Muhammad Baqer as-Sadr, *Lamha Fiqhiyya Tamhidiyya 'an Mashru' Dustur al-Jumhuriyya al-Islamiyya fi Iran* ('A preliminary legal note on the project of a constitution for the Islamic Republic of Iran'), Beirut, 1979; *Khilafat al-Insan wa Shahadat al-Anbiya'* ('Succession of man and testimony of the prophets'), Beirut, 1979; *Manabi' al-Qudra fid-Dawla al-Islamiyya* ('The sources of power in the Islamic state'), Beirut, 1979.

52. Muhammad Baqer as-Sadr, *al-Madrasa al-Qur'aniyya* ('the Qur'anic school'), Beirut, 2nd ed., 1981. (Lectures on the Qur'an given in 1979-80.)

53. An edition of the 'Collected Works' of Muhammad Baqer as-Sadr, of which 15 large volumes have now appeared, was started in 1980 by the Lebanese publishing house Ta'aruf. It includes, in Volume 13, a medium-sized booklet called *al-Mihna*. Other pamphlets on Shi'ism, *Bahth hawlal-Wilaya*

('Studies on the *wilaya*') and *Bahth hawlal-Mahdi* ('Study on the *mahdi*') were published separately in Beirut in 1977, but they were written earlier, and perhaps published as prefaces to other authors' works. (See the introduction of Sadr to 'Abdallah Fayyad's *Tarikh al-Imamiyya wa Aslafuhum*, Beirut, 4th ed., 1973.) The contributions on Shi'i history, *Dawr al-A'imma fil-Hayat al-Islamiyya* ('The role of the Imams in Islamic life'), and *Ahl al-Bayt, Tanawwu' Adwar wa Wahdat Hadaf* ('The household of the Prophet, diversity of roles and unity of goal') were lectures given between 1966 and 1969 and posthumously published. Muhammad Baqer as-Sadr also wrote numerous articles published in various journals. On all these works, see generally my 'Religious militancy'. Two other collections can be found in *Ikhtarnalak*, mentioned supra, and *al-Madrasa al-Islamiyya* ('The Islamic School'), Beirut, 1973. *Al-Islam Yaqud al-Hayat* ('Islam guides life') is the title of a series published in 1979, which is a collection of six pamphlets (Beirut, 1980). Three pamphlets deal with the constitution, and the three others are on economics and banking: *Sura 'an Iqtisad al-Mujtama' al-Islami* ('Picture of the economics of the Islamic society'); *Khutut Tafsiliyya 'an Iqtisad al-Mujtama' al-Islami* ('Detailed guidelines to the economy of the Islamic society'); and *Al-Usus-al 'Amma lil-Bank fil-Mujtama' al-Islami* ('General bases of a bank in the Islamic society').

54. Sadr, *al-Bank al-la Ribawi fil-Islam*, p. 25. This definition suggests that there is little difference with the classical definitions of Muslim jurists. On *mudaraba*, compare Sarakhsi (Hanafi school, d.1090), *Mabsut*, 30 vols., Cairo, 1906–12, vol. 22, pp. 18–19; Muhammad Kazim at-Tabataba'i al-Yazdi (Ja'fari school, d.1919), *al-'Urwa al-Wuthqa*, chapter on *mudaraba*, pp. 594–632; Ibn Hazm (Zahiri school, d.1065), *al-Muhalla*, vol. 8, pp. 247–50. See also the well-documented works of N. Saleh, *Unlawful Gain and Legitimate Profit in Islamic Law*, Cambridge, 1986, pp. 101–14; S.D. Goitein, *A Mediterranean Society*, vol. 1, *Economic Foundations*, Berkeley, 1967, pp. 170ff., 250–8; A. Udovitch, *Partnership and Profit in Medieval Islam*, Princeton, 1970, pp. 170–248.

55. Most noteworthy of the signatories of the query were Shamseddin and Ragheb Harb who was killed by the Israelis in 1984 for his resistance activities in the South of Lebanon.

Index

Husain, King of Jordan 198
Hussein, Saddam 255-7

ijma (secondary source of consensus) 7
ijtihad (legal practice) 7-9, 36, 179, 193
ikhtilaf (differences of opinion) 8
innovations (*bid'a*) 129
In the Shade of the Qur'an (*Fi Zilal al-Qur'an*) 160, 163, 174, 175
Iqbal, Allameh (Lahouri, Muhammad Iqbal) 3, 4, 8, 103
Iran 9; Assembly of Experts 92; Babi movement 14; Constitutional Movement (1905-06) 65; Islamic Republic of 184; Popular Movement 215-16; votes for women (1962) 86
Iranian Freedom Movement (IFM) 222, 223
Iranian Revolution (1979) 1, 184, 251
Iraq 1, 9
Isfahan 66, 67
Isfahani, Abolqasem Dehkordi 68
Al-Islam wa'l-Nasraniyya ma'al 'Ilm wa'l-Madaniyya 45
Islamic Coalition of Mourning Groups (*Hey'athay-e Mo'talefeh-e Eslami*) 87
Islamic Democratic Alliance IJI (Islami Jumhuri Ittihad) 119, 120
Islamic jurists (ulama) 5, 7-8, 34, 59, 67, 253
Islamic League of Nations 135
Islamic Liberation Organization (*Tanzim al-Tahrir al-Islami*) 179
Islamic Party *see* Jama'at-i Islami
Islamic Revolutionary Council 90, 91
Islamic Salvation Front 1
Islamic societies (*Al-Jama'at al-Islamiyya*) 177-8
Islamic Welfare Party 2
Islamiyah College 103
Islamology (*Eslamshenasi*) 228-33
Islam and the Problems of Civilization (*Al-Islam wa-Mushkhilat al-Hadarah*) 163
Ismail, Khedive 16-17
Israeli War (1967) 27-8

jahili 155, 162, 164, 171-3, 178
jahiliyya 161-2, 171-3, 177-8

Jam'at-i Islami 98, 104, 106; founded August (1941 in Lahore) 111; history and politics of 113-20; Mawdudi and 111-12; Punjab provincial elections (1951) 115; structure 112-13; structure, changes in 120-1; women's division 110; won only four seats in (1970) 117
al-Jami'a 52
jihad 41, 55, 142, 177-9
Jinnah, Fatimah 117
jizya (Muslim tax) 41
al-Jumblatt, Kamal 200

kafir (unbeliever) 40
Kafka, Franz 212
Karbala 9, 15, 67
Kashani, Ayatollah 81, 83-5, 216
Kashmir, insurgency in 114-15
Katov (Russian editor) 20
Kemal, Mustafa 2, 128, 130
Kemal, Namik 12, 18
Khadr, Shaykh Darwish 31
khalifat Allah (agent of God on earth) 46
Khamane'i, Hojjat al-Islam Ali 92
Khan, General Muhammad Ayub 116-18
Khan, Malkam 21, 34
Khan, Sayyid Ahmad 19, 34
al-Khatib, Muhibb al-Din 130
Khayyam, Omar 70
Khilafat movement 100-2
Kho'i, Ayatollah 85
Khomeini, Ayatollah Ruhollah 9, 64, 193-4, 199, 251-2; background 65-6; education 66-9; his interest in politics 76-90; *hudud* punishments and 107; marriage 69; mysterious death of son 89; rise of 184; as the ruler 90-3; in search of the Perfect Man 69-76; statesman bound by the Shari'a 93; Tehran then banishment 87; USSR and USA provoked by 94
al-Khu'i, Ayatollah Abu al-Qasim 193
al-Kwakibi, Abd ar-Rahman 3

Lahore Resolution (1940) 111
League for the Freedom of the Iranian People 215

CPSIA information can be obtained
at www.ICGtesting.com
Printed in the USA
LVHW080955210221
679533LV00034B/2675